UNMANNED COMBAT AIR SYSTEMS

Norman Friedman

UNMANNED COMBAT AIR SYSTEMS

A New Kind of Carrier Aviation

NAVAL INSTITUTE PRESS
Annapolis, Maryland

Naval Institute Press
291 Wood Road
Annapolis, MD 21402

Library of Congress Cataloging-in-Publication Data
Friedman, Norman, 1946-
Unmanned combat air systems : a new kind of carrier aviation / Norman Friedman.
     p. cm.
Includes bibliographical references and index.
ISBN 978-1-59114-285-0 (alk. paper)
1. United States. Navy—Weapons systems. 2. Uninhabited combat aerial vehicles. I. Title.
 VF347.F74 2010
 359.9'4835—dc22

                                                         2010020181

Printed in the United States of America on acid-free paper

14 13 12 11 10 9 8 7 6 5 4 3 2
First printing

Contents

List of Abbreviations   vii

CHAPTER ONE
Introduction: An Unmanned Combat Air System   1

CHAPTER TWO
A Changing Tactical Environment   15

CHAPTER THREE
A New Way of War: The New Technology   24

CHAPTER FOUR
The Need for Transformation   33

CHAPTER FIVE
What Pilots Do—and Need Not Do   46

CHAPTER SIX
The Economics of UCAS   55

Acknowledgments   61

APPENDIX I
Combat Use of Unmanned Combat Air Vehicles   63

APPENDIX II
World Military UAVs   69

Notes   249
Index   257

Abbreviations

ACTD	Advanced Concept Tactical Demonstration	CADI	Chengdu Aircraft Design Institute
ADD	Agency for Defense Development (South Korea)	CAIC	China Aviation Industry Corporation
		CAP	Combat air patrol
ADE	Aeronautical Development Establishment	CASA	Construcciones Aeronáuticas, SA
AGS	Alliance Ground Surveillance	CASC	China Aerospace Science and Technology Corporation
APC	Armored personnel carrier		
APID	Autonomous Probe for Industrial Data	CASIC	China Aerospace Science and Industry Corporation
ARCI	Acoustic Rapid COTS Insertion		
ARV	Aerial reconnaissance vehicle	CATIC	China Aero-Technical Import-Export Corporation
ASROC	Anti-Submarine Rocket		
ASTE	Affordable Surface Target Engagement	CC	Centralized controller
ASW	Antisubmarine warfare	CCD	Charge-coupled device
ATARS	Advanced Tactical Reconnaissance System	CEC	Cooperative Engagement Capability
ATLS	Automatic takeoff and landing system	CEP	Circular error probable
ATO	Air tasking order	COIN	Counterinsurgency
ATOL	Automatic takeoff and landing	COMINT	Communications intelligence
AVE	Aéronef de Validation Expérimentale	CPMIEC	China Precision Machinery Import-Export Corporation
AVIC	Aviation Industry Corporation		
AWACS	Airborne Warning and Control System	CSIST	Chang Shan Institute of Science and Technology
AWC	Aeronautical Complex and Air Weapons Complex		
		CTRM	Composites Technology Research Malaysia
BAMS	Broad Area Maritime Surveillance	DARO	Defense Airborne Reconnaissance Organization
BATES	Battlefield Artillery Target Engagement System		
		DARPA	Defense Advanced Research Projects Agency
BATMAV	Battlefield Air Targeting MAV		
BMDO	Ballistic Missile Defense Organization	DASH	Drone Anti-Submarine Helicopter
		DGA	Délégation Générale pour L'Armement
CAC	Chengdu Aircraft Corporation	DoD	U.S. Department of Defense

DRDO	Defense Research and Development Organization	ISR	Intelligence/Surveillance/Reconnaissance
DSEi	Defence Services Exhibition International	JASDF	Japan Air Self-Defense Force
DUSTER	Deployable Unmanned System for Targeting, Exploitation, and Reconnaissance	JCTD	Joint Concept Tactical Demonstration
		JDAMS	Joint Direct-Attack Munition System
		JGSDF	Japan Ground Self-Defense Force
ECM	Electronic countermeasure	JSF	Joint Strike Fighter
ELINT	Electronic intelligence	JUSTAS	Joint UAV Surveillance and Target Acquisition System
EMP	Electromagnetic pulse		
EO	Electro-optical		
ES	Electronic support	KAI	Korea Aerospace Industries
EUROCOM	European Command (NATO)	KAL	Korean Air Lines
EW	Electronic warfare	KARI	Korea Aerospace Research Institute
		KZO	Kleingerät für Zielortung
FCS	Future Combat System		
FEBA	Forward edge of battle area	LALE	Low altitude, low endurance
FELIN	Fantassin à Équipements et Liaisons Intégrés	LAMPS	Light Airborne Multipurpose System
FILUR	Flying Innovative Low-Observable Unmanned Research	LARS	Laser-Aided Rocket System
		LCS	Littoral combat ship
FLAVIIR	Flapless Air Vehicle Integrated Industrial Research	LIDAR	Light detection and ranging
		LIMA	Langkawi International Maritime and Aerospace Exposition
FLIR	Forward-looking infrared		
FPASS	Force Protection Airborne Surveillance System	LMM	Lightweight multirole missile
		Loran	Long-range navigation
		LRIP	Low-rate initial production
GMTI	Ground moving target indication	LSI	Leading Systems, Inc.
GPS	Global Positioning System		
		MALE	Medium altitude, long endurance
HALE	High altitude, long endurance	MALP	Multipurpose Air-Launched Payload
HERTI	High-Endurance Rapid Technology Insertion	MASS	Mini-UAV Modular Airborne Sensor System
HESA	Iran Aircraft Manufacturing Industry (IAMI in English)	MBB	Messerschmitt-Bölkow-Blohm
		MCMM	Multi Capteurs Multi Missions
		MEF	Marine Expeditionary Force
IAI	Israel Aircraft Industries	MEU	Marine Expeditionary Unit
ICAO	International Civil Aviation Organization	MidCAS	Midair Collision Avoidance System
IDEX	International Defense Exhibition and Conference	MTBF	Mean time between failures
IED	Improvised explosive device	NAL	National Aeronautical Laboratory
IFF	Identification Friend or Foe	NAVAIR	Naval Air Systems Command
INTA	Instituto Nacional de Técnica Aeroespacial	NAVSEA	Naval Sea Systems Command
IOC	Initial operating capability	NRL	Naval Research Laboratory
IR	Infrared	NSCT	Navy Special Clearance Team
IRGC	Islamic Revolutionary Guard Corps	NSP	National Sensor Platform
ISAF	International Security Assistance Force		

ONERA	Organisations Nationale d'Études et Récherches Aérospatiales	SOSUS	Sound surveillance system
ONR	Office of Naval Research	SP2S	Stealthy, persistent, perch and stare
OODA	Observe-orient-decide-act	STA	Singapore Technologies Aerospace
		STOL	Short takeoff and landing
PAAMS	Principal Anti-Air Missile System	STOVL	Short takeoff and vertical landing
PVO	Air Defense Force (Czech Republic)	STUAS	Short-Range Tactical UAV System
		SUAV	Swiss UAV
R&D	Research and development	TACMAV	Tactical Mini-UAV
RAF	Royal Air Force	TIHA	Türk Insansiz Hava Araci
RAPTOR	Responsive Aircraft Program for Theater Operations	TUMAV	Tactical Unmanned Multirole Air Vehicle
RFP	Request for proposal	UAV	Unmanned air vehicle
ROVER	Remote Optical Video Enhanced Receiver	UCAS	Unmanned combat air system
RPV	Remotely piloted vehicle	UCAV	Unmanned combat air vehicle
		UST	Unmanned Systems Technology
SAM	Surface-to-air missile	UUV	Unmanned Underwater Vehicle
SAR	Synthetic array radar	UV	Ultraviolet
SATUMA	Surveillance and Target Unmanned Aircraft	VACS	Variable autonomy control system
SIDM	Système Intermédiare de Drones MALE	VTOL	Vertical takeoff and landing
SIGINT	Signal intelligence		
SOCOM	Special Operations Command		
SORAO	Sottosistema di Sorveglianza di Acquisizione Obiettivi		

1

INTRODUCTION

An Unmanned Combat Air System

Northrop Grumman is developing an unmanned combat air system (UCAS), the air vehicle for which is the X-47B, for the U.S. Navy. Its system aspect makes it very different from the unmanned air vehicles, even armed ones (UCAVs), which are becoming commonplace. These vehicles are flown individually; each has its own pilot. In UCAS the vehicle and controlling system are much more tightly integrated. Typically the single ground system controls a group—a swarm—of air vehicles, each of which is usually not separately controlled. The operators assign targets to the swarm, and the system (under supervision) decides which air vehicle will attack each target, and largely how that will be done. The result is important new ways to fight—a transformation of U.S. naval aviation in the direction that other elements of U.S. national and technological strategy seem to point.[1] UCAS is likely to be the leading edge in a wider transformation of the U.S. military using unmanned vehicles to leverage U.S. technology and thus magnify the effect of limited numbers of U.S. airmen, sailors, and soldiers. The idea of such leverage is not new; it is why the United States fought a war of production in World War II. In that war the technological background was a mixture of mass production and the new technology of electronics. This time it is the continuing computer revolution.

Many years ago Adm. James Metcalf III, who was then director of surface warfare, reduced much of naval operations to putting ordnance on target. He had in mind surface ships armed with Tomahawk strike missiles, but he could just as easily have been describing carrier aviation. The point of naval warfare is to exploit the sea while denying it to an enemy. Currently, exploiting the sea generally means striking from the sea while freely transporting our own forces. Our enemies generally try to deny us the use of the sea, at least near their own shores. Classical naval strategy recognizes that our threat from the sea against the land compels an enemy to attack the fleet offshore and thus to expose his sea-denial force to destruction. Thus the strike forces both exploit command of the sea and gain it for other uses. Both an aircraft carrier and Admiral Metcalf's surface ship exemplify this combination. Each is a threat an enemy cannot ignore, hence each attracts attacks. In beating them off (the Tomahawk ship was also an Aegis air defense ship), each wipes out enemy antiship forces that would otherwise attack less heavily armed ships.

How can unmanned vehicles fit into such a strategy? What does air attack from the sea involve? In effect attack from the sea is the delivery of ordnance at the end of a long supply line reaching from the United States. The carrier or missile ship is the last transshipment point before the ordnance is delivered to its target. The same ordnance could be flown directly from the United States (which is why there is interservice rivalry between the Navy and Air Force), but flying it over relatively short distances makes for infinitely greater flexibility and timeliness—and for much more ordnance on target in any given length of

The U.S. Navy has bought the Northrop Grumman X-47B as its Demonstration Unmanned Combat Air System vehicle. X-47B is shown on rollout. (Northrop Grumman)

time. There is, after all, a vast difference between an hour's flight from carrier to target and ten or twenty hours from the United States. Another difference of course is that the carrier's fighters can destroy an enemy's antiship bombers, whereas that mission has nothing to do with a long-range bomber.

The New Way of War

A swarm of unmanned air vehicles, perhaps spread over a wide area, fits into a new style of warfare that has been adopted by the United States in recent years. This style is often called "network-centric."[2] Its first step is to create and maintain a current picture of *all* activity in a battle zone. This picture is to be precise enough for targeting, which increasingly means precise enough for attacks using navigationally guided (e.g., GPS-guided) weapons. This approach eliminates the warning enemies previously gained from the final reconnaissance step of the past, which was needed to bridge the gap between an approxi-

mate tactical picture and one that could be used for aiming (often this step was taken by the airplane actually making the attack). Given a good enough tactical picture, an enemy seeing one of our platforms no longer has the slightest idea of its significance. Virtually all attacks are surprise attacks. Too, comprehensive coverage may well make it easier to perceive enemy movements and even intentions, where the earlier approach might well miss things for which it had not been cued. The new approach also makes it far more difficult for an enemy to practice operational deception. This approach transforms the reconnaissance mission by enormously expanding the reconnaissance requirement. It is like the transition in air defense between acceptance of one or two channels per ship to demanding ten or more per ship.

The picture reveals an ever-changing array of potential targets. We already understand that we have to strike as many of them as possible as quickly as possible. That is why discussions of the new carrier design emphasize the

Many countries are now developing high-performance stealthy UCAVs. Showing that it was part of this trend, China displayed this model of its Anjian (Dark Sword) at air shows from 2006 on (this photo is from the 2007 Paris Air Show). Skeptics thought it unlikely that Chinese industry could build Dark Sword, but its presence at the show suggests a wider global trend. Stealth seems vital for a UCAV because it may be difficult for an unmanned vehicle to sense and recognize threats in an environment mixing friendly and unfriendly aircraft. Stealth may thus be its main defense against air-to-air and surface-to-air threats. (Norman Friedman)

ability to strike more targets per day. This is an issue of numbers of platforms versus numbers of channels. The ideal is to distribute the platforms over the targets as flexibly as possible.

In the past resources were limited, which meant that they could handle only a limited number of targets. Reconnaissance generally meant examining a particular pre-designated place, although there were attempts to gain area coverage by flying a planned path. In either case it was inconceivable that the whole of an enemy's territory would be covered, hence that reconnaissance in itself would provide insight into an enemy's overall dispositions. The only way to get true area coverage on a current basis was electronic reconnaissance, because the sensor range was so great. Thus the typical pattern was for electronic intelligence to provide the approximate position of a target of interest, which would then be overflown by a

reconnaissance aircraft. Important places might be overflown regularly. Generally, however, such patterns offered an enemy warning of impending attack. Armed reconnaissance could limit such warning, but only against a few targets at a time.

The Swarm as Virtual Air Base

The closer the carrier or other base is to the targets, the shorter the time line and the more efficient the delivery—not to mention that, if the ordnance is supporting a force on the ground, the timelier the delivery. UCAS suggests a new possibility, that because of their inherently long endurance, unmanned armed vehicles orbiting over an enemy's territory can act as a forward base from which strikes can be mounted quickly. The carrier in effect acts as a rear base feeding this sustained forward airborne base. In theory large aircraft could orbit for a sustained period,

Carriers are being redesigned to make it easier to turn aircraft around, so that they can carry out more sorties. This model of the next carrier, CVN-78 *Gerald R. Ford*, was displayed at the 2009 Navy League show. The island has been moved aft, eliminating the usual third starboard elevator and opening more space forward for aircraft servicing. The new arrangement has also been described as better suited to UCAVs. (Norman Friedman)

but they could not quickly replenish their weapon loads at a nearby forward area. Distributing the total weapon load among numerous vehicles makes it possible to sustain the weapon and fuel capacities of the group of vehicles on a continuous basis.

The UCAS design focuses not on the individual vehicle, as in the past, but on the swarm of vehicles that together create a new kind of air weapon. Control is distributed between the unmanned aerial vehicles (UAVs), which communicate with one another, and the base, which assigns targets.[3] The base can also monitor the operation of the UAVs, and it can take control of individual UAVs as necessary, for example, in emergencies. Communication among the UAVs makes it possible for the swarm as an entity to decide which UAVs are best suited to engage a given target, given factors such as their position, their fuel state, and what weapons they have on board. For example, different UAVs in the swarm may have different weapons on board, and the weapon mix will be replenished periodically as UAVs return to the carrier after expending their

weapons. Thus the swarm incorporates what amounts to a magazine continuously in the air.

Although each vehicle has only a few weapons and a finite fuel capacity, the swarm as an entity represents a sustainable air presence capable of mounting strikes as they are required. Like a carrier, it is also a target an enemy will find it difficult to ignore. The experience of carrier air warfare suggests that the swarm can be used to attract and destroy the most potent enemy antiair systems, his fighters.[4] That is, an enemy would feel compelled to use his fighters against the swarm. The stealthy high-performance UCAVs in the swarm would carry their own self-defense weapons, and the same sensors they would use to avoid collisions in mixed-use airspace would surely enable them to detect approaching enemy aircraft (the swarm would also benefit from sources of wide-area information about the positions of enemy aircraft, such as early warning aircraft).[5] Each UCAV would, moreover, keep track of the positions of others in the swarm, because that would be part of the shared information used by the

The X-47B has two internal weapon bays. About the size of an F/A-18, it also can carry weapons externally, at a price in stealth. (Northrop Grumman)

swarm, as an entity, to assign targets. Thus, particularly when it operated relatively far from friendly aircraft, the swarm would most likely be able to defend itself effectively without risking significant blue-on-blue attrition. In this way the swarm will tend to protect numerous other air activities over enemy territory, such as reconnaissance and resupply. This is much the way a carrier battle group is designed to attract and destroy antiship forces that otherwise would find it easy to attack less powerful seaborne targets, such as supply ships.[6] The swarm thus supports the kind of very flexible and fast-moving warfare the United States now favors. It is not clear how alternative forms of air power can achieve similar results.

Because the swarming vehicles are already close to the targets, routing them to targets is quicker and simpler than routing tactical aircraft from carrier to target or, as is now common, rerouting them in the air as targets pop up. The routing issue is particularly important in a tactical context, when targets are almost all transient, and when they have to be hit very quickly in order to support forces on the ground. It seems likely that future combat will involve more and more moving or transient tactical targets and fewer fixed or long-term ones. Current tactical air practice focuses on fixed targets because of inherent limitations in its command and control. Even respon-

sive measures against pop-ups are adapted from earlier fixed-target practice. For example, to provide support over Afghanistan, that country was divided up into zones, each of which was assigned to one aircraft available on a transient basis. From an air-control point of view, a zone was something like a spread-out fixed target; the airplane could be vectored as needed. The reality, however, was that persistent air cover was needed, with air platforms always available near potential targets. The closest the U.S. forces came to such cover was probably the Marines' use of Harriers at their fire base, because the Harriers were always on call at close range (the Marines thought of them as an extension of their artillery).

Aside from such bases, U.S. forces must rely on manned aircraft that spend most of their time en route to and away from the patrol or operating areas. The longer the flight, the more fatigued the pilot and the worse his judgment, which has caused friendly fire problems. Human judgment can always be faulty, but there seems little point in worsening the situation.

Moreover, the greater the fraction of its total mission time an airplane spends in transit, the more airplanes are needed to maintain some semblance of continuous coverage. Air coverage is vital. In effect it is an alternative to the artillery and surface-to-surface missiles ground troops

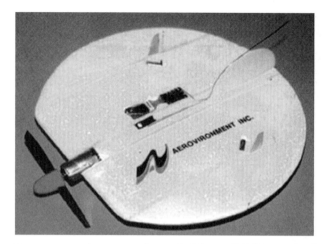

Swarm concepts are usually applied to small UAVs, each of which contributes to an overall picture of a situation. The controller of a swarm orders the swarm to execute some instruction (such as to attack a target at a given location), but the elements of the swarm decide among themselves how to conduct that attack. The U.S. Navy's Cooperative Engagement Capability program for air defense ships was probably the first to adopt this logic; CEC embodied a Force Threat Evaluation and Weapon Assignment for automated selection of the appropriate firing ship. In practice this feature was not adopted because the commanders of individual ships did not want to abrogate their responsibilities. That objection would not apply to unmanned vehicles. Swarm logic seems to be the only way to operate large numbers of unmanned air vehicles, particularly future ultra-small ones such as this AeroVironment Black Widow. A single Black Widow could report back to a single operator, but only a swarm of them can cover, say, an urban combat zone. X-47B takes this approach on a larger scale. (AeroVironment)

can deploy. The less such loads they carry with them, the lighter and more mobile they can be, without the sacrifice of firepower, the past price of such mobility. According to current thinking, mobility in itself is a major virtue because it can force an enemy to deal with faster-paced combat. More conventional forces should not be able to cope, and they may suffer collapse as a consequence. It really is important to be able to keep airplanes overhead, or within attack range, on a continuous basis, because the United States may be unable to support the logistical load a more conventional ground force would entail.

It appears that swarming UCAVs, maintained in the air by refueling aircraft, offer exactly the capability U.S. forces now need. If combat is near the sea, a carrier and its fighters can provide this sort of capacity, but we may find ourselves fighting at much greater distances. In future long stand-off may be imposed by enemy antiship capability, but even without that we have the example of Afghanistan, hundreds of miles from the Arabian Sea.

It may be objected that any acceptable U.S. operation will always attract partners who will provide nearby bases. That is by no means clear. Countries near Afghanistan were reluctant to host U.S. combat aircraft during the run-up to the 2001 attack, and it was apparent that many countries bordering Iraq were similarly reluctant in 2003. The experience of the first Gulf War (1990–91) suggests that it was the independent U.S. ability to operate from carriers in the Persian Gulf that convinced local governments to provide base facilities. The Afghan experience suggests further that although we may enjoy basing within, say, 1,500 miles of the combat zone, matters will be considerably more difficult closer in. Thus it may be possible to obtain rights to base noncombat aircraft such as tankers and electronic reconnaissance types, but using the same bases for tactical aircraft will likely cause us problems, including poor coverage of the combat area.

Some Tactical Implications

UCAS should demonstrate air-to-air refueling by the end of 2013; as this is being written, the Defense Advanced Research Projects Agency (DARPA) is already underwriting a demonstration of air-to-air refueling by the big Global Hawk UAV. Given the refueling capability, a carrier operating UCAS can stand off beyond the horizon of most enemy antiship weapons and sensors, while sustaining the swarm closer to potential targets. An enemy threatened by the swarm would have to concentrate on dealing with the stealthy UAVs constituting it. The swarm of UAVs would act as a lethal attraction for enemy air-to-air and antiair systems, and it would make a considerable difference that the UAVs could be controlled collectively rather than individually. This idea, that a sustained air presence can both exercise and gain air superiority, would be something new in air combat. In the past individual aircraft have never had more than a transient presence. Air battles have secured air control, but at a very high cost in aircraft numbers to gain sufficient presence. Here the great example is probably the use of heavy bombers over Germany to bleed the German fighter force and thus to preclude its use during the invasion of France in 1944. Even then an enemy has usually had the option of operating when our aircraft temporarily were not present. In either case it is very unlikely that we will ever again have

UAVs do not suffer from pilot fatigue and thus their endurance is limited only by fuel supply and reliability. Large surveillance UAVs are therefore more and more seen as intermediate between existing manned reconnaissance aircraft and satellites, enjoying the advantage that they loiter over an area of interest (but are also more vulnerable to enemy action). As reliability improves, fuel supply becomes the limiting factor, and work is currently under way on a means of refueling the big Global Hawk in the air. (Northrop Grumman)

the number of manned aircraft we have used in the past. Without very large numbers, aircraft operating on an individually transient basis cannot sustain presence. In Afghanistan we were able to maintain a few aircraft over the country continually, but they sufficed only because the tempo of combat was so slow that only rarely did airplanes have to hit more than one place at a time. This was not really sustained air presence, and it would not have sufficed against a more modern opponent.

Sustained air presence in the face of intact enemy air defenses is possible only because the UCAS air vehicle is a stealthy design. Obviously stealth cannot be absolute, but the effort required to detect and track these aircraft would be considerable and expensive. Enemy air defense resources will be finite. Concentrating on the lethal threat of the swarm would considerably reduce the threat to other U.S. aircraft. The UCAVs cannot take over all fighter functions because in some cases the fighter pilot's judgment is important. The human in the fighter is vital in situations that are neither entirely peaceful (aircraft never to be shot down) or clearly wartime (anything not answering an IFF [Identification Friend or Foe] challenge to be shot down). That was the case during the Cold War. Similarly the lack of pilot judgment proved disastrous in the 1988 *Vincennes* incident.[7] UCAS answers the problems of actual war-

fare, in which judgment is applied mainly in designating targets on the ground.

Ideally a stealthy UAV could come close enough to its target to deliver relatively short-range precision munitions, such as bombs guided by the Global Positioning System (GPS). As long as its weapons are guided to set coordinates, however, it does not matter whether they are short or medium range. Thus the UCAV can deliver some attacks from outside the range of the most sophisticated enemy air defenses. Previous experience of air defense suggests that such systems are always vulnerable to saturation, particularly if some UCAVs deliver decoys in the initial attack. It is very well to credit a modern air defense system with the ability to track one hundred targets at a time, but if it has only twenty ready missiles, it faces exhaustion by a mass attack.[8] That is why, during the 1980s, as it contemplated mass missile attacks delivered by long-range Soviet bombers, the U.S. Navy kept concentrating on the "archer," not the "arrows" the archer fired. All stand-off attackers force defenses to spend more of their efforts on the arrows. The effect of a stealthy airframe is likely to be a dramatic reduction in the effective engagement range of any air defense system. If the aircraft comes close enough, the system has enough opportunities to form a viable track, and a command-guided missile may

Tactical Tomahawk is effectively a one-way UCAV: It responds to operator commands based on what it sees (or can be sent on a preset mission). It loiters, awaiting those commands, or can observe a combat area so that the operator can decide what to do with it. It sends its data into a Link 16 network, and it receives its commands from a system which decides which of several such missiles should be used for a particular attack. That is very close to swarm operation. This prototype Tactical Tomahawk is shown with an F-14 chase airplane over China Lake, November 2002. (U.S. Navy)

well work (as it did against the F-117 over Serbia); but the stealthier the airframe, the closer "close enough" becomes. It may well be possible to detect stealthy aircraft at greater ranges using, for example, lower-frequency radars, but they provide warning rather than engagement data.

The swarm is probably best evaluated in terms of a campaign like those conducted over Iraq and Afghanistan. In each case, the first step was the destruction of the enemy's national air defense system. The swarming technique described above would be used to exhaust and then to destroy the limited number of expensive high-quality wide-area systems in the enemy inventory.[9] Once that had been done, the enemy would be limited to point defenses and most enemy air space would be safe for attackers. From the point of view of UCAVs, it would become possible to fly with larger weapon loads carried externally (the weapons themselves might still be stealthy, to penetrate the point defenses). This is much the way conventional aircraft would be used. The difference is that the sheer persistence of the swarm would probably make it easier to exhaust enemy air defenses. Conventional aircraft fly over and leave, but the swarm can easily strike the same target again and again.

UAV Control

Existing unmanned combat air systems, such as Predators carrying Hellfire missiles, are armed extensions of

existing unmanned air vehicles. Alternatively they might be imagined as much more flexible extensions of missiles. They are not so very different from Tactical Tomahawks, which loiter near a battle area, awaiting the command to attack designated targets. If a Tactical Tomahawk could release its warhead over a target and return for recovery, it would be an unmanned combat air vehicle. Conversely a kamikaze-style unmanned air vehicle is a missile. The Indians have gone so far as to develop their unmanned air vehicle (actually a target drone) into a cruise missile.

The characteristics of these vehicles suggest a next step. Armed Predators are effectively command-guided missiles. The human in the loop monitors what the vehicle sees and decides what to engage. The human also monitors the engagement. The number of human operators, much more than the number of vehicles, is the limiting factor on system engagement. The operators are necessary because the targets are enemy individuals whose identity must be verified (at least to some extent) before the attack. In effect the UAVs operate as high-tech snipers.

An individual UCAS air vehicle can operate this way, but more likely the sensor and the weapon will be connected far less directly. The U.S. armed forces are moving toward a style of warfare emphasizing the ability to engage large numbers of targets either in close succession or simultaneously. To do that we are separating the sensing element from the attacking element (although attack-

Predator became the first U.S. UCAV in service. This U.S. Air Force Predator was one of the first three to fly over Afghanistan after the 9/11 attacks; it flew a total of 196 missions there. It was the first to test fire the Hellfire C missile, and the first to fire it in combat. It was later modified (with a longer wing, new propeller, modified avionics, and modified engine cooling) as the prototype of the MQ-1L version. Below the Predator shown here is the stealthy Dark Star in the National Air and Space Museum, 2009. Unlike a swarming UCAV, Predator is exactly analogous to a manned airplane and is flown by its own pilot. In 2008 the U.S. Air Force was developing a UAV cockpit specifically for this kind of operation. Above Predator is the stealthy Dark Star. (Norman Friedman)

ers can still add their sensor data to the overall picture). This kind of separation makes it possible for one attacking vehicle to handle multiple targets in close succession. Judgment is exercised at the level of choice of target based on pervasive sensing. Thus descriptions of the new carrier mention the sheer number of separate targets the ship and its air group can engage each day, which is vastly more than the number that could be engaged in the past. The hope is that an enemy can be swamped by the sheer pace of warfare.

The new technique offers key advantages even for the current sniping role. We currently wait at a likely place for a prechosen target to arrive. Pervasive sensing would pick up that target anywhere in the area we can cover by air.

We would be much more likely to find such targets, and we would also be more likely to hit them rapidly and without warning. Moreover, the potential targets are surely aware of who they are and thus are likely to vary their routes more or less randomly. Without pervasive sensing, our ability to strike them can be frustrated. With more pervasive sensing, it is far more difficult for them to escape attack. To the extent that the current war on terror(ists) emphasizes individual attacks, it seems that we will be moving toward pervasive sensing, which in turn would best be linked to pervasive air presence and to the ability to engage multiple targets more or less simultaneously.

In the missile world the pace of warfare translates into the rate at which targets can be engaged—into the

As small UAVs gain endurance, they can provide pervasive surveillance but not pervasive attack capability. It may make sense to distinguish between swarms of surveillance UAVs and swarms of attack UAVs, which operate on the basis of the picture they create. An array of small but capable UAVs is shown at Patuxent River in June 2005, assembled for the U.S. Navy's 2005 Naval UAV Air Demo. Front to back, left to right: RQ-11A Raven, Evolution, Dragon Eye, NASA FLIC, Arcturus T-15, Skylark, Tern, RQ-2B Pioneer, and RQ-15 Neptune. (U.S. Navy by PH2 Daniel J. McLain)

factors that cause a system to be saturated. UCAS translates the antisaturation ideas of the missile world into the world of armed unmanned vehicles. In the missile world, the key to antisaturation was to give individual missiles sufficient intelligence that they did not require continuous guidance. Instead they could receive periodic commands so that the guidance system could be time-shared among them. This idea was the basis of successful antiaircraft (antisaturation) systems such as Aegis. The technological key was a programmable autopilot that could be reset remotely. A ship launches several missiles toward several targets. It continually tracks the targets and the rising missiles. Periodically the missile trajectories are reprogrammed (by command) to bring them closer to the targets. In Aegis the ship turns on illuminators (to provide individual guidance, in effect) only at the last moment. In some broadly analogous systems, such as the European PAAMS (Principal Anti-Air Missile System), the missile turns on its own guidance system at the end. Giving missiles a limited degree of intelligence or autonomy is a way to handle more targets, that is, to respond to a more complex situation.

For an unmanned vehicle the situation is more complicated. We can already program individual vehicles to fly to the vicinity of a potential target and to orbit there while an operator monitors their sensors. In this case the obvious barrier to quick target engagement is the operator's concentration on each single vehicle. However, there is also a subtler barrier. Flights are individually planned and individually tailored to particular targets. The flight from base to target imposes a substantial delay. Imagine what happens when a decision is made to attack some previously unplanned target. First the flight to the target must be programmed and inserted into a waiting vehicle on the ground. Then the vehicle must fly out to attack. Alternatively someone on the ground must decide that a particular target currently on the schedule can be abandoned in favor of the new one and that the vehicle already airborne but programmed for the first target can be reprogrammed in the air. In either case the process is anything but supple. At best it resembles the current attempt to retarget aircraft once they are airborne, which works but is probably limited to a few pop-up targets. What if *all* targets are pop-ups? How can they be engaged most efficiently? How can that engagement make the best possible use of the special characteristics of an unmanned vehicle?

Compared to a manned airplane, the most striking advantage offered by an unmanned one is that it does not suffer from pilot fatigue. It is as effective at the end of its sortie as at the outset, as long as it retains sufficient fuel and as long as its parts continue to function. If, as planned, the unmanned vehicle can be refueled in the air, and if it is difficult to shoot down, the unmanned vehicle offers sustained presence in a target area. The UCAS project envisages both. The absence of a pilot and cockpit should make it easier to design an unmanned vehicle for low observables, hence for better sustained survivability in the face of enemy air defenses. Moreover, to the extent that the unmanned vehicle depends on a network of external sensors to find its target, it should reduce its effective observability by reducing its own emissions. A pilotless design is probably also easier to provide with all-round sensing of other aircraft, which may be important for a UCAV armed with air-to-air missiles.

Imagine, then, that the preferred mode of unmanned vehicle operation is to loiter within attack range of potential targets waiting for the command to attack. Right now that is done singly, by Predators and their equivalents. However, the preferred mode of operation, consistent with other U.S. military developments, would be to separate attacker from sensor. The emerging U.S. style of warfare favors pervasive sensing rather than reliance on the sensors on board the attacking vehicle. Pervasive sensing in itself causes an enemy severe problems. He spends much of his effort trying to hide rather than concentrating on attacking us. Because sensing is pervasive, he cannot know when some observation will trigger an attack. He must therefore always be on the alert, which in itself is exhausting.

An Integrated System

Now consider the armed vehicles and the sensors and the decision makers as an integrated system. It has three main command and control functions. One is to assemble sensor data into a coherent picture that can be used for targeting. A second is to decide what to attack and when. A third is to program the armed vehicles to carry out their missions. Of these three, only the assembly of the picture and the decision making are inherently human functions. Mission planning, even for aircraft in the air, is increasingly automated. In the case of aircraft, the missions are planned using data inputs at a ground center. One of the inputs is the judgment as to which airplane already in flight is best placed to attack a pop-up target.

As computers become more powerful, it is no longer so clear where different computing functions should be located. UCAS is being designed to minimize the detailed control of different unmanned armed vehicles so that human operators can concentrate on the two functions that require their judgment. Each vehicle has more than enough computer capacity to accommodate a mission planner. Given a target assignment, it can develop an optimum mission plan to get there and return. Placing the mission planning function in the unmanned vehicle offers a new way of viewing such vehicles. They can operate together as a swarm, and the swarm can become the basic unit of force.

The vehicles of the swarm communicate with one another to decide which of them is best equipped to attack a given target on the basis of its fuel and weapon loads. Communication can also enable multiple vehicles to attack together. Communication between the human operator and the swarm concentrates on selecting and prioritizing assignments for the swarm as a whole. Human operators can intervene to redirect a particular air vehicle, but (as the system is envisaged) they never actually fly it.[10] Moreover, typically the swarm is controlled as a single entity; human operators do not assign particular targets to particular aircraft. This type of control is called state based, and it is likely to be applied to other massed systems as well. The human operator is mainly a system supervisor and a prime decision maker—which is the point of having human operators in the first place. The U.S. Navy already looks upon its strike missiles in much this way, demanding a man-in-the-loop but not continuous controlled operation. In this sense UCAV is a natural extension of current missile practice.

A focus on the swarm changes the way in which unmanned vehicle operation is understood. The swarm is a sustained presence within range of targets. The role of the system is to sustain it. That means periodically refueling its members and bringing them back to reload them with weapons as they carry out their attacks. The lifetime of a vehicle in the swarm is set either by its mean time between failures, by the rate at which it can be refueled in the air, or by weapons expenditure.

This type of operation *requires* that the vehicles in the swarm normally operate with minimum human intervention because their operation is coordinated in a way that would be extremely difficult for multiple remote human operators. The swarm *as a whole* is normally commanded by a single operator. Its efforts can be concentrated or distributed as required. It can also conduct mass strikes on particular targets (now typically the role of individual heavy aircraft) or for numerous strikes distributed in time and in space. Mass strikes may exhaust the swarm so that it has to be replaced en masse, but sometimes they will be worth that; similarly, the resources of a forward base might be exhausted by a high-intensity strike.

To some extent the swarming UCAVs are cruise missiles, a large part of which can be reused. The UCAVs do some things the missiles cannot possibly do: They refuel in the air to sustain their presence and they return to ship for reuse. However, the UCAS concept has enough of the missile in it to make past missile experience a guide to how a swarm of UCAS might work. One interesting example for the U.S. Navy is the Cold War use of a swarm of manned aircraft to maintain a missile presence. A swarm of fighters maintaining air-to-air missiles enabled the fleet to handle the threat of enemy bombers appearing relatively unexpectedly—unexpectedly enough that there was insufficient time to launch interceptors from deck. Sustained air presence was needed because the enemy antiship bomber force had a considerable window in which to attack, even if its takeoff time was known. On a carrier a single fighter control entity assigned the fighters to targets, much as a single controller might assign targets to the swarm. There were obvious differences, but

the parallel in sustaining an air presence is striking. Some lessons may also be applicable. The greatest problem was to maintain the swarm of defensive fighters (a Combat Air Patrol) despite limited fuel endurance (pilot fatigue was much less significant). In this case aerial refueling was rejected because the swarm was widely distributed, hence would have required too many tankers, and because of IFF problems every time a tanker flew back toward the carrier (fighters flying back presented similar problems). The swarm presented such problems that periodic attempts were made to abandon it in favor of surface weapons, which might be directed by a long-endurance airplane. Each time it turned out that the aircraft, closer to the threat, were far more attractive, just as UCAVs closer to their targets are more attractive than land-attack missiles on board ships.[11]

All of this means that at the least the individual UCAV has a navigational system that tells it where it is so that it can deliver ordnance as required and so that it can be directed. It needs a means of communicating both with its base and with other UCAVs of the swarm. These capabilities are not particularly exotic, though the swarm-control software is a new and important idea.

UCAS can accommodate reconnaissance sensors such as imaging radar and infrared (IR) or ultraviolet (UV) scanners. In theory, then, the same set of airframes could detect targets and attack them. Certainly it would be attractive to collect whatever the UCAS swarm detected for use in forming the tactical picture on which attacks would be based. However, it seems likely that the UCAVs will never be numerous enough to cover enemy territory well enough to find targets. Rather it seems likely that the relevant tactical picture will be formed from a wider variety of sensors, including those on board more specialized UAVs—plus, for example, spacecraft and various forms of ES (electronic support) and ELINT (electronic intelligence).

Where Are We Now?

How futuristic is the UCAS air vehicle? The answer is, not very much. We already operate large numbers of individually controlled UAVs, some of them armed, to the point where manned reconnaissance aircraft are scheduled to disappear some time in the next decade (there is

Among the challenges X-47B must meet is operating on a carrier flight deck. Such operation currently entails considerable skill on the part of flight deck personnel, as well as on the part of a pilot interpreting hand signals from the ground crew. A successful naval UCAV has to be integrated into a flight deck that uses such signals to control all other aircraft. Solutions may range from some means of recognizing the movements of specially modified gloves worn by the flight deck crew to simply having a crewman get on board the UCAV after it lands and before it maneuvers. (Northrop Grumman)

some dispute as to exactly when, but not whether). Cruise missiles are unmanned armed aircraft sent on one-way missions.

As for collective control, several missiles, such as the Tactical Tomahawk, embody a mixture of preplanned missions and man-in-the-loop intervention to conduct pop-up missions. Each missile orbits, awaiting commands, and then attacks if ordered to do so. If no order comes as its fuel begins to run out, the missile carries out a preset mission. Missiles do not have individual controllers. Instead, a collective system on board a ship decides which missile in the air is best suited for the desired mission. UCAS entails a leap in which the automated system is largely distributed on board the vehicles rather than on a surface station. That seems a reasonable extrapolation of current practice, and it has the important advantage of minimizing air-to-ground communication. Communication bandwidth will undoubtedly be limited, and moving most of the system to the air should make for the greatest possible number of air vehicles. It also offers the

best potential to continue swarm operations (albeit in degraded form) should communications with the ground station be disrupted.

We already deliver most weapons by sending them to GPS addresses, so the expected blind mode of delivery by UCAS is nothing unusual—it merely reminds us that the pilot's expertise is less and less used. Admittedly there are cases, particularly in close-air support, in which a pilot's ingenuity solves difficult problems—for example, skipping a bomb under a bridge—but they are few. All major changes in military technology involve the loss of important but relatively unusual capabilities, and UCAS is unlikely to be an exception. Its advantages far outweigh any such disadvantages. The point is that this is nothing new; military revolutions tend to sweep out previous methods because the combination of the new and the old turns out to be unaffordable.

There is already considerable experience of distributed systems that coordinate via short-range data links. The very successful Cooperative Engagement Capability

(CEC) is a case in point, and a far more complex one than UCAS. Aircraft carriers have been using automatic systems to land their aircraft in bad weather and at night for some time. Airliners also land blind. None of the systems involved is exactly that planned for UCAS, but the existence of such systems indicates that the system is feasible.

Two elements of UCAS remain to be proven: in-flight fueling and deck operation. The former is the more important because it ensures the important advantage of long endurance. The latter may involve some complexity, but if a planned system fails to materialize in time it is always possible to revert to the manual methods of the past.

Moreover the typical UCAS mission will be so protracted that recovery will be far less frequent than it is now, so the burden on the deck crew will be much less. Thus even a UCAS relying on primitive methods of deck handling should greatly reduce the load on the deck crew.

The aerodynamics and the controllability of the configuration was demonstrated in one flight by the predecessor X-47A Pegasus, and by multiple flights by the Boeing X-45A, which had a somewhat comparable tailless configuration. The evidence of numerous current operational systems would seem to show that UCAS is entirely practicable, with the sole exception of air-to-air refueling, which the program should be able to demonstrate in the future.

2

A CHANGING
TACTICAL ENVIRONMENT

The wars in Iraq and in Afghanistan are the first major post–Cold War conflicts faced by the United States. Do these linked wars represent the shape of future warfare? Or are they, in effect, distractions from classic large-scale high-tech warfare? In the past it generally was assumed that lower-intensity war was a lesser case of high-intensity warfare, so the weapons and systems bought for the higher end of the scale automatically sufficed for the lower end. Our experience during the Vietnam War should have suggested that this was not always true, but we seem to be relearning that lesson now. What is special about the new kind of war? What sorts of systems seem best adapted to it? What sort of air targeting is involved? These issues determine what sort of airpower is best adapted to particular kinds of war. This chapter will argue that the precision and endurance/persistence offered by UCAS is unusually (perhaps uniquely) well adapted to both the new kind of low-intensity war *and* classic large-scale warfare. It also fits well into evolving U.S. military technology, which is increasingly based on dispersed sensors whose information is fused together.

High-Intensity War

Classical high-intensity war involves the sorts of resources only a government can assemble and wield (an insurgency like that in Afghanistan or a wide-scale terrorist war like that against Al Qaeda is a different proposition). It is the realm of conventional tactics, the basis of which is the idea that defeating an enemy's organized military forces ends a war. Organized forces in turn are subject to attacks on their centers of gravity, such as their supply lines.

When approaching such wars, air forces have tended to emphasize attacks against fixed targets because it is far easier to specify target position, based on reconnaissance, and then have pilots navigate into position. Once near a target of specified position, they can use preselected landmarks to get them to the desired target. However, classical fixed strategic targets are rarely worth the attention they receive. It takes considerable time, for example, for the destruction of an arms factory to affect the level of supply in forward forces (if weapon stowage sites can be destroyed, that is another matter). Most of the worthwhile fixed targets will be small, and many will be difficult to identify from the air. They usually will be identified by analysts with access to a broad range of sensor information. The result of analysis will be the geographical position of a target. Pilots flying at high speed, even at the speeds common late in World War II, find it difficult to recognize small targets from the air. A small fraction of targets are attacked on the basis of armed reconnaissance, in which pilots seek out targets. Probably the most celebrated example would be train-busting in northern Europe in 1944–45 as a means of disrupting German rail communication. In Afghanistan enemies probably were often discovered when they shot at U.S. aircraft flying overhead (the problem was that people in Afghanistan also fired guns upward when celebrating). Note the connection between armed reconnaissance and free-fire zones: Pilots may recognize the sort of object that is of interest, but they are much less likely to know whether it is friendly or enemy.

The other kind of air support in high-intensity war is close air support, attacks on targets that become significant only because of how they figure in an ongoing battle. The less the fixed targets matter (as in places like Afghanistan), the more the only vital targets are those that occur in the context of ongoing operations. Close air support typically requires a spotter or forward observer. In the past the spotter used smoke rounds to indicate the desired target; now he can use GPS coordinates. An enemy may also sense that airpower is effective only against fixed targets, and he may therefore constantly relocate key resources. Nearly all worthwhile targets may be either mobile or relocatable. Much will depend on an ability to strike as soon as possible after targets are located and before they move very far.

As a case in point, during the 1990–91 Gulf War there was considerable effort to attack and destroy Iraqi mobile missile launchers. This effort consumed a large fraction of available attack aircraft for several weeks and presumably delayed the ground offensive. Aircraft were held in readiness in the air and vectored on the basis of observed missile trajectories. They reported numerous attacks. After the war it turned out that most or all had destroyed tanker trucks, which from the air resembled missile launchers.

In a wider sense the first Gulf War demonstrated that attacks on fixed targets had little impact on the course of the war. The weight of the initial air effort was directed at classic strategic targets in central Iraq, such as government facilities and arms plants. Their continued existence might have been crucial in a war lasting months or years, but the Iraqi army was unlikely to last more than a few days; Iraq was not a powerful modern country. These attacks may, however, have been intended as a means of disarming Iraq and thus precluding further near-term Iraqi aggression once coalition forces had stood down. For example, coalition spokesmen claimed, it turned out incorrectly, that the entire Iraqi nuclear infrastructure had been destroyed.[1] It turned out that the critical air attacks were those that wore down front-line Iraqi units so that coalition ground forces could defeat them. The whole war lasted about six weeks, but the decisive ground phase

was much shorter. It can be argued that the really crucial targets were those directly supporting the ground war, many of which were mobile or relocatable. These targets probably could be located only as the war progressed.

The second Gulf War (2003) showed, too, that the fixed targets the enemy really valued often could not be located. The United States certainly was able to deny the Iraqis Saddam Hussein's much-vaunted Battle of Baghdad, probably by hitting arms dumps in the city he thought he had concealed—precision strikes against fixed targets in known positions (known because of excellent reconnaissance). However, from Hussein's point of view, the most important target in Baghdad, after himself, was the television station he used to communicate with the country. Numerous attempts to destroy its transmitter all failed. The lesson is that Third World governments do have a significant ability to conceal their most important fixed resources (they are less likely to be able to conceal elaborate fixed bunkers). In both gulf wars Hussein survived by making himself a relocatable target. That should not have been a great surprise; he had spent many years evading assassination attempts, and air attack was only the latest of them.

Another significant factor in future war is the rising cost of military equipment, such as armored vehicles. Since World War II the size of armies (in terms of numbers of units, such as divisions) has been declining for this reason. Many Third World armies avoided this problem because the Soviet Union produced a flood of equipment, much of which was provided to them at little or no cost. With the fall of the Soviet Union, these countries face much the same economics as do Western armies. They are unlikely to replace equipment on anything approaching a one-to-one basis, and most of them lack the ability to produce the necessary replacement parts. One consequence is that the kind of units the United States can deploy on an expeditionary basis are likely to face smaller rather than larger enemy ground units. The leverage they can gain by using remote sensing and UCAVs is likely to make a decisive difference. In a world of small ground units, combat is likely to be decentralized, without a well-defined front line. The military objective will be the enemy's units rather than his territory. Such warfare makes reconnaissance and rapid-reaction air support vital.[2]

All of this suggests that in a future high-intensity war strikes will be mounted mainly on a quick basis, targets being assigned as sets of coordinates. A relatively small force of highly flexible attackers is likely to be more effective than a large force of attackers designed mainly to hit fixed targets. Close air support may be far more important than anything else. Precision will be particularly essential, because enemy forces will be close to friendly ones. Success will depend not so much on overall numbers as on numbers of aircraft continuously in range of the battle area—on a combination of persistence and precision, exactly the virtues that UCAS offers.

State-on-state war does not necessarily involve high technology on both sides. Vietnam was a case in point. U.S. strategists recognized that North Vietnam was the source of the war. Had it been politically possible to do so, overrunning North Vietnam would have ended the threat to South Vietnam. This sort of strategy was rejected because of fear that China would intervene (as in the Korean War) had U.S. forces invaded North Vietnam.[3] Thus the war in Vietnam was a classic state-versus-state war in which one of the combatants enjoyed sanctuary rights (at the outset the United States let China know that it did not intend to invade the north, the object being to preclude Chinese involvement on the Korean War model). Air attacks were mounted on North Vietnam in the hope that it could be damaged badly enough to convince its government to abandon the fight in the south. This part of the war was certainly conducted in high-tech fashion, by air attack and air defense over North Vietnam.[4] American strategists thought that the North Vietnamese regime would not willingly surrender the industrial base it had painstakingly built up over the previous decade. They did not realize that the main motivation of the North Vietnamese leadership was to maintain and extend their power. Industrial installations could be replaced once the war was over. In fact the only targets of critical importance in North Vietnam were those feeding the war effort by receiving war materiel from China and the Soviet Union. Hence the quick reaction, in 1972, when American aircraft mined Haiphong Harbor and thus jeopardized access to war materiel.

The North Vietnamese fought the war in the south using dispersed units seeking to control the rural South Vietnamese population and countryside.[5] Vietnam was a small-unit war without any front line because the logistic pipeline from North to South Vietnam could not support large units (the North Vietnamese did sometimes deploy higher-tech forces, including tanks, but never in large numbers). The North Vietnamese believed that they could continue this kind of warfare until the South Vietnamese population was so cowed that it would join a revolt. However, the attempt to combine invasion with a revolt during Tet in 1968 failed, and the Vietcong units fighting in South Vietnam were badly mauled.[6] U.S. forces sought to cut off their supplies (e.g., by attacks on the Ho Chi Minh Trail) or to force them to stand and fight U.S. units with far more firepower. The insurgent strategy failed; in the 1972 Easter Offensive the North Vietnamese felt compelled to mount a conventional invasion of South Vietnam, which was defeated by conventional means, including massive close air support strikes. Conventional air attacks on Haiphong convinced the North Vietnamese to accept a settlement of the war in 1973. By that time the U.S. public, weary of the war and hardly convinced that the settlement was any sort of success, no longer wanted anything to do with Vietnam. The North Vietnamese seem to have appreciated that the U.S. guarantees the 1973 agreement offered to South Vietnam were worthless, and in 1975 it mounted a successful conventional attack that overran South Vietnam.

On the face of it the Vietnam War thus suggests that an aggressive Third World government can profitably deploy a guerrilla force to overrun a neighboring country despite U.S. resistance. Clearly the nature of the war disenchanted the American public, to the point where North Vietnam won a conventional war in 1975. However, North Vietnam paid a very heavy price for that success. No other Third World government followed its path to success. North Vietnamese allies overran Western-oriented governments in other parts of what had been French Indochina (Cambodia and Laos), but they were deterred from going farther. In particular, guerrilla warfare in itself did not give the North Vietnamese the victory they sought.

Moreover, the sort of capability the United States is now developing, involving the extensive use of remote sensors to find targets, would greatly have improved performance both in cutting off the North Vietnamese logistics flow to the South and in supporting small-unit combat when the Vietcong were caught in the open. In both cases persistent air presence would have been essential. As airplanes have become more expensive, the numbers in air arms have shrunk dramatically, compared not only to those of World War II but also to those of the Vietnam War. The only substitute for numbers (assuming that airplanes are survivable) is persistence, which means a way of overcoming pilot fatigue. In this sense an extremely persistent survivable UCAV would seem to be a most valuable asset in a Vietnam-style war of the future.

Overall a U.S. capability to fight and win conventional wars provides us with a form of deterrence: a Third World government will not court the opportunity to be defeated. The U.S. capability is expensive, and it does not seem relevant to warfare against insurgents in places such as Afghanistan. Many now ask whether Iraq and Afghanistan show Third World governments that they can deal with conventional U.S. military power by adopting strategies closer to insurgency. Perhaps asymmetric war is the wave of the future, not only for insurgents but also for governments. If that is the case, then current U.S. investment may be a mistake.

A hostile government might hope that the threat of insurgency would be an effective deterrent. It seems that in 1991 the George H. W. Bush administration decided not to invade Iraq (and overthrow Saddam Hussein) partly for fear that to do so would ignite a guerrilla resistance war.[7] It seems to have reasoned that Saddam Hussein would fight a conventional war for Kuwait. If defeated there, Saddam could withdraw (hence preserve) his troops, particularly his Republican Guard, the buttress of his regime. There was some hope that further military action would not be necessary, that defeat would destroy Saddam's regime, given opposition within Iraq, particularly by Kurds and Shi'ites. Ineptitude in drafting the armistice terms (particularly allowing the Iraqis to continue to use helicopters in the no-fly zones) made it possible for Saddam to retain power and thus ultimately claim that he had won the war. There is no evidence that U.S. intelligence uncovered any Iraqi preparation to wage guerrilla war.

On the other hand, a government that mounts a guerrilla-style war is itself endangered. Government is ultimately about control of a population. A government tries to maintain that control through both victory and defeat. Most governments would rather surrender (and survive) than promote anarchy as a way of dealing with attackers. If they survive despite defeat, they can fight another day. A more anarchic movement may eject enemies from the national territory, but the government that promotes or unleashes it will not enjoy the fruits of that victory.

As a case in point, late in World War I, when the German army was collapsing, some in Germany suggested fomenting a "people's war" in which the whole of the German population would resist further Allied advances. They considered national resistance against Napoleon an inspiration. The German government rejected any such initiative because such a movement would transform German society in ways the imperial government feared and detested. Although the kaiser was forced to abdicate, in effect the pre-1914 German government survived (the point of the Allied policy of unconditional surrender was to prevent a future war by eliminating this government). Contemplating its own destruction in 1945, the Nazi government became interested in creating a postsurrender resistance movement. It was not particularly successful, but in a way this movement foreshadowed what has happened in Iraq. Saddam seems to have set up an insurgent organization, based on his Ba'ath Party structure, specifically to keep fighting after his government suffered a conventional military defeat.

When the Germans occupied Western Europe, governments surrendered but resistance movements formed. Some were at least nominally controlled by successor governments in exile. During the war these organizations received considerable publicity. It now seems generally agreed that none of them was particularly effective, at least up until the time when Allied forces landed on the Continent (after that they were often very useful auxiliaries). From governments' perspective, the important point was that some resistance movements were not under their control. They represented organizations, particularly Communist parties, that hoped to supplant the prewar governments. Thus resistance was very much a double-edged sword. After the Germans invaded the Soviet Union

(June 1941), the most aggressive resistance units were Communist-led, probably precisely because they were not interested in restoring the prewar governments but in creating new ones. Elements of the prewar systems, such as many police, remained in office after their governments surrendered to the Germans. All over Western Europe there was (and remains) ambiguity about the extent of collaboration. The Western European government that did not completely surrender, that of France, had the greatest interest in suppressing resistance movements because it wanted to retain its own power.

Eastern Europe was a different proposition. Resistance in Poland was a very powerful movement partly because the Germans made it clear that they would continue to attack the local population (not only minorities) after the Polish government felt compelled to surrender. The government in exile sponsored a Home Army resistance organization. Communist-led resistance had limited appeal because Polish nationalism was deeply opposed to the Russians. Resistance in overrun parts of the Soviet Union was different because the Soviet government never surrendered at all. It had an active interest in supporting partisans in the Germans' rear—and in suppressing any movements that did not place themselves under Soviet control.

A resistance movement creates new leaders whose military success makes them effective rivals of whatever earlier government fought and lost a war. That was the case in Afghanistan, during the war against the Soviet occupiers. To some extent it was also the case in Western Europe as a consequence of the resistance movement against the Nazis (resistance empowered Communist parties in Western Europe, which had been relatively powerless prewar).

All of these factors suggest that intact hostile governments are more likely to fight conventional than guerrilla wars. Guerrilla war might be attractive if the government believed that it could maintain control of the guerrillas *and* of the surrounding population. It is possible, for example, that Saddam imagined that his Ba'ath Party was sufficiently loyal that it could form the basis of a guerrilla army *and* that the Iraqi people would be so motivated by nationalism as to back that army. However, he was realistic; he knew that he ruled by terror. It was entirely possible that much of his population would prefer a foreign

invader to his own rule. The Shi'ites and the Kurds both welcomed the U.S.-led coalition in 2003; the question ever since has been whether that welcome was squandered, not whether Saddam's guerrillas themselves could have ejected U.S. forces.[8]

Decentralized War

It seems more likely that in the near term we will be fighting insurgents trying to overthrow relatively weak governments we back. That has certainly been the case in both Iraq and in Afghanistan. In both cases the wars began as conventional (state vs. state) wars against governments with relatively weak military forces, which collapsed quickly. The insurgents are fighting the governments we helped install after defeating the enemy government. Elsewhere insurgents threaten governments we already back, for example in the Philippines. Guerrilla war wins by exhausting or demoralizing an enemy rather than by defeating his forces. If the conventional enemy was not demoralized, he usually won, because guerrilla war imposes enormous costs on those executing it. The French defeat in Algeria is probably a prime example of victory by demoralization (the war in French Indochina was much closer to state-on-state conventional war). Examples of victory against decentralized insurgent war would be the British in Malaya and Northern Ireland. The Chinese used to make much of their guerrilla war against the Japanese, but there is little evidence that the Japanese suffered badly, and as late as 1944 (when they were losing the Pacific War as a whole) they were able to mount a very successful offensive in China. Popular support for the war depends partly on whether it seems important enough to be worth its cost, and partly on what it costs. If Americans feel that Afghanistan is about avoiding a future 9/11, they will support continued engagement. If they feel that it is about supporting a failed or corrupt government, and that the sources of 9/11 lie elsewhere, they will probably support withdrawal. A combination of remote sensing and UCAVs can enormously affect the perceived cost of such a war.

The insurgencies in Iraq and in Afghanistan are in effect the flip side of conventional military victory. In neither case did the government formally surrender, hence neither provided the winning coalition force with legitimacy, which is rare in any case in the Third World. In neither case was there the sort of protracted war that might have convinced civilians that further resistance was pointless. Instead the losing governments exhorted civilians to keep fighting, and in each case a substantial segment of the population agreed to do so. Quick conventional victory followed by guerrilla warfare is likely to be the outcome in actions against many Third World governments and against the failed states that may harbor Al Qaeda and similar organizations.

Typically the U.S. goal is to build a government that will resist intimidation by Al Qaeda and similar anti-Western movements. To do that the nascent government has to be preserved against insurgent attacks. It has to prove its ability to protect its own citizens against the insurgents. The military problem, which often seems impossible, is that the insurgents can always choose their targets and often cannot be identified, let alone intercepted, as they move about the country. Unlike in Vietnam, the insurgents are not fighting on a scale that requires extensive logistical support. As in Vietnam, the insurgents often enjoy sanctuary across a border. The most important current case is Afghanistan, the sanctuary being in Waziristan, the "tribal area" of Pakistan, in which central Pakistani governmental authority is tenuous.

Terrorists or guerrilla warriors try to convince the population to support them and thus to undermine the enemy government. Their methods include propaganda, but experience in places such as Vietnam suggests that it is frequently a product of terror: "Support the government and we will return to kill you." Another terrorist tactic is to mix with locals so that any counterattacks inevitably kill many civilians and sour the survivors. Thus one key to successful antiterrorist attacks is selectivity on our part: We will kill you *if* you are a terrorist, but you will be safe if you are not. Success requires that we "own" not only the day but also the night; in the past it was common for areas (as in Vietnam) to be safe in daylight but terrorist controlled at night.

In the case of Al Qaeda, it is sometimes claimed that the motive is simply to bleed the West as part of a plan to overthrow us, or at the least to sap our willingness to support Muslim governments Al Qaeda hates. Even then Al Qaeda needs the willing support of the populations with-

in which it moves, because without that support its operatives will not long survive (as they do not survive in many Muslim countries whose governments feel threatened by Al Qaeda). Another way to see Al Qaeda (and parallel) operations is as part of a plan to gain power throughout the Muslim world. Many people in that world resent the West for its dominance and power. Al Qaeda tells those people that it is leading a resurgent form of Islam that will overcome the West. In this sense operations like 9/11 are intended to demonstrate the power and reach of Al Qaeda, and thus to command support. They also seem to have been intended to force the United States into a war that Al Qaeda hoped would cause many Muslims to rally to it and to overthrow Muslim governments more or less allied to the United States. This hope seems currently to be playing out to some extent in Pakistan. It seems likely that the initial crushing Taliban defeat helped discourage many in Waziristan who might otherwise have rallied to the Al Qaeda cause. Conversely a U.S. defeat in Afghanistan might raise Al Qaeda prestige and thus ignite other wars. Ultimately an Al Qaeda dominated Muslim world would attack the West, but that is a distant rather than an immediate prospect. Because future Al Qaeda wars are likely to be widely dispersed geographically, the United States needs means of dealing with them that minimize the investment of heavy ground forces. Precision strikes by long-endurance UAVs seem to be an appropriate element of the necessary strategy.

Motives for resistance vary. In Afghanistan the Taliban were seen by many as a mechanism for control by the majority (or at least plurality) Pushtuns. Having tasted full control, many Pushtuns saw little point in the coalition's promise of a more pluralistic society. Their war against modernizing coalition forces is a war against both foreigners (Afghanistan has always been xenophobic) and the internal groups Pushtuns previously ruled. The situation in Afghanistan is complicated by the fact that the Pushtun tribal area straddles the frontier. Many Afghans simply do not recognize the legitimacy of the border (the Curzon Line), which the British imposed during the late nineteenth century.[9] Thus the border is not merely porous, but few on either side will support any attempt to seal it. For example, they will not consider cross-border commerce smuggling. That such smuggling includes the

The combination of precise navigation (currently using mainly GPS) and precision weapons makes it possible for a few observers on the ground to trigger air strikes against small targets that do not appear distinctive from the air. This combination was first used extensively in Afghanistan. Here an Air Force forward air control team awaits the attack it has called in. (National Museum of the United States Air Force)

weapons used against the current Afghan government and its coalition supporters is incidental; the substantial cross-border traffic cannot be stopped without attacking the legitimacy of Pakistani rule in northern Pakistan.

In Iraq the current war was initially a fight by Sunnis trying to maintain their Saddam-era dominance despite the fact that they are a distinct minority (moreover, a minority not located in oil-rich areas of the country). Their targets were thus not only coalition forces occupying the country but also the majority Shi'ites of the south. The situation is further complicated in that Iran is the only Shi'ite-ruled country in the Islamic world, and hence is a natural source of support for the Iraqi Shi'ites (on the other hand, Iran is unlikely to be happy with a Shi'ite government that is not theocratic). Partly because Shi'ites inhabit many key areas of Saudi Arabia, and because they are treated badly in Sunni Muslim countries such as Saudi Arabia, the Saudis have supported the Sunni rebels.[10] External support for various Iraqi insurgent groups means that they enjoy a mixture of sanctuary and support across both the Syrian and Iranian borders. So much trade crosses those borders that it would be impossible to stop any logistical support to insurgents that is buried in it.

Both wars are tied to a larger fight against terrorist attacks by Al Qaeda and its clones. Part of the strategy of that war is to deny such organizations the opportunity to build quasi-national organizations in sanctuary areas such as the tribal reserves of northern Pakistan. The difference between the fights in Afghanistan and Iraq and those in places like northern Pakistan is that U.S. and coalition forces can operate more or less freely in the former but not in the latter. Thus in the former we can use a combination of ground troops, riverine forces, and aircraft, but the latter are open, if at all, only to aircraft.

Both in Afghanistan and in Iraq, antiguerrilla war reduces to hunting guerrillas while seeking the support of the bulk of the population. Past antiguerrilla techniques, which often amounted to intimidation of the mass of the population, would now be rejected as reprehensible. Because the guerrillas try to blend into the mass of the population, hunting them down has often involved killing many innocent people, embittering others. That was the great complaint when U.S. forces employed too much firepower in places in Vietnam. Guerrillas are aware of the problem and often deliberately seek overreactions to gain support. In Iraq and in Afghanistan, as well as in other theaters of antiterrorist warfare, the United States has sought to solve this problem by hunting guerrilla leaders more than the rank and file (that has also been the Israeli technique). More and more that means precision air attacks. There is still embittering collateral damage, and our enemies still make propaganda use of it, but it seems that precision attacks offer a way to attack enemy forces and leaders without paying the typical prices of the past. Such attacks are hardly sufficient to win an insurgent war, but

they can be used to shield the population from oppressive insurgents.

Precision attack is typically based on intelligence. Modern surveillance systems can make it difficult for an individual to communicate quickly without disclosing his location, e.g. by cell phone. There is no question but that enemy commanders can evade such surveillance, but they typically do so at the expense of quick two-way contact with their followers.[11] In effect the threat of precision attack can reduce the efficacy of a guerrilla or insurgent leader by denying him quick communication. *If* the situation can be arranged so that the leader must push through rapid decisions, the tension between failing in combat and failing to communicate may prove fatal. The loss of insurgent leaders ultimately saps an insurgency. If the insurgency cannot keep disrupting the local government, that government has the chance to grow to the point where it provides its citizens with the security and other services they want and need. Conversely, the mere existence of persistent surveillance systems the insurgents think can detect and target them can have profound psychological effects. Similarly, surprise attacks on individuals and groups can be unsettling and disorienting to the insurgents. The United States is probably uniquely well placed to provide a combination of intelligence sensors and airborne means of using their information. As in close air support, much depends on having an airplane in place when information suddenly becomes available. The airplane, moreover, must attack a target with few if any visible distinguishing characteristics—it is little more than a set of coordinates. Whatever controls that airplane or weapon must be able to conduct very precise attacks whenever required. Only unmanned vehicles can overcome the relevant pilot fatigue factors.

In addition to insurgent leaders, it may be possible to conduct quick responsive attacks based on observed enemy behavior. Anyone planting an improvised explosive device (IED) is unlikely to be friendly or neutral. Night infiltration of a village, to attack those who support government forces, would similarly seem to identify insurgents. It may even be possible to recognize a suicide bomber by some characteristic kind of motion, for example, by a change in gait. In each case sudden prompt action may be essential. It is unlikely that ground troops can ever provide sufficient persistent presence to conduct such attacks, let alone be sure of hitting the right targets. Orbiting UCAVs are a different proposition. That is not to deny the value of ground troops altogether. Villagers worried about night attacks do not see the UCAV overhead or the surveillance UAVs. They are unlikely to rely on unseen presences. Visible troops give them vital confidence (in Vietnam the U.S. Marine Corps placed small units in villages with great success). However, killing off enemy troops and, more important, enemy leaders may actually end the problem. The widespread perception that our enemies feed from a bottomless pool of dedicated manpower is wrong.

3

A NEW WAY OF WAR
The New Technology

The United States is developing a new way to wage war: network-centric—or, more properly, picture-centric—warfare. This new concept seems especially well adapted to the changing character of war, and UCAS systems seem particularly well suited to exploit-ing it.

This new way of war is described in various ways. It is called "precision strike warfare," in which limited numbers of very precisely targeted weapons replace the mass strikes and perhaps even the nuclear weapons (which had mass effect) of the past. Limited numbers seem appropriate to a situation in which the United States usually wages expeditionary war—a kind of war requiring rapid reaction against enemies far from this country (and from any permanent bases we have). This type of warfare should be characterized by sudden surprising attacks (which exploit the lighter-weight forces implied) and ultimately by tactics that speed up the pace of combat, getting inside the enemy's operating cycle or "OODA loop" (the cycle of military operations: observe-orient [interpret]-decide-act). Associated with this type of warfare is a shift in military resources toward reconnaissance/surveillance from platforms delivering weapons. The logic of the shift is that in the past most weapons have been wasted. A combination of effective targeting (due to much better reconnaissance/surveillance and better interpretation and use of the resulting information) and great precision (to exploit that information) should make a much higher percentage of weapons count.

Conversely if we cannot find and destroy small units, an enemy can operate on a low-tech basis to field surprisingly large numbers of fighters. It is up to us to force our enemies to invest in higher technology, which may help put them out of business. If our own units are too small, moreover, an enemy may imagine that he can mass to overwhelm them. In land warfare there is in effect a lower limit to effective unit size because individual soldiers act as sensors and as a means of dealing with enemy infantry attack. The new kind of warfare does have vital implications for how such infantry should be supported, for example, how much organic firepower it should have to carry with it. Conversely, the amount of organic firepower helps determine just how mobile the ground unit is. The ideal is the greatest possible mobility to impose the greatest possible stress on the enemy's OODA loop.

We still must be able to destroy massed enemy forces such as armor. To that end we now have dispersable precision weapons that should be able to destroy multiple vehicles on a single pass. Multiple aircraft can threaten massed tank forces effectively.

The ideal, then, is to buy platforms and systems that can execute both mass *and* dispersed precision attacks. Too, the threat of attack must be available on a sustained basis, because an enemy evading mass attacks will probably hide much of the time. Whatever systems we use must be able to wait and then to react as needed. The chief alternatives are missiles and various kinds of air systems. Missiles offer quick reactions, but their numbers are lim-

A key question is whether, as in the past, UCAVs individually find and identify targets or whether they are cued by a broader constellation of sensors, which creates a wide-area picture of the tactical situation. UCAVs like the new X-47B have their own sensors, but it is not clear whether they will be used to detect their own targets or mainly for reconnaissance as an alternative function, the UCAV attacking targets based on positions determined by a wider system. This image is intended to remind the reader that X-47B has a very capable sensor suite, including a multimode radar and electro-optics. (Northrop Grumman)

ited. A missile is self-contained, and often it is a wooden round that requires only periodic maintenance. That makes it attractive in the field. Every time the missile is fired, however, the entire package of warhead, guidance, and propulsion is expended. The package is not cheap, and often it is relatively large. As a consequence missile production runs are relatively short (except for the smallest or simplest weapons), and small units cannot carry very many rounds (compare numbers with, say, artillery rounds). Replenishment can be difficult.

Naval forces are an extreme case. Individual missile ships may carry up to about one hundred long-range missiles in vertical launchers. That may mean fewer than a thousand in a battle group. More important, the missiles cannot be transferred at sea, so whatever ships begin a battle will probably have to see it through. However sophisticated the targeting, missiles cannot be reused, so they cannot be used on a protracted basis. This is apart

from their other limitations. For example, current strike weapons are subsonic, which dramatically limits their ability to substitute for a ground unit's organic artillery.

Carriers offer radically different possibilities. Their strike platforms—their aircraft—are reusable as long as they can survive in the face of enemy antiair systems. Moreover, weapons can easily be transferred to a carrier at sea, so that in theory its potential to keep hitting is limited only by the supplies on board ships replenishing the carrier. The major supplies involved are aircraft fuel and weapons. Although each airplane is far more expensive than a single missile, the combination of aircraft and their weapons are far less expensive on a shot-by-shot basis, when attacks are sustained. Anything that makes carrier operations less expensive greatly increases these ships' advantages over surface combatants as strike platforms. As we shall see, UCAS seems to fit exactly that bill.

The Picture

The essence of the new way of war is to create a precise map of the current situation, hence of potential targets. Given weapons that can be delivered to precise points using navigational methods such as GPS, the map becomes the basis for attacks. This may not seem particularly impressive; reconnaissance is hardly new, nor is the idea of dispatching attacks on its basis. What is new is a combination of precision and near-real-time reconnaissance. This combination makes for a war of surprise attacks (which have considerable psychological effect on an enemy) conducted at an unprecedented pace (which also has considerable effect on an enemy). Attacks are surprises because there is no need to deploy special reconnaissance platforms to prepare for each of them; information already in hand suffices. Without any need for specific reconnaissance of a chosen target, attacks can be mounted more rapidly.

In the past reconnaissance or surveillance and strike operations were separate. Reconnaissance revealed targets, but the strike function usually required a closer look to vector a strike airplane to the target. Reconnaissance and strike are always part of an OODA cycle, but in the past the cycle was stretched out for two complementary reasons. First, reconnaissance was slow and target location was often imprecise. Second, aircraft could not fly to precisely stated target locations. Considerable effort was needed to assemble sufficient information for a pilot simply to locate the target at all. In many cases that meant an intermediate level of reconnaissance to improve target data. Reconnaissance and strike could be considered parts of a larger system, but it could hardly be described as tightly integrated or particularly responsive. This is not to mention the extensive effort required to plan missions once reconnaissance data had been used to choose strike targets. The reconnaissance-strike effort of the past limited the number of targets that could be engaged in short order. It encouraged rigid strike planning, perhaps symbolized by the air tasking order (ATO) technique developed by the U.S. Air Force and used in the 1991 Gulf War.

As in any other military field, there is a cycle (with a characteristic cycle time) associated with unintegrated reconnaissance and strike, using an ATO. In the 1991 war the cycle time exceeded twenty-four hours. One consequence was that the system as a whole could not engage Iraqi targets being relocated on a shorter cycle, such as the aircraft the Iraqis moved around their cities. The very quick relocation of Iraqi missile launchers was handled by assigning aircraft to patrol particular areas, waiting for cues to attack. Besides being unsuccessful (even then the cycle time was too long), this tied up a large fraction of limited strike resources.

Toward the end of the Cold War the Soviets recognized that the next major military development would be an integrated reconnaissance-strike entity. If its cycle time could be compressed sufficiently, such an entity could destroy the sort of massed armored forces they operated in Europe. For the first time, it would be possible to defeat a Soviet land offensive without resorting to nuclear weapons. The Soviets saw this system (Assault Breaker) as a direct threat to their ability to coerce Western Europeans. For the first time, a nonnuclear defense of Western Europe might be not only possible but even attractive. On this basis Nikolai Ogarkov, chief of the Soviet General Staff, began writing about 1979 that the Soviet Union was doomed unless it could match (or, better, neutralize) the reconnaissance-strike system NATO (the North Atlantic Treaty Organization) seemed to be erecting. It seems that Mikhail Gorbachev was made general secretary precisely because he promised to solve the Soviet computer production problem, which in turn made it impossible to solve Ogarkov's problem. He in turn found it necessary to try to reform Soviet society because, unlike Nikita Khrushchev, he could not cancel existing programs to make space for the new computer ones he needed. He did not realize how suicidal that would be.[1]

In effect the new kind of warfare employs exactly the sort of reconnaissance-strike system ("complex," in Soviet-speak) Ogarkov feared. We generally have not appreciated how revolutionary it is, and can be. Existing forces were not designed specifically to exploit the new capabilities. We now have about a decade of experience, however, and we may be able to glimpse what is needed. We are, moreover, being pushed toward the new style of war because existing techniques are becoming unaffordable or are poorly suited to the post–Cold War expeditionary world. Were we to build forces from scratch

The symbol of picture-centric warfare is the GPS-guided weapon. Unlike most earlier precision weapons, its accuracy does not decline with range from the aimer. In theory such weapons are effective only against fixed targets, although experiments have shown that periodic updates make it possible for them to hit some moving targets. Even without such updates, a small seeker can add the ability to lock onto a moving target, such as a truck, near the designated aim point. Raytheon displayed this Multi-Purpose Loitering Missile at the 2006 Navy League show. It was relatively simple to develop because it was built around a universal (GPS) seeker plus a data link by means of which the seeker could be updated as required. This kind of missile can be very effective when directed against a target whose coordinates have been designated by some other system, but if it had to find and track a target using some other kind of seeker, it would become anything but affordable. The GPS (or other navigational) seeker is in effect universal because many specialized sensors go into creation of the picture on the basis of which the GPS seeker is set. (Norman Friedman)

to reflect new conditions and capabilities, they probably would look quite different from what will actually materialize. The "transformation" pressed from 2001 onward was ill defined, but its core was probably directed toward the sort of capabilities envisaged here.

In effect weapons are air-mailed to addresses discovered by the reconnaissance-surveillance elements of the system. If these elements are good enough, there is no need for further human intervention; the human in the system is the one interpreting the mass of surveillance data. Such interpretation may well require considerable reference to other data, and it may also require reference to rules of engagement and to the boundaries of free-fire and no-fire zones. The key capability is to ensure that all the surveillance data and the targeting data are registered

to the same system of coordinates, so that the data can be fused effectively. That seems to be less and less difficult, as computer capacity increases. For the United States this revolution happened because of the advent of GPS, but any precision means of navigational guidance would offer much the same tactical consequences. In the absence of GPS, some form of correlation guidance (e.g., using an imaging radar) would offer similar capability, albeit at a higher cost. This point is important because without it there would be a valid argument that the new kind of warfare could be compromised if GPS signals were jammed over a wide area.

The new kind of war is called "networked" because a network of sensors creates the picture and because the strike elements (or those commanding them) have access to the entire picture via a targeting network. In the past effort was generally concentrated on a particular target. Thus, among other things, the reconnaissance and target reacquisition effort indicated which target was about to be hit. So the new style of war requires persistent surveillance that detects targets, some means of assigning priorities to them, and some means of providing accurate and precise target locations. Attack systems deliver weapons to those locations. This type of system works, at least in theory, for both fixed and moving targets. If surveillance is pervasive enough (though not continuous) it can provide target tracks and thus predictions of the positions of moving targets. If target positions are measured frequently enough, a weapon can be commanded to the predicted target position. The weapon may perhaps need a very short range sensor to lock onto the moving target. This concept was demonstrated some years ago in the ASTE (Affordable Surface Target Engagement) program. The U.S. Navy has investigated very inexpensive short-range terminal seekers for navigationally guided bombs.

If future air attacks and missile attacks are nearly always executed by navigationally guided weapons, what is the role of attack pilots? When they deliver GPS-guided bombs, they have little input into the attack. They monitor aircraft systems, and they evade enemy action en route to the target and home. Our experience with system monitoring has been that once systems become sufficiently reliable, it is not really needed. Does that leave attack pilots with the task of evading enemy fire? If so, to what extent can evasion be automated?

Pervasive reconnaissance and surveillance offer no clues as to our action, because a potential target never knows what will be done with their output—he may or may not be chosen for attack at any time. If targeting-quality information is always available on a very wide range of potential targets, then it cannot be clear to an enemy which one we plan to hit or which course of action we plan to take. In reality surveillance cannot always cover a very wide area, so there are some indications, but an enemy may be unable to be sure of where our surveillance assets are and of how they work. This is, incidentally, an argument for stealthy reconnaissance/surveillance assets. Conversely, if all enemy assets are always subject to sudden attack, the enemy must devote disproportionate

resources to guarding against it. In a low-tech world such as Afghanistan, that would mean moving cautiously and always seeking cover—slowing the enemy's OODA cycle and giving us interesting opportunities. In a higher-tech world an enemy would spend more resources seeking effective warning, and that in turn might limit his offensive capabilities.

Persistent Strike Capability

The complement to persistent reconnaissance and surveillance should be persistent strike capability. Although missiles offer some of what is needed, it would seem that airborne assets closer to the potential target area offer a more responsive solution. Also, airborne assets can be replenished as needed with more weapons, whereas a missile is expended on each mission. Given limited numbers of expensive long-range missiles, recoverable aircraft may be the only way to fight sustained wars on the basis of the new style of combat.

No single aircraft can provide sustained persistent strike capability because it must return to base as soon as it has expended its weapons. However, a swarm of aircraft is a different proposition. The swarm can maintain its attack capacity by detaching individual aircraft as they expend their weapons, replacing each with a fresh aircraft from base. Similarly, aircraft of the group can peel off to fuel in the air as required, returning to the swarm as they finish doing so. As long as the swarm can survive in the face of enemy area air defense, it continues to present a threat to surface targets. Survivability would emerge from factors such as stealth, routing to avoid areas of particular enemy air defense strength, and jamming or the destruction of enemy threats.

Persistent strike capability would seem to require both long endurance on the part of the striking aircraft and limited distance between their base and the target area. Any one strike vehicle has limited endurance, but a swarm of vehicles, replaced as they run out of endurance, provides pervasive air presence—*something not currently available*. It is the need for quick replacement, for example, as vehicles expend their weapons or as they require maintenance, which suggests the need that the vehicles providing the pervasive strike threat be based near the target area. Single large aircraft may be able to orbit for long periods, but maintaining even one on station thousands of miles from a base requires a stream of replacements, and the need for large numbers makes such aircraft uneconomical in the pervasive strike role.

Carrier aircraft offer an unusual advantage. A carrier can operate persistently without basing permission. Often the only U.S. land bases not tied to local restrictions are distant. They can support intermittent air presence, but not the sort of sustained presence the carrier can provide.[2] A carrier operating long-endurance UAVs can maintain presence more or less continuously, assuming the air vehicles involved can survive in the face of enemy air defense. A swarm can deliver either a mass strike or its vehicles can hit numerous discrete targets, either in a pulse or as a sequence of strikes over whatever time period is desired. The important parameter is clearly vehicle endurance. Aircraft can remain airborne for lengthy periods by refueling. If they are manned, the pilots are probably the limiting factor in endurance. Moreover, the farther the patrol area from the base, the more of the pilot's finite endurance is taken up in transit, hence the less effective endurance he has left—even if time in the air can be stretched by refueling. Obviously there will be cases in which the carrier is far from the battle area.[3] In that case pilots cannot spend much time in the battle area. Unmanned aircraft with a refueling capability would not be subject to any similar limitation. This consideration suggests that a carrier could set up a swarm at a considerable distance, increasing its effectiveness as it approached the battle area. That is, the initial swarm could present a continuous threat, but once it began to fight it would be unable to replenish itself very quickly. As the carrier approached, the time for an individual vehicle to return to replace its weapons would be cut and the swarm would gain reattack or sustained attack potential.

Persistent Strike Capability Now

We already have examples of a kind of sustained or pervasive strike capacity in the use of armed UAVs against important terrorist leaders in vehicles. In these cases there was apparently intelligence indicating that the target was likely to pass along a given road or drive toward a known place. It was not clear exactly when that would happen. The solution was to have an armed UAV orbit the area, keeping an electro-optical sensor pointed at the relevant area of road. An operator monitoring the output of that sensor could decide whether a given vehicle was or was not the designated target. The UAV could be commanded to designate and attack the vehicle with its onboard missiles. Enough successes of this kind have been reported that it seems worthwhile to consider why unmanned vehicles are typically used.

One reason is their endurance at low speed; there is little point in using a fast jet roaring past the potential target area. Another reason is the monitoring. Again, there is little point in having a pilot try to remember whether what he sees resembles the target vehicle. An operator with access to intelligence data is far better placed to make that decision. He can even command the sensor on the UAV to zoom in to provide better data. It is often suggested that the most important advantage of the UAV is that it can be used in an area nominally denied to U.S. forces, so that its actions can be denied and its loss, if that occurs, does not provide a hostage in the form of a pilot. Of the three reasons this is probably the least important, because such aircraft generally operate in areas of low antiaircraft threat. Endurance and precision command and control are surely far more important.

Sustained surveillance and sustained strike capability have made it possible to kill many enemy leaders to the point where the life expectancy of such a leader may be noticeably reduced. That has tactical and strategic implications. Tactically it means that enemy leaders generally have too little time to build experience and hence are more likely to make mistakes with significant battlefield consequences. Strategically it means that all such leaders spend more of their time trying to avoid exposure, which in turn may make it more difficult for them to exercise command in the first place. Particularly in the current war against terrorists, command on the enemy side probably requires considerable face-to-face time. At the least we can exert pressure to make that so by spreading deceptive messages in alternative command channels such as radios and the Internet.

The ability to strike at will is coupled with extensive, almost pervasive, surveillance. Many of our enemies already know that it is dangerous to use radios and satellite phones because we can localize them and then set up attacks from the air. That forces them to use work-arounds such as runners and emissaries who cross borders to use the Internet. These techniques certainly counter our surveillance techniques. However, they also drastically slow the enemy's reaction cycle. They present opportunities: We can win by either speeding our OODA loop or slowing the enemy's (or, preferably, both). This is the sort of tactic the new style of warfare encourages.

Precision Strike

Another capability, which seems allied to pervasive striking power, is precision strike—the ability to lay down fire on precisely specified places. *If* striking power is always available, and *if* deployed units can generally specify the locations of enemy forces they wish to hit, it is not nearly as important that they always have organic heavy firepower with them. They can live with much smaller logistical tails, so they can be far more maneuverable. More maneuverability plus good surveillance ought to make for new kinds of tactics that can defeat larger but conventional forces. In an expeditionary world marked by sudden outbreaks of violence (e.g., as Al Qaeda colonizes a string of failed states), the ability of small U.S. forces to win would seem to become extremely important. We would never have time to build up massive stockpiles to feed our local wars. For that matter it is already vital that relatively small forces deployed to Iraq and to Afghanistan can fight and win because we would much prefer not to deploy much larger ones. In many places, moreover, there are logistical barriers to deploying large U.S. forces. In land-locked Afghanistan all supporting materiel must come through either Russia or Pakistan, neither of which would probably enthusiastically support a massive U.S. presence.

We can increasingly trade off one kind of firepower for another because precision no longer depends on firing range (thanks to GPS and, to a much lesser degree, seekers) and because we enjoy good communications between those needing fire support and the shooters. Right now the main candidates for stand-off support of ground forces from the sea are new guns (AGS, rail gun) and new hypersonic missiles (speed needed for prompt delivery). Neither is particularly credible. Even the large new destroyer carries relatively few gun rounds. A fleet offshore would have even fewer missiles, each of them very expensive and carrying a very limited payload. That makes air platforms loitering above a ground battle area, with the ability quickly to replenish their ammunition, extremely attractive.

There is also armed reconnaissance. We may often find ourselves hunting down dispersed enemies. It appears that in Afghanistan one tactic was (and probably still is) to show our aircraft and then attack anyone who seemed to be shooting at them. As currently exercised such tactics have some major drawbacks. One is that a pilot may mistake something for ground fire. The best known case in point was a pair of Air National Guard pilots who attacked a Canadian live-fire exercise. In theory such incidents should have been precluded by a requirement to clear such attacks through a controlling AWACS (Airborne Warning and Control System) airplane. It is not clear why that failed. One possibility is that pilots considered the ground fire so immediate—and so transitory—a threat that they informed their controllers rather than waiting for clearance (the Canadians were skeptical, arguing that the pilots should simply have accelerated away). The frailty of this explanation suggests that instead pilots were used to attacking because ground fire seemed the clearest way to know that those on the ground were hostile. In either case, the weapons used were imprecise enough (500-lb bombs) that they would certainly have killed others than the shooters. Other cases, which could not have been avoided by controllers, were attacks on wedding parties celebrating (in a traditional way) by firing guns into the air. It is not clear whether some form of automation could have solved that problem, but it does seem clear that no human pilot would have managed to do so. In both cases attacks had considerable ill consequences for the coalition effort.

The implication may be that even in armed reconnaissance, which is usually considered to require human judgment, the human best placed to use judgment may be at a base where geographically oriented information (such as prohibited attack zones) is easier to obtain, assimilate, and use. This is a profound shift in the way air wars are likely to be fought. If—and this is perhaps a major if—we can rely on geographically oriented information, the man in the cockpit may be almost the worst one to use it.

On the whole the new kind of low-intensity war

revolves around pop-up targets, mostly human ones. Engaging them requires a combination of long endurance and sustained alertness, neither of which can be assumed for manned aircraft. This is not the airpower of the past. The character of targets is changing (or perhaps we are learning to understand targets better). In the past we assumed that most target sets were fixed. We could either destroy them at the outset, en masse, or we could attack them progressively. In either case sufficient reconnaissance could identify them at the outset. That was the basis of strategic air attack. Now we are generally interested in changeable situations in which even the significance of particular targets depends on the situation. There are still fixed targets, but there are many fewer of them. The initial mass strike, as in Afghanistan, may still be well worthwhile as a means of destroying national air defenses, but that is a means to the larger end of gaining freedom of air action. Once we have that freedom, we can deal with the changing or moving targets that really matter. Those targets may be objects or even individuals, as in the Hellfire strikes from Predators.

Future Warfare

U.S. forces employing picture-centric tactics and resources gain considerable potential advantages. By this time our potential enemies are well aware of what these ideas mean. The Chinese in particular have been writing about asymmetric warfare, which to them often means blinding our sensors so that we cannot employ our new techniques. Some Americans feel that their attack on one of their own satellites was a wake-up call that they not only understand us but also plan to execute such anti-picture-centric strategies. Others argue that they are aware of our fears but cannot yet execute such strategies. But it may already be time to think through means of maintaining our surveillance capability in the face of serious countermeasures. They will include not only attacks on our sensors but also, probably, anti-GPS warfare.

We have considerable potential to maintain our surveillance capacity. Satellites in low earth orbits are clearly vulnerable, but many of ours fly substantially higher. We may find aircraft, whose paths are fundamentally unpredictable and that are relatively easy to replace, vital substitutes. We are already fielding unmanned aircraft

in substantial numbers, and we have spent considerable sums to devise stealthy surveillance vehicles. Given the endurance involved, it seems clear that the future surveillance constellation will be largely or entirely unmanned. If that is already satisfactory for a satellite placed in orbit for years, surely a lack of manning will work for an airplane flying for hours or days. In some cases the airplane is preferable because its crew can refocus surveillance on the spot, in response to what it detects, but we may well find that we can do almost as well via remote control.

Presumably our enemies will find it preferable to adopt something more like our own new style of war, including their own approaches to pervasive surveillance. How would a net-on-net war play out?

This would be a war of precision strikes, with a threat of mass strike to keep forces on both sides dispersed. The emphasis would be on finding key targets and hitting them before they moved out of sight. Much would obviously depend on quick assessment, using all available information—something best done at an intelligence center. Each side would spend considerable effort on concealment, using remotely controlled strike assets so that its enemy would find it difficult to associate a strike with the location of the enemy command center (the main target).

At least at the outset reach would be valuable, because enemy surveillance activities would probably be concentrated in a limited operational area. Outside that area an enemy would enjoy only intermittent surveillance capacity. To the extent that the strike base(s) were mobile and operating outside enemy pervasive surveillance range, that would also help frustrate an enemy's ability to predict our own operations. On the other hand, once the enemy surveillance and control system had been damaged, it would be valuable, probably vital, to increase the intensity of pervasive strike power. This combination suggests that the ideal strike system would begin with the longest possible range but would be able to close rapidly as enemy capability declined.

This is very nearly a description of an aircraft carrier operating a strike swarm. Nothing land based offers the same flexibility and the same ability to quickly exploit success. Much obviously depends on the ability of the carrier to support sustained operation by the swarm at a great distance.

This is a very abstract argument, but it sketches the end result of the transformation we are now carrying out. Transformation does not begin with some genius sketching a road to a future thirty or fifty years away. It begins incrementally. However, once the technology is in place, those who can understand the way it can be developed and exploited tactically enjoy great advantages.

We know as much because we know a great deal about past attempts at transformation. Blitzkrieg is a famous example. The British and the French introduced tanks on World War I battlefields, and once they had been minimally developed, some visionaries, such as J. F. C. Fuller, saw how they could change war. Had the war continued into 1919, Fuller's vision might have been realized in something resembling the tactics the Germans actually employed in 1940. As it was the technology was developed by all countries between the two world wars, but it seems that only the Germans fully understood its implications. They seem to have understood that a combination of tanks and tactical airpower could accelerate the pace of war to the extent that their enemies would literally disintegrate. It proved irrelevant that French tanks were far superior technically; what counted was the understanding of what the new technology could mean. In this case the new technology was an amalgam: not only tanks but also tactical radio (probably including the Enigma cipher machine) and a combined-arms approach using tactical airpower under army control.

It would be a pity if we developed the means to realize a transformation that we failed to exploit because we did not understand how vital unmanned attack aircraft systems—swarms using the fruits of pervasive surveillance—could be.

4

THE NEED FOR TRANSFORMATION

UCAS is a new kind of system offering a different way of using naval aviation to help fight our wars. It is best seen as part of a move toward transforming our overall military capabilities. Transformation was widely promoted during the first few years of this century. Skeptics argued that it was not needed. The U.S. military, which had performed brilliantly in Iraq in 1991, was still much superior to the forces that other countries fielded. Why change what was so successful? Much the same arguments can still be made.

Militaries adopt revolutionary technology and tactics because they cannot go on the way they have been operating. In some cases, such as ours, circumstances make the existing way of war either literally impossible or unaffordable—or there are new requirements that existing forces cannot meet. In others the general adoption of some new technology makes it impossible to go on as before. For example, we may need a new way to apply airpower to overcome current attempts to deny us access to various places.[1] Different forces, in different countries, typically adopt some mixture of new technology and new tactics and operational practices. Experience shows that the winners are the ones who are most willing to understand how their tactics must be transformed to exploit the new technology. UCAS offers revolutionary tactical potential, not just in what is inside the platform or in its distributed control system but in the way it can be used.

So why invest in new ways of fighting, and in new technology? There are two key reasons. One is that we are being forced by circumstances to shift toward expeditionary operations in which our forces will usually fight outnumbered and, moreover, will have to get to the theater and set up their support when they arrive. They will need new kinds of leverage in order to win. This is the argument of chapter 2: The tactical environment is changing. The great difference between expeditionary operations and those of the Cold War, from which most of our current systems are derived, is that we are unlikely to be able to build up massive forces in peacetime. The essence of NATO strategy was twofold. One was the assumption that war would begin with a massive Soviet attack; the other was that the forces already in place would be enough to slow that attack. It was, for example, argued that the Soviets would hardly chance an all-out attack on NATO. Any war would more likely grow out of some local problem that, unaccountably, spiraled out of control. It followed that NATO's real strength would be the ability to mobilize the enormous power of the West during a protracted buildup on both sides. Hence, for example, the importance of a struggle to maintain control of the North Atlantic sea-lanes. How much of this bears much resemblance to current or likely scenarios?

The second reason for transformation is that the current conventional way of war is less and less affordable overall. Existing systems are expensive partly because they require the sort of massive logistical tail that was rational during the Cold War but cannot become expeditionary. It also seems that existing systems and their offshoots do

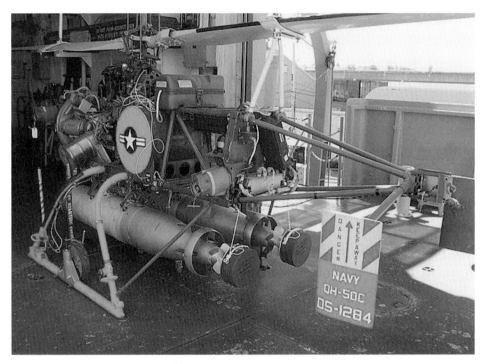

New technology provides an opportunity for transformation, but that opportunity is not always taken. Military organizations tend to be conservative because failed innovations are so expensive in blood and money. The U.S. Navy's DASH drone exemplified the problem; it was a step much too far. DASH was, in effect, replaced by the manned LAMPS light helicopter. Here a QH-50C DASH is shown on board the museum ship USS *Joseph P. Kennedy*, with its lightweight torpedo underslung. (U.S. Navy)

not fully exploit technologies, such as microelectronics and software, which matured late in the Cold War. The civilian economy has been dramatically transformed by the new technology; surely the military economy ought to undergo a parallel series of changes. Exactly what those changes can and should be has hardly been resolved, however.

The current economic problem dramatizes the need to achieve considerable savings in defense. Usually the argument is that we are in trouble because we have become addicted to increasingly complex (one term used in the past was "baroque," another is "gold-plated") weapon systems. The reality is that relatively simple improvements are less and less affordable. We need some alternative way to fight. This is not a new situation. In the past transformation often was driven by the unaffordability of existing ways of fighting. Typically the sheer numbers available using earlier technology become unaffordable due to new developments.

This may not seem obvious, because the old way of fighting died out. World War I infantrymen were rela-

tively inexpensive, so the shift to mechanized forces seems to have added cost. However, an infantry force designed to fight a mechanized force would have to add enormous defense in depth, as the mechanized force would almost certainly smash through a World War I–style line. To support an army several times the size of a World War I army covering much of the western front would have been entirely unaffordable, in both human and money terms.

As another case in point, during World War II the United States produced about 100,000 fighter aircraft (although nothing like that number served at any one time). The U.S. Navy, at its peak, had about 35,000 combat aircraft. With the shift to jets, such numbers became entirely unaffordable. The shift to much smaller numbers was concealed, in effect, by the increasing longevity of the aircraft—once technology had stabilized to the point where aircraft did not become obsolete within two or three years. To some extent, too, smaller numbers were justified by much greater capability, although that had to be balanced against an enemy's improved capability. For example, during World War II the expected lifetime of a Hellcat fighter was so short that there was no point in buying replacement engines. An F-14 Tomcat, on the other hand, might serve for twenty years or more.[2] The tacit assumption was that aircraft were also much more survivable, so that the lifetimes designed into them in terms of wear and tear were their actual lifetimes. In Vietnam the United States suffered heavy losses in combat that could not be made up because affordable production levels were in effect keyed to the inherently long lifetimes (and high unit costs) of the aircraft. Since Vietnam overall numbers of aircraft have declined rapidly because aircraft unit costs have risen faster than inflation. The change was not the shift in type of aircraft but a shift in the way aircraft were used. Jets were never used for the kind of mass raids that became common in World War II, because they were never available in the requisite numbers.[3] Precision attack (or at least an attempt at such attack) became the norm after World War II.

The solution to limited aircraft numbers has been an unsung transformation using precision munitions released outside the range of enemy air defenses, their targeting based largely or entirely on netted systems. Precision also dramatically reduced the number of sorties (exposures to enemy air defense) entailed in destroying a target. If aircraft are less and less vulnerable to destruction by those enemy defenses, their effective lifetimes are more closely related to the nature of their structures. It is possible to maintain a large enough force by extending aircraft lifetimes, given a more or less steady production rate. However, this logic collapses if the enemy regains any substantial counter-air capability. Hence the continuing importance of stealth, which in theory limits enemy counter-air capability.

That is, the solution to the economic crisis in tactical aircraft has not been better tactical aircraft operating in the way of the past but to move most or all of the targeting function outside the aircraft. This transformation has been hidden, in effect, because the aircraft themselves have not seemed terribly different from those of the past. The key change has been in command and control, which is always more or less invisible. Without this transformation, tactical attack aircraft would already be unaffordable, because it would be impossible to produce enough

of them to keep up with losses to current (not to mention future) air defense systems.

It is often suggested that some new technology offers such potential that it is foolish not to leap at transformation. That was one explanation given in the 1990s for the adoption of new ideas such as networking. In practice military organizations are conservative because errors due to overenthusiasm can have fatal consequences. They are willing to experiment on a small scale, but they understandably resist attempts at wholesale change, including rejection of entirely workable existing modes of operation. What typically drives transformation is disaster: What has worked in the past either clearly can no longer work (as in the case of the adoption of nuclear weapons) or is patently unaffordable. Typically, too, there is an attempt to meld the new kind of force with existing types of forces. The result is attractive but typically unaffordable, so the new replaces the old more completely than might seem wise.

For example, during World War II the U.S. Navy operated a powerful carrier force. Contrary to much received opinion, well before the war senior naval officers had expected carriers to become preeminent (the question was when, not if). During the war the Navy discovered that carriers plus conventional capital ships formed a very potent synergistic combination. Battleships provided valuable cover against both air and surface attack; limits on carrier night operations made it possible that an all-carrier force could be surprised and destroyed by enemy surface warships.[4] Thus plans for a postwar fleet included both a large carrier force and a substantial number of battleships. Carriers provided reach, but it seemed that battleships were still important for screening, even against a non–sea power such as the Soviet Union (which did have significant numbers of surface warships and for a time after World War II planned to build modern battleships). The combination was affordable for a few years. However, as defense budgets collapsed after the war, and as money was desperately needed for new weapons such as jet aircraft, a hard choice had to be made. By 1949 only one battleship, the USS *Missouri*, remained in commission, as a training ship. Others were recommissioned later for shore bombardment, but the choice had been made in favor of the new carrier navy and against the old battle-ship force.

Much the same can probably be said of the more or less contemporary U.S. Air Force decision to drop propeller-driven fighter/attack aircraft, which offered superior ground support capability, in favor of exclusive reliance on jets, which, as Korea proved, were (at the time) almost useless in that role (the U.S. Navy retained a propeller-driven attack airplane, the A-1 Skyraider, into the 1960s, precisely because it considered close air support a vital mission). The Air Force abandoned all such aircraft after Korea, and even before Korea had explicitly decided to retain the propeller fighter least well adapted to ground support, the P-51 Mustang, rather than the P-47 Thunderbolt, which was a better support airplane. It was assumed that neither could survive encounters with jet fighters, but the U.S. Navy clearly thought otherwise (the Air Force found itself obtaining Skyraiders from the Navy for the specialized close-support missions it flew in Vietnam).

The current need for transformation was perceived in the mid-1990s. Many defense analysts spoke at that time of a coming "defense train wreck," when Cold War weapon systems would need replacement and unit weapon costs would rise catastrophically due to both shorter production runs and the need to incorporate new technology. Shorter production runs raise costs sharply because the overhead per unit increases: The producers must be kept alive, and their fixed costs do not fall, or at least do not fall very steeply. Even continuing to produce existing weapons would be expensive. Most forecasters expected the "train wreck" about 2002. A sharp increase in defense spending, due to the onset of the Global War on Terror, deferred the problem but could not possibly solve it. In some ways the war exacerbated it, because the hot wars in Iraq and in Afghanistan wore out much existing equipment far more quickly than had been expected.

These wars coincided with a shift in Defense Department emphasis toward various forms of netting, which were advertised as the solution to the train wreck. Whether or not that was the case, money flowed into new generations of computers and into links between them, including new-generation communication satellites. At the same time, however, existing weapons needed replacement as they reached the end of their planned lifetime. Aircraft,

for example, have finite fatigue lives; at one point the U.S. Air Force threatened to ground most of its F-15s, and the Navy had to ground many P-3Cs. Changes in procurement policy appeared to raise unit costs because they included life-cycle costs in the usual totals. By late 2008 it was clear that further increases in defense funding were unlikely. The train wreck had arrived.

Secretary of Defense Donald J. Rumsfeld entered office in 2001 with an explicit mandate to transform the U.S. military into a post–Cold War force. He created an Office of Force Transformation, initially under retired Vice Adm. Arthur K. Cebrowski. Unfortunately neither Rumsfeld nor Cebrowski pointed out (or pointed out clearly enough) that transformation was inescapable because of defense economics. Both gave the impression that they were pressing for transformation either because change was inherently attractive or because exciting new technology was on the table. Neither argument proved particularly convincing, and there was a good deal of transformation for transformation's sake.

The underlying reality was the train wreck. The reference to a post–Cold War world suggested that there was also a kind of tactical or strategic train wreck: Existing forces, particularly land-based ones, were ill suited to the new world of expeditionary warfare. It did not help that the major war of the time, against jihadis in Afghanistan and then Iraq, was and remains ill defined, so that it is hardly clear exactly what new technology is needed to fight it. When the new Obama administration entered office early in 2009, the one obvious reality was the combination of ongoing warfare and the economic train wreck—and it is clear that U.S. defense policy will need a fundamental review. That is exactly the climate that demands transformation, and it is the climate that has led to transformation in the past. The question is not whether transformation will come, but what sort of transformation the United States is likely to adopt.

One way to imagine the changes is to think in terms of the number of deployed personnel needed to achieve desired military effects. Ultimately this number helps determine the footprint of an expeditionary force. The desired effect might be a particular level of destruction of key targets, or a particular psychological effect on the enemy leadership. Those pressing for transformation argued that new technology, particularly microelectronics, had reached a critical mass that made it possible to change the way U.S. forces fight—and that such a change would regain both affordability and the sort of mobility that expeditionary warfare demands. These ideas may seem very abstract, but their meaning becomes obvious given the rapidly rising cost of individual military personnel, particularly the heavily trained ones who operate advanced equipment. Those personnel include both pilots and those who maintain their aircraft. For an air offensive incidental costs include the cost of providing fuel for each flight, including proficiency flights, and the cost of maintaining and transporting spares required for each flight hour.

Past Transformations

The push to transform the U.S. military began with the perception that a different kind of military was needed for a post–Cold War world. Many studies of past transformations, or military revolutions, were conducted. The central conclusion was that transformation or revolution entails not only new technology but also a new way of fighting. Buying one without the other has generally been a recipe for disaster.

Studies of earlier military transformations show that they follow much the same path that our current one does. Transformation is born of intense pressure. Military organizations are conservative because mistakes are literally deadly. The failed introduction of a new weapon can lose a war. The classic case is the French *mitrailleuse*, a primitive machine gun championed by French emperor Louis Napoleon (Napoleon III). He thought it would be so devastating that he kept it secret even from most of his own army. As a consequence no tactics were devised to exploit it. It looked like a conventional artillery piece, and when war broke out against Prussia in 1870, it was used as one. Unfortunately, it had nothing like the range of artillery. The disparity between the new technology and the irrelevant tactics was devastating. France lost the war for many reasons, but the *mitrailleuse* had a real potential to overcome them.

Another way of looking at the *mitrailleuse* saga would be to say that it was an exciting new technology that was not properly adopted because no one involved

had any pressing reason to use it. Like the *mitrailleuse*, UCAS offers wonderful possibilities, but it would be of little importance if the United States were not currently feeling a desperate need for military transformation to deal with new conditions. Given that need UCAS is well worthwhile. Its characteristics suggest a new and very attractive way of using airpower. UCAS technology is vital because of the *tactical potential* the technology offers.

It can also be suggested that the United States squandered an early lead in UAV technology developed before and during the Vietnam War (see Appendix II), much as the British squandered their World War I lead in developing tanks and aircraft and cooperative tactics for both. The result for the British was that they did not envisage how such tactics could develop, hence they did not understand how to fight an air-ground force in 1940. The British failure resulted in large part from the assignment of all British aircraft to the separate Royal Air Force (RAF), which had a very specific idea of how air forces could achieve decisive results—by strategic bombing. The RAF actually refused to bomb German troops in 1940 on the grounds that such raids would not be worthwhile. In the U.S. case, not developing UAV technology after Vietnam made it impossible to envisage what UAVs could do. Fortunately no hostile power developed UAVs aggressively and used them against us, so that we did not suffer badly for our lapse. We may not be so fortunate in the future; the Chinese, for example, are certainly very interested in a broad range of UAVs. At the very least that will give them insight into our capabilities and vulnerabilities.

A Case in Point: Tank Warfare

The classic example of a successful transformation is tank warfare. The Allies introduced tanks, sometimes with devastating results, during World War I, because it was impossible for their armies to advance in the face of machine guns and trenches. That is, they had to transform because their existing tactics and technology were unsuccessful. It is by no means clear that tanks were the only available solution. Thus the Germans developed breakthrough tactics to deal with much the same reality, and the final successful Allied offensive of 1918 did not involve large tank forces. However, by the end of the war there was certainly a perception that armies should be

The reconnaissance UAV program suffered after Vietnam because the main remaining area for which such aircraft were wanted was China—and after the post-1971 rapprochement (and improvements in satellites) there was no longer any desire to fly reconnaissance aircraft, manned or unmanned, over China. The twenty-eight Ryan 154 drones (AQM-91) designed specially for this role were mothballed, then scrapped. This model survives at the National Museum of the United States Air Force. (National Museum of the United States Air Force)

transformed to deal with the horrific failures experienced during World War I.

Overall the problem of World War I was that no offensive could get deep enough into enemy-occupied territory before the enemy's forces could close the gap or, at worst, make the attacker's position untenable by attacking his flanks. In a way the problem was the inevitable result of the industrial revolution, which had already transformed European countries. The revolution created mass armies, because now they could be fed and armed. It also created railways that could move troops to planned destinations. However, troops conducting an offensive had to walk, or crawl, forward. Ultimately the enemy's forward railways could always deliver more troops faster to the area of the enemy offensive.

In 1918 the Germans tried to solve the problem by focusing their artillery fire on a limited part of the front. This fire destroyed enough of the defense for small groups of shock troops to infiltrate through, bypassing surviving enemy strong points. Such tactics had failed in the past because it took large numbers of troops to provide much firepower. The German solution was to arm shock troops with weapons offering unusually high firepower with great mobility, such as submachine guns and wheeled mortars. This solution worked for a time, but even it failed—the shock troops still had to walk, and the Allies still had their

own railways behind the front. The Germans first tried such tactics in 1917 on the eastern front, which was far more lightly held than the western. In March 1918 they tried to win the war by using shock attack tactics on the western front. So much had been hoped for that the failure of the 1918 German offensive broke the spirit of the German army, and the Allies began to push it back. The Germans talked of falling back into new defensive positions, but they were unable to stabilize the situation.

None of this gave much confidence that the breakthrough problem had been solved. Through the interwar period, the French army staff argued that the main lesson of 1918 was that breakthrough was impossible because no hole in the front could be maintained in the face of massed reinforcements. Enormous effort went into operations analysis to prove this comforting thesis, in ways that would now be familiar.

We might see the French arguments as a claim that nothing had happened to transform the situation; what had worked reasonably well in 1918 should work as well in, say, 1940. However, things had changed. Technologies embryonic in 1918 were well developed twenty years later, particularly the internal-combustion engine, the airplane (relying largely on such engines), and radio for rapid communication. The new technologies in effect accelerated the possible pace of a war. We now understand the impact of pace in itself, when we refer to the OODA loop, the observation, orientation, decision, and action cycle that characterizes many activities, including warfare. Few if any at the time made the explicit connection between the new technology and the pace of combat, but this connection seems evident in some of the new ideas developed between the World Wars.

The offensive failures marking World War I were so bad that several combatants embraced alternative kinds of transformation as a way to avoid any repetition. Those making this choice rejected the French conclusion; the Allies had won the war, but in so unacceptable a way that they might as well have lost. Thus studies of military transformation often concentrate on the interwar period. German blitzkrieg tactics were a case in point, as was interest in strategic bombing (as a way of avoiding ground combat) and interest in offensive submarine warfare (again, as a way of limiting ground combat). Having lost the war, the Germans were obviously most interested in an alternative way to fight, but the British and the Italians, both on the winning side, were also intensely interested in alternatives. The Soviets too were intensely interested. The British actually pioneered new ways to use tanks, but they abandoned this effort about 1930 partly because their political leadership promised that they would never again fight in Europe; the British army concentrated instead on policing its empire, until it was far too late to modernize completely, in 1939. The British hoped, too, that a powerful bomber force would deter any potential Continental enemy. This hope (and the belief that bombers could be decisive) presumably paralyzed their leadership when the Germans built their own bomber force and showed no particular interest in being deterred. The point of all this is that the British agreed with the Germans that some sort of military transformation was needed.

In each case it is easy to emphasize the new technology, but the great lesson is that success went to those who understood how to change tactics and even strategy to make the best use of that technology. Conversely one might rate examples of the new technology in terms of how well they were adapted to the appropriately transformed tactics and strategy.

In 1940 Germany confronted France with fewer, and individually inferior, tanks. The French had many tanks that were better protected and better armed. They had had, after all, much more experience in tank development. Yet the Germans won, and they won very quickly. Why?

The usual answer is that the Germans, but not the French, understood that tanks could be part of a new kind of warfare adapted to their speed and striking power. In 1940 the French still thought of infantry as the primary arm of an army. Their infantry were relatively immobile. Moreover, French communications were poor, adapted to the slow-moving warfare of 1918. The Germans, furthermore, understood that they could use dive bombers (Stukas) as highly mobile artillery in support of fast-moving ground forces. The French did not appreciate this potential, so they did not realize how fast the Germans could move or provide their army with sufficient means to deal with the Stukas. In theory they had enough fighters, but they did not maintain sufficient readiness. Worse,

French direction of the war was far too sluggish. They assumed that, as in 1918, fire support meant guns on the ground, which could not move very fast. Neither they nor the bulk of the German army was mechanized, but the Germans had enough fully mechanized armored units to shatter the French. One consequence was that French airpower was too slow to react and concentrate against the initial German bridgehead at Sedan.

In effect the Germans mechanized the breakthrough tactics they had tried in 1918. Their new force could be larger, and it could take much more firepower with it, in the form both of tanks and self-propelled guns and of the accompanying Stukas. In addition, this firepower, particularly from the air, could range over a wider area to prevent French infantry from massing. The timescale had changed dramatically, but the French were unable to handle it. One analyst pointed out that there were only two telephones at the French headquarters at Vincennes.[5] French accounts of the German attack are full of German units popping up unexpectedly, which means that the French picture-keeping system was unable to keep up with events on the ground. The French seem to have collapsed because they could not react nearly quickly enough.

Accounts of 1940 make it seem that the highly mechanized German army faced a French army operating mainly on foot. That was hardly the case. The Germans had a few armored divisions in a largely horse-drawn army, but these few smashed through enough of the French defense to win the Battle of France. Apart from one armored division, the French distributed their tanks throughout their army as infantry support weapons— much as the Allies had used tanks in 1918. The basic French reasoning was correct; any deep attack through their lines would be vulnerable to flanking attacks. However, the French lacked the ability to locate or to attack the oncoming Germans.

Had the French been able to track the situation, they would still have had to concentrate enough force to smash the oncoming German units. Infantry could not move quickly enough. If a German unit happened to cross the front of a French armored division, conditions would have been right for just such an attack—which was conducted, as it happened, by General de Gaulle. Otherwise the French needed more mobile weapons for such

Modern UAVs were adopted not as substitutes for manned aircraft but because they offered something new, for example, endurance not limited by pilot fatigue. The Global Hawk exemplifies this change. (Northrop Grumman)

attacks. In 1940 the only such weapons were aircraft, and the French lacked the ability to direct their bombers and to coordinate them with either supporting fighters or with the ground units they should have been supporting. France suffered a command and control disaster as much as a disaster of antiquated technology.

Another way to look at the 1940 comparison is to observe that the Germans, but not the French, installed radios in many of their tanks and used radio to coordinate ground and air movements. German tanks might have been flimsier than their French counterparts, and poorly armed in comparison, but generally they did not face French tanks. They wiped out the French infantry defenses. To do that they needed mobility and excellent command and control. Only later, when the German armor faced masses of Allied armor in North Africa, in northwestern Europe, and in Russia, did it matter whether German tanks were sufficiently armored and armed. Even in Russia the disparity in quality was not immediately decisive, but that was because Soviet units were poorly trained and led (and in many cases had just received their new tanks).

What counted was that the Germans understood the tactical and operational implications of the new weapon,

whereas the French did not. They bought not just tanks but also a tactical system in which speed itself helped win. Their success in 1940 is much like that which current advocates of OODA-loop warfare hope to achieve for U.S. forces. The argument is that relatively small forces (as in a comparison of the German armored force to the whole French army) can win if they move so fast that the enemy cannot react. The enemy's failure is a combination of limited technology and limited communications, the latter including the ability to assimilate a changed situation. Because the French did not appreciate how fast armored forces might move, they did not invest in the sort of flexible forces needed to destroy them—such as large numbers of dive bombers of their own.

In an important sense the Germans were doing what we may now have to do. We had a garrison force that would have fought a defensive battle in Western Europe based on enormous preparation. Assuming the force survived, it would have been reinforced to the point where any further Soviet attack would have been frustrated. Because they were interested in overrunning Western Europe, the Soviets had an offensive doctrine similar to that which the Germans used in 1940, albeit very different in terms of how responsibility was distributed and in terms of the sheer masses of troops and bombardment involved. Attempts by the United States to adopt a similarly offensive doctrine in the late 1980s ran into the political problem that NATO was an essentially defensive alliance, unwilling to adopt as a war aim the liberation of Central Europe. The great irony of the first Gulf War was that U.S. forces adopted a somewhat Soviet-style doctrine of offensive warfare to defeat the Iraqis, whose defensive doctrine was often described as British-based.[6]

Now, however, we are unlikely to begin with a massive garrison. Instead, we are likely to find ourselves fighting offensively and seeking to win despite being badly outnumbered. Although in 1940 overall German numbers matched or even exceeded those of the French, in fact the hard core of the German army was small, limited by treaty until 1935 to 100,000 men. They became the core of a rapidly expanded force. German victory in 1940 showed that in effect the long experience embodied in the French officer and noncomissioned officer corps was either irrelevant or actually counterproductive in the face of a transformed enemy. Similarly the mass of French equipment left over from victory in 1918, and built up between the two world wars, proved largely irrelevant.

Those arguing in Germany for fighting in new ways managed to experiment continuously and often illegally, but they could not field the new military they envisaged. It had to be built rapidly. Despite considerable German industrial resources, that was a difficult task. The limits of German industry showed, for example, in the inferiority of German to French tanks in 1940. Aircraft were a different matter, because technology was changing so rapidly that Germany and France started from much the same position in the 1930s. However, the real difference between the German and French armies, and by far the decisive one, was that the Germans understood that new weapons had to be used in a new way and that the new way offered a very different potential. The French could not accept that the new technology could radically change the tempo of warfare, and it appears that they crumpled because they could not react quickly enough. For them it was still 1918.

The Germans had their own limits. They were able to equip a limited number of panzer divisions, but in 1940—even in 1945—much of their army was not too different from that of 1918, including its horse-drawn transport. This limitation probably had important consequences when the Germans faced a more fully mechanized U.S. Army in 1944–45 in northwestern Europe, and indeed as the Soviets became more mechanized. The Germans also suffered badly because they were unable to maintain the degree of air superiority needed to use their close air support, in effect the mobile artillery intended to support their tanks.

Too, the Germans had a strategic problem. They designed their forces for attack. Their new technology and tactics were much less adapted to defense, particularly under conditions of air inferiority. Prewar the Germans assumed that they could fight quick wars, not least because Hitler feared that his regime would crumble under the stress of a drawn-out war such as World War I. That is another way of saying that the Germans were aware that their potential was limited and hoped that they could overcome that limitation by superior offensive action at the outset (sustaining a defensive would give their enemies time to develop their military potential into actual strength). The belief in an early decisive offensive had driven the German general staff in 1914, and it can be argued that the Germans lost that war to precisely the same industrial weight that destroyed them in World War II. This experience might be interpreted to mean that the Germans might have fared better had they been able to combine the relative defensive power of 1918 with the offensive they developed before 1940. Both offensive and defensive became more expensive during World War II, as they had to take into account tanks and modern aircraft and modern communications. The Germans could not afford both. Even in 1918 they found it difficult to develop sufficient offensive power while maintaining a defensive so that the Allies could not simply attack somewhere the Germans were weak. It is also possible that, given their industrial strength and their inability to convince conquered populations to support them enthusiastically, the Germans had little hope of matching the Allies whatever they did. Even in their best year, 1942, they were grossly outproduced.

Offensive orientation made major intelligence failures (which may have been inevitable in the fragmented and highly politicized German system) seem tolerable.

Now that UAVs have shown their value and reliability, the next step is to use them in traditional combat aircraft roles. Northrop Grumman's X-47B prototype is shown here with its wings folded (for carrier stowage) after rollout in December 2008. At that year's Navy League show, the Naval Air Systems Command displayed a nominal future carrier air wing consisting of about 44 strike fighters (F/A-18, F-35, F/A-XX), 5 electronic attack aircraft (EA-18G), 5 airborne early warning aircraft, 19 helicopters (MH-60R/S), of which 8 would be dispersed to the ships working with the carrier), 2 onboard delivery aircraft, and 8–10 Navy unmanned combat air systems (N-UCAS). The implication was that the N-UCAS would be reserved for specially dangerous missions. However, if UCAS proves successful, it may replace a much larger proportion of the fighter-attack force, perhaps with enormous consequences. (Northrop Grumman)

Operational intelligence was less important to a rapidly moving blitzkrieg, which mainly needed information on the targets as they existed at the beginning of the battle. On the eastern front after 1942 the Germans succumbed to Soviet deception again and again, concentrating their forces in the wrong place.[7]

Naval Transformation after 1945

The U.S. Navy of the late 1940s offers another case in point. In 1935 German army officers were trying to solve much the same strategic problem they had faced in 1914. In 1945, however, U.S. naval officers saw an entirely new strategic problem. They had just won the greatest maritime war in history against Japan. Now the most likely opponent was the Soviet Union, the greatest land power in the world. What would be the role of naval forces in a war, hot or cold, against such a power? There was also new technology, in such forms as nuclear weapons, jets, guided missiles, and fast submarines. New technology would be needed to deal with them in any naval context, but how should the U.S. Navy transform itself?

The choice was hardly obvious, because U.S. national strategy was in flux. Was the problem to secure the inter-German border against a Russian steamroller? In that case the most important naval role might be to protect shipping bringing U.S. reinforcements to Europe or supporting land-based nuclear bombers. The U.S. Navy preferred to emphasize its ability to cause the Soviets problems by transporting troops or carrier bombers to strike around the periphery of the Soviet Union. Detractors pointed out that carriers could not deliver anything like the number of bombs offered by big land-based bombers. Proponents pointed out that bomber routes were rather predictable. The Navy's arguments attracted vigorous opposition from both the U.S. Air Force and the U.S. Army. However, as NATO commander, Gen. Dwight Eisenhower recognized the value of naval threats to the flanks of any Soviet army advancing through Western Europe—the main threat as then understood. As president he continued to support the Navy's ability to deal with the small wars he envisaged around the periphery of Europe. This high-level thinking was reflected in urgent development of new nuclear-capable carrier-based bombers and then in new carriers. Much U.S. naval effort also went into countering the large Soviet submarine fleet. However, the striking transformation was from a navy designed mainly to win by destroying an enemy navy to one designed to win by attacking the enemy on land, exploiting the unique mobility of seaborne forces. This new direction still defines the modern U.S. Navy.

Looking back the choice seems obvious. It even turned out that the ability to strike land targets offered a solution to the long-standing problem of the large Soviet submarine fleet and to the Soviets' ability to attack shipping in the North Atlantic using land-based naval bombers. As late as the 1980s, however, many argued that instead of trying to find a place in operations ashore the U.S. Navy should concentrate on countering Soviet submarines—on something close to classic navy-on-navy warfare. The U.S. Navy certainly wanted to retain the ability to deal with an enemy navy, and to some extent it did. Ultimately, however, there was not enough money for a transformed navy plus a more modern version of a classical navy intended mainly to win sea control by defeating an enemy fleet. For example, there was no possibility of replacing the vast antisubmarine fleet of convoy escorts that had helped win the Battle of the Atlantic. Something different was needed. The U.S. Navy learned to exploit the leverage offered by new means of ocean surveillance (both the SOSUS [sound surveillance system], inaugurated in 1956, and improved shore high-frequency direction finders and other forms of signal intelligence [SIGINT]). Given ocean surveillance,

U.S. antisubmarine thinking turned from waiting for submarines to attack convoys (which was now unaffordable) to a more offensive orientation, using aircraft such as the P-3 Orion.[8] The Navy also learned to operate its submarines in forward Soviet areas. Once the Soviets developed ballistic missile submarines of their own, they had naval assets they felt compelled to protect. The threat of U.S. submarine attacks on these craft helped force the Soviets to use much of their submarine fleet to protect them. The offensive U.S. Maritime Strategy helped concentrate Soviet naval assets on defense rather than offense—a very different situation from that in the Atlantic in World War II. Much of this multilayer transformation took place without notice because it was relatively slow and so much of it depended on highly classified advances in ocean surveillance. It is obvious only in retrospect.

Now

In the U.S. case, in the wake of the Cold War many advocates of transformation simply saw numerous new opportunities in the technology now available, particularly in new applications of computers such as networking. Their opponents pointed out that existing equipment and tactics worked; why change? Transformation was poorly defined because it was not clear that it was needed, and hence it was not clear just what sort of transformation was needed.

In fact a great deal was changing. During the Cold War the West confronted the Soviet Union from a more or less fixed position in Europe. Enormous infrastructure was built up over the decades of the Cold War, including both bases and fixed communications. Vast amounts of materiel were stored against the threat of a sudden attack. Nuclear weapons were deployed. Perhaps as important, the terms of a possible future war were more or less fixed, so that contingencies were well understood and plans elaborated. Everything changed as technology improved, but change was relatively slow. A less obvious factor, at least in the West, was that although computer technology as a whole developed rapidly during the Cold War, until the 1970s or even later only military applications required maximum computer capability. As a consequence the rapid developmental cycle of civilian computers had little impact on the military, whose computers

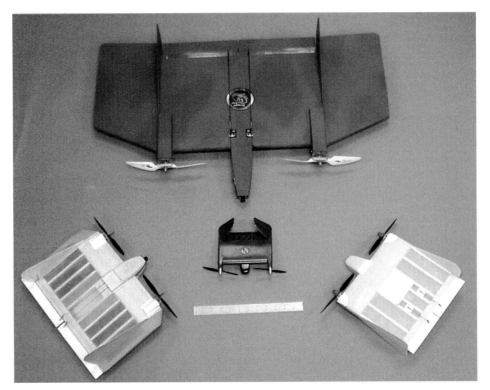

At the other end of the scale, mini- and micro-UAVs offer capabilities in sizes that no manned airplane could possibly match. The U.S. Naval Research Laboratory displays a variety of small, electrically powered UAVs, a ruler giving an idea of their size. (NRL via UVS International)

were so advanced by comparison. Thus the slow military development cycle did not seem, at least until the late 1970s, to cripple military command and control.

The end of the Cold War naturally cut military funding. But when the Cold War ended, the world did not suddenly become peaceful. Deterrence did not apply to local conflicts, so the sorts of national and even subnational aspirations that had been submerged by the Cold War boiled over in many places. Some of them touched U.S. national interests and thus demanded U.S. intervention. The United States' attempts to help manage the disintegration of the Soviet Union also demanded changes in U.S. force posture, for example to support new guarantees to post-Soviet states.

What is the future likely to be? Perhaps the best guess is that it will be full of surprises, cases such as Afghanistan in which we suddenly must project power into the most unlikely of places. Limited U.S. forces—limited by the need for mobility—will have to deploy rapidly to unprepared places abroad. These inherently light forces may have to deal with heavy local forces (as in a conven-

tional war) or with widely dispersed insurgents (Iraq, Afghanistan). The first kind of requirement emphasizes focused firepower. The second would seem to emphasize a need for intelligence gathering and for quickly deployed or persistent means of reacting to that intelligence (e.g., finding and attacking insurgent leaders). Both needs are foreign to our established patterns, and both have become expensive. The question now is how to leverage current U.S. superiority in military technology to solve such problems. This seems to be a major opportunity for the United States.

At the very least the analysis suggests that we cannot escape some sort of military transformation because we really do face a different situation. If we fail to understand the change, we will likely pay heavily. The French collapsed in 1940 because, ultimately, they failed to understand that they faced a new situation made possible by new technology. In their case the strategic situation—the confrontation with the Germans—was unchanged. In our case the technology is evolving, but the basic strategic situation has been transformed beyond recognition. That is quite aside from the problem that the existing force structure seems less and less affordable.

So how do we defeat enemy forces that may outnumber ours? Our deployed force will enjoy good support from those assets that we do have in place, thanks to the fact that space-based assets cover nearly the whole world. It seems inevitable, then, that we must find a mode of combat that emphasizes the values of reconnaissance (or sensing) and communication. Together they suggest the value of suppleness.

Unmanned air vehicles are a natural candidate for transformation because they can operate more cheaply than conventional aircraft (on a capability basis; see the next chapter). At least in Iraq and in other Middle Eastern areas, it seems, moreover, that armed unmanned vehicles can execute key antipersonnel missions with less political fallout than can manned aircraft. In wars that focus on individual terrorists, that is an enormous advantage. But the unmanned vehicles will not offer much greater suppleness than manned aircraft if, as is now often the case, each requires its own pilot or controller. Nor do current unmanned aircraft rival manned ones in their ordnance loads; they are antipersonnel or anti-automobile weapons, nothing more.

Yet suppleness demands that limited numbers of vehicles do as much as possible, because the fewer the vehicles, the more maneuverable the force as a whole. It also demands the most efficient kind of control, meaning the fewest controllers. The Germans won in 1940 because the key part of their army was much more maneuverable, and much faster-moving, than anyone else's. They were forced in that direction by the need to build an army rapidly from almost nothing and thus to concentrate on

a small offensive force within a much more conventional mass army. We are forced in an analogous direction by the need to be truly expeditionary.

Suppleness requires excellent fast communication based on an accurate picture of an evolving tactical situation—what we currently call network-centric warfare. Netting in turn is best adapted to weapons (in the widest sense) that are keyed to that picture. The UCAS system seems well adapted to exactly this mode of operation. Individually controlled aircraft and UAVs can achieve the same effects but at a much higher cost not only in money but also in total footprint, which means at a high cost to our overall mobility.

In effect that is the lesson of 1940. A conventional French army *could* have defeated the Germans if there was enough of it. It could have presented a defense in such depth that the Germans would never have broken through, but that would have taken many times the number of troops as the French could possibly have fielded. The French failed in 1940 because they did not realize that warfare had changed and they did not adopt the practices needed to fight faster-moving wars. Even a modicum of such transformation might have made all the difference in 1940, when the French deployed many superior tanks and a substantial air force but got very little out of either. Without any such transformation, it would have taken a far larger army to make up for German suppleness, because it would have had to be in many more places at the same time (since it would not have had the command and control to react properly to where the Germans actually were going). We can achieve our goals without transforming our forces, but only at an unacceptable cost.

5

WHAT PILOTS DO— AND NEED NOT DO

Just where an unmanned combat air system fits in the larger scheme of U.S. defense depends on what the pilot, who is absent from it, does. What is the effect of changing technology on his role? The success to date of various UAVs shows that the pilot is not always needed. However, it also seems clear that pilots are still needed—and may always be needed—for some functions. Where does the boundary lie between missions that still require pilots and those that do not? For that matter there may be (we argue that there are) missions that are best performed without pilots, even new kinds of missions for which human pilots are unsuited.

At the very least humans offer creativity and decision-making ability when information is scarce or a situation is unexpected (including situations in which existing equipment fails or is damaged). Against that, humans often cannot hold complex situations or rules in their heads. They are subject to fatigue, they require life support, and they impose limitations on vehicle performance. At least in theory a pilot provides a given airplane with enormous flexibility.[1] Moving the pilot off the airplane eliminates some limitations but raises the question of communications bandwidth and reliability: What does the airplane do when communications are cut or jammed? How does it deal with tactical deception? To some extent missiles have already encountered and dealt with such problems, but they are generally less autonomous than future unmanned aircraft, and their missions are both more specialized and shorter.

Much of the history of weapons has been the replacement of manpower by machinery and then by automation. This trend goes back as far as the shift from spears to arrows (propelled by a very simple machine). It led to stand-off combat, and it has led repeatedly to radical transformations of tactics and of national strategy. In each case the question has been the same. What does the human in the system contribute that a machine cannot? Or should not? Generally the human element is gradually concentrated where it absolutely has to be, while everything possible is automated. Automation cuts the number of expensive valuable people, and often it provides capabilities that otherwise would involve absolutely unaffordable numbers of people. In the case of airplanes, because the single pilot does so many tasks, there has been little incentive to decide which ones are essential and which ones can or should be automated.

The paragraph above refers to weapon systems rather than weapons because the weapon is part of something larger. It is usually the most visible part, and it is the part on which people generally concentrate. However, the overall system in which the weapon is embedded is what fights. Generally a weapon *system* involves some sort of sensor, some sort of decision maker, and the weapon that executes the decision. Sometimes all three are concentrated together. For example, a pilot flying an attack airplane on an armed reconnaissance mission spots the target with his eyes (sensor), decides to attack, sets up the fire-control system on the airplane, and then fires his weapons. On the

Humans provide an essential element of judgment in military operations. Their direct intervention may be most crucial in those missions just short of unrestrained combat. For example, we probably would prefer not to rely on an unmanned system to interpret the intentions of an unfriendly aircraft approaching the fleet in a tense but not wartime situation. Nor would we want to assume that communication with such an aircraft (were it not manned) would be altogether reliable. How high a price should we pay for that capability, and how many fleet aircraft are needed for such missions? Here an F-14 escorts a Soviet Bear D (Tu-95RTs) maritime reconnaissance and targeting airplane. The period that might lead up to a war demands particularly fine judgment. Soviet naval doctrine called for getting in the first shots (the "Battle for the First Salvo")—by surprise. Aircraft such as this Bear D had to be present to support those shots, but they were also present when the Soviets had no intention of fighting. During a war game in the 1980s, the gamers tried to solve the problem by declaring that any approach to within fifty miles of task force center was an act of war, but that was clearly no solution. Much depended on what the crew of the F-14 actually saw—on their very human perceptions. That is radically different from whether a pilot instructed to hit a surface target with given coordinates can make a human decision. (U.S. Navy photo via *Naval Aviation News*, August 1976)

other hand, if the same pilot is ordered to destroy a fixed target, the situation is radically different. The sensor is whatever form of reconnaissance detected the target.[2] The decision to hit that target is probably made at the wing or squadron (or higher) level. More and more we can specify the target location precisely enough (via GPS) that the pilot has only to navigate to within attack range, where he releases a weapon that heads for the specified coordinates. The U.S. Navy still wants to keep a man in the loop, because a decision taken minutes or hours before the moment of attack may be negated by something happening at or near the target in the interim. However, it is not clear that the man need be on board the attacking platform. That is certainly not the case for several missiles, such as Tactical Tomahawk.

Looking at the history of weaponry this way raises a central question: Will war ultimately reduce to a strug-gle between machines? Anyone looking at a new level of automation, which UCAS certainly is, must consider such questions. There is a sense that unless humans are willing to risk their lives in combat, our military power is both unconvincing and hollow. For example, it now appears that the decisive move in Afghanistan in 2003 was the Marine Corps' establishment of a forward base near the Taliban stronghold of Kandahar. In effect the Marines were proving the determination of U.S. forces, and that determination in turn convinced many Afghans to defect from the Taliban. Unmanned vehicles are often promoted specifically as a way of reducing pilot casualties in particularly dangerous situations, such as the destruction or suppression of enemy air defenses. It seems arguable that these are exactly the situations in which the pilot's judgment and creativity are most important, that unmanned vehicles offer their greatest advantages in more routine missions (such as ground attacks, which may still be quite dangerous).

Were war merely a contest to destroy machines or targets, it could be argued that the best weapon systems are the ones that extract the lowest cost in U.S. casualties to accomplish such ends. But war is something quite different. Clausewitz is still relevant: War is the extension of policy by other (violent) means. In other words the point of war is to convince the enemy to accept our own will. That may mean, as it does right now, convincing the enemy to abandon attempts to kill us or to overthrow our system. The key difference between war and propaganda or diplomacy is that it involves violence. It also often involves a willingness on our part to risk the consequences of the enemy's violence so as to prove our own determination. All of this may read like bad political theory, but the point is that we replace humans with machines not to save our own lives (though we probably will do so) but to gain military effectiveness. War is not a struggle between machines but between humans. Generally we cannot destroy everyone on the other side, so we fight in a way designed to change the enemy's perceptions.

An enemy perception that he was suffering losses in blood, while U.S. losses were generally merely to machines, might be particularly depressing to the enemy. Note, however, that psychology varies radically from place to place. A U.S. force depending mainly on machines is represented by the Taliban leadership as gutless and not manly enough to fight; at one point during the Afghan War Mullah Omar, the Taliban leader, said in effect that carpet bombing was all very well, but what would count would be man-to-man combat. The presence of U.S. Marines near Kandahar, at their forward fire base, may have supplied the visibly courageous element needed to convince Afghans to switch sides to the coalition we led.

Ultimately what counts is probably a credible threat to an enemy's ability to make war or, ultimately, an enemy's population. Some writers argue that enemies surrender because their struggle comes to feel hopeless. The current U.S. theory that an enemy can be shattered if we can get inside his operating cycle (i.e., if he can no longer keep up with us) fits this model.[3] It emphasizes the need for flexibility and speed of execution.

There is another way to look at the issue of man and weapon. There are usually two alternative paths to automation or mechanization. One is to automate parts of an existing system. In the case of an airplane, that path would replace the pilot with either an artificial-intelligence computer or with a computer taking orders from a remote pilot (the vehicle would be called a remotely piloted vehicle [RPV]). The alternative is to rethink the entire system. That is the case with UCAS, and it is the reason that the acronym includes the letter *S* for "system."

If the point of our current tactical thinking is to achieve maximum flexibility, then where does a pilot fit? Is he the system element that makes for flexibility, or does that come from somewhere else? Consider air attacks on surface targets. They may be planned in advance, they may be assigned to an airplane already in flight to strike another target, they may be assigned by close air support forward observers, or they may be the result of armed reconnaissance in which the pilot initiates action. In all but the last case, the flexibility comes from whoever assigns the target, not from the pilot. The pilot affects flexibility by the extent to which he can adapt to rapid mission change, either before or after taking off. In the case of armed reconnaissance in anything but a fully free-fire zone, the freedom of action afforded the pilot is limited in some way, and the pilot's effectiveness depends in considerable part on whether he can keep in mind mission restrictions (usually geographical) while seeking targets. His ability to do that may depend on the way in which information is laid out in the cockpit (see the U.S.-Canadian example below).[4]

Increasingly we envisage masses of distributed sensors that contribute to a tactical or strategic picture on the basis of which targets are selected for attack. For about two decades we have been developing the techniques that will most likely be used by future unmanned attack aircraft, though clearly not for this purpose. The two key parallel developments were the rise of automated mission planning and the rise of mission computers on board aircraft. Mission planning began as a way of avoiding enemy defenses en route to a preset target. It is an intricate process because it has to take account of factors such as aircraft fuel usage (on alternate paths to and from the target) and the areas of effectiveness of enemy air defenses. Even when several aircraft attack the same target, each needs its own mission plan so that all can attack from different angles to overcome target defenses. Thus planning for missions such as the strikes against Tripoli or the Bekaa Valley attack in 1986 took weeks. A last-minute delay in the Bekaa strike ruined all that work because instead of coming out of the sun, the aircraft were visible as they approached the target. Two were shot down.

For the U.S. Navy the result of the Bekaa Valley experience was pressure to automate strike planning so that it could be much quicker—and much more flexible, because plans could be recast much closer to the actual attack. Automation emphasized that the flexibility of the system as a whole resided mainly in the strike planners, not in those flying the airplane. This conclusion was somewhat clouded by the fact that, once the target had been chosen, the individual pilots developed their own flight plans.

Strike planning tends to be iterative, because a route to the target that seems attractive at the outset may entail unexpected problems, such as those imposed by terrain. To some extent a pilot developing a strike plan (as is standard) takes into account his own ability to deal with enemy defenses by maneuver and other countermeasures. At least in theory this is a creative issue, because the pilot responds to what the defense throws up, not to the theoretical or known defense capability. As defenses become more sophisticated, however, it seems that reliance is placed much more on hardware defenses such as stealth, antiradar weaponry, and jammers.

By 1986 aircraft already had mission computers that, among other things, navigated them between waypoints en route to a preselected target. The waypoints embodied the mission plan, so naturally the automated mission planning systems eventually produced data cartridges that could load strike plans into aircraft mission computers. By the 1990s this combination had reduced the pilot's efforts in flight to taking off, flying from waypoint to waypoint (as indicated by the onboard mission system), conducting the attack itself, flying the waypoints home, and landing (and, if need be, taking on fuel in the air). While flying, of course, the pilot had to defend against enemy missiles and fighters, very much not an automatic function. The pilot was needed for the attack proper because he had to recognize the particular aim point and set the aircraft fire-control system to attack it (the mission plan merely placed him in position to begin the attack itself). However, with the rise and improvement of GPS, it became possible for a mission computer to do more and more of the attack itself, with minimal (or no) pilot intervention. All that mattered was that some external system determined the GPS coordinates of the preselected target. Even in cases in which GPS coordinates are not available, it can be argued that images of the target may suffice for a fully automated attack, using, say, electro-optical sensors. That is, it is not clear that for target designation the pilot's eye and brain are significantly different from a machine. A multi- or hyper-spectral machine may do even better, because it may be able to see through camouflage or to ignore the effects of different sun angles.

By the early 1990s it seemed that the only surface targets that could not be attacked more or less automatically were pop-ups or time-sensitive targets such as those identified by forward air controllers and by UAVs. In fact, the forward air controllers could measure GPS coordinates using hand-held lasers. Pilots still did have to identify targets located by UAVs, because UAV imagery was not always suitable for GPS measurements. In such cases imagery was fed to the pilot, who locked his weapons onto the indicated target. However, even that barrier seems increasingly frail. In 2002 the U.S. Navy demonstrated an all-GPS attack on a pop-up target whose GPS coordinates had been measured by the UAV that detected the target in the first place. Clearly there will still be cases in which a target's coordinates cannot be measured in advance, so a pilot (or some other entity) will still have to recognize the target on the way in, but such cases seem less and less likely to account for the bulk of what attack aircraft will do in the future. In the case of Hellfire-firing Predators we already see orbiting UAVs attacking targets whose images they relay back to a controller, who commands them to designate and then attack the chosen target. That might be much less practicable in a jamming environment. However, a manned airplane would hardly orbit on a sustained basis waiting for the right automobile to come into firing range because it would be far too exposed—and would give the potential target far too obvious a warning.

The question is always where in the larger military system (of which the airplane is a part) humans are needed. Humans may be simpler or more flexible ways of doing what a programmed machine can do, but ultimately they are special because they can make crucial choices and can find creative solutions to the problems they meet (advocates of artificial intelligence may disagree). It can also be argued that pilots make airplanes flexible. They make it possible to swing a carrier's air wing from one role (say, fleet air defense or air superiority) to another (strike), but it is not clear that much of that flexibility cannot be supplied by a UCAS operator. Unmanned vehicles might be better for strike. They may also prove ideal for long-endurance combat air patrol against an unambiguous threat, where any potential targets that are found (relatively easy in the sterile air-to-air environment) should be attacked. On the other hand pilot choice is crucial to fighter operations under the ambiguous conditions that apply when the situation is warlike but there is no war. It takes a pilot to decide whether to fire a missile at an incoming airplane that does not return IFF signals and then turns out to be an airliner when he comes within visual range. Probably the appropriate view at this stage is that the fleet would benefit from a combination of manned and unmanned aircraft, but that unmanned aircraft offer essential new capabilities that should not be ignored.

From the point of view of air attack, the fixed targets of the past are likely to matter less and less, at least in anything short of a prolonged central war (a few vital fixed targets, such as command centers and weapon bunkers, are important exceptions). We are likely to find ourselves in dynamic situations in which the importance of targets changes rapidly. It may well be that we want to design our forces specifically so that they can recognize changes in a situation, take the appropriate decisions, and apply force as needed to execute such decisions more quickly. It is not at all clear that classic air attack systems (not just the aircraft) are best designed to meet such requirements.

It takes humans to identify the targets that currently matter because of a dynamic situation (e.g., a battle) or because other humans (on the enemy side) perceive their value. This evaluation is *not* what pilots generally do. It is done on two levels: at a central headquarters aware of the tide of battle or of larger issues and at the level of the forward air controller. In either case, the role of the pilot is to deliver his ordnance on target as needed. In some cases that involves considerable ingenuity (creativity), for example, to reach a target largely hidden by, say, a viaduct.

Often proposals for automation evoke a subtler issue. War often seems to be about heroism and sacrifice. Cold machines do neither. How can an unmanned machine be compared to a pilot braving enemy fire to make a precision attack? Fortunately we have a way of seeing how such concepts play out in a type of warfare that went from close human combat to long-range machine combat: naval warfare. At one time a fight between two ships really was decided largely by hand-to-hand combat by their crews. You can see that sort of battle in movies about the age of sail. By 1900 combat was a matter of gunnery at ranges of miles, and what counted was the skill of crews in using guns and in controlling damage to their ships. Now it is generally seen as a fight between a ship's largely automated defensive systems and antiship missiles. Ideas such as controlling the sea or denying sea control are as valid as they were two centuries ago. Admittedly many military enthusiasts find naval warfare too cold-blooded to be exciting, but that is not the point.

So where does UCAS fit? UCAS is best seen not as a further advance in automation but as a step toward more efficient human control. The key is in the last letter of the acronym, *S*. The visible element of the system is the unmanned armed air vehicle. It is part of a larger system (hence the *S*) in which human decision making has been moved from the air vehicle but is still very much present. An important issue in system design is the extent to which a distant controller can suffice. There are two key factors here. One is the time lag due to the distance between vehicle and controller and the way in which the controller, who is not on board the vehicle, acts. A second is the reliability of the communications links that carry information from the vehicle to the controller and commands back from controller to vehicle. Problems involving the first include feedback from machine (vehicle) to control. The second issue raises the question of backup:

What does the vehicle do when it cannot receive what it needs? When the links exist but are too noisy? And how does the vehicle distinguish appropriate data from erroneous commands and data?

We are already part of the way to such systems. The new Joint Strike Fighter (JSF) is more and more characterized as a network node, an information-gathering platform as much as a conventional airplane. The pilot depends heavily on information from other aircraft and from other external sensors, relayed via radio and satellite links. His own perception of the situation around the airplane depends not only on sensors dotted around the airframe (giving him a virtual 360-degree field of view as well as a view below the airplane) but also on external data melded with his own sensor data. If this vision is realized, how important is it that the pilot is sitting in that airplane? How different would it be if the data were all concentrated somewhere else? The concept of the JSF is to give the pilot access to the mass of data normally held by the Air Operations Center, the idea being that evolving computer technology makes that possible. It is not at all clear, however, that the single pilot, rather than multiple analysts on the ground, can effectively use that mass of data. As it developed forms of netted warfare, the Navy's slogan was "sensor to shooter connectivity," but that turned out to mean that sensor data were transformed by a data fusion center into a form the shooters could easily use. The JSF may be the ultimate expression of the idea, very common in the computer world, that more is always better. However, human perception seems to be a fixed bottleneck, and feeding in more data really precludes good decision making.

What do the people in weapon systems do? They do a combination of things. One is to operate the system skillfully, which includes solving routine problems. For a pilot that might mean being able to land successfully or to negotiate airspace in which there are other airplanes. Another is to apply their strength as needed to carry out entirely routine tasks. For a pilot that might mean keeping an airplane on course as required, say, between way points during a mission. Note that this role has largely been automated away by autopilots, which have existed for many decades. Then there is a third role: creativity and

decision-making when it is not at all obvious what to do, for example in many kinds of combat. People are still far more flexible than any programmed machine, and they can still deal with unexpected situations that will defeat any computer.

Human judgment or, in a larger sense, creativity may mean making up for errors inherent in an automatic system (as in a controversy in the pre–World War I Royal Navy about gunnery): Are men the problem in a system (because they make mistakes) or are they its saviors (because they make up for design or operating errors in a machine)?[5] The savior view is that human creativity makes up for inevitable failures on the part of those who design the machine. That would apply as much to our digital age as to an earlier analog one. In this case the balance would be between the errors that men impose and the ones they solve. Human problem solving to save a complex system requires considerable training and the choice of the right humans. It can be argued that even though the best operators may do things a computer cannot, the computer will outperform average operators, tired operators, or operators who have lost their edge because their training has faded.

There are already many examples of computers taking over operators' tasks. In the past radars employed human detectors. A human operator decided that something visible on the screen represented a real target rather than noise. The screen itself considerably filtered the information available to the radar, but the operator could tune the filtering to allow in more real targets mixed with noise, and he could often distinguish one from the other in subtle ways—very much an application of human creativity. During the 1970s it became possible to digitize radar output. A computer associated with the radar could see which targets produced echoes above a set threshold, and it entered them as real targets. The computer was generally programmed to set the threshold to hold the false alarm rate to some acceptable figure. Experience showed that good operators could often detect targets before the computer could. However, operators could not maintain their edge for many hours of inaction. On average the computer was better. Moreover, as computer power increased, the computer could also examine the apparent motion of the apparent targets, rejecting ones behaving randomly. It was coming closer to the subtle clues the human operators were using when they detuned their scopes. It had access to a great deal more detailed data than the human operators, because it could constantly monitor detailed characteristics of the noise, and it could also adjust its criteria for where the target might be found (for an air search radar, noise will be different, for example, near the ground). Many modern radars still offer raw video (like that the old operators saw) as an option, to check computer performance, but humans generally act as system monitors rather than as system operators. Many radars operate altogether unmanned.

Thus at the least it can be argued that an unpiloted vehicle offers greater inherent endurance, if it can survive in a combat area, simply because it does not tire. That may have important tactical consequences. In a dynamic situation sustained air presence translates into shorter reaction time to pop-up targets, which may be the only ones that really count.

We currently operate aircraft that require a highly trained pilot to, in effect, make up for the limits of the machine. We use the pilot for a combination of routine and emergency tasks and as a system monitor. It can be argued that the system monitor role is needed mainly in cases in which human passengers would be endangered by a computer failure. We know from the successful use of UAVs that most in-flight tasks can be automated. The one automated task not yet commonly seen is operation in mixed-use airspace, the requirement being a collision avoidance system on the UAV equivalent to collision avoidance (including pilots) on, say, an airliner. Effective systems have been demonstrated; the current question is the field of regard over which the UAV detects other aircraft. Unfortunately the FAA requirement is for a demonstrated level of safety rather than a specified field of regard, which cannot yet be translated directly into a safety level. Collision avoidance would also make it possible for multiple UAVs to operate freely in close proximity. UAVs, unlike conventional aircraft, do not entail continuous proficiency training. That might be very important for an aircraft at the end of a long logistical pipeline in a forward expeditionary area—of the sort in which we currently find ourselves.

It is sometimes argued that decisions as to when and whether to fire should be left to human judgment. That is not usually an issue for an air strike against a preplanned or assigned target.[6] As noted, in current UCAVs the decision is left to a remote human controller. There have long been attempts at automatic target recognition, which implies automatic attack at long range.[7] They generally apply to land vehicles; we would very much like to be able to hit wheeled armored personnel carriers, for example, but not buses filled with civilians. It is not at all clear that a pilot flying at high speed and low altitude can do much better than a machine in such cases.[8] Either neither can be trusted to distinguish or the machine may actually do better at pattern recognition.

If communications were both perfect and instantaneous, it could be argued that all pilot functions could be carried out by ground-based controllers. In reality communications will often break down and there will be a dramatic difference between the situational awareness of a pilot and the awareness of a controller on the ground (although new forms of synthetic reality might change the situation dramatically). It is probably possible to provide a UAV with enough to complete its mission even if continuous communication fails, particularly once a target has been assigned. An alert pilot may well be much better at air-to-air combat, at delivering ordnance to poorly defined targets, and perhaps at dealing with enemy air defenses. Switching to an all-UCAS force would be unacceptable because it would open us to obvious communications countermeasures, but in more and more cases the pilot acts more as chauffeur than as creative actor. The usual path to automation is to eliminate humans in routine jobs. Machines are often more reliable and more effective in such roles.

The human pilot also imposes limitations on aircraft operation. Some missions cannot be ordered because they are patently unsafe, for example, missions in marginal weather. An enemy aware of such limitations knows that he is safe. We now fly cruise missiles—in effect, one-way UCAS—under adverse weather conditions, but generally the number of such weapons in theater is limited, and they are often ineffective against pop-up or ill-defined tactical targets. At least for naval missiles such as Tomahawk, the limit is not due to the cost of the weapons but to limited shipboard launcher capacity (and nothing more capacious is in sight). Even in good weather, pilot fatigue limits the number of sorties aircraft can fly.

It is not always obvious that a mechanized system should duplicate an existing one, simply replacing people by machines. Often it is much better to rethink the system altogether. For example, a pilot flying an armed reconnaissance mission decides that a patch of color on the ground is a valid target. Direct automation would insert a robot with some sort of artificial intelligence. Rethinking, however, would move the decision to a command center in which a person looking at the image (perhaps in hyperspectral mode) would make the decision, ordering an unmanned vehicle to attack (to some extent this is already happening even in the manned world). Moving the point of decision would carry a tactical cost—for example, in delay and in demanding continuous connectivity—that might or might not be acceptable. The shorter the available time for decision making, the less attractive this degree of automation.

When automated command and control was proposed in the U.S. Navy in the 1950s, the counterargument was that decision-making responsibility should always remain with humans. No one could be sure that any machine would make the right choices. The answer was that automation replaced functions that supported decision making, not decision making itself. In this particular case decisions were already being made on the basis of a displayed tactical picture. Automation made the picture much more timely, which was critically important for humans trying to deal with more complex faster-moving tactical situations. Automation also made it easier for the same humans to understand available options. In effect automation eliminated routine human roles. The central role of decision making was not affected. Attempts to automate decision making on a limited scale (e.g., to engage incoming aircraft automatically) have generally been rejected. Ironically, in the most prominent case of erroneous engagement, when the USS Vincennes shot down an Iranian Airbus airliner over the Strait of Hormuz in 1988, the system had been set in nonautomated mode specifically to avoid catastrophic errors in judgment. It now seems that the machine might never have fired at the airliner had it been left in automatic mode.[9]

The Vincennes incident is interesting as a way of understanding what automation can and cannot do, and what human decision making requires. One reading of the incident is that automation did not go far enough: The picture presented to the watch standers in the ship's combat direct center gave an unintentionally misleading idea of whether the approaching airliner was within the defined civilian air traffic corridor. This problem was due to limited computer capacity, but in a larger sense it reflected assumptions inherent in the design of the ship's combat system. The key problem may have been that the ship's system was little more than an automated version of earlier manual systems. Automation in effect underestimated the role of human judgment in what seemed to be routine functions, in this case detecting and plotting air targets.

The lesson of about half a century of automated decision support has been that the design of the systems imposes decisions and choices of which the human user is often ignorant or forgets in the heat of the moment. That does not negate the basic idea of computer support, but it does emphasize the need for better or more informative support. Computer support has generally meant assembling and winnowing tactical information to support a decision maker then automating the response the decision maker orders. Decision making itself remains a human responsibility. In some cases response time is so short, and the situation apparently so simple, that decision making is taken out of human hands. Examples are automatic-response tactical antimissile systems and self-designating antitank weapons (self-guided bomblets). In the former case, at least for naval missile systems, commanders typically switch off the automated feature and prefer semiautomatic operation. Even the automated version offers a human veto. It is automatic, but it is not autonomous; it follows a logic, dictated by humans, which a human can reject. The bomblet is autonomous because there is no provision for human intervention once it is released. Its template for deciding that a target is legitimate is simple and cannot easily be altered.

The wider lesson seems to be that successful automation is not merely translation from human-operated to computer-operated systems with humans left in place to make key decisions. It is, rather, to rethink the entire system to decide how to support the very necessary human decision maker. Sometimes a machine simply substitutes for a person, as in an airplane's autopilot. Sometimes the human decision maker needs not only the information nominally provided by the unautomated system but also much more information that it turns out that the human was supposed to have but often missed.

What does all of that mean? In the case of *Vincennes*, the humans in the system were supposed to know, for example, that their computer was showing only the centerline of the airliner flight zone, not its edges (within which the Airbus was flying). That information was in the backs of their heads. They were trained to concentrate on the picture they actually saw, and on that picture, the Iranian airliner was outside the line.

The Air National Guard pilots in Afghanistan who attacked Canadians conducting a live-fire exercise in 2002 were another, more complex, case in point. They had been dispatched to bomb a suspected enemy position. However, it was well known that the enemy might reveal himself by firing at a passing U.S. airplane, in which case the natural counter was to attack those firing. These instructions were, if you like, in the fronts of the pilots' minds. At the morning briefing, the pilots were told about the Canadian exercise. Like the information about the width of the airliner corridor, that information was in the backs of their minds. Their cockpits were ill adapted to emphasize exactly where they were at any given time relative

to friendly or other forces; the systems were designed to navigate them from point to point. Position information was certainly present in the airplanes' mission computers, but it did not seem vital in the usual context in which aircraft attack designated targets. In theory an additional layer of command, supplied by a ground center, should have exercised a veto over an attack in the wrong place, but apparently it did not.

As in the *Vincennes* incident, this problem reflected unstated assumptions in the way in which the fighters' cockpit displays worked. The cockpit systems were designed to support attacks on targets the pilots saw, the object being maximum accuracy in a single-pass strike. Other parts of the airplane were designed to bring the pilot into position to attack a target whose coordinates had been fed in prior to takeoff. The hidden assumption was that whoever planned the mission would be responsible for avoiding targeting errors. That would have been fine for fixed, prechosen targets, but in Afghanistan most targets were pop-ups. And worse, that is likely to be the case in future. In this case the difficult part of the mission is deciding whether to attack a particular target. The problem of actually hitting it once it has been chosen is far less difficult (at least as long as systems like GPS work). It might seem natural to concentrate on the human who decides what to attack. Apparent enemy fire is a useful cue, but it must be considered in the context of where friendly forces are.

6

THE ECONOMICS OF UCAS

The UCAS air vehicle is comparable to many other modern fighter or attack aircraft. It lacks provision for a pilot, but presumably that makes only a small difference in the cost per pound of the airplane. It is usually assumed that aircraft are bought by the pound, so that if UCAS weighs about as much as, say, an F/A-18, it ought to have a similar cost. It may be that, as the electronics on board such aircraft becomes more complex, cost is set by airframe weight plus electronics complexity. What matters in the end is the life-cycle cost of a fleet of these air vehicles. That depends on individual life-cycle cost and on the number of air vehicles required. In both factors a UCAS fleet would almost certainly differ radically from a conventional fleet of manned aircraft.

Ultimately the fleet performs some number of combat or operational missions. However, each pilot must fly frequently to maintain proficiency, particularly if that pilot is to operate in a demanding carrier environment. Thus the number of sorties conducted by a manned aircraft squadron, for example, depends on deployment time, not on combat or other operational requirements. Combat flights are likely to represent only a small fraction of total aircraft flights. An unmanned airplane has no need to fly except in combat or operationally. Presumably test equipment will suffice to confirm that the airplane is ready when needed. That is certainly the way missiles, which are in effect unmanned (but not reusable) airplanes, work.

Maintenance and spares requirements are typically written in terms of maintenance man-hours per flight hour. The more complicated the airplane, the worse the ratio between the two; hence, the more expensive each flight hour is. Improved electronics has drastically reduced electronic maintenance hours, but it seems unlikely that mechanical systems and engines are subject to similar improvements. There is some hope that aggressive in-flight monitoring can help focus maintenance to reduce hours and spares loads. This development would apply equally to unmanned and to manned aircraft. Thus cutting sorties to, say, a tenth of those usually imposed on airplanes would cut maintenance costs proportionately. Fuel costs would also be reduced proportionately.

It can also be argued that the UCAS air vehicle should be less expensive to maintain. In the mode of operation sketched here, the swarm of air vehicles spends more time in the air and lands much less frequently on the carrier. From a structural point of view, landing and launching (and climbing and descending) impose considerable loads on each airplane; it may even be that the measure should be maintenance man-hours per *flight* rather than per *flight hour*. In that case the swarm, which it is posited can remain in the air by being refueled there, will impose a considerably smaller burden on carrier maintainers per flight hour. Manned aircraft take off and land much more frequently.

This difference also would be significant from a fleet lifetime point of view. Many aircraft are grounded not because they are obsolete (aircraft technology has been fairly stable for a long time) but because they can no longer stand the stress to which they are subjected; they are fatigued out. If the main causes of fatigue in naval aircraft are landings and takeoffs, then the UCAS flight vehicle benefits in two ways. First, it flies far less often, so at a given age it has experienced far fewer flight hours. That has already been taken into account from a maintenance point of view. Second, during those hours it is likely to experience a great deal less fatigue, say, by a factor of five or ten (depending on how much longer the UCAS air vehicle normally remains in the air). The stealth of the air vehicle may reduce another source of stress, the need to fly low to evade enemy air defenses. The use of external targeting has already dramatically reduced the need for most tactical aircraft to fly low.

Some proportion of the total purchase of any type of airplane is accounted for by expected operational attrition. A UCAS fleet ought to experience much less attrition than a fleet of manned aircraft, simply because the aircraft will fly far less frequently (that is a different question than attrition per thousands of flight hours) and thus last much longer. In that case money not spent on early replacements could go into improved systems and into the weapons the UCAS vehicle delivers. Constant system upgrades would make maximum use of the rapid improvement of electronics.

Nowhere here, incidentally, is there any assumption that the UCAS air vehicle would be less vulnerable to enemy action than a conventional manned airplane; there is no reason to imagine that it would be much *more* vulnerable.

From a naval point of view, these possibilities have additional implications. An aircraft carrier is manned and fitted to maintain its squadrons for several months at a time. A dramatic reduction in their maintenance needs would probably mean a reduction in spares and, perhaps, maintainers—and there is currently enormous pressure to reduce manning, which is very expensive. To some extent, moreover, carriers must receive stores in forward areas. It might be possible to eliminate or to reduce dramatically any such requirement.

The carrier typically has enough fuel on board for about a week's air operations. It must therefore periodically take on fuel from a consort—a time of increased vul-

nerability. The consorts themselves must fuel periodically, and they too need protection. In recent years the consorts have been moved to the Military Sealift Command and disarmed, the theory being that U.S. sea control is such that offshore areas are safe. This assumption would collapse in the face of any sophisticated enemy. To remain viable the U.S. Navy would find itself arming its auxiliaries and probably assigning major combatant ships to protect them as they moved toward fueling rendezvous. Carriers would probably pull farther back from an enemy coast to fuel and to take on weapons. Anything that made that more necessary would reduce the effectiveness of the carrier force. Conversely, anything that would increase the interval between fueling would both make the carriers more effective and reduce the need for supporting ships (there would still be a need, of course, for ammunition ships).

A dramatic reduction in proficiency flying in forward areas might, then, have dramatic implications. A carrier that did not have to sustain such flights during its move toward the target area would have its full aviation fuel load available for operational and combat flying. It would still have to replenish its load of weapons, and it would still fuel (to support air operations) from time to time, but the load would be considerably reduced. Moreover, the carrier's movements would become much less predictable. It seems arguable that an enemy with limited ocean surveillance resources would find it easier to track the slower auxiliaries than a fast nuclear-powered carrier (and consorts that fuel from it).

Say, for example, that combat operations are only 10 percent of overall flying once a carrier is at sea. Fuel sufficient for a week might then stretch considerably, perhaps long enough that the carrier would not have to take on fuel at all while anywhere near a combat area. The carrier would still fuel its escorts, so the idea of not fueling at all is probably utopian. Even so, reducing fueling dramatically would undoubtedly improve carrier survivability in the face of blue-water threats such as submarines. For example, diesel-electric submarines, which represent the great bulk of the underwater threat to carriers, are probably largely ineffective against a nuclear carrier running at high speed but have a fair chance against one replenishing, particularly if the submarines are vectored by an external system. If that seems unreal, the interception of the USS *Kitty Hawk* by a Chinese diesel-electric submarine a few years ago almost certainly demonstrated the existence of a Chinese ocean surveillance (cueing) system.

There is another factor, too: the pilot. Training a human pilot is extremely expensive, and a pilot is not inexpensive to maintain once trained. Training requires substantial numbers of dedicated airplanes, each of which eats fuel and consumes spares and maintenance man-hours. All calculations of aircraft requirements, for example, include a considerable percentage for the training pipeline.

Without its pilot a UCAS air vehicle would entail no pipeline cost at all, except for a few vehicles on which maintainers would practice. There might also be a limited requirement to teach remaining pilots how to deal with these unmanned vehicles in the same air space. In either case the pipeline requirement would be substantially less than that assumed right now.

All of these savings would be very important. Right now aircraft carriers are by far the most expensive warships to build and operate. They are also, often, the most valuable vessels in the U.S. arsenal. They are, for example, the only U.S. warships that can take their primary weapons on board at sea, and hence they are the only U.S. warships that can impose sustained combat pressure on an enemy. There is little or no reason to imagine that this situation will change in the near future, because there is still no simple way to replenish cruise missiles at sea (an electric rail gun might use replenishable ammunition, but it is still a very distant prospect). Anything that makes carrier operation more affordable helps the U.S. Navy do its vital duty of projecting U.S. power.

Finally, consider the lifetime cost of an airplane from the point of view of changing technology. One lesson of about fifty years of jet fighter development is that aerodynamics and even engine technology change relatively slowly. Airplanes become obsolete mainly because they cannot accommodate new radars and computers and data buses and thus cannot live in new tactical environments (in the information sense) and deliver new precision weapons (newer airplanes are often also less expensive to

operate). The same sort of upgradability the U.S. Navy has put into its submarines and its surface ships, with programs such as ARCI (Acoustic Rapid COTS Insertion), is surely applicable to airplanes. It is, then, possible to imagine stretching the life of airframes over very long periods. That could dramatically reduce the ownership cost per airplane, which would make it much more affordable to maintain a large fleet.

There are, however, important caveats. It is vital to hold down the attrition rate, which is probably proportional to flight hours per year (but might be lower with unmanned aircraft). It is also vital that the airframe last as long as possible. It appears that the newest composite airframes are essentially impossible to rebuild or rewing—they last a fixed number of flight hours. If the path to a more affordable tactical air force is to make the individual airplanes last longer, that is disastrous—unless the number of flight hours per year can be slashed *without any cost in loss of tactical competence*. Experience suggests that simulator hours cannot be substituted for real flight hours. It seems that unmanned aircraft are the only solution to this particular problem.

These notes suggest that adopting a UCAS-based attack aircraft complement would dramatically reduce the cost of carrier operation. Apart from all the arguments given, we can guess as much because cruise missiles—unmanned but one-way aircraft—are so inexpensive to operate. We do not even think of them as aircraft because they fly only once in their lives. However, it is not difficult to imagine a cruise missile that could drop a weapon—instead of diving into a target—and therefore could be recovered. We even know that in the 1980s a Russian design organization, Chelomey, designed a missile, Meteorit, which would drop a bomb on one target and then proceed to another. That is not too far from having the missile attack and then return. Such a weapon would not cost very much more (if at all more) than current one-way missiles. The only real difference is that we tend not to think of cruise missiles as unmanned aircraft, which is what they are. There is even an example, in India, of a UAV serving as the basis of a cruise missile. For that matter, during the test stage of some early cruise missiles, such as the U.S. Navy's Regulus, vehicles were produced that returned to

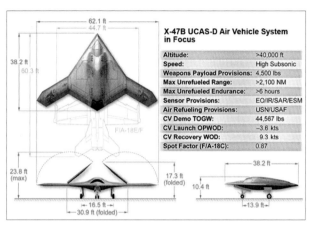

The X-47B is about the size and weight of an F/A-18E/F and is likely to cost about as much in production quantities; increased software costs will probably offset the savings of not supporting a pilot. However, its economics may be radically different because it will fly almost exclusively on combat missions. (Northrop Grumman)

land as airplanes (though they were hardly what we would now call UAVs).

A UCAS airframe with roughly the performance of a current jet attack aircraft should cost about as much (in fact there will be some saving because it has no life-support system, but they may be balanced by software investment).

Typically 20 percent of the aircraft of any given type are needed to train pilots on a full-time basis. Pilots who have been trained and are operational must continue to fly daily to maintain their proficiency. It is reasonable to suppose that only 10 percent of overall flight time after training is combat flight time, and we know that flight accounts for 60 percent of overall aircraft program cost. Flight cost presumably includes wear and tear on the airplane and the costs of spares and maintenance. All of these figures are crude, but they give a reasonable idea of the overall costs.

In an unmanned force there would be no pilot training at all, so for the same number available for combat only 80 percent as many aircraft would be bought. In fact the number should be far lower, because only part of the total combat air force is deployed at any one time. Yet to maintain proficiency, all of the undeployed units operating piloted aircraft must be filled out. If there were no need to maintain proficiency, aircraft could be cross-decked when carriers deployed, much as expensive missiles are.

For example, we currently consider ten carrier air wings a dead minimum (and perhaps too little) to support the ability to surge-deploy six of them. If, however, we needed only six air wings' worth of aircraft (plus attrition spares), then we would not buy 40 percent of the operational aircraft we currently buy (which are 80 percent of the total of operating aircraft). That is, 10 operational air wings currently cost at least 12.5 air wings' worth of aircraft. Buying only 6 air wings' worth would avoid buying more than half of the aircraft of any given type we currently buy.

Current plans envisage four fighter squadrons per carrier, a total of forty-eight aircraft. Current plans also envisage buying two squadrons of F-35s and two of a future fighter, which might be UCAS. Buying only six carriers' worth of UCAS on this basis would mean *not* buying 156 airplanes, not to mention their attrition spares. The effect is to more than halve the purchase of these aircraft, from (typically) 361 to 144 for a future fighter. At about $100 million per airplane, *not* buying 217 airplanes saves $21.7 billion, which does not count savings in fuel and maintenance. Since 60 percent of an airplane's lifetime cost goes into these factors, the saving is actually far greater. Each conventional airplane would cost $250 million over its lifetime (taking the 60 percent of lifetime cost into account). Not buying 217 airplanes thus directly saves over $54 billion. However, each UCAS costs much less to fly—10 percent flying time might cut the usual 60 percent lifetime to the point where each of the airplanes we *do* buy costs us $115 million instead of $250 million. That is a further saving of $135 million per airplane—about $19 billion. The alternative, the 361 conventional aircraft, could cost as much as $90 billion to buy and operate. The UCAS alternative costs about $17 billion, mainly because these aircraft are so few and because they fly relatively rarely. All of these figures are slightly high because the numbers bought include attrition aircraft, but they give an idea of the savings possible. The cost of the aircraft dwarfs the cost of buying and operating the carrier.

At one time it was usual to equate the purchase cost of a carrier air wing with that of the carrier and to assume that a carrier would operate two full air wings during its fifty-year lifetime. Carrier operating cost is likely to be far less than carrier purchase cost. If the cost of the carrier air wing and its operations can be more than halved, then for the same amount it is possible to buy and operate many more carriers.

Say the carrier purchase price is C, and the carrier operating cost (over the ship's lifetime) is 80 percent of purchase price. If the purchase price of each carrier air wing is another C, then total operating and purchase cost of a carrier plus its aircraft amounts to 6.8 C (2.5 C per air wing). This costing imputes to the carrier the appropriate fraction of overall aircraft system cost, including training and so forth. If the appropriate figure for each air wing is only 1.15 C, then total program cost is 4.1 C, which is about 60 percent of the current cost. On this basis three carriers cost less than two current ones, without any sacrifice in capability.

That is a very attractive option in a world in which crises are widely distributed and are likely to be simultaneous. The alternative usually suggested is a dramatic cut in individual carrier capability in hopes of increasing numbers. But the resulting ships, which are not as survivable, cannot operate high-end (i.e., survivable) aircraft and cost much more per aircraft. Nor do the smaller ships operate tactically efficient numbers of aircraft. This combination of limitations explains why the small carriers operated by foreign navies are not comparable to current U.S. carriers.

Acknowledgments

I am grateful to David C. Isby and Steven Zaloga for their advice and insights, particularly historical, and particularly concerning the use of UAVs in ground operations. Richard D. Fisher and Steven Zaloga very kindly supplied some of the photographs. For assistance with illustrations, and with information and insights, I am grateful to many within the UAV industry. I hope I have accurately described their aircraft and their ideas. My wife Rhea has lived with this project for about two years. I could not have completed this book without her loving encouragement—and her patience.

Appendix I

COMBAT USE OF UNMANNED COMBAT AIR VEHICLES

The United States has had combat experience with two kinds of armed combat air vehicles: cruise missiles, particularly the Tactical Tomahawk, and armed versions of earlier surveillance UAVs such as the Predator and now Reaper. Putting the two together, rather than treating them very separately, emphasizes the range of possible missions and also the range of ways in which such air vehicles may be used.

The Tomahawk attacks much the same range of targets as tactical aircraft, except that it is not used in snap attacks against pop-up tactical targets and it cannot by itself conduct anything like armed reconnaissance. The missile is not intended to find the targets it strikes. Instead it is part of a larger system in which targets are found by dedicated surveillance sensors (Tomahawk could contribute to such a system, but at least as currently configured, it does not). The parallel between Tomahawk and an airplane (manned or otherwise) was initially obscured by its designation as a missile rather than as a one-way unmanned airplane. Few appreciated the extent to which pilots as well as missiles depended on mission planning to hit their fixed targets. The role of mission planning was obvious for the missile and was largely ignored for the airplane. In fact the planning process was not too different for missile and airplane. This similarity was emphasized when the U.S. Navy bought its first automated air planning system, which was based on the Tomahawk mission planner. That system in turn was wanted in order to make air strikes more flexible (it was bought after inflexibility

caused an operational disaster in a strike on Lebanon's Bekaa Valley).

Prior to automation it took several days to plan a strike against a defended target and replanning was extremely difficult. Tomahawk was, incidentally, bought by the same U.S. Navy organization, Naval Air Systems Command (NAVAIR), which bought the Navy's attack aircraft. Initially Tomahawk was also much affected by the limitations of its terrain-comparison midcourse guidance technique; missions were difficult to set up, and the area involved had to be mapped in great detail. For example, what was then the Defense Mapping Agency spent about six months of twenty-four-hour days mapping Iraq so that Tomahawk could be used in 1991.

There were several striking differences between Tomahawk and aircraft strikes against fixed targets in Iraq. On the plus side, the missile could be used in any weather, but pilots did not attack when visibility was very poor. Tomahawk was considered far more precise than a piloted aircraft. On the minus side, in 1991 mission planning was so computer-intensive that it had to be done ashore. The fleet took packages of mission plans to sea. It could change only the final parts of a mission. That was why Tomahawks approached Baghdad via only a few routes, and the Iraqis eventually shot some of them down once they realized that. That limitation was due in part to an under-appreciation of the inherent stealth of the missile; planners flew it at very low altitude, and to do that they had to tap into a database of all buildings more than fifty feet high. Planning for terrain-following was laborious, because a route that seemed attractive might dead-end in a mountain or cliff too steep for the low-powered missile to climb. Later it became clear that a stealthy missile could fly at twenty thousand feet without much chance of loss, and mission planning became much simpler. At about the same time computers became so much more powerful that the planning function could move to sea.

The most striking difference between the Tomahawk and an airplane was that the missile was a one-way shot. That pushed up the cost per Tomahawk warhead delivered to a target, and it also pushed up the cost per Tomahawk in terms of shipboard space. The largest U.S. missile cruiser can carry about one hundred Tomahawks, say, one per one hundred tons of ship. An aircraft carrier (100,000 tons) carries about two thousand tons of aviation ordnance, and it can be replenished at sea in order to keep up attacks. That makes the reusable aircraft on the carrier about four times as efficient, in terms of tons of ship per ton of ordnance delivered, as the ship firing one-way missiles.

Tomahawk, moreover, cannot easily be transferred from ship to ship at sea, not because of some inherent limit but because the U.S. Navy long ago adopted vertical missile launchers, having found it difficult to transfer surface ship missiles at sea. Once a Tomahawk-armed missile cruiser exhausts its weapons, it withdraws to a base or to very calm water to rearm. Carrier missiles are transferred horizontally and hence can be replenished at sea. That difference in effect provides a carrier with an infinite magazine, since rearming ships can keep arriving with more weapons.

When Tomahawk was conceived in the early 1970s, these were essentially irrelevant comparisons. Antiaircraft firepower was so effective that the important difference between manned and unmanned systems was in the human cost associated with manned aircraft. The great surprise of the 1991 war against Iraq was that it was possible to decapitate an enemy's air defense system so effectively that aircraft could roam at will. Stealth offers much the same possibility. If the human cost per sortie is nearly zeroed, efficiency in terms of cost per ton of weapon delivered becomes a much more meaningful considera-

tion. General acceptance of automated air mission planning makes much clearer the similarity between a long-range (or long-endurance) cruise missile and a manned attack bomber or a UCAV.

With the advent of GPS navigation, Tomahawk no longer depends on premapping of a target area. A combination of fast computers and the exploitation of the missile's inherent stealth greatly simplified mission planning, as the missile no longer usually flies at very low altitude. The missile can therefore respond to quick changes in mission, requiring only very limited updates. It therefore has the potential to loiter in an area waiting for a designated target. Because the missile cannot be recovered, it has to be launched with a default target. The loitering potential is realized in the current Tactical Tomahawk. Loiter time is of course limited, but for all practical purposes Tactical Tomahawk does what the swarming concept envisages for UCAS. The major difference is that UCAS is conceived as a cooperative swarm, in which a target is broadcast to the vehicles in the swarm, and they compare their status to decide which vehicle conducts the attack. In the Tactical Tomahawk this function is conducted on board a ship controlling the fleet's tactical strike assets based on the known situations of the Tomahawks orbiting awaiting orders. Too, given its sensors UCAS will sometimes, perhaps often, find its own targets, which the current Tomahawk cannot do (but which antiship Tomahawks certainly did).

At present the most important case of retargeting once aircraft are launched is probably the evolving practice of RTIC, meaning either Real-Time in the Cockpit or Retargeting in the Cockpit. The Navy view has been that RTIC is set up by the controlling air operations center, which passes the aircraft the necessary heading to the target and enough information for the pilot to distinguish the target. As reconnaissance improves it is entirely possible that such information will be discarded in favor of target GPS coordinates. The alternative Air Force view has been that the pilot should be data fusion manager, deciding for himself to attack a pop-up target which he (or, more likely, a constellation of sensors) detects. This view seems to be embodied in the current Joint Strike Fighter (JSF).

Tomahawk clearly reflects the Navy view. It can evolve to use simple visual clues, using some sort of correlation processing, but it would need a leap of artificial intelligence to approach what is envisaged for JSF. Arguments about the legal status of self-targeting weapons clearly apply to the AI approach, but that is not envisaged here. Incidentally it seems that the data fusion to be embodied in JSF is among the immature technologies that may sink the project.

What is *not* done is also interesting. Tomahawks do not have individual operators. The shipboard (fleet-wide) missile control system coordinates their flight plans and keeps them out of the way of manned aircraft—which may be operating in much the same air space. The same system applies other naval weapons, including missiles and even long-range guns, to targets ashore. This practice is possible because the aircraft are under more or less positive control through their data links, and the shipboard system keeps track of all air vehicles anywhere near the fleet offshore. No one assigns an individual Tomahawk or other missile to a particular target, because no individual can easily comprehend what capabilities and status each of the swarm of aloft missiles has. Nor can individuals pilot the missiles through so complex an airspace.

Tomahawk has evolved this way (and other missiles are handled similarly) because it was never imagined as a stand-alone device. It was always part of larger systems, and it was handled like other missiles. It is true that at one time missiles were command-guided by individual operators, but for decades it has been appreciated that such operation limits the number of targets that can be engaged simultaneously. Most of the time such limits are potentially fatal, particularly if the resources of the naval force using the missiles are limited.

The system is, however, designed so that a man can easily be inserted into the loop when needed. Tactical Tomahawk has an onboard camera, and its images can be beamed back. An operator can intervene to designate a desired target. That does impose time lags, but they do not seem to present insuperable problems. Another navy missile, SLAM-ER, has an automatic target recognition module that makes it possible for the missile to lock onto a target whose image has been inserted. Just as aircraft can currently receive such images via their data links to hit

pop-up targets, it would seem that images can be inserted into the missile as desired for final lock-on. Presumably they can be adjusted so that the missile sees the image properly as it approaches the target (correlation seekers can accept a considerable degree of distortion, so such operation should not present problems). Such insertion is attractive because it would exploit data links that might not work effectively closer to the target because the image would be sent earlier.

SLAM-ER is air-launched, and the launching pilot locks it onto its target. Tomahawk is ship-launched, but with the advent of numerous over-the-horizon data links it is no longer obvious that its shipboard operator is much worse placed to control it. The real difference is in the size of the missile, which has some (but not too much) effect on its cost.

On this basis UCAS is Tactical Tomahawk plus the ability to return to base and probably plus aerial refueling for extended endurance.

This is not to say that all problems inherent in UCAS have already arisen (and have been solved) by experience with Tactical Tomahawk. For example, it may be more complicated to arrange for air traffic control for returning aircraft than for aircraft leaving a carrier or a base because the aircraft spread out as they leave but come together as they approach for landing. Pilots on approach may have to maneuver to avoid emergency situations, and thus aircraft may not be entirely under positive control. However, civil aircraft approaching airports are increasingly under positive control, and indeed the problems seem to arise mainly when they are not being controlled from the ground. It may be that fully positive control on approach requires much higher scan rates than at present, which can be provided by electronically scanned control radars. Moreover, if aerial refueling is successful, UCAS air vehicles would have much longer cycle times than conventional aircraft, so they would present fewer problems (in any given time interval) on approach. A few individuals could handle all such approaches. In addition it would be far more acceptable to ditch a UCAS air vehicle that was behaving badly than to ditch an aircraft carrying a pilot and, perhaps, a crew.

Some current loitering missiles are closer to UCAVs. The U.S. Army and the U.S. Navy are buying versions of a Non–Line of Sight (N-LOS) land attack missile. Both employ an attack missile that flies to a designated spot and cannot be confused with a UCAV. However, the Army version also employs a loitering missile that sends a picture of the potential target area back to the operator. The operator designates targets on this basis (the loitering device has a warhead, and it attacks). In the Navy version the target detection and designation task is done by other systems.

Several loitering antiradar missiles, the first of which was the Israeli Harpy, are often included in lists of UAVs. Their role is to shut down enemy radars by threatening to attack any that operate. The UAV element is that they cruise around the potential target area rather than being predirected to a specific target. The device itself decides that a particular possible target should be attacked, and then it executes the attack. Is it a missile or a UCAV? The current British Shadow Fox applies much this technique to attacking vehicles. In both cases the UCAV is attractive because its sustained presence exerts tactical pressure on an enemy.

Few would recognize Tactical Tomahawk as the UCAV it already is. The more recognizable case is Predator, armed with Hellfire antivehicle missiles. Predators were being used for covert surveillance of Afghanistan prior to September 2001. It was immediately obvious that their surveillance systems could pick up individuals. In a celebrated case in point, a CIA Predator seems to have spotted Osama bin Laden himself. Legal objections to attacking specific individuals were resolved, and within a short time Predators were being armed with Hellfire missiles. They have been used extensively against senior terrorists in Afghanistan, Pakistan, and Yemen. The Israelis, who invented modern low-speed long-endurance surveillance UAVs, have used armed ones against terrorists in places such as Gaza and southern Lebanon. Although they are shot down from time to time, these aircraft seem remarkably difficult to shoot down. That is probably because terrorists have been given IR-guided antiaircraft missiles to deal with conventional air attackers and the UAVs have small IR signatures. Because they are used for surveillance, the UAVs become a fixture in the skies above terrorist camps, their presence giving no warning

of impending attack. At least as described publicly, they have been extremely effective.

Unlike a Tomahawk, an armed UAV is far more self-contained. It carries its sensors and its weapons. Its individual operator monitors what it sees, just as a pilot monitors the ground over which he flies. Because the UAV flies slowly, the view on the ground is excellent. Low speed also minimizes the effect of the time lag inherent in the communications link back to the operator. Low speed also limits the amount of ground the UAV can overfly, so, like the Tomahawk, it relies to some extent on a larger intelligence picture. In this case the larger picture indicates where the UAV should orbit awaiting its prey. The operator is personally responsible for deciding that a particular target should be hit, but the system makes it possible for him to pass the decision up the line to someone more senior. This combination makes it practicable to attack an individual house or car. Even though it cannot fuel in flight, the UAV has far more endurance than a conventional airplane, so the system as a whole can deal with targets that are expected but may appear at any time over a period of many hours.

Because the armed Predator is handled like an airplane in combat, it is natural to handle it like an airplane throughout its flight. It is an individual weapon. Numbers are tied to the number of pilots or operators rather than to some more abstract factor such as the bandwidth of available communications links or the capacity of the onboard computer. As currently operated by the U.S. Air Force, each UAV needs its own operator. That is true of UAVs used for tactical surveillance; the operator in effect detects targets as they are seen and passes information to other users. That is what a pilot does on board a slow airplane directly supporting ground forces. One of the great advantages that such UAVs offer troops on the ground is the sort of look "at the other side of the hill" that the earliest reconnaissance aircraft offered. Modern jets are too fast to offer that sort of service, so the slow UAV is seen as an enormous advantage.

In effect the slow UAV is the unmanned equivalent to the turbo-prop counterinsurgency (COIN) aircraft conceived for the Vietnam War in the early 1960s. Its great advantage is long endurance without pilot fatigue:

A UAV can orbit apparently endlessly waiting for a target, such as insurgents in a car, to turn up so that it can deal with them. Long endurance also makes for effective surveillance of, say, a key road. Surveillance by fast aircraft is necessarily very intermittent, the pilot having little time to think about what he sees.

The great question is whether this kind of operation is inevitable or has been adopted as a kind of historical accident. The broader trend in air operations has been to centralize control in an air operations center, which collates reconnaissance information and assigns targets to attack aircraft. It is distinctly not an asset providing a tactical picture to deployed troops on the ground, although it may pick up targets of interest to them, and although it may assign aircraft to support them. This disconnect explains the use of forward air controllers, who are controlled by ground troops and therefore can identify targets of direct tactical interest to them.

In this style of operation, reconnaissance is a relatively scarce resource that is assigned to particular places on the basis of cueing information usually provided by intelligence or by broad-area surveillance systems such as satellites. The availability issue is the main reason that maritime patrol aircraft have been so popular with troops in Iraq and in Afghanistan: They are slow, they have lots of sensors, and—most important—they are assigned more or less directly to particular ground units. The great issue

in UAV operations has been whether UAVs should serve centralized operations centers or should be owned, in effect, by ground units. The needs of the ground units have been met by masses of small UAVs, which they can control individually. One question is whether such UAVs so fragment the overall picture of what is happening that they render a disservice to higher levels of command. The ideal would be to provide their pictures to those needing them, but also to provide those pictures up the line so that they contribute to overall situational awareness. Ultimately the issue is how to allocate scarce troop resources as much as how to make those resources, once committed, most effective.

The network-centric concept suggests a very different approach in which surveillance is made as pervasive as possible and the fruit of that surveillance is available to a wide variety of users. Ground units ought then to be able to assign weapons or attacks on the basis of the picture to which they are privy. Right now those units like organic UAVs because they control them. If surveillance is pervasive enough, control becomes a much less urgent issue. When surveillance assets are scarce, moving them into place is a kind of attack warning. One important lesson of Predator and equivalent operations is that surveillance that is nearly permanent offers no warning and thus opens an enemy to sudden attack.

Appendix II

WORLD MILITARY UAVS

This appendix covers all large military UAVs currently in service or advertised (weight 50 kg [110 lbs] and above) and, to the extent possible, all military UAVs, including small ones, in current or recent service. Some interesting developmental UAVs are also included, as are UAVs of historic interest (to indicate trends). It is striking that many current airframes are difficult to distinguish from UAVs flown or even fielded as many as three or four decades ago. The differences, which are very important, are internal—in the control systems of the aircraft and in their sensors. There is, for example, a vast difference between the first U.S. Army reconnaissance drone, which carried a 95-frame camera, and a UAV carrying a camera, which sends images back in real time. Similarly there is a difference between an analog flight-control system, which is essentially an autopilot, and a digital system, which decides how to fly the aircraft to reach a designated waypoint or target, taking into account wind and other influences en route, and can often take off and land automatically.

This appendix excludes the very large category of target aircraft, many of which were converted into UAVs (and are so described in what follows).

For conciseness this appendix also excludes many mini-, micro-, and nano-UAVs currently advertised but not in service (and in some cases unlikely to enter service). Numerous types of UAV have been built or advertised because—particularly at the lower end of the scale—they are often inexpensive to build (but as often not durable

enough). Many are difficult to distinguish from model aircraft. As a consequence many countries have entered the UAV market in preference to trying to enter or survive in the full-scale aircraft market. The most striking case is the United Kingdom. It appears that the decision was made to build a UAV industry while surrendering aircraft design and production to pan-European organizations, which often seem not to use British expertise. Someone in the British defense establishment seems to have decided that the future belongs largely to unmanned rather than manned aircraft. The low entry cost of such an industry is somewhat illusory, because the real costs of UAVs are generally in the sensor package, in the mission-control system, and in the links to a ground-control station. In some cases the control systems are standardized but the airframes are not. It is not at all clear which of the UAVs described in this appendix are likely to enter service in any numbers.

Note that this appendix excludes loitering attack missiles such as the U.S. N-LOS and Tactical Tomahawk and the Israeli Harpy, although it includes one-way surveillance devices. The line between UCAVs and such loitering munitions is fuzzy at best. Many accounts of future electromagnetic weapons (i.e., nonnuclear electromagnetic pulse, or EMP, blast weapons) claim that they will be carried on board UAVs, on the theory that the effects of such weapons might well cause the loss of the vehicle carrying them. It is not clear how to distinguish such UAVs from cruise missiles, although they may be recoverable. UAVs

The Israeli Harpy loitering anti-radar device is often described as a UAV. Like other UAVs it follows a long-endurance path through the air, using its sensor, a radar signal receiver, to detect objects of interest—into which it then dives. Unlike most UAVs, however, the Harpy is not intended to be recovered; however, there are now a fair number of one-way UAVs. Is Harpy a missile or a UCAV—and how much difference is there? This Harpy was photographed at the 2007 Paris Air Show. (Norman Friedman)

have also been used as jamming platforms, again on the theory that losses to enemy home-on-jam weapons would be acceptable. Again, the line between a cruise missile and a UAV is not very clear.

Note the increasing interest in nano-UAVs, which may operate in swarms. In some formulations, nano-UAVs are the size of small birds or even insects, and they may penetrate buildings.

Dimensions and weights in this appendix are metric; ranges and speeds are in nautical miles and knots. Weight is maximum takeoff weight, unless otherwise specified.

Drones, RPVs, and UAVs

Originally unmanned aircraft were called drones. During and immediately after the Vietnam War the usual designation was remotely piloted vehicle, or RPV; the term was probably first applied to the Firebees used extensively for reconnaissance during the Vietnam War, and it apparently was applied to make these aircraft more attractive to air forces. The current term is unmanned air vehicle, or UAV, suggesting a much greater degree of autonomy

(although Vietnam-era RPVs flew hundreds of miles or more without human intervention).

Most aircraft described as drones (and often listed as UAVs) have preset mission parameters, and many of them have analog rather than digital controls (i.e., analog autopilots) and fly preset missions with very limited ability to handle operator interaction. They have nothing that could be described as a modern mission-control system (they may have sensor control systems, however). Modern UAVs are unmanned recoverable aircraft with a digital—hence programmable—mission-control system and a data link that receives commands and downloads data gathered by the aircraft. Digital mission control also makes it possible for the UAV to sense and deal with in-flight contingencies to an extent that an analog system (essentially an autopilot), which cannot revise its program to deal with changing circumstances, cannot. Thus, at least in theory, a UAV does not require continuous intervention by a pilot; one operator can handle several aircraft. However, air forces that operate UAVs sometimes seem to see them as direct replacements for manned aircraft, each requiring a full-time rated pilot. In at least one case, a U.S. UAV crashed because the pilot, who was familiar with much faster aircraft, took the wrong action when it went into a spin. Probably the implication is that UAVs that can fly themselves should do so except in extreme circumstances when intervention is necessary. Recent U.S. experience on this point is interesting. The U.S. Air Force assigns a pilot to land each of its Predator UAVs. The U.S. Army automatically lands its version of the same UAV, the Warrior. The Army experiences a much lower landing accident rate.

Networking implies that the UAV transmits its data back in real time via a data link. To achieve sufficient capacity, downlinks must operate at high radar frequencies. That in turn limits them to line of sight, which for a vehicle at 10,000 ft is only about 130 miles. Long-range UAVs such as Global Hawk therefore have satellite links, the dishes for which account for the cockpit-like fairings atop their noses. Many existing unmanned aircraft still return with their film or other sensor information, and cannot download it in real time.

A Saab presentation published in October 2006 distinguished three generations of modern tactical UAVs: a first generation beginning about 1985, a second beginning about 1990, and a third beginning about 2000. A fourth generation is due to begin about 2010. The presentation contrasted operations/maintenance cost and production/development cost. For the first generation, characterized by the early Israeli UAVs, these two costs were about equal. For the second generation, operations and maintenance cost was about the same as before, but production/development cost more than doubled as much more capable airframes were used. This cost increased yet again in the third generation, characterized by the Franco-Dutch Sperwer, and operations/maintenance cost grew somewhat. For the fourth generation Saab expects lower operations and maintenance cost but about the same production/development cost, so that for the first time the net cost of UAVs of a given type will actually fall.

Unmanned aircraft first appeared in World War I as attempts to develop what would now be called cruise missiles. During the interwar period several countries developed drone (radio-controlled) target aircraft, partly because new attack tactics such as dive bombing could not be simulated by towed targets. Just before and during World War II both Germany and the United States developed unmanned combat aircraft (as well as one-way missiles), but these developments had no apparent effect on postwar thinking. By way of contrast, developments from the 1950s on had a sustained effect, to the extent that some current systems are directly descended from airframes first developed at that time. Thus the modern history of UAVs properly begins with the reconnaissance systems developed in the 1950s, initially in the United States and the Soviet Union.

Successful UAV use in Vietnam prompted some, at least in the United States, to argue in the early to mid-1970s that such aircraft (then called RPVs) would or should soon supplant manned tactical aircraft. Heavy losses of tactical aircraft during the Vietnam War and during the Yom Kippur War (1973) made it appear that the battlefield would soon be too dangerous for manned aircraft. The advent of stealthy aircraft and stand-off weapons seemed to reverse that judgment, and from the 1991 Gulf War onward tactical aircraft have been extremely successful and survivable. Thus much of the modern interest in UAVs stresses qualities that no manned aircraft can match, such as persistence (no pilot fatigue) and quantity (manned aircraft are increasingly expensive). Current interest in high-performance UCAVs suggests a swing back to interest in wholesale replacement of manned aircraft.

Despite considerable interest the military UAV market was small through the 1990s. Thus although IAI (Israel Aircraft Industries) dominated it, through 1998 that company produced only about six hundred UAVs (and fewer than one hundred systems). The 1991 Gulf War probably saw the first large-scale tactical use of UAVs that could transmit data on a real-time basis (the U.S. Navy's Israeli-built Pioneers). Three years later in Kosovo NATO deployed UAVs again, including Predator, Hunter, and CL-289 PIVER. This war demonstrated the vulnerability of slow UAVs, twenty-seven being lost (some to operational problems rather than air defenses).

Most UAVs were designed for low-speed surveillance, the idea being that at low speeds it is far easier to pick up tactically important details. Low speed may dramatically reduce survivability, but that may be acceptable if the UAVs are inexpensive enough. In any case the loss of low-speed UAVs does not cost human pilots. However, it may be difficult to make up for losses among forward-deployed UAVs, whatever their unit costs. As in the world of manned aircraft, one way out of the problem is to increase speed, but that costs clarity of low-altitude vision. A way around this problem would be to fuse the outputs of multiple fast UAVs following crossing paths. The result might be equivalent to a picture provided by a few low-speed UAVs.

Categories

The U.S. government classifies UAVs according to their altitude and endurance, so that HALE means a high-altitude long-endurance aircraft and MALE is a medium-altitude long-endurance aircraft. HALE typically means operation above 50,000 ft, or even at 70,000 or 75,000, and probably at 90,000 in the near future. The payload is typically greater than 400 kg (880 lbs); some current HALES carry 1.2-ton payloads. Endurance is typically 24 hours or more, and the data link is via a satellite, for long range. Often the 24 hours is loiter time, when the UAV is 1,000 nm (or more) from its base. Global Hawk is the main case in point. However, there are also projects for ultralight ultra-long-endurance aircraft, typically solar-powered. MALE typically indicates a UAV operating at 20,000 to 40,000 ft, carrying a 150- to 400-kg payload (330 to 880 lbs) with an endurance of at least 12 hours. Such a UAV might operate 500 nm from its base, relying on a mixture of satellite and line-of-sight radio communications. The Predator is a good example. A recent account suggests an additional Maxi-MALE category (e.g., Reaper): operation between 40,000 and 50,000 or even 55,000 ft, internal payload 200 to 300 kg plus external payload 400 to 600 kg (up to 1,320 lbs), and endurance 18 hours. Several countries are now developing what they call LALE (low-altitude long-endurance) UAVs. Flight altitude might be 150 to 30,000 ft, and endurance greater than 24 hours.

Other categories, not currently used by the U.S. government, are listed in Table 1. All of these figures are approximate, merely to give some idea of different ranges of performance.

Another U.S. categorization is by tier, the higher tiers indicating higher altitudes. Some UAVs, which provide data directly to ground units, are described as tactical.

Despite their considerable variety, surveillance UAVs generally carry similar sensors: stabilized electro-optical balls carrying both IR and optical sensors and, usually, a laser designator. Some larger UAVs also carry radars and even passive electronic (SIGINT) arrays. Given their association with ground combat, UAV radars typically offer high ground definition (by synthetic array radar [SAR] techniques) and/or ground moving target indication (GMTI). The EO (electro-optical) sensor packages are generally located below the UAV's nose. The need to accommodate such sensors and to provide them with the widest possible field of view explains the near-universal use of pusher propellers. Most UAVs use a short fuselage with tail booms to accommodate the pusher; a few place the propeller at the tail of a more conventional fuselage. This appendix omits most UAV sensors because nearly all UAVs have much the same electro-optical devices, albeit with considerable differences in capacity, and because it is likely to be relatively easy to modify UAVs with different electro-optical turrets.

For ground forces UAVs are characterized by the unit level that uses them: platoon, company, battalion, brigade, regiment, division, corps, and so on. The lower the level, the lighter and more portable the UAV must be. Thus platoon or company level generally means a hand-held, hand-launched vehicle, which is often called a mini-UAV. There is considerable interest, at least in the United States, in micro-UAVs, which might be launched as a swarm to cover a complex area of interest, such as part of a city; they fall outside these classifications. One such vehicle is described as a robotic cockroach, capable of crawling inside a building or flying within it.

Emerging Types of UAVs

Some potentially important emerging types of UAVs are under development mainly in the United States. At one end of the scale, DARPA has shown intense interest in ultra-long-endurance craft such as solar-powered lightweight UAVs intended to fly for up to five years without landing. Another current DARPA project is a large unmanned blimp carrying a phased-array radar, which could be positioned near a battle area to track enemy forces (and enemy missiles). The radar and the blimp would use solar power during the day, which would break down water to

TABLE 1

	MASS	**RANGE**	**ALTITUDE**	**ENDURANCE**
Micro	<5 kg	10 km	800 ft	1 hour
Mini	<25 kg	10–150 km	N/A	<2 hours
Close range	25–150 kg	10–30 km	10,000 ft	2–4 hours
Short range	50–250 kg	30–70 km	10,000 ft	3–6 hours
Medium range	150–500 kg	70–200 km	15,000 ft	6–10 hours
Medium-range endurance	500–1,500 kg	>500 km	25,000 ft	10–18 hours
Low-altitude deep penetrator	250–2,500 kg	>250 km	150–30,000 ft	0.5–1 hour

provide electrical energy on a 24-hour basis. The radar array already exists, and a blimp may fly in 2010. Such a platform would provide the sort of tactical picture on which the UCAS described in this book would rely.

Also in the large-UAV category are projected unmanned cargo aircraft, which are apparently of particular interest to the Marine Corps. Kaman has developed a large unmanned helicopter (K-Max Burro) specifically for tasks such as ship-to-ship replenishment, and it is easy to imagine its extension to the cargo role. For that matter it is not clear that the delivery of pallets of supplies should be distinguished from the delivery of weapons, in which case even weapon-delivery UAVs may in future have a ground force logistics support role. Although such craft carry smaller loads than dedicated cargo craft, their high speed may give them an attractively high throughput, assuming that the cargo pallets are guided into their targets.

There is also increasing interest in air-launched UAVs. The old reconnaissance drones were often air-launched (the most dramatic example was Lockheed's supersonic D-21, launched from an SR-71 reconnaissance airplane). Those currently contemplated are much smaller, but the idea is to extend the reach of surveillance using platforms the loss of which would be much more acceptable than the loss of aircraft. Too, an airplane might launch multiple UAVs, extending the area under continuous surveillance. Probably the most important part of any UAV-based surveillance system is the data fusion center that melds the discrete pictures provided by the UAV into a more or less continuous tactical picture. At least in the United States, there is also interest in submarine-launched UAVs that can land in the water and submerge for recovery. The precedent for such dual-medium aircraft would be an abor-

tive U.S. project for a submersible jet aircraft, presumably for intelligence work, carried out in the 1960s.

ATLS and Collision Avoidance

There also are some important emerging types of UAV avionics: automatic takeoff and landing systems (ATLS) and automatic collision avoidance systems. At least in theory, both should dramatically reduce operator workload, making it easier for a few operators to handle multiple aircraft. ATLS is a current reality, mentioned in some of the UAV descriptions below.

Collision avoidance (sense-and-avoid) systems are more complex. The International Civil Aviation Organization (ICAO) sets a goal of reducing the probability of midair collision to one in 1 billion flight hours, of which one in one hundred is attributable to failures in air traffic control and the rest to aircraft or pilot failure. As a context airline traffic in the United States currently amounts to 18 million hours per year, so the ideal would allow for perhaps one collision every fifty-five years. These figures, incidentally, make it nearly impossible to test any actual system in service, so approval of systems rests on simulations. Normally protection against midair collision is achieved by nesting a series of systems. At long ranges, beyond perhaps 200 miles, safety is achieved by traffic separation based on Air Traffic Control procedures. From 200 miles to 30 miles, it is the responsibility of an Air Traffic Control system. UAVs benefit from both as much as manned aircraft do. Inside 30 miles aircraft rely on collision avoidance systems, which famously order a pilot to climb or dive to avoid trouble. At very short ranges pilots must rely on their own eyes, and that is where a UAV needs help. A collision avoidance system must

Global Hawk (RQ-4) is the premier HALE aircraft in current service. Long-range operation requires a satellite link; the dish is inside the bulged nose. (Northrop Grumman)

detect nearby aircraft, track them to decide whether they are threats, prioritize threats, and determine and enforce the necessary evasive maneuvers. Sensors of current interest are microphones, radar, laser radar (light detection and ranging, or LIDAR), and cameras (EO or IR).

Systems may be closed or open loop, in the latter case involving human intervention. The U.S. Air Force's Global Hawk Program Office has sponsored a Multiple Intruder Autonomous Avoidance program led by Northrop Grumman since 2006. It employs a Learjet 25 programmed to fly like a Global Hawk. Tests have had intruders coming from all directions around the airplane. The initial sensor is a pair of cameras (110-degree field of view), one on each side of the airplane's nose. They

are obviously limited by night and by cloud cover. Even so, in 2007 the Learjet typically detected other aircraft at twice the range at which a human pilot could do so. It has proven difficult to match radar resolution, scan volume, and scan speed to the camera. A successor system is to fly in 2013 and hopefully to be fielded sometime after 2015. It is also possible that a ground-based sense-and-avoid system, work on which began in 2007, will make it possible for a high-flying UAV such as Global Hawk to avoid air traffic well enough to be allowed to fly in mixed airspace until it reaches an operational altitude above normal air traffic. The Marine Corps hopes to use this approach to erect a tunnel through which their Shadow UAV can pass from controlled to restricted air space.

The goal is a closed-loop system that would make a UAV equivalent to a manned airplane from the point of air traffic control. Current thinking seems to envisage sensing and avoidance within a sphere of about 500 ft diameter. This is actually far stricter than what is required of a human pilot.

There are at least two European initiatives seeking similar results, the British ASTRAEA (Autonomous Systems Technology Related Airborne Evaluation and Assessment) and a new project (MidCAS, for Midair Collision Avoidance System) sponsored by the European Defense Agency. The first phase of ASTRAEA concluded in 2008 with a simulated flight through nonsegregated British airspace. The second phase tests technologies on board a manned surrogate aircraft. Originally a UAV flight was envisaged for 2012, but that date will not be met. MidCAS is a four-year program sponsored by France, Germany, Italy, Spain, and Sweden and led by Sweden. It is to develop both sense-and-avoid technology and a new regulatory standard. Apparently it will exploit technology developed for the Neuron UAV. The partners are Saab, Diehl, DLR, EADS Deutschland, ESG, Alenia, Selex, SAGEM, Thales, and Indra.

Artillery Targeting and Battlefield Surveillance

Unmanned reconnaissance aircraft first became important to Western armies with the advent of army-controlled beyond-horizon weapons in the form of nuclear artillery rockets. These weapons were intended to destroy massive attacking Soviet army formations, and as such required something close to real-time reconnaissance information from beyond the usual range of ground reconnaissance formations. The advent of tactical nuclear weapons promised to rescue NATO from a position of disastrous weakness compared to the Soviet ground forces, but only if the weapons could be used relatively far from NATO ground units, hence not endangering them. Briefly the U.S. Army imagined that it could protect its troops in armored vehicles while using nuclear weapons nearby, but tests showed that it would not work. Thus the need for reach in both the weapons and in the means of targeting them. Tactical nuclear weapons intended for use against moving enemy formations were important to

NATO thinking nearly to the end of the Cold War. Even after they had been superseded, NATO depended heavily on beyond-horizon area denial weapons such as 155-mm guns strewing land mines—again, useless without some means of reconnaissance.

In both cases the usual air reconnaissance conducted by fast jets was useless because it was intended to find less-mobile targets (it had too lengthy a turnaround time). The early unmanned reconnaissance systems were controlled by the U.S. Army formations that were expected to use the weapons. To some extent they can be seen as efforts by the U.S. Army to gain back the sort of tactical reconnaissance capability that the newly independent jet Air Force could not or would not provide. The interservice reconnaissance issue is still an important factor in UAV development.

The U.S. Army led this evolution because it had the first important tactical nuclear weapon, the Honest John (MGR-1) rocket, with a range of up to 30 miles. The U.S. Army replaced Honest John with the longer-range Lance in 1973, but the earlier rocket remained in NATO service until 1985. Given time lags and the expected speed of a Soviet advance, any reconnaissance system associated with Honest John had to reach more than 50 miles beyond the front line. Honest John first flew in 1951 and was deployed in January 1953. Presumably the Army initially planned to use light artillery spotting aircraft to support it, but instead it adopted its standard Radioplane (now Northrop) antiaircraft target drone as a reconnaissance drone, the system being designated USD-1 (the drone was eventually designated MQM-57 Falcon). It was a small propeller-driven aircraft of conventional configuration. The basic drone was built under license by the Italian Meteor company and thus was presumably the inspiration for the original version of its Mirach UAV.

Falconer development, as a derivative of the existing MQM-33 Quail (first flown 1945 as a modification of an earlier target drone with a new engine and initially designated OQ-19), began in 1955, mass production beginning in 1959. This MQM-57 (Radioplanes RP-71) remained in service until 1966, a total of 1,445 being built. Range was 100 miles; typical mission endurance was 30 minutes. Speed was 185 mph. The payload was either a daylight camera (95 photographs) or an infrared camera (10

Radioplanes' Falconer was the first U.S. reconnaissance UAV. It seems to have inspired the Italian Mirach-20 and, by extension, the Chinese ASN-105. This U.S. Army SD-1 was photographed on 15 January 1959. Radioplanes is now the Ventura Division of Northrop Grumman. (U.S. Army)

photos). Film development time increased system dead time, but contemporary television cameras, which could have provided real-time data, were considered unacceptable (the problem may have been data linking at extreme range). Typically the aerial surveillance and target acquisition platoon of a division had twelve Falconers. The U.S. Navy operated the MQM-33 target drone under the designation KD2R and apparently also used a reconnaissance version (presumably for the Marines). Photographs exist showing KD2R-5s (MQM-36 Shelduck rather than MQM-33) rigged for other purposes, apparently torpedo delivery and radiation sampling. The British army received thirty-two Falconers under the name Observer. It is not clear whether Falconer was given to any other NATO armies, but it was made under license in Italy by Meteor and hence contributed to the development of the Mirach UAV series. By the 1980s this series was called the Basic Training Target; more than 73,000 of all versions were built.

Falconer was part of the first series of successful U.S. drones, originally intended as aerial targets (the source of several UAV series). They were conceived in the 1930s by Reginald Denny, a Hollywood actor and model-airplane enthusiast, whose first few Radioplanes were literally radio-controlled model airplanes. During World War II his Radioplanes Corporation built 15,374 of these targets, which became the natural basis for the first U.S. reconnaissance drones. These aircraft were all flown by radio command, limiting their effective range to the horizon and requiring radar tracking to keep them on course. For example, the initial version (RP-1) used a telephone dial to generate tones for left-right and up-down commands. Targets were essential because real aircraft towing the usual sleeves could not simulate aircraft maneuvers, particularly dive bombing (the first realization of just how devastating dive bombing could be came when antiaircraft gunners tried to shoot down maneuvering targets).

On 15 January 1957 the Army Combat Surveillance Agency was created, presumably because the new pentomic division concept (using weapons such as Honest John) required over-the-horizon battlefield surveillance. Apparently Falconer was seen as an interim solution to the unexpected Honest John targeting problem. In 1957 the new agency held a competition for a new system.

There were two prototypes. Rheem Manufacturing (which was bought by Aerojet) developed the USD-2 (later MQM-58) Overseer, a tractor-like USD-1 but with considerably higher speed (350 mph); it had an IR sensor and a real-time data link. Its most obvious new features were tip tanks and a vee tail. USD-2 may have been used to test a side-looking radar. USD-2 had interchangeable sensors. It used a form of Loran (long-range navigation): The command link was repeated back by a slave station, the time difference between master and slave reception giving UAV position. The technique offered an accuracy of 5 ft out to a 50-nm range but was probably unreliable; navigational problems reportedly led to cancellation of the program in 1966 (by which time the Vietnam War had absorbed the funds involved). The USD-2 never entered service, thirty-five having been made. Republic's USD-3 Snooper or Sky Spy (which did not get an MQM designation) must have been the first twin-boom/pusher-propeller UAV. The prototype flew in January 1959, and fifty were made, but they did not enter service. Range was 160 km, comparable to that of the USD-1. Speed was considerably superior: 300 mph. Apparently production of one of the 300-mph drones was also planned for the Navy, but that seems not to have happened.

By 1957 the U.S. Army was building missiles with much longer ranges. It therefore became interested in longer-range reconnaissance UAVs, which needed higher performance in order to survive in the face of increasingly sophisticated tactical air defenses (air defense missiles were just beginning to appear). In 1960 the Army let a contract to Republic Aviation for a supersonic USD-4 (Swallow), with interchangeable nose sections for photographic, radar, or IR sensors. Range would have been 300 miles. The program was canceled in January 1961; none ever flew. In 1957 the first U.S. Army surface-to-surface guided missile, Corporal (ultimately designated MGM-5), was just entering service, having flown in August 1952 (units began to train with this weapon in April 1954). Maximum range was 130 miles. In 1962 the Corporal was replaced by the follow-on Sergeant (MGM-29, 75-nm range, solid rather than liquid fuel). Longer range (175 nm) was associated with the Redstone (PGM-11), which entered production in 1955 (the first production missile flew in 1956,

and the first operational unit deployed to West Germany in June 1958). The date of cancellation suggests that Swallow, and probably an associated Army missile, were about to enter production when the Eisenhower administration left office. That administration left production decisions of this kind to the incoming Kennedy administration, and incoming Secretary of Defense Robert S. McNamara badly wanted to rationalize programs between the Air Force and Army.

Broadly parallel to Swallow was Fairchild's USD-5 Osprey, another high-performance (in this case subsonic) jet reconnaissance UAV, which received a contract in 1958 and first flew in May 1960. It had a longer range, 1,000 miles (1,600 km), and was to have become operational in 1964. Osprey was derived from Bull Goose, a ground-launched decoy developed for the Strategic Air Command (U.S. analysts of large-scale air defense considered ground-launched decoys a devastating way of neutralizing them by simulating masses of manned bombers). However, it was canceled in November 1962. The range suggests that it was initially associated with the Jupiter intermediate-range ballistic missile (IRBM), which was conceived in 1954 as a 1,000-mile missile (in November 1956 the Air Force was given authority over missiles with ranges beyond 200 miles, hence over Jupiter). Pershing in turn arose from 1956 U.S. Army studies of a missile with a range of 500 to 750 nm, which led to removal of the 200-mile limit. The name Pershing was assigned in January 1958, and the contract for full-scale development awarded in March. The first missile was launched in January 1960, and deployment began in 1964. Presumably USD-5 was canceled because conventional air and even satellite reconnaissance sufficed at the ranges Pershing was intended to reach.

The U.S. Army's need for tactical reconnaissance persisted well beyond 1966, when USD-1 was retired. There was apparently no follow-on program; by 1966 Vietnam was consuming available development money. The USD-1 role was filled by a complementary battlefield reconnaissance airplane, the Grumman OV-1 Mohawk, which was built to a 1956 joint Army–Marine Corps specification (the Marines later withdrew). Its payloads included side-looking radar (in service in 1963), which would have pro-

USD-5 Osprey. (U.S. Army)

vided sufficient depth from behind U.S. lines to see Honest John targets. Various forms of SIGINT may have been considered adequate for targeting missiles like Sergeant.

NATO armies became interested in short-range UAVs as they obtained nuclear missiles about 1960, beginning with Honest John. Thus the Canadians, British, and Germans teamed to produce the Canadair CL-89 Midge (and its CL-289 derivative). About 1960 NATO issued a battlefield UAV requirement (it is not clear whether CL-89 was involved). The Belgians produced the Épervier. The French developed a reconnaissance version of their CT 20 jet-powered target. The Italians produced the Mirach series, which was unusual in that it employed two very different air vehicles. Versions of these systems (except the French one) are still in service.

After France left NATO, the French army received its own tactical nuclear missile, Pluton, comparable to the U.S.-supplied Lance and Sergeant (range 120 km, equivalent to 74.5 miles). The Pluton entered service in 1974 as an artillery weapon; note that French short-range UAVs (which appeared considerably after 1975) are operated by artillery units.

Real-Time Tactical Reconnaissance

About 1972 DARPA became interested in a new generation of tactical UAVs. Unlike the earlier ones, they were intended specifically to improve situational awareness for troops. Beginning in March 1972, DARPA let contracts to Philco-Ford (later Ford Aerospace) to develop reconnaissance and target designation UAVs under the designations Praeire and Calere (meaning, respectively, "to precede" and "to give heat"). Praeire was a day-only UAV using a television camera and a laser designator; Calere used forward-looking infrared (FLIR) for night or reduced visibility. Each had two-man control, one man flying the UAV and the other operating its sensors, indicating that at this point autonomous flight between commandable waypoints was not yet possible. The air vehicle had a high wing. Praeire I and Calere I had a span of 3.05 m, and weighed, respectively, 34 and 38.6 kg at takeoff (Praeire I payload was 11.3 kg). Range was about 10.4 nm. Praeire II/Calere II were designed both to reduce radar cross section and to improve sensor field of view. They were of high-wing pod-and-boom configuration, with pusher engines mounted above the wing trailing edge. The sensors were in a transparent dome; the nose rotated 180 degrees after takeoff to bring them into viewing position without compromising landing characteristics. Praeire IIB showed an endurance of nearly 6 hours and carried a high-performance data link. Some Praeire IIB were sold to Israel in 1977, presumably for comparison with the initial version of Mastiff. Flown in 1976, Calere III was part of DARPA's LANDSS (lightweight advanced night/day surveillance system) program. Praeire IIB: span 3.96 m, length 3.35 m, weight 61.7 kg (payload 8.6 kg), endurance 6 hours (speed 75 kt), ceiling 10,000 ft.

In 1973 DARPA let a contract to Lockheed to develop another tactical UAV, Aequare (Equalize), a twin-boom air-launched pusher intended for target acquisition and definition in the face of high surface-to-air missile (SAM) threats. It would relay data back to the ground station via the launch aircraft. Aequare would illuminate the target with its laser, designating it for laser-guided bombs and missiles. UAV dimensions were set by the launch device, a modified SUU-42 flare dispenser pod. It was intended for launch (by an F-4 Phantom) at 25,000 ft, after which it would descend by parachute to 14,000 ft before flying free. Alternatively, Aequare could be ground-launched. Only the payload pod was recoverable. The result was about the size of Praeire/Calere: span 2.29 m, length 2.26 m, weight 63.5 kg, endurance 2 hours (speed 100 kt, range 174 nm).

The DARPA tactical UAV program was intended to spur U.S. Army interest (Praeire and Calere were dem-

onstrated to all three services). In 1974 the U.S. Army initiated a "small r" program to develop a tactical reconnaissance UAV (presumably "large r" indicated a longer-range system). The Army chose Lockheed to develop its tactical UAV, the Aquila (XMQM-105), which first flew in December 1975. The demonstration program was completed in 1979, and full-scale development began on 31 August 1979, with IOC (initial operating capability) expected in 1984. That did not happen, and even this timescale was grossly protracted, presumably reflecting limited interest on the part of the Army (in 1983 planned purchases were scaled back from 995 to 548 air vehicles; as cost rose, that was cut further to 376 in 1985, with a unit cost rapidly approaching $1 million, four times the original estimate). The problem seems to have been requirements creep. Aquila began as a 120-lb vehicle with a 30-lb payload. By 1988 its endurance had doubled to 3 hours (with more possible), and the vehicle weighed 265 lbs (but was far stealthier). It was also touted as an all-weather system, when many UAVs were operable in fair weather only. Aquila was a flying wing with a ducted pusher propeller: span 3.88 m, length 2.08 m, weight 150 kg (payload 52 kg). Endurance was 3 hours, but an extended-range (150 kg) version offered 10-hour endurance (speed 113 kt, cruising speed 73–94 kt, loiter speed 70 kt). Ceiling was 15,000 ft. An export version, Altair, flew in 1987 (it attracted no buyers).

Aquila problems were a major reason for the 1987 freeze of UAV programs, leading to its cancellation and then to a series of joint programs (jointness was being promoted very actively in the wake of the Goldwater-Nichols Act, which was intended to force the U.S. services to cooperate more completely).

Higher up the scale, in the mid-1970s the Army financed development of BQM-74D, a version of the MQM-74C Chukar II jet target drone with a precision navigation system and target sensors. The related BQM-74C Chukar III target had a digital flight-control system (probably among the first in a drone) and was evaluated (but not adopted) in a reconnaissance role by the U.S. Navy in the 1980s. Chukar was built under license by Meteor in Italy and presumably fed into that company's Mirach program. Chukar seems to have been a reversion to the sort of deep reconnaissance longer-range assault

Lockheed's Aquila was the first modern U.S. tactical UAV. This one is shown on its launcher, 4 September 1979. According to a Lockheed press release, the company began work on UAVs in 1970 with the "two boomer," a test platform (span 13 ft, length 10 ft, 35-hp Wankel engine) using tricycle landing gear. A ground operator dialed instructions to the UAV instead of flying it remotely. This was apparently a private venture, leading to work with the Air Force, Army, and DARPA on what were then called mini-RPVs (weighing under 200 lbs). Two Army studies followed: FASTAR (Family of Army Surveillance and Target Acquisition Requirements) and RPAODS (Remotely Piloted Aerial Observer and Designator System). In 1973 Lockheed contracted with DARPA to develop the air-launched Aequare (170 lbs, span 12 ft, length 8 ft), which could be carried underwing by an F-4 fighter. The Army's "little r" contract followed, work beginning in December 1974. Early in 1975 the program was renamed Aquila. The complete system required five standard Army trucks. The sensor was an unstabilized pan-and-tilt TV camera and a 35-mm panoramic camera or a stabilized TV camera with selectable field of view and a laser rangefinder designator. By August 1979 Lockheed was also developing the Harassment Vehicle for the Air Force, similar in concept to the Israeli Harpy but smaller. (Lockheed)

systems demanded. In the late 1970s the U.S. Army was developing Assault Breaker, which was intended to use long-range nonnuclear missiles to break up approaching Soviet formations. The alternative sensor was a big airborne SAR radar capable of detecting moving targets. Initially it was to have been mounted on a stealthy airplane, but ultimately it became J-STARS, carried behind U.S. lines on board a converted airliner. Presumably the airliner's persistence made it far more attractive than a short-endurance UAV.

Short-Range Naval UAVs

The U.S. Navy lost interest in UAVs as its Drone Anti-Submarine Helicopter (DASH) program, at the time

the most ambitious tactical unmanned aircraft program in the United States, died. It appears that DARPA promoted a short-range naval UAV in parallel to the Army program that created Aquila. The naval program was at least initially called STAR (Shipboard Tactical RPV). The stealthy delta-wing configuration chosen, at least for the Teledyne Ryan contender (Model 262), was so close to that of Aquila as to suggest that both emerged from the same program. Span was 2.29 m, weight about 75 kg, and endurance was up to 8 hours. The power plant was an 18-hp pusher engine. Three prototypes were built, flying in 1976–77. The program probably died because of the success of the LAMPS (Light Airborne Multipurpose System) manned shipboard helicopter, which provided small warships (such as frigates) with longer-endurance organic reconnaissance (and with an ASW capability a UAV lacked altogether). After 1977 U.S. Navy interest in small long-endurance UAVs concentrated on their use as jammer or electronic decoy platforms, but no production aircraft emerged.

Tactical Reconnaissance: Replacing Manned Aircraft

In contrast to the army-oriented battlefield reconnaissance role, air forces became interested in long-range unmanned reconnaissance on two levels. One was replacement or supplements for existing converted fighters. Fast manned reconnaissance aircraft became increasingly vulnerable as surface-to-air missiles developed. The United States was the first to use such aircraft in combat, during the Vietnam War.

Prior to the war the U.S. Air Force experimented with an antiradar missile, the Crossbow (GAM-67), which had several alternative missions including tactical reconnaissance. It was based on a Radioplanes jet target, and it would have been air-launched. Work began in 1953 (as MX-2013), and the drone first flew in July 1956 (the first guided flight was in May 1957). The antiradar version was killed in July 1957, and all development stopped in 1960. A follow-on WS-121 Longbow was also abandoned. Crossbow seems not to have influenced later UAV work.

The much more significant Ryan Firebee series is a case study in the rise and fall of past UAVs in the face of air forces more interested in piloted aircraft. Firebee was conceived in 1948 as a target drone with much the performance of a modern (subsonic) jet fighter. It first flew in 1951 and was widely used. In April 1955 Ryan publicly pointed out that a Firebee could be modified for reconnaissance, but nothing was done. Presumably this was in the context of U.S. Army efforts then producing aircraft like the MQM-33 and a series of jet reconnaissance drones. There was no Air Force interest. In September 1959 the chief of the Air Force's Reconnaissance Division asked what would happen if the U-2, then flying missions over the Soviet Union, were shot down. His camera expert suggested placing cameras in a drone instead of a manned airplane, referring to the only U.S. target drone then in service, Firebee.

At the time there was no Air Force interest in unmanned reconnaissance other than the very secret satellite system then being developed. There certainly seems to have been no interest in using the developing Army reconnaissance drones to provide strategic intelligence like that offered by the U-2. Ryan formed a reconnaissance drone division in January 1960 to modify the current version of the Firebee (then designated Q-2C, later BQM-34A) for the purpose. The nose was extended (with a characteristic shark snout) to provide a reconnaissance payload, the wings were extended for greater altitude (to 67,000 ft), and a fuselage plug added fuel or payload. The new version also had reduced radar signature (using mesh over the inlet, nonconductive paint, and blankets over the engine) and improved flight controls. Early estimates showed that range could be increased from the usual 660 nm to 1,200–1,400 nm, making it possible to overfly considerable areas of denied territory, particularly in Asia. Ryan estimated that with a new wing and an uprated version of the engine, a modified Firebee could fly 2,500 nm, sufficient to overfly from the Barents Sea to Turkey or from India to South Korea or Japan. For such ranges the Firefly would be provided with a new inertial navigation system—it was essential that it follow the required flight path in order to photograph the right targets.

At the suggestion of Air Force officers in the Reconnaissance Division, Ryan produced a proposal, but there was no money until after Francis Gary Powers' U-2 was shot down over the Soviet Union in May 1960. A first "summer program" contract was let on 8 July 1960 for two (later four) modified Q-2Cs (Ryan Model 124s). Plans called for development of a specialized reconnaissance vehicle, Ryan's Model 136, with long, straight (rather than swept) wings and with its engine moved to atop the fuselage to reduce IR detectability from below. This Red Wagon program was suspended in November 1960 pending the change of administration and not revived despite analysis suggesting the value of such an unmanned system. A follow-on and more sophisticated proposal, Lucy Lee, died in January 1962. Ryan then reverted to proposals for a simple evolutionary design, which the Air Force's Big Safari quick-acquisition program accepted in February 1962 as Firefly. Four more Q-2Cs were now modified on a ninety-day basis as Ryan Model 147A, to achieve a 1,200-nm range and cruise above 55,000 ft. The aircraft would be launched from a modified C-130, which could bring it close to the border of the denied area it was to cover. The Air Force became really interested after October 1962, when a U-2 was shot down by a Soviet SA-2 missile over Cuba during the missile crisis. Note that although the Firebee was described as an RPV, it was designed to fly autonomous preprogrammed missions. Externally identical to the BQM-34A target drone, the AQM-34A (Ryan Model 147A) had a new navigation system and increased fuel capacity.

The Air Force ordered Model 147B, with an extended wing (27-ft rather than 13-ft span) for longer range (the A version had its span extended to 15 ft, compared to the 13 ft of the Q-2C target drone, and its fuselage—and that of the B version—was 27 rather than 22 ft long). A parallel 147E version revived the ELINT role of the 147D, this time for use in South Korea. Unlike the D version, it saw combat (in Vietnam). On 13 February 1966 a Ryan 147E picked up the SA-2 command link before being destroyed by the missile. The sole 147F, a converted 147B, tested the Navy's ALQ-51 electronic countermeasure (ECM) device operationally before it was installed on board combat aircraft.

While the B version was being developed, seven 147Cs, short-wing versions with contrail suppression, were ordered in October 1962. In addition two 147Ds, modified specifically to measure proximity fuse and transponder beacon waveforms on Soviet SA-2 missiles used in Cuba, were ordered for the CIA, the idea being that they could transmit this data back to a controlling airplane or to a surface ship before the missile destroyed them. The waveforms were wanted for countermeasures development. In this case the UAV's radar signature would have been increased to simulate a real airplane and hence elicit a missile launch. They were declared operational in December 1962 but were not used operationally because by the time they were ready it was no longer likely that a Cuban SA-2 battery would fire at them.

The 147B drones were first used over China, the Republic of China's air force having lost U-2s there. Although the aircraft were called remotely piloted vehicles, in fact, they flew programmed paths, since there was no

drone operator on the DC-130 launch aircraft (the D ironically meaning "director," since if it were launching target drones it would control them). In any case the drone soon flew far beyond the horizon of the aircraft. Control was exerted (generally from the ground) only as the drone approached the recovery area. Typically the DC-130 flew from Okinawa, launching the drone to overfly Hainan and the area of China near the coast to the north; drones were recovered on Taiwan.

The first five missions were flown early in September 1964. A Firebee (147B) was shot down over southern China on 15 November, possibly in a mission intended to stimulate air defenses so that their emissions could be picked up by U.S. aircraft. The 147Bs flew a total of 78 operational missions, returning from 48 of them; one survived 8 missions (the average was 2.6). A new high-altitude version, 147G, was ordered in March 1965, using a new uprated engine (1,920-lb rather than 1,700-lb thrust) for higher altitude and a further stretched fuselage (29 ft). This version also had a new contrail-suppression system, the earlier one apparently proving unsuccessful. It became operational in October 1965; note the very quick tempo of development, which seems characteristic of UAVs. To achieve still better altitude performance, the new engine and a further stretched body (30 ft) were mated with an even longer wing (32 ft, the first wet wing in the series) in the 147H version (AQM-34N), the range of which was 2,415 nm compared to 1,455 for the 147G. This version could reach 70,000 ft as its fuel ran out and could operate regularly at 65,000. This version introduced countermeasures, including an evasive maneuver program triggered by the standard MiG airborne radar (a later version also responded to ground missile control radars). The last 147H missions were flown in 1972, the drones carrying ELINT equipment to obtain enemy surface-to-air missile emissions (SA-2 missiles; the missions were called Compass Cookie). A 28 September 1972 mission collected the required data.

Despite the efforts made to reduce observability, by late 1965 the North Vietnamese were regularly shooting down these drones, particularly after the December 1965 bombing pause removed most U.S. aircraft from their airspace. Ten standard target drones were converted into decoys (147N) to dilute defenses. The idea was to mix them with the actual reconnaissance drones. They survived so often that later ones were modified with parachutes for recovery as 147NX.

The high-altitude versions were useless during the monsoon (November through March), because they flew over, rather than under, cloud cover. Ryan received a contract for an interim low- and medium-altitude version (147J) in October 1965. It flew in November and was operational in March 1966 (147H/AQM-34N became operational about a year later). The 147J retained the long wing of the high-altitude versions but had a low-altitude barometric control system that allowed it to fly at 1,500 ft.

For effective low-altitude reconnaissance the Air Force ordered Model 147S. While it was being developed, the decoy version (147N) was modified into a low-altitude photo version (147NP) combining a slightly stretched wing (15 ft) with a stretched fuselage (28 ft). Four aircraft were modified for night reconnaissance (147NRE) with strobe lights (earlier drones used flares) to deal with increased enemy night activity intended to evade U.S. daylight bombing. Other low-altitude versions were 147NX and 147NQ; NQ may have been unique in that it was controlled from the DC-130. There was also a photo version of the short-wing decoy NC version, NC (M-1: Modification 1; AQM-34J). In February 1971 eighteen M-1s were transferred from the Strategic Air Command, which was responsible for photo reconnaissance, to the Tactical Air Command, giving that organization its first drone reconnaissance capability. There was also a leaflet-dropping version of 147NC (AQM-34H), which flew twenty-nine missions between July and December 1972.

Model 147S was the most-produced version. To hold down airframe cost, it retained more of the original target drone than did versions like 147G or 147J, for example, the 13-ft wing. This was an analog airplane, so every increase in flexibility required some new control system. For example, the barometric system in the J version operated at a single altitude; the modification to a multi-altitude flight plan was significant enough to require a new designation (147SB), which allowed for three preselected altitudes between 1,000 and 20,000 ft, to be repeated throughout the flight as desired. The SC version (AQM-34L), account-

ing for the bulk of Firebee reconnaissance UAV production, was delivered beginning in mid-1968; it flew 1,651 operational sorties, with an 87.2 percent success rate. It had a Doppler navigation system. There was also an SRE night version (AQM-34K) corresponding to the NRE. Some aircraft equipped with real-time television cameras and data links were designated AQM-34L/TV. The AQM-34M (Model 147SD) was a production version with the real-time link; -34M(L) (Model 147SDL, Compass Robin) had Loran for better navigation. It was intended to operate at 300 to 500 ft altitude. The previous SC version had to be updated by the drone control aircraft to make sure that it was on course to cover the required targets. The SD version offered better precision (within 200 to 250 ft) and was self-adjusting, because Loran gave the actual location of the drone. The AQM-34L was built under the Compass Bin program. The Loran version appeared during the 1972 bombing of North Vietnam (June 1972) and was intended specifically for the new drone reconnaissance program associated with that bombing campaign (Buffalo Hunter). This campaign also involved heavy SC activity.

The U.S. Navy became interested in a ship-launched drone reconnaissance capability; the Navy had been using intelligence collected by the air-launched drones (operated by the Strategic Air Command) but did not consider it timely enough, as photographs had to be delivered physically to the ships (and as the Navy could not task the drones). The Navy therefore let a contract for a ship-launched version of the normally air-launched Model 147S, which would be recovered at sea (147SK). Surface launch involved different structural stresses, and different aerodynamics as the drone took off. This version was first successfully tested in August 1969, including launches from the carrier USS *Bennington*. In October it deployed experimentally to Vietnamese waters on board the attack carrier *Ranger*; the drone control aircraft would be the ship's airborne early warning aircraft, and the drones would be recovered in the air by helicopters (some of these capabilities were not yet ready, however). Drone control involved placing the drone at its initial point and taking control when it returned to the recovery area. On the first flight (23 November 1969) the drone flew successfully, but the drone control aircraft was unable to take

AQM-34L (Model 147SC) accounted for the bulk of Firebee (sometimes called Firefly in the reconnaissance role) sorties over Vietnam. (National Museum of the United States Air Force)

control; the drone had to be maneuvered from the ship. That introduced enough of an error (2 miles) to move the strip photographed by the drone away from the area of interest (the photographs were technically excellent but useless). A second mission was entirely successful, and flights continued through June 1970.

The Air Force was still interested in high-altitude reconnaissance, so early in 1967 it ordered Model 147T (Compass Dawn: AQM-34P), with a new 2800-lb-thrust engine (45 percent more than the original) plus reduced radar reflectivity (HIDE) and a jammer to deal with the only high-altitude surface-to-air missile it was likely to encounter, the SA-2 (Rivet Bounder). Model 147T had the same airframe as the earlier high-altitude Model 147H; with the increased thrust it could operate at greater altitudes (66,300 ft when 220 nm from launch, 75,000 ft at fuel-out). Range was more than 2,400 miles. More than three-quarters of the 28 missions flown over China and North Vietnam between April 1969 and September 1970 ended in successful recovery, but at least one was

recovered by the Chinese and reverse-engineered as their WZ-5 (see entry below). Note that the 147H version, which was very similar, flew 138 missions, two-thirds of them successful, between March 1967 and July 1971.

As the 147T reached operational status, the North Koreans shot down a U.S. EC-121 ELINT aircraft. Ryan proposed an ELINT drone version of 147T. Obviously it could not incorporate the intelligence of the operators on an ELINT airplane, only the receivers. Instead the receivers could operate on a relay basis, operators receiving their outputs controlling them (this concept originated with Melpar, later E-Systems). Four prototype 147TEs (AQM-34Q) were built, first flying on 25 November 1969 (six months after the loss of the EC-121); the first operational flight came on 15 February 1970. Production aircraft followed.

The idea of simplifying the ELINT mission by using remote control was later picked up by the Navy in the form of BGPHES, the Battle Group Passive Horizon Extension System, using sensors on board an ES-3A or

AQM-34Q (Model 147TE) was an ELINT version of the Firebee. It was used extensively near North Korea after a U.S. EC-121 was shot down (January 1969). (National Museum of the United States Air Force)

a U-2. Given its limited payload, the TE had to be fitted for either COMINT (communications intelligence) or for ELINT, the two versions being called HARC and HARE (high-altitude reconnaissance, COMINT or ELINT); the ELINT role was later eliminated. The program was called Combat Dawn. Given its very-high-altitude capability, 147TE could detect enemy emissions as much as 300 miles away, and it could link to a ground facility as much as 300 miles away, for a total effective reconnaissance range of 600 nm. COMINT drones could be identified by the radome atop their tail fins for their ten-channel (for ten receivers) wideband data link back to base. Among other things the COMINT package could pick up ground-control instructions to fighters attempting to intercept the aircraft, and, since it was within link range of its ground control, it could be maneuvered to evade. Later aircraft had external fuel tanks to increase their endurance. A follow-on 147TF (AQM-34R) could conduct either COMINT or ELINT missions. With external tanks, this drone weighed 6,600 lbs, which was about the

limit for air-launch from the usual DC-130 aircraft. To meet demands for higher altitude and greater capability, Ryan proposed a longer-wing 147TL, which would have required a new (and much more expensive) launch aircraft. It seems not to have been built. The TE version carried out 268 missions between February 1970 and June 1973; the TF version, 216 missions between February 1973 and June 1975.

The Firebee was the first drone used in combat on a large scale. Between 20 August 1964 and 30 April 1975, 1,016 Firebees ("Lightning Bugs") flew 3,435 sorties over China, North Vietnam, and North Korea; 544 were lost (one-third to mechanical failures). A Firebee was expected to survive through 2.5 sorties, but in practice the average was 7.3 missions, and one Firebee (Model 147SC, "Tom Cat") managed 68 missions before failing to return on 25 September 1974 (others with similar records were "Budweiser" [63 missions], "Ryan's Daughter" [52], and "Baby Buck" [46]). North Vietnamese fighter pilots claimed eleven drones, but several fighters were lost in the process, sometimes when one fighter's missiles missed the small drone and locked onto another fighter (one Firebee was considered an ace because it was involved in five fighter shoot-downs). In some cases MiGs crashed while trying to intercept the drones.

Given the widespread and very successful use of Firebees during the Vietnam War, it might have seemed obvious that UAVs (then called RPVs) would have been retained operationally and their use would have been expanded in the 1970s. There was certainly sentiment to that effect in the U.S. defense development community (e.g., DARPA), and the Vietnam experience seems to have led to DARPA's interest in using UAV technology to support small-unit ground combat (ultimately in the Army's Aquila program). The U.S. Air Force was substantially less interested; cynics would say that it had no interest in reducing pilots' roles. It went so far as to reject senior congressional direction to retain RPV units. In effect the Firebee force was retired (and proposed successors terminated; see below) in favor of restarting the U-2R/TR-1 production line. Thirty-three refurbished AQM-34s went to Israel but probably were not reactivated because the Israelis preferred ground-launched UAVs.

The Firebee experience did lead to interest in Israel. The Israelis first became interested in drone reconnaissance in 1965, when Israel depended mainly on France for weapons. An internal suggestion to acquire a license for the R20 drone was rejected by the then-chief of the Israeli Air Force and his deputy, both former fighter pilots. The chief of staff and chief of intelligence were more supportive, but arrangements could not be made, and the Israelis decided to try to reverse a U.S. decision not to export Firebee. All of this seems to have happened about the time of the 1967 Mideast War and the consequent French decision to stop selling weapons to Israel. In 1969–70 the Egyptians moved numerous surface-to-air missiles into their side of the truce zone around the Suez Canal to fight the War of Attrition (Soviet crews were involved). In mid-1970 Israeli Air Force interest in drone reconnaissance revived after several Phantoms were lost late in this war. Although the U.S. drone operation over Vietnam had not been described officially, by this time it was an open secret. Ryan offered a modified version of its Model 124 Firebee target, which it designated Model 124I

(Mabat in Israeli service). It was, in effect, a Model 147 drone (span 14.5 ft, length 31 ft, ground-launched). Model 124I was roughly equivalent to the 147SD then under development, but it also offered an alternative high-altitude capability (56,000 ft ceiling). Some features developed for 124I were incorporated back into 147SD. The drone first flew in Israel on 23 August 1971. The drones flew numerous missions during the 1973 Yom Kippur War. By this time Ryan was developing a supersonic Firebee II target, and the Israelis were interested in a reconnaissance version; they eventually opted for more 124Is because of the delay involved in developing an entirely new aircraft. The 124I was still in service as late as 1990, albeit in dwindling numbers. It is not clear whether the Israelis developed or sought a comparable follow-on; their later interest was in UAVs with much lower performance. It is possible that the attraction of the later kind of UAV, first proposed soon after the 1973 war, was that it would offer much the same capability at a much lower price. In this sense the Israeli Firebee was the bridge between the U.S. Vietnam experience and the Israeli experience in 1982, which in effect launched modern UAVs.

In addition to Mabat, the Israelis acquired a reconnaissance version of the smaller Northrop (formerly Radioplanes) Chukar drone. Both Mabat and Chukar served in 1973 with the new 200th Drone Squadron (Chukar may have been used mainly as a decoy). Chukar (MQM-74A) was a smaller jet target drone first flown in 1965; it was intended to reach 400 kt. A total of 1,800 were made between 1966 and 1972 for the U.S. Navy and export customers, including Israel. For comparison with Firebee, Chukar data: span 1.69 m, length 3.46 m, weight 143 kg without boosters, range 143 nm at sea level (237 nm at 20,000 ft), maximum level speed 400 kt at sea level, 425 kt at 20,000 ft. Note that Chukar was license-produced by Meteor in Italy, leading to the Mirach-100 series of jet UAVs, including reconnaissance types. A later air-launched Chukar III was repeatedly considered by the U.S. Army and Navy for reconnaissance. Span was 1.76 m, length 3.95 m, weight 199 kg when air-launched, speed 530 kt at 20,000 ft, range 450 nm.

The Israeli experience inspired Egyptian interest. In April 1983 they approached Teledyne Ryan to develop a UAV reconnaissance system for them. The main new feature was the extensive use of composite materials in a UAV initially designated Model 124RE, which was eventually designated Model 324 Scarab. Like the high-altitude UAVs developed by Teledyne Ryan, it had its turbojet engine above rather than below the fuselage, blended into the body near its tail (as the company had planned to do in its Model 275 follow-on to the Model 235 prototype Cope-R). The engine was derived from that of the Harpoon missile. For details see the entry below.

Perhaps inspired by its experience with the carrier-launched Firebee reconnaissance drone, by 1974 the U.S. Navy was interested in what it called a "midi-range" RPV. At that time it was clear that the Vietnam-era RA-5C Vigilante reconnaissance aircraft would soon be retiring, and some replacement was needed. The interim replacement was a combination of electronic surveillance aircraft and the converted RF-8 Crusader fighter, but the Crusader was also unlikely to survive for much longer.

Presumably the Crusader replacement became more and more urgent through the early 1980s, so that in 1985 the U.S. Navy issued a formal requirement. In September 1987 the Navy awarded seven-month design contracts to Northrop (probably offering a reconnaissance version of the BQM-74C jet target, using a television nose) and to Martin-Marietta/Beech (probably for a derivative of the Beech MQM-107A target drone, which that company offered as the Raider UAV), one of which would receive a prototype contract leading to production beginning in fiscal year (FY) 1989. By this time a version of the Italian Mirach-100 had already been rejected. The program was frozen by the congressionally mandated freeze on UAV development.

The Navy's UAV became the medium-range JSCAMPS (Joint Services Common Airframe Multi-Purpose System) and the competition was reopened. That gave Teledyne Ryan the opportunity to bid a UAV derived from its Egyptian Scarab. It won the contest in June 1989 with its Model 350 Peregrine (BQM-145). By that time JSCAMPS had become the MR (medium-range) UAV. (The Joint Projects Office differentiated between short-range, medium-range, and long-range [SR, MR, and LR] UAVs.) Model 350 could be launched either from the ground or from fighters. The primary payload was a new filmless optical/IR reconnaissance system, ATARS

(Advanced Tactical Reconnaissance System). Plans initially called for five hundred aircraft for use by the Air Force, Navy, and Marine Corps. However, the Navy and Marines were to have been the primary ATARS users, the U.S. Air Force already having abandoned fighter photo reconnaissance. When ATARS was canceled in 1993 (due to budget shortfalls), the Navy and Marine Corps withdrew, and BQM-145 itself was canceled that October. The Navy reconnaissance mission was to be conducted by conventional fighters carrying pods or with palletized equipment installed (on board F/A-18s). At that time six aircraft were being made, and the first of these flew in February 1997; all six were delivered for use by the U.S. Air Force Battle Lab. Northrop Grumman, which had taken over Teledyne Ryan, attempted to market Model 350 (as a general-purpose UAV) without success. Data: span 3.20 m, length 5.59 m, weight 980 kg, endurance 2 hours (speed Mach 0.85, mission radius 350 nm), ceiling 40,000 ft. Model 350 was jet powered (tail exhaust) with twin tail fins and conventional swept wings and horizontal tail surfaces. The engine was a 1,000-lb-thrust Teledyne CAE F408-CA-400 turbofan. For the United States BQM-145 was effectively the end of developing high-performance jet UAVs until they reappeared as part of the UCAV program.

High-Altitude Reconnaissance

The other type of long-range reconnaissance was high-altitude long-endurance reconnaissance and sensor monitoring, which for the U.S. Air Force generally meant replacement for the high-flying slow U-2. Initially it seemed that the appropriate replacement would be a much faster airplane, which became the A-12 and then the SR-71 Blackbird. After the U-2 was shot down, a drone version of the A-12 was proposed, but its designer, Kelly Johnson, argued that it was too large and complicated; he suggested a supersonic drone be designed for the purpose. The initial concept was a ramjet that an A-12 would launch at high speed. The mother aircraft was redesignated M-21, and the drone (daughter) became D-21 Tagboard (initially it was designated Q-12). The mockup was ready by 7 December 1962, a full-scale development contract awarded in March 1963, and the design was finalized in October 1963. D-21 made its first captive flight on

D-21B Tagboard drone. (National Museum of the United States Air Force)

board an M-21 on 22 December 1964; release was a problem, and it did not make a first flight until 5 March 1966. A contract for fifteen aircraft was let in April 1966, after one of them had reached 90,000 ft and a speed of Mach 3.3. Designed range was 3,450 miles. Given problems with the M-21, operational drones were launched from B-52s, using large boosters to reach ramjet operating speed. The operational program, designated Senior Bowl, began with an overflight of the Chinese nuclear test site of Lop Nor on 9 November 1969. Although the drone was never spotted by the Chinese, it did not return. Like the Russian Tu-123, D-21 was designed to deploy a data recovery package; the drone itself was never re-used. On the first flight the D-21 crashed in Siberia, the wreckage was recovered by the Soviets, and Tupolev was assigned to develop an equivalent, Voron (which was never built). The D-21 program was canceled after four operational flights, on two of which data capsules were ejected but lost; on the last flight (20 March 1971) the D-21 was shot down.

Of thirty-eight aircraft built, twenty-one were expended in tests or operationally.

U.S. attempts to develop long-endurance but low-speed unmanned aircraft began in the 1960s, initially to service the Igloo White ground sensor system in Vietnam. This function illustrates the value of an unmanned aircraft that can remain aloft, conducting a repetitive operation without succumbing to pilot fatigue. Initially ground sensor data were collected by a manned EC-121, whose operators could also process it. The alternative was a UAV that could collect sensor data radioed by the ground sensors and downlink it to a sensor fusion station on the ground. The EC-121s were replaced by single-seat versions of the Beech Bonanza (QU-22As) operating as radio relays (Pave Eagle program). Six YQU-22A were converted for evaluation (Pave Eagle 1) and another seven converted for operational use (QU-22B Pave Eagle 2). On-station endurance was about 18 hours; ceiling was 19,000 ft. Although the Bonanza could operate as a drone under data-link control, typically it did not. The Bonanzas suffered high losses due to engine failure, and they were withdrawn late in 1972.

The Compass Dwell program sponsored a long-endurance UAV (Model L-450F) developed by LTV Electrosystems specifically for the Igloo White program. It was a modified Schweizer sailplane powered by a turboprop, with extra fuel tanks. The prototype flew in February 1970 (in piloted form). It crashed, but a second prototype completed flight tests, and a third, without a cockpit (XQM-93), flew early in 1972. Four were ordered, but the program was canceled in 1972, presumably due to the withdrawal from Vietnam. Data: span 17.4 m, length 9.14 m, weight 2,090 kg (payload 320 kg), endurance 30 hours (range 5,220 nm/6,000 miles), cruising speed 91 kt (105 mph). Data are for the manned version. Martin Marietta's competing UAV, Model 845A, was also based on a Schweizer sailplane. It flew in 1971, and one prototype remained in the air for 28 hours.

Roughly contemporary with these efforts was a new attempt to develop a high-altitude long-endurance version of the Firebee (Compass Arrow program) specifically to overfly China at sufficient speed and altitude to be immune to interception. The resulting AQM-91A (Ryan Model 154) had its fuselage reshaped to reduce radar reflectivity from below, and the engine was moved from below to above the fuselage to reduce IR signature. The tail fins were slanted inward, both to contain the exhaust stream and to reduce radar reflectivity from the sides and below. The aircraft was air-launched and parachute-recovered (on command). The main sensor was a film camera (1,500 exposures). The contract was let in 1966, and it died when relations with China were opened and overflights were no longer desirable; all aircraft were placed in storage in July 1973. Reportedly they were later scrapped. Even so the success of the program must have indicated that high-altitude reconnaissance was entirely practical. Like Firebees, Compass Cope was air-launched. The launch aircraft (two UAVs) had a 2,300-nm radius, and each UAV had a 5-hour endurance and a range of 2,000 nm. Data: span 14.63 m (48 ft), length 10.36 m, weight 2,379 kg (5,245 lbs). The power plant was a 5,270-lb-thrust J97-GE-100 turbojet.

Compass Cope was a different long-endurance program intended to develop a U-2 replacement and begun about 1970. It was conceived as a long-endurance rather than simply long-range platform, loitering above the jet stream, its operation not limited by crew endurance. In this sense it presaged the current Global Hawk. Missions would include SIGINT, communications relay, battlefield surveillance, ocean surveillance, photo reconnaissance, and atmospheric sampling (e.g., to detect nuclear tests). Many of these missions were already being conducted by the Korean surveillance UAVs (Models 147TE, 147TF). The relay role was new. It was intended as a way of extending the coverage of the new Precision Location Strike System, which used what became Link 16 to create an airborne precision location net. Because Link 16 operated only in the line of sight, extension beyond the horizon relied on relay aircraft. Ocean surveillance was becoming important to the U.S. Navy, particularly in the Mediterranean, and by 1970 there was interest in using a U-2 for this purpose. Even so this was a highly automated role, and using a UAV would eliminate the serious problem of pilot fatigue. Such considerations explain later interest in aircraft such as Global Hawk.

Goals were an endurance of more than 20 hours (given as 24 hours by Teledyne Ryan), a ceiling of more than 55,000 ft, and a payload of 700 to 1,500 lbs (317 to 680 kg; the payload requirement was given as 750 lbs by Teledyne Ryan). Unlike previous reconnaissance UAVs, this one would take off from and return to a runway, like a conventional airplane. Runway recovery would reduce the wear on the UAV on landing.

The contract went to Boeing for its YQM-94A Compass Gull (Cope-B). Boeing began design work in September 1970, two prototypes being ordered on 15 July 1971, one flying on 28 July 1973 (it soon crashed). There was speculation at the time that Boeing had received the sole-source contract specifically to create an alternative to Teledyne Ryan, which was then the sole U.S. builder of reconnaissance RPVs. However, Teledyne Ryan was brought in as competitor in 1972, producing the YQM-98A (Model 236) Cope-R, which rolled out in January 1974. Cope-R was similar in configuration to Compass Arrow but had much longer wings and had conventional landing gear for runway recovery. It first flew on 17 August 1974, and on the fifth flight it set an endurance record, remaining airborne for 28 hours 11 minutes and exceeding an altitude of 55,000 ft. Boeing won the competition, but the contract was canceled in July 1977, the U.S. Air Force stating that the planned payload was unlikely to mature in time.

The YQM-94A data: span 27.43 m (90 ft), length 12.19 m, weight 6,531 kg (payload 317.5 kg); estimated operational performance of a 7,559-kg aircraft: endurance 27 hours (maximum range 8,600 nm). The YQM-98 data: span 24.75 m (81 ft), length 11.68 m, weight 6,490 kg (payload 317.5 kg for a 24-hour mission); estimated endurance was 30 hours (cruising speed Mach 0.5 to 0.6), and operating altitude would have been 50,000 to 70,000 ft.

About 1983 DARPA began a black program, Teal Rain, to develop a long-endurance high-altitude UAV powered by a piston engine. It seems to have paid for two programs, Condor, developed by Boeing, and Amber, developed by Leading Systems, Inc. (LSI). Boeing's Condor was revealed in March 1986. Said to have been the first robotic U.S. aircraft, it flew in October 1988. It may have introduced lightweight composite honeycomb structure. About 60 percent of the loaded weight was fuel, all of it carried in the long narrow wing. The power plant was a pair of 6-cylinder 175-hp Continental piston engines using 2-stage superchargers, driving tractor propellers. Span was 61 m (200 ft), length 20.7 m, weight 9,070 kg (empty weight 3,630 kg); endurance was 2.5 days (cruising speed 200 kt/230 mph) and ceiling was 65,000 ft. Despite its spectacular performance, Condor did not lead to any known further program.

Amber was a very different proposition. It resulted from a $40 million contract issued in 1984 to LSI to develop the reconnaissance UAV. The Army, Navy, and Marine Corps were all interested, and the Navy became lead service. Span was 8.54 m, length 4.6 m, and weight 335 kg; the power plant was a 4-cylinder 65-hp liquid-cooled engine driving a pusher propeller in the tail. The wing was carried on a short pylon above the fuselage, and there was an inverted vee tail. In addition to the UAV version, there was a cruise missile version. Endurance was at least 38 hours. Amber first flew in November 1986, and its existence was declassified in 1987, when the program was killed in the UAV freeze described above. The contract called for three A-45 cruise missiles and three B-45 reconnaissance prototypes. When the program died, LSI sold out to General Atomics to avoid bankruptcy.

In 1988 LSI began work on an export version, Gnat 750, which first flew in 1989. The Gnat 750 was somewhat larger (span 10.75 m, length 5 m, weight 517 kg), and its wing was mounted under the fuselage rather than above it. It was powered by an 85-hp Rotax 912 piston engine. Endurance was increased to 48 hours, and ceiling was 25,000 ft. The CIA bought Gnat 750s, deploying it to Albania in 1994 to conduct surveillance of the former Yugoslavia. Gnat was considered successful despite weather limitations and extremely bad terrain (a low-powered UAV, like a low-powered cruise missile, cannot easily deal with steep mountains in its path). An improved Gnat or I-Gnat 750) had a turbocharged engine and reliability and maintainability improvements. The next-generation Gnat 750-45 was Predator, described below. General Atomics proposed a tactical UAV (Prowler) based on Gnat 750. It was smaller (span 7.31 m, length 4.25 m, endurance over 16 hours), but it did not sell.

Probably as part of this program, in 1985 Teledyne Ryan proposed a HALE it called Spirit (Model 329). Its characteristics give some idea of what was wanted at the time. Like Amber, and unlike its earlier high-altitude UAVs, Teledyne Ryan planned to use a liquid-cooled piston engine, in this case a Teledyne Continental 6-cylinder engine producing 155 to 160 hp (the 4-cylinder version powered Rutan's "Voyager" around the world in December 1986). The Naval Air Development Center was apparently principal sponsor, but it could not find sufficient funds or allies to fund the project. Spirit would have been a twin-boom pusher with an inverted vee tail; missions included monitoring large sonobuoy fields (roughly analogous to Igloo White) from high altitude. The payload would have occupied a modular nose. To minimize weight, the structure would have been built from composites. Span would have been 25.91 m, length 12.19 m, and takeoff weight about 2,041 kg (136- to 544-kg payload, 1,134 kg empty); endurance would have been 80 hours at 50,000 ft, equivalent to a range of 14,000 nm. Ceiling would have been 75,000 ft.

Compass Cope-R rollout, 1 April 1974. (Teledyne Ryan [now Northrop Grumman])

The U.S. Air Force considered Gnat 750 as Tier I; Predator was Tier II. Tier III was reserved for a much larger UAV comparable to a B-2 bomber (a very large UAV code-named Quartz was considered in the late 1980s and early 1990s but dropped as too ambitious). Quartz was revived but dropped in the late 1990s, and in its place the Air Force decided to develop a stealthy UAV, Dark Star, and a super Predator (Tier II Plus), which became Global Hawk. See below for a description of Dark Star.

Teledyne Ryan proposed a considerably smaller shorter-endurance Model 410 for the Tier II requirement, but Predator won. Model 410 flew in October 1987 and used a different 160-hp engine (Avco Lycoming flat-four). Span was 9.45 m, length 6.60 m, weight 736 kg (payload 136 kg); endurance was 48 hours with reduced payload (45.4 kg) or 24 hours with full payload (maximum speed 190 kt; typical speed range 85–140 kt). Model 410 was proposed in 1993 as a Tier II system, responding to a

I-Gnat 750 reconnaissance UAV, January 1998. (General Atomics)

request for proposal (RFP) from the UAV Joint Projects Office; Predator was selected in January 1994.

Prestrike ECMs

Late in 1967 the Air Force asked for ECM drones to support its strikes. The existing N model was modified to carry a pair of chaff-dispensing pods as Model 147NA (AQM-34G). The modified 147NC (AQM-34H) offered programmable flight patterns (multiple altitudes). The first drone unit was declared combat ready in August 1968, but on 1 November President Johnson announced a bombing pause (which would last through 1972). The chaff drones did demonstrate their capability in Tactical Air Command exercises in 1970–71. By 1971 some drones were carrying the external jamming pods normally carried by F-4 Phantoms. This program was called Combat Angel.

ECM drones were not apparently used during the 1972 bombing attacks on North Vietnam, but Tactical Air Command remembered the idea, and immediately after

the war it promoted a revived version. A contract for this AQM-34V (Model 255) was awarded in September 1974; the aircraft were heavily modified AQM-34H airframes; the program was called the Combat Angel update modification program. The first flew on 13 May 1976. The aircraft carried an onboard ECM system and a pair of chaff pods underwing. It was extensively demonstrated during a triservice (Air Force, Navy, Marine Corps) Gallant Eagle exercise over the Gulf of Mexico, 30 October to 1 November 1978. The drones were used to lay down a chaff corridor that manned ECM aircraft (EB-57s) flew using their jammers and spreading more chaff. In effect the combination reflected typical Soviet naval air techniques for massed attacks against carriers, and the object of the exercise may have been to show that drones could provide fleet training less expensively than a fully manned force.

Attack

Firebees dropping chaff or leaflets crossed a subtle line between the UAV as pure reconnaissance platform and the UAV as delivery platform. Experience in Vietnam showed that defense suppression was both dangerous and difficult, as the attacking aircraft had to expose itself to enemy air defenses in order to detect and destroy them. The Israeli experience attacking Egyptian air defenses along the Suez Canal in 1970 dramatized the problem for U.S. decision makers. Ryan had proposed a bomber version of Firebee as early as 1964, but apart from the Army it had attracted little interest. In 1971, however, interest revived, as it seemed likely that the Soviets in Europe would field an interlocking air defense system even more formidable than that they had provided the Egyptians. A new defense suppression program (Have Lemon) was funded, one item in which was an attack version of the Firebee (BGM-34A, Model 234, placed under contract in March 1971). It would be armed with Maverick television-guided bombs and with a version of the Air Force's television-guided glide bomb, Stubby Hobos. Television guidance was specified because the usual anti-radar weapons could be neutralized when an enemy simply turned off his radar. The drone was needed because getting close enough to see the radar (hence to lock on the weapon) would be extremely hazardous. It carried a television camera with a zoom lens, the image being carried back to a human decision maker via a data link. The first successful flight of this much-modified Model 147S was carried out on 14 December 1971. An air-launched version was demonstrated in February 1972. U.S. bombing of North Vietnam resumed in December 1971, and not surprisingly North Vietnamese air defenses were considerably more effective than they had been in 1968.

Unfortunately the television seeker planned for BQM-34 was not likely to be effective in the face of excellent North Vietnamese camouflage. The Air Force therefore began a program (Have Onyx) to develop an IR system to see through the foliage and camouflage.

Meanwhile Tactical Air Command became interested in a tactic in which drones would form the first wave of the attack, absorbing enemy air defense missiles and leaving the way more open to follow-on manned aircraft. This went well beyond the antiradar concept. The Air Force became interested in quick production of attack drones, asking in late January 1972 how many missile-equipped

147SC and 147SD could be provided. A new prototype strike version, BGM-34B (Model 234A), was rolled out in February 1973 after about a year's engineering work. Compared to BGM-34A, the new version had a larger engine, modified tail, and enlarged control surfaces. Like BGM-34A it could launch Maverick, and it tested a self-propelled laser guided bomb, SPASM (Self-Propelled Air-to-Surface Missile). In a Pathfinder version the usual nose "snout" was enlarged to house a laser designator (for SPASM and some versions of Maverick), a low-light-level television, and a conventional television.

BGM-34A was demonstrated in West Germany in November 1974 under a cooperative program called Coronet Thor. The success of this effort seems to have inspired further German interest in armed UAVs, leading ultimately to Tucan and to the current Barrakuda. However, the U.S. Air Force proved uninterested in unmanned alternatives to manned aircraft.

Having developed both a strike version of Firebee and an ECM version, in 1972 Ryan proposed a multi-mission version using interchangeable noses and a tail radome (for data link) for strike: BGM-34C (Model 259). Under a November 1974 contract, Ryan modified five AQM-34L drones (Model 147SC); a DC-130 provided remote control during flight. The prototype was rolled out in August 1976, at which time it was expected that twenty would be produced per year beginning in July 1977 (for FY 1978). The flight test program was completed in April 1978 (fourteen reconnaissance, twelve EW (electronic warfare), and one strike flight to test the wide-band video data link). The program included a simulated escort jamming run by two drones in formation (November 1977). The Office of the Secretary of Defense (OSD) considered a proposal to manufacture 145 drones over six years (FY 1978–84).

Nothing came of this idea; by 1976 it was being reported that the Air Force considered the drones a burden, competing with the B-52/cruise missile combination then under development. In 1979 the U.S. Air Force shut down its only drone unit, the 432nd Tactical Drone Group, and its more than sixty Firebees were placed in storage. At the time Senator Strom Thurmond, who resisted the decision, stated that manned aircraft would now have to fly missions into dangerous areas that already could be flown by RPVs.

Probably the most important early armed UAV came out of an entirely separate program, the U.S. Navy's QH-50 DASH drone, conceived in the mid-1950s to deliver homing torpedoes. DASH was attractive because it required much less of the operating ship than the contemporary ASROC (Anti-Submarine Rocket) missile but could also be operated in bad weather (because it had no pilot to risk). By about 1957 it was intended to equip all U.S. destroyers (and many destroyer escorts) not large enough to accommodate ASROC. The DASH first flew on 12 August 1960, and it was first deployed in January 1963. By 1969 the U.S. Navy had bought 810 drones and had modified 240 ships to operate them. DASH had only the most rudimentary autopilot, and a lack of feedback made it difficult to fly reliably (it seems to have had an unfortunate habit of returning to its ship upside down). Many destroyer commanders came to hate DASH so much that they ran their ships over drones that had fallen into the water. By the summer of 1970, about half the drones (440) had been lost, and MTBF (mean time between failures) was 145 to 185 hours. That was unacceptable in peacetime but might have been reasonable in a hot war. DASH was retired in 1970–71, replaced by the small manned LAMPS helicopter. An important factor in retirement was that the smallest of the DASH-operating ships were retired at about the same time, leaving ships large enough to accommodate LAMPS. With DASH the all-weather nonmissile capability was lost. The Japanese Maritime Self-Defense Force acquired another twenty-four DASH drones. It showed that careful attention to detail made it possible to operate DASH reliably. In 1986 the Israelis acquired three U.S. DASH drones and modified them as sensor platforms called Hellstar. During the Vietnam War a few DASH ("Snoopy DASH") were modified to spot for naval gunfire.

Data on the QH-50D DASH: rotor diameter 6.10 m, length 2.33 m, weight 1,055 kg (ordnance load 416 kg; Nite Gazelle ordnance load 136 kg). Typical mission radius was 40 nm (increased from 26 nm in the original QH-50A), and non-ASW range was 393 nm; ceiling was 15,700 ft and hover ceiling was 10,200 ft. Speed was 80 kt. The power plant was a 330-shp Boeing T50-BO-12 turboshaft.

DARPA modified QH-50Ds under the Nite Panther and Nite Gazelle programs, begun in January 1968. Panther involved installation of a day/night television camera, motion and still cameras, and a laser target designator, plus other sensors. Gazelle was an armed version using Miniguns, a high-velocity gun, a grenade launcher, bombs, bomblet dispensers, and the LARS (Laser-Aided Rocket System). There have been several attempts to develop vertical takeoff and landing (VTOL) UAVs using the DASH rotor system and power train, none leading to a successful program.

Current UCAVs, such as Predator/Reaper, were derived from surveillance UAVs and share their limited speed. They operate as hunter-killer aircraft, the surveillance system on board the UAV picking up the potential target, locking on, and designating it to a missile (such as Hellfire) by laser. This is efficient if the UAV must loiter to watch for the approach of a particular target, such as a vehicle carrying a terrorist leader. However, it is also possible to envisage a separation of functions in which numerous passing surveillance UAVs together maintain coverage of a place where the terrorist may pass (providing him no tactical warning). The resulting picture may be precise enough that another platform can easily deliver the weapon.

The Israeli Experience

A third source of UAV thinking was the development, in Israel, of much lower performance vehicles that could carry real-time sensors such as television cameras with data links. Reportedly the Israelis first became aware of the potential of unmanned aircraft when they took heavy aircraft losses during the 1973 Yom Kippur War. They already had Firebees, though that was not publicized at the time. They quickly modified some Chukar target drones as decoys to counter Egyptian surface-to-air missiles along the Suez Canal. After the war the Israeli Air Force reportedly asked IAI and Tadiran to develop small tactical surveillance RPVs offering real-time data to ground forces. Firebees did not offer this capability; they were higher-level strategic or operational-level reconnaissance assets, and usually they provided time-late film footage (it is not clear whether real-time capability was coming in 1973). Ultimately the Scout and Mastiff UAVs (originally called mini-RPVs in comparison with aircraft such as Firebee) were developed. Later Israeli accounts suggest that the idea of developing (in effect) enlarged model aircraft was not only revolutionary but also in distinct contrast to what the Israeli Air Force originally had in mind. During the June 1982 war in Lebanon, small, low-performance Israeli UAVs apparently drew fire, while reconnaissance aircraft at higher altitudes used that fire to locate the enemy missile units. The higher-altitude aircraft may have been Israeli Firebees.

The Israelis came to see their low-performance UAVs as sources of real-time tactical information, which could be used to guide ground formations. Their use of UAVs during the 1982 Lebanon War inspired considerable interest in many armies, because UAVs seemed to offer an inexpensive form of reconnaissance over the dangerous battle space. Probably the same armies were also frustrated by air forces' inability or unwillingness to supply them with the sort of dedicated short-range reconnaissance they needed, at least on a timely basis.

Israel apparently did not directly replace the high-performance Firebee with a higher-performance drone, preferring to invest in special versions of the F-4 Phantom. It is possible that the Israelis came to believe that they could use specialized loitering drones (Harpy) to neutralize enemy air defense radar systems so effectively that they did not need high UAV performance for survivability, at least in tactical operations.

Recent Combat Experience

The United States used Pioneer UAVs during the first Gulf War. Although the system was bought by the U.S. Navy, it was also operated by the Army, which received its first system in 1990. During the war forty-three U.S. Pioneers were deployed, flying 330 sorties (more than a thousand flight hours). Army Pioneers supported the "left hook" by detecting all potentially threatening Iraqi artillery so that it could be destroyed. Navy Pioneers spotted for the battleships' 16-in. fire; famously, Iraqi troops on an oil rig surrendered to one of them. The Marine Corps, which had retired its RF-4 Phantom photo reconnaissance aircraft, used Pioneer camera footage as a replacement. In 1995 nine systems were operational: five

U.S. Navy, three Marine Corps, and one assigned to the Joint UAV Training Center at Fort Huachuca, Arizona.

Kosovo (1999) was probably the first war in which modern UAVs provided a large percentage of reconnaissance capability. NATO losses amounted to seventeen U.S. craft (three Predator, nine Hunter, four Pioneer, one undetermined), seven German (probably all CL-289), five French (three Crécerelle, two CL-289), and fourteen British (Phoenix), plus four others of unknown nationality. Of these aircraft CL-289 was a standard classical drone, preprogrammed to take pictures and return. Of these twenty-eight were combat losses and nineteen were noncombat. For the United States, Operation Iraqi Freedom was the widest use of UAVs in any U.S. operation up to that time, nine different systems being involved (Global Hawk, Predator, Silver Fox, Pioneer, Dragon Eye, Shadow 200, FPASS [Force Protection Airborne Surveillance System], Pointer, and Hunter). Global Hawk flew 16 sorties (as of 12 May 2003) totaling 357 hours, locating thirteen SAM batteries, fifty launchers, three hundred canisters, three hundred tanks (38 percent of known Iraqi armor), and seventy missile transporters. Predator flew 93 sorties (1,354 hours) as of the same date, directly servicing six targets but providing buddy lasing and talk-on target for other targets. Hunter flew 190 sorties as of 22 May, Shadow 200 flew 172 (688 hours), and Pioneer flew 388 sorties (1,344 hours as of 4 June).

Once coalition forces were engaged in Iraq, they found that UAVs were vital—not only for standard reconnaissance but also to ensure the security of roads down which convoys were moving (it was often said that convoys would not be despatched without UAV cover). Typical usage was tens of hours per day in 2003, 100 in 2005, and about 500 by 2008. In 2003–4 the U.S. Army flew UAVs about 1,500 hours per month; that increased to 9,000 in 2005 and to about 55,000 in 2007.

One irony of the U.S. operation in Afghanistan was that large UAVs operated by the U.S. Air Force did not provide this sort of service; they were controlled centrally and dedicated to more strategic missions. The U.S. Marine Corps in particular used large P-3C maritime patrol aircraft as, in effect, manned UAVs simply because its ground units could control them directly.

Abu Dhabi/United Arab Emirates

The UAV Research and Technology Center of Abu Dhabi has teamed with the South Korean Ucon Systems to offer a range of mini- and tactical UAVs. The United Arab Emirates (UAE) armed forces let a contract to Ucon in August 2004 to develop a UAV ground-control station and signed a memorandum of understanding (MoU) with the UAV center in April 2005; the center had displays at the 2007 International Defense Exhibition and Conference (IDEX 2007) in both the Korean and the UAE areas. It showed the Korean RemoEye 002, 006, and 015. This firm also produces a new launcher for the Austrian Schiebel Camcopter UAV, which is used by the UAE. The new system is called Al Saber.

The UAE-based Adcom group has operated an Advanced Target Systems division since 1992; at IDEX 2005 it showed a modified target drone configured as the Yabhon-M UAV. Yabhon-R and -RX were later added. Yabhon-H may have been the first in the series. It uses a blended wing-body design with swept wings and unswept canard surfaces plus twin swept fins and rudders at its wingtips. It is powered by a piston pusher engine. Its EO sensor is mounted in its nose. Span is 3.28 m, length 2.50 m, weight 62.5 kg (payload 5 kg); endurance is 8 hours (maximum speed 94 kt, cruising speed 84 kt, stall speed 37 kt); ceiling is 10,000 ft. Yabhon-M is similar but larger (and has wing flaps and landing gear); it can carry the usual EO and thermal imagers or a laser range-finder-designator. Span is 5.70 m, length 4.30 m, weight 280 kg (payload 30 kg, empty weight 180 kg), endurance 12 hours (speed 240 km/hour [129 kt], endurance speed 210 km/hour [113 kt]); ceiling is 15,000 ft. The power plant is a 60-hp ME 684 piston engine. The next step up is Yabhon-R: span 6.56 m, length 5 m, takeoff weight 500 kg (payload 30–50 kg, empty weight 320 kg). Endurance is 30 hours (speed 240 km/hour [129 kt]; endurance speed 210 km/hour [113 kt], stall speed 95 km/hour [52 kt]); ceiling is 15,000 ft. The power plant is an 80-hp 4-cylinder 4-stroke engine. By way of contrast Yabhon-RX has a conventional twin-tailboom configuration. It is intended for long range and long endurance. Span is 9.68 m, length 5.56 m, weight 535 kg (payload 60 kg). Endurance is 42 hours (maximum speed 167 kt [310 km/hour], cruising speed 151 kt [280 km/hour], stall speed 53 kt [97 km/

hour]). Ceiling is 24,500 ft. Presumably this is the RX-6 flown in 2006, on the basis of which Adcom is developing a 1250-kg Yabhon RX-18 MALE aircraft.

At IDEX 2009 (February 2009), Adcom displayed its Smart Eye HALE aircraft (21-m span), the largest it had yet offered. Development began in 2002, the final configuration being set early in 2008. Smart Eye has much the same twin-tailboom configuration as Yabhon-RX, and may be RX-18. Smart Eye has a primary propeller engine (pusher-propeller, twin-boom configuration) with a secondary jet engine boost performance. Maximum payload is 550 kg (two sensor turrets). Estimated endurance is 125 hours (maximum speed 220 km/hour) on 700 liters of fuel (150 in each wing). Ceiling is 18,000 ft (26,000 ft with the jet engine). At IDEX Adcom claimed that it had a customer (although Smart Eye had not yet flown) and that it expected to build three prototypes.

Argentina

The Argentine navy began a two-year program to develop a surveillance UAV, Guardian, in 2007. Construction of the platform was completed in August 2007. It has a pod-and-boom configuration using a 17-hp pusher-propeller engine; span is 5 m, weight 77 kg (payload 30 kg), mission radius 27 nm (cruising speed 65 kt), ceiling 10,000 ft. By 2009 this program was still incomplete. It is apparently an internal Argentine navy program.

The Argentine army R&D organization began work on the Lipán M3 brigade-level tactical UAV in 1996; as of 2007 it was reported in service. Lipán uses a conventional twin-tailboom airframe with an inverted vee tail and a pusher propeller. Sensors are in a stabilized underslung nose turret. A system comprises three air vehicles and a control station. M3 is the operational version developed in 2006–7. It is reprogrammable in flight. Span is 4.38 m, length 3.43 m, weight 60 kg (payload 20 kg), endurance 5 hours (mission radius 21 nm, maximum speed 91 kt, loiter speed 43 kt), ceiling 6,500 ft. The first system was delivered to Combat Intelligence Detachment 601 of the Argentine army in December 2007, a second following in 2008, the third due in 2009, and a fourth in 2010.

In addition to these official efforts, the Nostromo company of Córdoba has developed several mini-UAVs: Cabure, Yagua, and Yarará. Cabure is a preprogrammed

Yabhon-H (Yabhon-M is similar). (Advanced Target Systems)

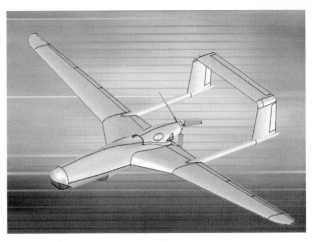

Yabhon-RX. (Advanced Target Systems)

The Argentine Lipán II UAV at the 23 May 2008 Argentine army exhibition. (Joaquin Alvarez Riera)

UAV intended for law enforcement but also evaluated by the Argentine air force and marines. As of 2009 the company had built ten and had orders for a total of twenty-eight. Yagua is a special forces mini-UAV announced in 2007, intended to operate at a range of 16 nm. Yarará is a small tactical UAV, design of which began in 2005–6; the first was delivered in August 2006, and it was apparently the first Latin American UAV to be exported (to the United States). It was first displayed at the Argentine air force show in August 2006. Two systems were deliv-

ered to an unidentified U.S. customer in 2006, one to an Argentine oil company in 2007, and one Yarará-C to the U.S. Department of Defense (DoD) late in 2007. By 2008 a total of twelve air vehicles had been delivered (there were orders for fourteen). The unidentified U.S. customers were likely pass-throughs for special operations in Central or South America, perhaps in Colombia. A system comprises three air vehicles and a control station. The air vehicle has a single boom, its engine mounted on a pylon above the trailing edge of its shoulder-mounted wing.

Span 3.98 m, length 2.47 m, weight 30 kg (payload 5 kg), endurance 6 hours (maximum speed 79 kt, cruising speed 62 kt, mission radius 27 nm), ceiling about 10,000 ft.

Austria

Schiebel's 200-kg Camcopter S-100 helicopter has been ordered by three countries, among whom the UAE ordered forty systems (eighty air vehicles) with an option for twenty more air vehicles as Al Saber (Watchkeeper). The nine prototypes were delivered in October 2005, and acceptance trials were completed in March 2006. The first thirty were delivered late in 2006, and two were deployed with UAE troops in Afghanistan. Thales UK hopes to sell it to the Royal Navy, and it was successfully tested by the German navy in 2008. It flew at the 2009 Paris Air Show, the first UAV to do so. The system consists of a ground station and two air vehicles, which use a C-band data link. The ground-control and mission-planning elements are network-based. Schiebel has displayed S-100 with a lightweight multirole missile (LMM) on each side; LMM is derived from the Short Blowpipe/Javelin/Starstreak family. The S-100 first flew in mid-2004. Schiebel opened a plant with an annual capacity of 100 to 150 Camcopters in 2006, but it is not clear that anything like that many (if any) were being ordered. Data: rotor diameter 3.40 m, length 3.09 m, takeoff weight 200 kg, payload 50 kg. Empty weight is 100 kg. Endurance is 6 hours (with 55-lb payload), ceiling 18,000 ft, speed 120 kt. The power plant is a 55-hp Wankel engine.

A smaller Camcopter 5.1 has been used to evaluate antiterrorist defenses and used by the U.S. Army to detect land mines. It has been bought by the U.S. military (three systems for the U.S. Army, presumably only for trials), France, the Egyptian navy (two Mk 2 systems), and the German army (selected for its airborne minefield surveillance technology program). Thales bought three systems for payload demonstrations. Camcopter 5.1 superseded an earlier Camcopter 5.0 in 1998 (more powerful engine, wheeled landing gear, reconfigured ground control), and a Mk 2 was announced early in 2000. Main rotor diameter is 3.09 m, fuselage length is 2.50 m, and weight is 68 kg (payload 25 kg including fuel); endurance is 6 hours (cruising speed 49 kt, mission radius 5.4 nm with standard data link), ceiling 10,000 ft (hover ceiling 5,600 ft).

Mk 2 has a 38- rather than 22-hp engine, offering a greater hover ceiling (12,500 ft) and more power, plus, eventually, a satellite link.

Belgium

The Belgian army bought the Belgian-made Épervier battlefield drone, developed to meet a NATO requirement formulated in March 1964. It was demonstrated on 24 April 1965 (X-1 prototype version), and on 11 July 1969 the Belgian government offered financial support for development. Épervier was reportedly based on an unsuccessful U.S. Radioplanes design (RP-99 of 1962). A first series of forty-three was ordered in 1974 and delivered in 1976, equipping two platoons of the Belgian army in Germany. Asmodeé, a non-NATO export version, attracted no sales. Épervier last flew operationally on 3 September 1999 and was replaced by B-Hunter. It is retained here to show the continuity between the efforts of the 1960s and current systems. Épervier was a cropped-delta with vertical surfaces at its wingtips (and a conventional vertical tail), powered by a small jet engine (110-lb-thrust Lucas CT 3201). Control was by autopilot with radio remote control. Sensors were day or night film cameras (for night operation Épervier could carry sixteen flares); alternatively Épervier could carry an IR linescan or a low-light level television camera, both offering real-time transmission. Span was 1.72 m, length overall 2.38 m, takeoff weight 147 kg (payload 20 kg), endurance more than 25 minutes (meaning that it could not loiter). Effective range was about 50 nm. Cruising speed was 270 kt (310 mph, or 500 km/hour). The manufacturer was MBLE (Manufacture Belge de Lampes et de Matériel Electronique), which had participated in earlier Belgian avionics programs.

Canada

After having gained experience with a variety of UAVs, in 2008 Canada announced a competition for a next-generation Joint UAV Surveillance and Target Acquisition System (JUSTAS) initially for a high-performance UAV for use in Afghanistan. The candidates are Predator A, Heron, and Hermes 450.

Canadair (later Bombardier) was responsible for a standard NATO reconnaissance drone, CL-89/289.

Camcopter S-100 at the 2009 Paris Air Show. (Norman Friedman)

Both are preprogrammed recoverable drones using film. Canada, Germany, and the UK teamed to buy the CL-89 Midge (USD-501 in the AN-series of designations), sharing 282 drones. Canadair had begun work in 1961, initially with Canadian and British funding. Germany joined the program in 1965 (flight tests began in 1964). Production began in the early 1970s. CL-89 looked more like a missile than a drone, with cruciform flying surfaces. In all, twenty systems, forty launchers, and more than five hundred drones were made for Canada, Germany, the UK, Italy, and France. They set the pattern for the current CL-289. CL-89 was a division-level recoverable drone carrying a day or night camera, launched from a ramp by booster rocket. It was powered by a Williams WR2-6 turbojet (125-lb thrust) and had a wingspan of 0.94 m and a length of 3.73 m; weight was 108 kg (payload 17–20 kg). Maximum speed was 400 kt, ceiling 10,000 ft, range 32 nm (38 nm with extended-range fuel tank), and endurance 12 minutes. The Midge was deployed to the Gulf in 1991 by the British army.

The next-generation CL-289 PIVER (Programmation et Interprétation des Vols d'Engins de Reconnaissance) or USD-502 is a somewhat larger (span 1.32 m, length 3.61

m, 220 kg), faster derivative; ceiling is reduced to 3,900 ft; range is 108 nm (endurance 40 minutes). In this project Canadair was teamed with the German Dornier company. The CL-289 was developed as a trinational project by Canada, France, and Germany, entering French and German service (Canada decided not to procure it). The PIVER became operational with the German Army in 1990 and with the French in 1992. About 1995 the French 7th Artillery Regiment had four PIVER batteries (54 air vehicles). These drones operated over the former Yugoslavia, typically flying 400-km missions lasting 30 to 40 minutes, relaying their imagery back by data link as long as they were in line-of-sight contact, then storing it on film. French CL-289s operated in Afghanistan in 2001–2. The Italian army replaced its CL-89s with CL-289s in 2002 (its 20 CL-289s were part of its commitment to the new European Rapid Reaction Force). In January 2001 EADS Dornier received a NATO contract to upgrade 160 French and German PIVERs with GPS and improved flight software; deliveries began in April 2003. This version uses a digital data link and offers nearly online distribution and exploitation of the IR imagery collected by the drone. By 2007 French and German CL-289s had exceeded one

CL-289 drone test-fired at the German Meppen firing range, August 1986. (U.S. Army)

thousand flights; the French did not expect to replace this system until 2011–12.

Canadair/Bombardier also produced a series of helicopter UAVs (CL-227 Sentinel/Puma, CL-327 Guardian, and CL-427). They seem not to have attracted any sales.

China

Chinese firms have developed (or proposed) numerous tactical UAVs, whose operational status is unknown. In 2008 the Israel Defense Forces' air force used one or more Chinese UAVs to develop anti-UAV tactics to deal with potential threats from UAVs (Hezbollah flew an Iranian-supplied Ababil down the Israeli cost in November 2004, the flight being neither detected nor intercepted). In 2009 it was reported, not entirely credibly, that China was trying to buy South African UAV technology through the China New Era Corporation. Denel has claimed that China tried to acquire its A-Darter air-to-air missile (although there was no sale, Denel claims that the Chinese PL-ASR is nearly identical to A-Darter in external

design). The designs of interest to the Chinese are apparently Seraph and Bateleur, which the article quoted refers to as Angel and African Eagle.

Ten different UAV models were displayed at Zhuhai 2006, including the Tianyi (Sky Wing) and Xianglong (Soaring Dragon) high-altitude reconnaissance aircraft. Chengdu Aircraft Design Institute/China Aviation Industry Corporation (CADI/CAIC) showed a jet UAV with a joined wing (main wings swept back, tail surfaces swept forward to meet them at the wingtips), with a hump forward presumably housing antennas for data links and perhaps a satellite link. The air intake was over the fuselage, the engine being located in the tail.

In appearance Chengdu's Xianglong HALE is a scaled-down Global Hawk, with the same bulged nose for a satellite link and the same top-mounted engine between vee tails. Estimated Xianlong data: span 25 m, length 14.3 m, weight 7,500 kg (payload 650 kg), range 3,780 nm (speed 400 kt), operating altitude 60,000 ft. In 2006 this aircraft was in the concept design stage; at the air show it

AVIC's Long Haul Eagle HALE aircraft at the 2008 Zhuhai air show. (R. D. Fisher Collection)

was stated that flight testing would begin in 2009 and that the UAV might enter service in two to three years (i.e., 2010–11). A video of taxi tests appeared on the Internet in the fall of 2008. The stated mission is maritime patrol. The name Tien Chi has also been applied to this aircraft.

At Zhuhai 2006 and at the 2007 Paris Air Show the AVIC (Aviation Industry Corporation) export agency displayed a model of a stealthy Anjian (Dark Sword) UCAV. Anjian was designed by the Shenyang Aircraft Design Institute. It is apparently questionable whether it can actually be built by Chinese industry.

Many UAVs were shown at Zhuhai in 2007, ranging from concepts to existing aircraft. They included the CH-3 MALE craft by the China Aerospace Science and Technology Corporation (CASC). Its spokesmen stated that CH-3 had completed tests and was now in production. CH-3 also was described as a UCAV. It is a canard with twin tails and a pusher propeller; it was displayed with AR-1 air-to-surface missiles designed specifically for UCAVs (45 kg with 10-kg warhead, semiactive laser guidance, 8-km range). The configuration is apparently that of the Rutan Vari-Eze home-built airplane, also used for the Indian Rustom-H.

A purported Chinese document leaked in October 2008 described a China Aerospace Science and Industry Corporation (CASIC) program to develop a HALE (like Global Hawk) within two years. This may refer to the Xianglong endurance UAV tested (at least on the ground) by Chengdu Aircraft Corporation (CAC).

CAC displayed models of UAVs under development at the November 2008 Zhuhai show. One such model was shaped like Global Hawk but carried four missiles underwing: two TY-90 lightweight air-to-air missiles and two AR-1s. Also displayed at Zhuhai was a models of CAC's Wing Loong, which was said to be comparable to Pre-dator. It could carry four A2G missiles (not previously described) or two 50-kg precision-guided munitions (presumably comparable to the U.S. SDM). Weight was given as 1,150 kg (payload 200 kg), endurance 20 hours, seed 240 km/hour, and ceiling 5,000 m (16,400 ft). Wing Loong was reported under test. Beijing University displayed a twin-boom pusher tactical UAV. The Dark Sword model was also on display.

Another model at Zhuhai was Warrior Eagle (by AVIC 1), which broadly resembles Western UCAVs such as the X-47B and Neuron. The AVIC 1 stand also showed a HALE resembling Global Hawk (Long Haul Eagle) and Tian Yi-3, described as a conceptual UAV for reconnaissance (it had also been shown in 2006), which resembled Soar Dragon. AVIC 1 includes CAC, which is developing Soar Eagle (taxiing video of which was displayed at the show).

At the November 2002 Zhuhai air show CASIC displayed a micro-UAV similar in configuration to the Israeli Mosquito, a flying wing with roughly semicircular wings, two vertical fins (about halfway along the wing rather than end-plates), and a tractor propeller. Development of three such vehicles, of different sizes, apparently

Anjian (Dark Sword) at the 2007 Paris Air Show. (Norman Friedman)

The CH-3 UCAV at the 2008 Zhuhai air show. (R. D. Fisher Collection)

began in 1999. One of the versions, this time in camouflage, reappeared at the November 2006 show, labeled LT Series. Span was 300 mm (12 in.), weight was not given, but endurance was said to be 30 minutes (mission radius 5.4 nm [10 km], cruising speed 38 kt), ceiling 2,600 ft (800 m). Current status is unknown.

The Harbin Institute of Technology displayed Chinese ducted-fan micro-UAVs in the same class as the U.S. T-Hawk (RQ-16) at the 2005 and 2006 Zhuhai shows.

In addition to these programs, the Chinese have converted numerous fighters into target drones needed to test air-to-air missiles (there is speculation that some of the fighters would be used as decoys in a future attack on Taiwan). They have stated that experience with such conversions taught them how to move from parachute recovery of UAVs to conventional landings. One consequence was that the Chinese lost interest in buying Firebee (or Firefly) UAVs from the United States, presumably during the 1980s, when the United States was willing to export such aircraft.

CH-1/WZ-5

The first Chinese UAV was the reverse-engineered Ryan Firebee (BQM-34N), CH-1 (Chang Hong 1) or WZ-5 (Wuren Zhenchaji, "pilotless reconnaissance"), which follows a preset course and returns with its exposed film. It has no data downlink, but it can be radio controlled using an analog link and analog electronics. Work on it began in 1969, based on Firebees that crashed in China, and the prototype flew in 1972. The prototype seems to have used some material from the crashed drones; two more proto-

types were built entirely of indigenous materials. Small-scale production began in 1981. Reportedly prototypes were used during the 1979 Sino-Vietnamese War. Like its U.S. counterpart, this drone is air-launched, typically from a modified Y-8 transport. Data: span 9.76 m, length 8.97 m, weight 1,680 kg; ceiling over 57,000 ft, range more than 2,500 km (1,350 nm), and cruising speed 800–820 km/hour (432–443 kt). Major development problems were the Doppler navigation system (which measured speed over the ground and draft) and the compact engine. Note that some sources distinguish WZ-5 and CH-1.

The Chinese reverse-engineered the Soviet La-17 as their CK-1 target drone, but unlike the Russians apparently did not develop a reconnaissance version. The split with the Soviets precluded a Chinese version of the Tu-123/143.

ASN-15

Xian Technology's mini-UAV is powered by a piston engine on its parasol wing. It apparently belongs to a later generation than the ASN-104/105 described below, with a (presumably digital) data link. It is hand-launched and belly- or parachute-recovered. The system includes three air vehicles, a control station, and a reception/recording station using a videotape recorder. Data: span 3 m, length 1.8 m, weight 6.5 kg, operating altitude 50–500 m, endurance 1 hour (radius 10 km, speed 90 km/hour).

ASN-104/D-4RD

Development of Xian's analog army surveillance drone began in 1980, followed by a first flight in October 1982

Wing Loong 002 at Zhuhai 2008. (R.D. Fisher Collection)

and limited production beginning in 1985. The air vehicle is similar in configuration to a number of target drones (ASN-7/9, or Ba-7/9), with a conventional tractor design. The configuration recalls that of the U.S. Radioplanes target drones and the related Italian Mirach series. The system consists of a ground-control vehicle and six aircraft. Data: span 4.3 m, length 3.32 m, weight 140 kg (with 18 kg of fuel; payload 30 kg); endurance is 2 hours (range 300 km [162 nm], speed 150 km/hour [81 kt]), and ceiling is 10,500 ft. Remote control range is 60 km. The power plant is a 30-hp HS-510 4-cylinder piston engine. Sensors were film and television cameras, but it is not clear whether the drone could transmit its picture back to a ground station. It was intended for surveillance up to 60 to 100 km from the forward edge of the battle area.

Roughly contemporary with ASN-104 was Xian's D-4RD, designed for aerial survey but also used by the Chinese military. It flew in 1982. D-4RD is normally radio-controlled but can be preprogrammed. Data match those for ASN-104, and it may be an alternative designation for that UAV.

ASN-105B

Xian ASN Technical Group's UAV was exported to Pakistan, where it is currently in service. Presumably a derivative of ASN-104, it uses the same 30-hp engine, but it has a stabilized multimode optronic system using both day and low-light-level television cameras, still film cameras, and

WZ-5 drone. (R. D. Fisher Collection)

an IR linescanner. Data are transmitted by downlink. The operator can associate the downlinked image with a spot on a map on the console. In addition to such images, the UAV returns with video recordings and film negatives. The UAV can use either GPS or the Russian GLONASS navigational satellite system. Data: span 5 m, length 3.75 m, weight 170 kg (payload 40 kg); ceiling 6,000 m, endurance 7 hours (radius 150 km/81 nm at 2,000 m [6,500 ft], maximum speed 200 km/hour[108 kt]). This UAV can be controlled up 100 km (54 nm) from a ground station.

ASN-105B was (or is being) supplanted in Chinese service by ASN-206/207. ASN-105 itself was a target. ASN-106 is either a derivative or an alternative designation for ASN-105B; a photograph distributed by UVSI (and presumably supplied by Xian) shows much the same configuration.

ASN-206/ASN-209

Xian Technology's twin-boom pusher UAV is intended for battlefield surveillance. The system consists of a vehicle for ground control plus six to ten aircraft. Design and prototype construction were completed in December 1994, and ASN-206 was shown at Zhuhai in November 2006; it may currently be in production. Tadiran of Israel may have been involved in this program; ASN-206 broadly resembles Israeli UAVs such as Scout. The sensors are located in a gyro-stabilized turret under the nose, the modular design of which allows for sensor interchange. As an alternative to electro-optical payloads, ASN-206 can carry a JN-1102 EW suite, which can scan, intercept, and jam ground-to-air communications in the 20–500 MHz band. Apparently the intercept system feeds a ground-control station that sets the jammer and activates it. ASN-206 was offered to Turkey late in 1998. Span is 6 m, length 3.8 m, and takeoff weight 222 kg (payload 50 kg). Endurance is 4–8 hours (range 150 km [81 nm]), ceiling 5,000–6,000 m (16,000–20,000 ft), and speed 113 kt (210 km/hour). The power plant is a 50-hp HS-700 4-cylinder piston engine.

ASN-209 is a slightly smaller UAV similar in configuration and operation to ASN-206, with a circular rather than square-section fuselage. A CATIC (China Aero-Technical Import-Export Corporation) brochure distributed at the 2009 Paris Air Show described ASN-209 as a medium-altitude medium-endurance UAV, with a maximum payload of 50 kg.

ASN-207

The ASN-207 is a theater-tactical system intended to operate to a depth of 600 km (324 nm) beyond the battle line. The system employs two identical airframes, one for reconnaissance and the second for communications relay from the low-flying reconnaissance UAV. Both are piston powered. Navigation is inertial/GPS. In addition to the usual EO sensors the reconnaissance UAV has ELINT, radar warning receiver, and ECM elements. Span is 9.3 m, length 6 m, empty weight 250 kg; takeoff weight 480 kg for the reconnaissance version and 410 kg for the relay version (payloads 100 and 30 kg, respectively); ceilings 6,000 and 8,000 m, respectively; endurance is 16 hours (combat radius 600 and 200 km [324 and 108 nm], respectively; speed 180 km/hour [97 kt]).

PW-2

CPMIEC (China Precision Machinery Import-Export Corporation) surveillance and artillery support UAV has a twin-boom pusher configuration. PW-2 was announced at DSEi (Defence Services Exhibition International) 2005 in London as an improved version of the earlier W-50 announced at Zhuhai 2000 (PW-1 was a developed version of W-30). These are all twin-boom UAVs with pusher propellers, PW-1/2 having constant-chord wings without the tapered outer sections of the earlier aircraft. They also have shorter and more rectangular fins and rudders. Landing gear is twin skids. Guidance is described as autonomous, with a GPS mode, with real-time image and telemetry transmission. CPMIEC stated that W-30, W-50, and PW-1 were all in Chinese military service as of 2005. The PW-2 was shown at Zhuhai in November 2008, so presumably it was in service by that time. Takeoff weight is 210 kg (maximum payload 30 kg). Endurance is 6–7 hours (endurance speed 140–160 km/hour [76–86 kt]) and ceiling is 4,600 m (15,000 ft). Mission radius is 200 km (108 nm).

SH-1

A model of the SH-1, a flying-wing jet UAV or UCAV, broadly similar to models of the European Neuron, appeared at the 2008 Zhuhai show (November 2008). A blurry photo from the 2006 show may also be of this UAV, or of its model.

SW-1

AVIC distributed a brochure describing the SW-1, a twin-boom pusher UAV, at the 2009 Paris Air Show. Data: span 4.179 m, length 2.465 m (not including pitot tube projecting forward), weight 85 kg (payload 16 kg). Endurance is 2 hours (radius 80 km [43 nm], presumably data-link range; maximum speed is 160 km/hour [86 kt], cruising speed 80 km/hour [43 kt]). Ceiling is 3,000 m (about 10,000 ft). The illustration was a painting, so it is not clear whether SW-1 actually exists.

SW-6

AVIC distributed a brochure describing the air-launched SW-6 at the 2009 Paris Air Show. Like some earlier U.S. projects, the UAV has a cylindrical body suited to weapon

ASN-106 mini-UAV. The ASN-105B is similar.

dispensers. After being dropped by a fighter, it descends vertically by parachute until it reaches deployment altitude. It has two sets of tandem wings, the forward wings being stowed atop the fuselage and the after wings folding to fit under it. The tail surfaces seem to be stowed around the after end of the body. The illustration in the brochure suggests UAVs radiating toward a stealthy U.S. aircraft carrier (an abandoned concept), presumably locating it for strike aircraft. Data: span 2.4 m (rear wings 2.39 m), length 1.6 m, weight 20 kg (payload 5 kg). Endurance is 1.5 hours (cruising speed 80 to 100 km/hour [43 to 54 kt]). Cruising altitude is given as 1,000 m (about 3,300 ft). All illustrations in the brochure are paintings or drawings, so it is not certain that SW-6 is more than a concept.

U8E

CATIC's main brochure distributed at the 2009 Paris Air Show included a photograph of the U8E, an unmanned helicopter that broadly resembles the U.S. Fire Scout. Maximum payload is 40 kg. Endurance is 4 hours. No other details were given. The same brochure carried photographs of ASN-209.

WZ-9/WZ-2000

CAIC's WZ-9 (Wu Zhen-9, meaning "unmanned vehicle") was first shown in model form in 2000. During the show it was renamed WZ-2000. The model showed a jet with a delta wing and a vee tail, the twin-turbojet power plant lying above the fuselage and between the canted vertical tails (in the revised design later adopted it is a single WS-11 turbofan buried in the after fuselage). The low wing was blended into the bottom of the fuselage. Sensors were an IR camera and SAR radar, relaying data via Satcom, the antenna for which is in a bulging nose (the original model showed a sharply tapered nose). All of this suggests similarity to Global Hawk, but on a far smaller scale. CAIC showed another model at Zhuhai 2002 (bulged nose, swept wing instead of delta), and a more accurate one at Zhuhai 2004. WZ-2000 first flew on 26 December 2003, the remote sensing system being tested successfully in August 2004. Data: span 9.8 m, length 7.5 m, weight 1,700 kg (payload 80 kg); ceiling 18,000 m (59,000 ft), endurance 3 hours (speed 800 km/hour [430 kt], combat radius 800 km [496 miles]). An improved WZ-2000B is reportedly under development. Note that data for the original WZ-9 were for a much smaller UAV: span 3 m, length 4.5 m, payload 50 kg (overall weight not given), maximum speed 459 kt.

YILONG

Photos of October 2008 tests of CAC's MALE UAV were shown at Zhuhai in November 2008. It is described as

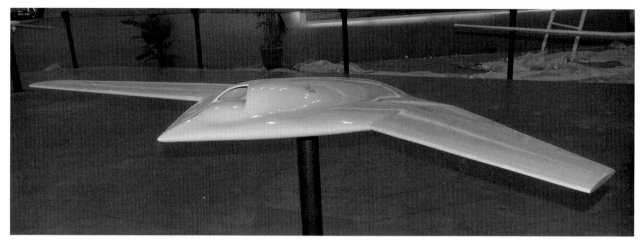

Warrior Eagle Chinese UCAV fighter at Zhuhai 2008. (R. D. Fisher Collection)

similar to RQ-1 (Predator). Development began in May 2005, and the UAV first flew in October 2007. Data: take-off weight 1,180 kg (payload 200 kg); endurance 20 hours (maximum speed 240 km/hour), ceiling 5,000 m. The power plant is a 100-hp turbocharged engine.

Croatia

Croatia developed the MAH-1 UAV in 1991–92 at the time of the civil war, reportedly with Israeli (Malat) assistance; it strongly resembles Malat UAVs. The first version flew in 1992, using film cameras. By 1993 Croatia had a real-time EO version, which was used in the July 1995 Storm offensive (on at least one occasion UAVs dropped pamphlets).

A development program announced in May 1998 called for both a tactical and an operational (presumably MALE) system. Neither seems to have materialized.

Sono ZI's twin-boom pusher B-4 is intended to detect land mines as well as for the usual reconnaissance and artillery support. Span is 6 m, length 4.2 m, takeoff weight 200 kg (payload 50 kg). Endurance is more than 10 hours (endurance speed 120 km/hour [65 kt]), and mission radius is 150 to 200 km (81 to 108 nm).

Czech Republic

VTUL a PVO Praha's twin-boom pusher Sojka (Jay) III/TVM 3.12 is intended for tactical surveillance. Sojka III emerged from a program begun in the early 1980s using UAVs patterned on the new Israeli ones. The E50 target

was tested beginning in 1986, and the E80 target/reconnaissance craft beginning in 1990. Sojka III was considered ready for production in 1993; the developer was formerly the PVO (Air Defense Force) research institute. Hungary joined the program after the dissolution of the Warsaw Pact but did not buy any systems. The Czechs were responsible for the air vehicle, payload, and launcher, the Hungarians for the ground-control station. The Czech army operationally evaluated the system in 1995, it took part in air defense exercises in 1996, and it was fully operational in 1998. The upgraded TVM version entered service in 2001. At least one system was operational during the Duha air defense exercise (1996). An upgrade project began in 2004. It is to provide a modular payload. Span is 4.5 m, overall length is 3.8 m (fuselage length 2.5 m); takeoff weight is 145 kg (empty weight 97 kg, payload 25 kg). Endurance is 4.5 hours (mission radius 100 km, endurance speed 160 km/hour), ceiling 4,000 m. The power plant is a 36-hp gasoline engine. This UAV has landing skids rather than wheels. Each system includes three or four air vehicles. Sojka III/TVM 3.12 is used by both the Czech army and the Czech air force.

Track System announced the Heros helicopter UAV at a NATO Day exhibition in September 2008 (development began in 2007). It uses coaxial rotors and hence has no tail rotor. Heros uses a proprietary Track System flight-control system as well as an "advanced" anticollision system claimed capable of recognizing objects as small as 10 cm. Rotor diameter is 4.21 m, length 4.675 m,

WZ-2000 at the 2002 Zhuhai air show. (R. D. Fisher Collection)

Sojka III disassembled for transport at Waddington, 4 July 2009. (South Wales Aircraft Group)

weight 465 kg (payload 120 kg), endurance 4 hours (maximum in hover, 2.5 hours; maximum speed 97 kt, cruising speed 75 kt, mission radius 135 nm).

Finland

The Finnish army operates the Patria mini-UAV, part of the Mini-UAV Modular Airborne Sensor System (MASS). Patria was apparently conceived in 2004, was first shown at the 2006 Paris Air Show, and was ordered in quantity in June 2007. Although plans called for buying one MASS (six UAVs), Finland eventually bought two systems (five UAVs each). An earlier program was deferred due to the high cost of the F/A-18 fighters Finland bought; the alternatives were the U.S. Outrider, Oerlikon Ranger, SAGEM Sperwer, and MATRA Tucan, of which Ranger was declared the winner in August 1999 after 1998 tests.

The Patria UAV has a conventional configuration with a high wing, a vee tail, and a propeller in its tail. Span is 1.5 m, length 1.05 m, weight 3 kg (empty; payload 0.5 kg), endurance 60 to 75 minutes (operating range 10–15 km, maximum speed 120 km/hour, cruising speed 60 km/hour), and operating altitude is 50 to 150 m (about 150 to 500 ft). Payloads include nuclear and biological sensors, and all versions include a fixed see-and-avoid camera. A system includes one to three UAVs and can be operated by two personnel.

France

Sometime in the 1960s Aérospatiale developed a reconnaissance drone version (R 20) of its CT 20 jet target, which was produced between 1958 and 1962 (Sweden

used CT 20 as the basis of its Rb08 naval antiship missile). CT 20/R20 resembled a small jet fighter, with wingtip pods and a vee tail (plus a ventral vertical tail surface). It was considerably smaller than a fighter: span 3.72 m over the pods, length 5.71 m, launch weight 850 kg (plus boosters; payload 150 kg). Operating altitude was 200 to 10,000 m (660 to 32,800 ft; typical altitude was 1,000 m), and operating radius at low altitude was 86 nm (160 km). R 20 could carry standard NATO cameras; typically it was equipped with three cameras to capture a swath of territory (it could photograph 77 square miles during one sortie). A reference to a radio data link suggests the alternative use of a linescan or television sensors. Over-target accuracy at a range of 54 nm from launch was given as 300 m (985 ft). A total of sixty-two were made for the French Army, production ending in 1976. It is not clear whether R 20 was developed to meet the same NATO specification as Épervier. For a time Aérospatiale advertised a reconnaissance version of its follow-on target drone, C 22, but it was not bought.

During the 1991 Gulf War, French forces were supported by the ALTEC Mini-Avion de Reconnaissance Tactique (MART II). They were the only European-built UAVs used during the war. The MART was developed in the 1980s. It was deployed in an artillery platoon of the 8th Artillery Regiment in 1989 and was deployed to Saudi Arabia in February 1991. It carried video, film, IR, or linescan sensors or a jammer or a communications relay package. Span was 3.4 m, length 3.2 m, and weight 110 kg (payload 25 kg); endurance was 4 hours, maximum speed 119 kt (cruising speed 48–65 kt), ceiling 10,000 ft, range

Patria MASS at the 2009 Paris Air Show. (Norman Friedman)

54 nm. The power plant was a 25-hp Meggitt 2-cylinder 2-stroke piston engine. An upgraded MART-S or S-MART (span 3.4 m, length 3.0 m, 144 kg with 30-kg payload, speed 97 kt, range 81 nm) flown late in May 1996, was credited with 7-hour endurance. Based on Persian Gulf experience, the French issued an urgent requirement for the tactical UAV, which became Crécerelle. It was a modified Banshee target drone. After the Gulf War, Altec Industries bought the rights to MART and advertised a MART II; apparently there were no takers.

As of 2003 the French expected to have an interim MALE they called SIDM (Système Intermédiaire de Drones MALE) to replace the existing Hunter early in 2004. They chose the Israeli Heron (see that entry). At that time it was expected that the full MALE would be delivered in 2010, as many as twelve air vehicles being required. The Netherlands was invited to join the program. This program collapsed into the larger European one described in the International section. In 2008 Dassault, Thales, and Indra (Spain) announced a modified IAI Heron TP they called SDM (Système de Drone MALE). In February 2009 it was announced that three SIDM systems would be deployed from Bagram, north of Kabul. These aircraft are operated by the French air force (the smaller Sperwer is operated by the army).

French companies have also published sketches of HALEs: Aerospatiale's Frégate and SAROHALE, and a Dassault HALE. As of about 2005, the French military intelligence directorate wanted five HALE systems in service by 2012. There is also interest in a long-endurance UAV to support the antimissile version of the SAMP-T (Aster missile) air defense system. Late in 2006 Délégation Générale pour L'Armement (DGA) invited proposals for MIRADOR (Moyen Infra-rouge Aéroporté pour la Détection et Observation Rapide antimissile).

French thinking about the lower end of the scale is indicated by a September 2005 DGA presentation on small UAVs to be used for "contact combat." The presentation distinguished small UAVs (handled by two soldiers, endurance 1 hour 30 minutes, UAV weight less than 10 kg, range 10–15 km) from mini-UAVs (endurance 15 to 45 minutes, weight less than 5 kg, size less than 70 cm, range 1 to 3 km) and from micro-UAVs (range 100 m, weight less than 0.05 kg, size less than 15 cm). Plans called for a possible DRAC II successor to enter service about 2012; it might be a VTOL. The existing Hover-Eye demonstrator would be succeeded by a MAVDEM (demonstration mini-UAV), then by a demonstrator about 2010. About 2015 an Urban mini-UAV might enter service, followed by a micro-UAV from 2020 onward.

The first DRAC contract had just been signed (December 2004). HoverEye was expected to fly in 2005 and to be tested by the French army in mid-2007. Plans called for a mini-UAV operational demonstrator to lead to an operational mini-UAV system in 2015, based on results and experience gained with HoverEye, MAVDEM, DRAC, some DGA-funded several mini-UAV contests and a program to develop avionics for mini-UAVs (SUAV). In 2005 DGA hoped to begin a three-year program, based on army requirements, in 2009. In addition to the more or less conventional craft described, DGA sponsored a flapping-wing nano-UAV demonstrator (MAV4G-1) beginning in 2003, using wings powered by artificial muscles (span 6 cm, weight 0.12 g, 180,000 muscles/wing). It had a tandem-wing configuration. A somewhat larger micro-UAV won the French 2005 Science and Defense Award. Work on these ultrasmall UAVs was ongoing.

DGA's Soldier UAV program envisages a DRAC (see below) successor to be fielded about 2010. It is to be part of the Fantassin à Équipements et Liaisons Intégrés (FELIN) infantry system program, which envisages 31,000 systems, of which 22,588 would be provided to French infantry and another 9,000 to supporting arms. Unlike DRAC, the future short-range UAV would feed its data into a network that would carry them to all interested users. FELIN is roughly analogous to U.S. infantry automation concepts that include individual data links and a tactical picture displayed on the infantryman's visor. Trials began with 350 systems delivered in 2008. A typical infantryman would carry a 24-kg pack effective for 72 hours, with batteries rechargeable at section level. The three key vehicles are the wheeled VBCI and VAB Revalorisé and the tracked AMX 10P. Related projects include UGVs and a nano-UAV. Definition contracts were awarded to Thales and SAGEM in 2002, and in March 2004 SAGEM received a thirty-month development and production contract. Trials of 40 FELIN systems were completed in June 2008, and another 358 delivered (for a nine-month trial) that July. First production deliveries to the first regiment of FELIN troops were planned for July 2009, the first four regiments being complete at the end of 2009, and production to be completed in 2013.

FELIN envisages UAVs to operate at company, platoon, and perhaps even squad level. Initially the baseline was the Bertin HoverEye (mission radius 1.1 nm, speed 19 kt [10 m/second; loiter speed 5.5 kt], endurance 0.5 hour, duct diameter 40 cm, overall height 60 cm, weight 3.5 kg, payload 0.2 kg, for a day or night [uncooled] camera), which was designed to operate with mechanized infantry. It uses ducted contraprops for lift; after taking off vertically it flips over for flight, the pod leading the wing-propeller. HoverEye is fully stabilized, responding to high-level navigation commands (i.e., need not be remotely flown); it has a radar collision avoidance system. Bertin began work on such UAVs in 1999. The prototype Smart Ball (2001) was too vulnerable to gusts, but DGA supported work leading to the more stable HoverEye, which appeared in 2004. HoverEye is the basis for the SAGEM-Bertin ODIN system.

The French may have decided to buy Novadem's NX110m, developed in cooperation with the Institut Polytechnique of Grenoble, instead of ODIN. The NX110m was one of two MAVDEM candidates, the requirement being higher speed (20 m/second, 39 kt). It uses four sets of propellers to maintain stability in flight, and was displayed at Eurosatory 2006 show. NX110m weighs less than half a kg (payload 90 g), has an effective range of 1 km (endurance 25 minutes on battery power). The sensor is a color TV camera. The less successful competitor was a more conventional helicopter with contraprops.

Bertin also offers the smaller Mini-Rec.

SAGEM also offers a Merlin light UAV for missions in open terrain. It has an unusual twin-boom configuration with tandem wings, small tails, and a short centerbody carrying an underslung sensor turret. An electric motor provides power, presumably driving a pusher propeller on the centerbody (illustrations are unclear). Span is 1.6 m, length 1 m, weight 6 kg (payload 0.8 kg), endurance more than an hour (cruising speed 55 to 75 km/hour, range [set by downlink] about 7 km). SAGEM claims that the tandem wings make for a square configuration that is particularly robust.

ONERA (Organisations Nationale d'Études et Récherches Aérospatiales), the French defense research organization, produced a Mirador mini-UAV in the same class as the Israeli Mosquito and the U.S. Wasp. Its unusual feature is the use of fuel cells to power its electric motor

HoverEye mini-UAV. (Bertin via UVSI)

(endurance is 20 minutes). Span is 25 cm (0.25 m), length is 25 cm, there is no autopilot (Mosquito and Wasp both have autopilots), and range is more than 1 km (compared to 2 km for Wasp and 1.5 km for Mosquito).

At Eurosatory 2008 (June 2008) Thales displayed an ultralight (less than 1 kg) Spy Arrow, which appeared to be a model airplane (illustrations show a dummy cockpit). Thales claimed that it was fully autonomous, and hence could be deployed by a single operator without special training, and that it could carry day or night cameras or NBC detectors. The configuration may be intended to fool enemy troops into thinking it is a more distant real airplane.

In addition France is participating in a MAVDEM program with Italy, Norway, and Spain.

As of 2003 the French navy hoped that in 2006 it could begin a maritime VTOL UAV program, Drone Maritime Tactique, for use on board the new multimission FREMM frigates. In December 2006 DGA released a request for proposal for a DVI (drone VTOL Interarmées, i.e., "interservice"). Contenders include Orka (see below), the Thales (teamed with Boeing) Little Bird (a UAV version of the MD-530), and the SAGEM/Bell Textron Eagle Eye tilt-rotor.

CRÉCERELLE/SPERWER

SAGEM developed the Crécerelle (Kestrel) under a 1993 contract on the basis of the Meggitt Banshee target drone. It was based on SAGEM's proposed ATAOS (autonomous tactical attack and observation system). Crécerelle entered French army service in 1994, and it supported French forces in Bosnia (deployed November/December 1995) and during the 1999 Kosovo war. The French fielded two platoons and a total of twelve air vehicles. In 1999 the French Ministry of Defense awarded a contract for additional Crécerelles to form a UAV communications-jamming platoon. France lost three Crécerelles and two CL-289 drones during the Kosovo war. The Crécerelles and PIVERs were transferred to the 61st Artillery Regiment beginning 1 July 1999. French operations in Macedonia alongside CL-289s and German LUNAs showed the need for additional speed and range.

Crécerelle became the basis of the Dutch army's Sperwer-A (CU-161), winning a 1995 Dutch competition to acquire long- and medium-range UAVs. Unlike Crécerelle, Sperwer had twin vertical tails and larger air intakes feeding an improved power plant. Meggitt sells a target drone with a similar configuration as Spectre. Deliveries began in 2002 (four systems, each with three

Novadem quad-copter UAVs. The military version is on the right. (Novadem)

air vehicles [early reports claimed nine air vehicles per system]). Dutch Sperwers deployed to Afghanistan in December 2006, at least two air vehicles being lost. The name means "kestrel" or "sparrowhawk."

The French DGA then competed a next-generation SDTI (Système de Drone Tactique Intermediare); Sperwer-A won against Matra (offering the CAC Ranger) and Silver Arrow. Plans originally called for fifteen systems, each with a ground station and three air vehicles, plus an overall reserve of five air vehicles. Later this was scaled down to four systems and eighteen air vehicles. Service trials were conducted in 2003, two systems being delivered for troop trials in 2004. The system was formally accepted into service by the 61st Artillery Regiment in April 2006, replacing Crécerelles. The regiment has two batteries of CL-289 PIVER drones and two of Sperwer-A. Each of the latter has two systems and nine air vehicles. France later bought six secondhand Sperwers from Canada and ordered three more from SAGEM in June 2009. As of the fall of 2009, France was operating four Sperwer UAVs and one launcher in Afghanistan. As of November 2009, of eighteen Sperwer deployed to Afghanistan, seven had been disabled. One complaint was that the optronic window (bubble) could be damaged both by catapult launching and by landing in rough terrain.

The 2003–9 French defense program envisaged development of a new multirole UAV, the MCMM (Multi Capteurs Multi Missions) and a new long-endurance reconnaissance UAV. This program was deferred and renamed SDTT (Système de Drone Tactique Terrestre). As an approach to MCMM, at the 2005 Paris Air Show

SAGEM displayed a Sperwer carrying a Rafael Spike antitank missile, and it showed an armed Sperwer-B at Eurosatory 2006 (see also Surveyor, below). Flight tests of a longer-range Sperwer-B began in June 2006, and that year SAGEM received a contract from Finland to demonstrate Sperwer-B armed with Spike as a hunter-killer UAV. As of 2003 the French Army hoped to buy eighty MCMM aircraft, but the program collapsed.

Merlin light UAV. (SAGEM)

Thales' Spy Arrow being launched by a soldier. (Thales photo by Bernard Rousseau)

Sperwer on its launcher at the 2009 Paris Air Show. (Norman Friedman)

Sweden ordered three Sperwer systems late in 1997 under the designation Ugglan (Owl; the first was delivered in 1998, the other two in 1999). The Swedes considered this a battalion- or brigade-level system. Denmark bought Sperwer (three systems, ten air vehicles), which became operational in 2001. After problems experienced in Iraq in 2006, they were sold to Canada. Canada had also bought two systems (six air vehicles) directly from France in 2003. France is replacing its current Sperwers with the type operated by Canada. Greece bought Sperwer from France in 2002 (for delivery in 2003–4), eight air vehicles being delivered (four per year).

France used Crécerelle in Bosnia in 1993–96 and in Kosovo in 1998–99. French forces used Sperwer in Lebanon in 2006 and possibly also in Kosovo in 2007. Canada and the Netherlands have used Sperwer in Afghanistan.

As of 2009 a longer-range Sperwer Mk II or Sperwer-ER was being marketed, with improved performance, updated sensors, and better deployability. It has a 6.2 rather than 4.2 m wingspan and has been shown (as

Sperwer-B) with canard control surfaces. Both the longer wings and the canard surfaces were developed for the HV version. In 2009 SAGEM claimed that it had delivered more than twenty systems and more than 120 aircraft to five users, three of which had deployed Sperwer to Afghanistan: Canada, France, and the Netherlands.

A SAGEM-Dassault consortium was created to develop Sperwer-HV (Haute Vitesse), which was first shown at the 2001 Paris Air Show. Intended as a deep penetrator, it is turbojet powered (Sperwer uses a propeller), for greater speed, allowing it to penetrate defended areas. Competitors included the EADS Italian CARAPAS, evolved from Mirach. Plans called for buying fifteen systems and about eighty aircraft during the 2003–9 program, but in the summer of 2004 DGA deferred MCMM pending experience with the new Sperwer. DGA let a contract to SAGEM in 2006 to study a UCAV distinct from Neuron.

Crécerelle data: span 3.30 m, length 2.75 m, takeoff weight 115 kg (empty weight 45.4 kg), payload 35 kg. Endurance is 3 hours (speed 135 kt, mission radius 80 km), ceiling is 10,000 ft. Transmission range is 50 km.

Configuration: cropped delta wing, single vertical tail, cylindrical body, and pusher propeller. The power plant is a 25-hp WAE 342 rotary engine.

Sperwer/Ugglan data: span 4.21 m, length 3.51 m, take-off weight 330 kg (payload 45 kg). Endurance more than 6 hours (speed 90 kt, mission radius up to 180 km), ceiling 15,000 ft. The power plant is a 65-hp 2-stroke engine.

Sperwer-B data: span 6.8 m, length 3.9 m, takeoff weight 350 kg, payload 100 kg. Endurance is 12 hours (endurance speed 80 kt), and ceiling is 20,000 ft. The power plant is a 70-hp engine. Line-of-sight data-link (Ku-band) range is 150 km. Beyond the line of sight Sperwer-B can use a satellite link. Unlike Sperwer, Sperwer-B has canard foreplanes.

Sperwer-LE (long endurance) data: span 6.5 m, length 3.5 m, weight 350 kg (payload 100 kg, as in Sperwer-B). Endurance is 12 hours at 20,000 ft. This is essentially Sperwer-B without the canard foreplanes, but with similar performance. It can carry over 60 kg of weapons (e.g., the Spike antitank missile). Sperwer-LE first flew in 2001.

ORKA 1200

EADS' helicopter UAV is intended for shipboard use. It is a contender for the French interservice VTOL UAV competition. The French navy experimented with the Canadian CL-227 Sentinel in the summer of 1995, but the effort lagged and was restarted in the fall of 2002 when DGA ordered the ONERA research organization to study two possible maritime UAVs, one for carriers and large amphibious ships and the other for frigates. At that time it hoped to have a UAV ready for deployment in 2012. Late in May 2005 DGA issued an RFP for a "Devil" helicopter UAV suitable for both army and navy, with hopes of having a deployable system by 2008. Requirements included 700-kg takeoff weight, 150-kg payload, endurance of 14 hours, and a speed of 90 kt. By this time the large-ship and frigate requirements had merged.

Orka is derived from the small Cabri G2 helicopter. EADS is teamed with Vertivision, a consortium of Eurocopter and Hélicoptères Guimbal. Rotor diameter is 7.2 m; fuselage length is 6.22 m. Takeoff weight is 680 kg (payload 180 kg). The helicopter carries an EO/IR ball under its nose and a radome under its belly. Endurance

Orka 1200 helicopter UAV. (EADS)

is 8 hours (speed 195 km/hour), and ceiling is more than 3,600 m. Reportedly Orka 1200 may be adopted by the German navy in preference to the Seamos UAV previously evaluated and dropped. It is derived from a light helicopter made by Helicopter Guimbal of France.

PATROLLER/BUZARD

SAGEM's long-endurance surveillance UAV was shown at Paris in June 2009; it first flew on 10 June. As of the Paris Air Show there was no formal program behind it. Patroller is apparently related to the earlier Buzard, which was advertised for maritime surveillance. Span is 18 m, weight 1,100 kg, endurance 25 hours, cruising speed 150 kt. Buzard was an optionally piloted powered sailplane with a tractor propeller (the Patroller shown in Paris had no cockpit). A brochure described Buzard and later Patroller as a collaborative effort between SAGEM, ONERA, and the German firm Stemme (which makes high-end light aircraft), a flying laboratory for future UAV development. In addition to its main fuselage bays, Buzard can carry two wing pods. The positions of objects on the ground are given with an average accuracy of 20 m, moving targets can be tracked, and onboard time-difference analysis of imagery conducted, so that the UAV can return to an area of interest. Span is 23 m, weight is 980 kg (payload 180 kg), endurance is 18 hours (10 hours on average, or 20 hours at a range of 125 miles [200 km] and an altitude of 25,000 ft; cruising speed is 150 km/hour). Range is more than 5,000 km (2,700 nm); ceiling is 26,000 ft.

Patroller at the 2009 Paris Air Show, with Sperwer under its wing. (Norman Friedman)

SCORPIO

EADS' small battlefield surveillance helicopter is made in conjunction with SurveyCopter. In 2004 Scorpio 6 became the first UAV ever demonstrated at a British civil airport (Aberporth, which had been designated a UAV center of excellence). Originally it was characterized as a technology demonstrator and as a complement to the company's Tracker (DRAC). EADS considers vertical flight and hovering capability particularly important in urban combat (presumably this was a reason the U.S. military bought T-Hawk). The sensor turret, for either an EO or an IR payload, is gyro-stabilized, and there is a digital data link. The name is sometimes rendered Skorpio. Scorpio 6 data: rotor diameter is 1.8 m, length 1.7 m, weight 13 kg. Endurance is 1 hour (speed 35 km/hour); ceiling is about 7,000 ft. Propulsion is electric.

The Scorpio 30 is a larger version announced in 2002 (rotor diameter 2.2 m, length 2 m, weight 38 kg [payload 15 kg], speed 50 km/hour [27 kt], endurance 2 hours, ceiling about 7,000 ft) for urban and maritime environments (i.e., for operation from small warships).

French forces used Scorpio 30 in Afghanistan, in the Ivory Coast in 2006, and probably also in the Democratic Republic of the Congo in 2006. Scorpio 30 was also sold to undisclosed South American customers, and one system was bought by the UK Ministry of Defence for its joint UAV experimental program. Thirty-eight Scorpios had been sold by mid-2003. One system was delivered to French special forces in 2005. In 2008 EADS reported that a "major Western army" was testing Scorpio 30 for missions including urban warfare.

SurveyCopter markets its own Copter 4, presumably using much the same airframe as Scorpio 30 (but without the fairings of that aircraft): rotor diameter 2.2 m, length 2 m, weight 25 kg (maximum payload 10 kg), endurance 15 hours (cruising speed 40 km/hour), ceiling 5,000 ft, range 8 km. Saudi Arabia acquired some Copter 4s in 2007. As of 2009 SurveyCopter was developing a new data link to extend effective range from 10 to 30 km (16.2 nm), the latter apparently being much preferred by users.

In addition to helicopter UAVs, SurveyCopter produced a fixed-wing UAV, DVF 2000, comparable to DRAC but with a single motor. This twin-boom UAV is driven by a pusher propeller (at the after end of the main body) with folding blades. The bent-wire landing gear extends from the fore ends of the booms. Data: span 3

Scorpio surveillance helicopter. (EADS)

m, length 1.2 m, weight less than 7.8 kg (payload 1 kg), endurance 1.5 hours (cruising speed 60 km/hour, range 4 to 8 km), altitude 8,000 ft.

Saudi Arabia acquired DVF 2000 UAVs in about 2007.

SURVEYOR 600/CARAPAS/SURVEYOR 2500

EADS-Galileo's high-performance jet UAV is a modified Mirach-100-5 airframe (see Italy section) using the same navigational system, but its 2.5-m wing had two hard points for additional sensors or stores. Maximum takeoff weight increases from 340 to 450 kg. It was intended to fill the French army MCMM requirement. The MCMM was conceived as a fast/slow replacement for both Sperwer and CL-289, to be ready by 2010; Surveyor 600 covered the fast (CL-289 replacement) part of the requirement. Unlike CL-289, it could loiter in an area. It could also use its ESM sensors to detect radiation sources worth investigating. Surveyor 600 was announced at the 2003 Paris Air Show, and was still being marketed in 2009. As of 2003 DGA had funded construction of a prototype with a dual ESM and EO/IR payload, to fly during the first half of 2005 (later moved to the end of 2005) in a demonstration program called CARAPAS (Capacité Drone Rapide

Antileurres, or fast antidecoy drone). Because it is based on the same airframe, CARAPAS is analogous to the Italian Nibbio.

Surveyor 600 is powered by a Microturbo TMS 18 engine. Span is 2.3 m, and length is 4.06 m; takeoff weight is 450 kg (payload 65 kg). Range is 400 km, endurance is 3.5 hours, and speed is 260 to 458 kt (also given as Mach 0.25 to Mach 0.65). Operating altitude is 300 to 33,000 ft. The payload includes an underbody radar canoe. Roles include not only the usual surveillance and targeting but also ECM, SIGINT, and sampling and measuring in an NBC environment. Unlike Nibbio, Surveyor 600/ CARAPAS has a real-time data link.

EADS' long-endurance Surveyor 2500 was the slow (Sperwer replacement) companion to Surveyor 600. Announced at the 2003 Paris Air Show, it was based on the DynAero MCR S4 manned light aircraft, which has a tractor configuration. The aircraft would be catapult-launched and runway-recovered. Span is 6.9 m (with upturned wingtips), and length is 5.5 m; takeoff weight 450 kg (maximum payload 100 kg). Endurance is 12 hours at 200 km. The power plant is a rotary engine.

CARAPAS antidecoy drone. (EADS via UVSI)

SAGEM also competed for the MCMM requirement. Note the modified Sperwer described above. In addition beginning in 2002 SAGEM offered a tactical stealth aircraft based on Dassault's AVE Moyen-Duc (see the entry for Neuron, below). It was described as "slow-fast," offering both halves of the MCMM mission in a single versatile aircraft. This aircraft was described as capable of flying at Mach 1.6 but also of loitering at 120 kt for 3 to 4 hours. These figures were probably gross exaggerations; another account credits it with a high speed of 720 km/hour and a low speed of 216 km/hour, not far from figures claimed for CARAPAS; endurance would have been 3 hours, and high-speed altitude about 1,000 ft. A sketch shows a faceted fuselage (for low radar cross section) with straight wings and a vee tail, the intake for the jet engine being atop the body. Weight would have been about 500 kg (payload 50 kg). The SlowFast was never built.

TRACKER (DRAC)

The Tracker mini-UAV is made by EADS. The program is DRAC (Drone de Reconnaissance au Contact), and sometimes the UAV is called DRAC rather than Tracker (the system is based on SurveyCopter's Tracker, developed in partnership with EADS). The configuration is twin-boom (with a tractor propeller in each boom), with a pod above the wing carrying the sensors, flight electronics, and data link. It was conceived as an "extended-range pair of binoculars" using an 8-kg air vehicle. Each system consists of two backpack-carried UAVs, a two-unit ground station, and an automatic tracking antenna. The French army acquired four U.S. Pointers and used them in 2004 in Haiti, acquiring the experience that helped to formulate the DRAC requirement.

When EADS was awarded development of the UAV in March 2005, it was the largest European acquisition program for a close-range battlefield reconnaissance system; Tracker won out over the EMT/Bertin Aladdin, the SAGEM Merlin, and the Thales/Alcore Azimut 2. DGA awarded EADS a contract to develop, test, and manufacture an ultimate total of 160 systems, each employing 2 air vehicles. The initial order was for 25 systems. In July 2008 EADS announced an order for 35 systems, bringing the total to 60. Initial trials (September 2007 to September 2008) were conducted by the French army (mainly the 7th Armored Brigade, 21 aircraft) and by a new brigade intelligence unit (4 DRAC within the 2nd Armored Brigade). Further operational tests were conducted in Kosovo between July and September 2008 by the 1st Marine Artillery Regiment (RAM) within the Multinational Task Force–North (10 DRAC). DRAC has been exported (it was acquired by Saudi Arabia in 2007). DRAC reportedly performed poorly in Afghanistan. In October 2009 design problems, causing interference and motor problems, were reported. At that time 110 DRAC had been ordered and 25 delivered, but it was unclear if the last 50 of the planned 160 would be ordered.

Data: span 3.30 m, length 1.40 m, weight 8.2 kg (payload 1.0 kg), endurance 2 hours (range 19 km, cruising speed 60 mph), ceiling 8,000 ft. Propulsion is electric. DRAC is hand-launched.

Surveyor 2500 jet UAV. (EADS via UVSI)

Germany

Like other NATO countries, Germany became interested in battlefield reconnaissance drones in the 1960s, Dornier working with Canadair in the CL-89/289 programs. Plans originally called for delivery of 11 PIVER (CL-289) battery sets to the German army, the first in 1988; the first was actually turned over on 29 November 1990. Production for Germany was completed in June 1993, the Germans receiving a total of 188 air vehicles and the planned eleven ground stations. Twenty-one vehicles deployed to Kosovo with the German army; they flew 237 missions and suffered five losses. A proposed extended-range KWS-289 (2001) attracted no interest.

Dornier also developed a tethered helicopter UAV, the Peewit (Do-32/34), but it was not adopted. In 1977 the company displayed a model of a UCAV it called UKF (Unbemanntes Kampfflugzeug), its entry in a Federal Defense Ministry competition. Tasks would have been

strike, electronic warfare (including defense suppression), and tactical reconnaissance. The model had a conventional configuration with high wings, a dorsal jet engine, and a vee tail; span was 3.80 m and length 6.50 m. The program was suspended in 1981, but Barrakuda is in effect its successor.

Dornier also displayed mini-UAVs in 1977 and continued to develop them through the 1980s. In 1978 this vehicle was offered for a joint Luftwaffe/Bundeswehr UAV program (antiradar and target acquisition/fire control for artillery); it was also offered to the U.S. Air Force (with partner Texas Instruments) in the German/U.S. Locust antiradar program. Later a version of the drone was offered for attack (as Hornisse, or Hornet) mainly against tanks, and then for the antiradar role. These requirements were still alive as late as 1987, but they never began production programs. However, they were clearly predecessors of the program that produced Tucan. The

Tracker mini-UAV. (EADS)

Dornier drone was a delta with wingtip vertical surfaces powered by a 26-hp pusher-propeller engine. Span was 2.10 m, length 2.0 m, weight 70 kg (payload 15 kg); endurance was 3 hours, ceiling 3,000 m (about 10,000 ft), and cruising speed was 135 kt (190 km/hour); maximum diving speed was 194 kt (360 km/hour). The delta configuration is reminiscent of the Israeli Harpy.

In the 1980s the German Ministry of Defense called for a larger UAV under its KZO (Kleingerät für Zielortung, or small device for target location) program. Dornier offered a version of the Israeli Pioneer. Messerschmitt-Bölkow-Blohm (MBB) offered a UAV it called Tucan (RT-900). After showing two prototypes, MBB flew RT-900 in November 1979 (the follow-on RT-910 was intended for the Locust program). Development flying ended in 1985, three hundred flights having been made. Tucan had straight wings and no horizontal tail; it was powered by a 22-hp pusher piston engine. Span was 3.30 m, length 2.055 m, and launch weight 100–140 kg (payload 30–50 kg); endurance was 4 hours 30 minutes (maximum speed 135 kt [250 km/hour]), and ceiling was about 10,000 ft. Operating radius was 38 nm (70 km/43 miles), including 30 minutes holding time). The KZO version had a circular radome atop the vertical tail for a data link. The stabilized FLIR sensor occupied the nose, with optional onboard processing and recording (but typically using a real-time downlink). For precision navigation Tucan used Rho/Theta radio navigation with map/image correlation. Endurance was given as more than 3 hours 30 minutes, although other details matched those of RT-900. As of 1987 MBB expected to place KZO in service in 1993, but it had not yet received a development contract.

In April 1983 MBB joined with Matra of France to develop a new Brevel reconnaissance system, described as suited to rapidly deployable mobile batteries. Brevel used the MBB Tucan air vehicle and a Matra ground system (Matra was working on the Scorpion mini-UAV for the French government). Brevel in turn became the German-French Eurodrone program, from which France withdrew in 1997. The Germans persisted with Tucan, described at the time as an austere variant of Eurodrone (Brevel).

Presumably the long gap between Eurodrone/Tucan and the programs of the 1980s can be attributed to the collapse of German military funding following the decline of the Cold War in 1989.

From the German point of view the Euro Hawk HALE replaces the ageing navy Breguet Atlantic SIGINT aircraft. Northrop Grumman reportedly hopes that the Germans will also buy Global Hawks with imagery and maritime surveillance payloads. The Germans hope to leverage their Euro Hawk purchase into the creation of a European center of excellence for HALE operations at Schleswig-Jagel, which could become an important part of the new NATO Alliance Ground Surveillance (AGS) initiative. It in turn might employ both Advanced UAV and Agile UAV (Barrakuda follow-on) demonstrators.

The most important current German requirement is apparently a MALE, SAATEG (Systeme für die Abbildende Aufklärung in der Tiefe des Einsatzgebietes, or System for Imaging Reconnaissance in the Depth of the Battle Zone [also rendered in-theater imaging reconnaissance system]). In effect the SAATEG MALE fills a gap between the Euro Hawk HALE and KZO. For some years the German government has sought a UAV replacement for the Tornade manned reconnaissance jets currently supporting the ISAF (International Security Assistance Force) in northern Afghanistan; they should have real-time imaging capability. In 2008 two off-the-shelf options were being considered, but in April 2009 both options were dropped by the German defense ministry in favor of leasing. The options had been Predator (offered by General Atomics and Diehl) and Heron TP (IAI–Rhinemetall). The scale of the project is indicated by the possible Reaper (Predator B) sale announced to Congress in August 2008: five air vehicles and four (up from two) mobile ground stations. Requirements reportedly included a ceiling of 40,000 ft and an endurance of at least 24 hours. As of 2008, the winner would have been fielded in 2010, the system reaching full capability in 2012. Predator and Heron are still the likeliest choices, leasing meaning that the Germans will not have to develop as much maintenance infrastructure (or pay as much on a first-cost basis). EADS' advanced UAV (see the International section) is an outside possibility; Heron is favored as a less expensive alternative. Rhinemetall, which would be responsible for the ground station, has argued that a non-U.S. solution will provide better technology access.

About the beginning of 2009 the German arms procurement agency was interested in the WAPEB concept:

an ISR (Intelligence/Surveillance/Reconnaissance) UAV would guide a loitering attack missile to its target, the latter having its own terminal sensor. The observation UAV would be Rhinemetall's KZO. The strike platform might be the Israeli Harpy loitering antiradar missile.

Apart from the specialized antiradar role, the Germans are not currently interested in UCAVs for places such as Afghanistan. However, as the cost of manned aircraft rises, that may change. Although the SPD failed to win in the fall of 2009, its promise to cut the number of Eurofighter wings from five to four suggests that some such cuts are likely in the future. The Tornados are ageing and are poorly suited to the new environment typified by Afghanistan. UCAVs may be quite attractive.

The German navy experimented with a helicopter UAV, Seamos , whose flight elements were based on those of the U.S. Navy's old DASH (QH-50) helicopter drone. Dornier received a development contract in 1992, and shipboard trials began in 2002. The project was canceled in 2003. The German navy has considered both Orka and the U.S. Fire Scout as replacements. The Schiebel Camcopter was demonstrated on board German warships, including a K130 class corvette, in the summer and fall of 2008 (one report has the Germans ordering six S-100s for K130 class corvettes, but that seems premature). These trials were an outgrowth of a partnering agreement between Schiebel and Diehl of Germany. The initial platform would presumably be the K-130-class corvette, which has a shore attack role using RBS 15 missiles and therefore needs a helicopter (but lacks the facilities for a manned aircraft).

ALADIN

The Abbildende Luftgestütze Aufklärungsdrohne im Nächstbereich (airborne reconnaissance drone for close-area imaging, or Aladin) is associated with armored and mechanized reconnaissance units and hence with their Fennek scout vehicle (used by Germany and the Netherlands). EMT's UAV won a German competition and entered low-rate production (six systems) in August 2002; follow-on orders for 115 systems worth $32 million followed in April 2005 (deliveries began that August). Aladin is used by both the German and Dutch armed forces in Afghanistan. The Netherlands acquired an

Aladin Mk 3 reconnaissance drone. (EMT)

initial series of 10 from the German production series specifically to support Afghan operations. The Dutch apparently also ordered 6 systems of their own in April 2006. Norway also bought Aladin. By April 2008 German Aladins had flown more than two thousand missions.

EMT's mini-UAV is electrically powered, with a tractor propeller and a conventional configuration (it has a prominent landing skid). Data: span 1.46 m, length 1.53 m, takeoff weight 3.2 kg. Endurance is typically 45 minutes (15-km range, speed 45–90 km/hour); operating altitude is 100 to 650 ft.

BARRAKUDA/AGILE UAV

EADS financed the Barrakuda as the basis of a future German UCAV to be built around 2020–25; the Germans also used the term URAV (Unmanned Reconnaissance Air Vehicle). EADS saw Barrakuda as an element of its modular approach to developing the necessary technology. The prototype flew on 2 April 2006. Both Spain and Switzerland were also involved in this program. The prototype crashed on 23 September 2006 due, it was said, to problems with its flight-control system. A second prototype completed in November 2008 was flying by late July 2009. Barrakuda may have been the low end of the joint Franco-German-Spanish program to produce a series of twin-turbofan modular UAVs, the high end of which became EADS' Trillium.

The second prototype was built under the "Agile UAV" program to produce an "Advanced UAV" for tactical reconnaissance and strike (a model of the Agile UAV showed twin engines rather than the single engine of Barrakuda). The Advanced UAV, to be about twice the size of Barrakuda, was to have been available in 2010, but that is not possible. Barrakuda uses swept wings and tail surfaces, with its jet engine mounted atop its after fuselage, between tail fins. It has conventional landing gear. EADS suggested that a follow-on could complement or replace Eurofighters as early as 2013–14. Span 7.22 m, length 8.24 m, takeoff weight 3,350 kg (payload 300 kg, empty weight 2,300 kg). The power plant is a P&W Canada JT15D-5 turbofan (650 lbs of thrust). Maximum speed is about Mach 0.85. Ceiling is 20,000 ft.

As of 2009 Barrakuda or the Agile UAV was being touted as a possible successor to the current Tornado ECR for suppression of enemy air defenses. Funding may not, however, be available.

FANCOPTER

The German armed forces ordered two preproduction systems of EMT's VTOL system in 2006 and in 2007, and then a production series (nineteen systems) in October 2008. Fancopter is a "backpack" UAV usable in buildings, due in part to its electric propulsion. Diameter is 50 cm, height is 60 cm, and weight is 1.3 kg; endurance is 25 minutes. When perching (no flight power) the battery can keep internal electronics and the data link alive for more than 2 hours. Mission radius is more than 500 m. The configuration is two unducted rotors above and below the main body, the lower one between three undercarriage legs and the upper one between three guards extending up from the legs, with sensor electronics above and below the rotors. EMT sees Fancopter as a civil as well as a military UAV.

KZO/TUCAN

The KZO/Tucan system is an outgrowth of the earlier Franco-German Brevel program (Eurodrone), from which France withdrew in 1997. The air vehicle is Rhinemetall's KZO (Kleinflugerät für Zielortung, or Small Device for Target Location). It is tailless, with a straight wing, and a circular data-link radome atop the vertical fin. The system is STN Atlas Tucan. KZO development began in 1980, and it first flew in 1995. The tenth KZO system was delivered in 2009. The Tucan order was placed in August 1998.

Barrakuda UCAV at the Berlin air show, 11 July 2006. (Jean-Patrick Donzey)

Each system consists of two ground stations and ten air vehicles; the original plan was for eight systems (eighty air vehicles), but six were bought (sixty air vehicles, twelve ground stations), the first being delivered in November 2005. The first system deployed to Afghanistan in 2006. Span 3.42 m, length 2.25 m, takeoff weight 161 kg (payload 35 kg). Endurance is 3.5 hours (maximum speed 220 km/hour, endurance speed 150 km/hour, mission radius more than 100 km), and ceiling is 11,500 ft. Configuration: tailless with swept wings. The power plant is a 32-hp Schick SF2350S piston engine.

The German government also considered Brevel as a basis for an antiradar drone (Taifun) and a communications jammer (Mucke). Both were abandoned when the 1997 budget was cut. In 2005 Rheinmetall displayed the Tactical Advanced Reconnaissance Strike System (TARES), a modified KZO with an optical sensor and a data link allowing it to attack selected targets. The TARES has a ventral fin. It and the shorter dorsal vertical fin (compared with KZO) carry electronic pods, one or both carrying the antenna of the synthetic aperture radar. The UAV carries a combination shaped charge and fragmentation warhead. Dimensions are different (span 2.26 m, length 2.09 m, and height 1.03 rather than 0.90 m); takeoff weight is reduced to 150 kg. Endurance exceeds 4 hours (mission radius 250 km, speed 145 kt, ceiling 4,000 m).

Although the warhead is integral, TARES is intended to be recoverable in the event it does not strike a target.

Teledyne Brown Engineering licenses KZO in the United States as Prospector.

LUNA X-2000

EMT Penzburg's tactical mini-UAV entered German army service in 2000, initially for artillery targeting (it is assigned to artillery reconnaissance battalions). It was deployed for the first time to support German troops in Kosovo. The LUNA (Luftgestütze Unbemannte Nahaufklärungs-Ausstattung) was a requirement originally set in 1995, calling for a UAV to support ground troops with an effective operating radius of about 10 km. Proposals were due in April 1997, by which time two experimental X-2000 systems had already been tested for brigade support. EMT defeated seven competitors (three German, two French, one British, and one Swedish) to win the LUNA contract in October 1997 (originally the Germans had planned a fly-off between two downselected UAVs, but ultimately they bought only X-2000). The prototype flew in September 1996. X-2000 was first used in Kosovo beginning in March 2000 (174 sorties in support of Kosovo Force [KFOR]). Three systems deployed to Macedonia in June 2002 conducted 139 more sorties in support of a multinational brigade. The X-2000

Fancopter "backpack" UAV. (EMT)

was deployed to Afghanistan in April 2003 (two systems, twenty air vehicles), and it has been used in Iraq. By early 2009 LUNA had flown over 4,300 operational sorties in the Balkans and in Afghanistan. As of 2009 the German army planned to deploy thirteen units, each with four ground-control vehicles and twelve UAVs. In mid-2009 the German army ordered four more systems (forty air vehicles). Sensors are television and FLIR.

Data: span 4.17 m, length 2.36 m, weight 32 kg. Endurance is 4 hours (range 40 km, probably set by data link); ceiling is 4,000 m (13,000 ft). Maximum speed is 160 km/hour (about 80 kt); stall speed is 70 km/hour. Configuration: conventional with high wing and pusher engine on a pylon atop the trailing edge of the wing. The X-2000 is a motor glider, capable of operating silently near a target by turning off its engine, restarting once out of earshot. The LUNA is the only UAV permitted to fly in German civil airspace (over thinly populated areas).

The Pakistani army bought three systems (sale reported March 2006).

A LUNA system comprises ten air vehicles, two launch catapults, and two control stations. Span is 4.17 m, length 2.28 m, weight 40 kg (payload 5 kg); endurance is up to 5 hours (loiter speed 26 kt, cruising speed 38 kt, maximum speed 70 kt), typical operating altitude is 1,640 ft (500 m), ceiling 4,000 m. Mission radius, set by data-link range, is 54 nm. Glide ratio is 18. The power plant is a 6-hp piston engine. The payload space has a volume of 10 liters and can accommodate up to five cameras.

EMT Prenzburg also offers the Mikado mini-UAV (span 50 cm, takeoff weight about 0.5 kg, with a mission endurance of better than 15 minutes and a mission radius of better than 500 m). It has a flying-wing configuration, with a tractor propeller and an underslung pod; the sensor is a video camera linked back to the system operator. EMT also offers the Museo helicopter UAV.

SHARC

EADS' Scouting and Hunting Autonomous RotorCraft is not to be confused with the Swedish SHARC UCAV demonstrator. It is a helicopter with contrarotating rotors, development of which began in 2005; it first flew on 14 June 2007. The rotor arrangement is taken from the defunct Seamos (and thus from the old U.S. DASH). SHARC was apparently conceived specifically for the German navy. Takeoff and landing are automatic. The name suggests something more than the reconnaissance system with data link listed for this craft. The SHARC is officially a technology demonstrator. Rotor diameter is 3.20 m, length 2.65 m, weight 200 kg (payload 60 kg); estimated performance: endurance 4 hours, maximum speed 86 kt (cruising speed 54 kt).

KZO tailless drone. (Greg Goebel)

LUNA X-2000 mini-UAV. (EMT Penzburg)

X-13

EMT Penzburg's developmental flying-wing UAV (with a pusher propeller) can be land- or ship-based. It is catapult-launched and net-recovered. The design was announced in 2004 (by September 2004 EMT was flying a half-scale model), but it is not clear when (if at all) a full-scale X-13 flew. Span is 5.10 m, and takeoff weight is 130 kg. Endurance is 6 hours (mission radius 200 km [set by downlink range, without relay], speed 100 to 180 km/hour), and ceiling is 10,000 ft. Speed is 100 to 180 km/hour. The UAV can take off and land in seas up to Sea State 5 (this feature suggests that it is an alternative to the helicopter UAV for the German navy; it seems to have been developed specifically to replace the failed Seamos helicopter UAV for the navy). The sea state is apparently set by the software the UAV uses to track the ship on which it lands. The power plant is a 35-hp heavy-fuel piston engine. Two small vertical control surfaces are located about halfway between centerline and wingtips. The hump housing the engine is surmounted by a small circular data-link antenna, and an EO ball projects from the bottom of the center section. There is also a synthetic aperture radar.

Greece

The Pegasus (E1-79) reconnaissance UAV was developed by the Hellenic Aerospace Industry (HAI or EAB in Greek); development in collaboration with the Hellenic Air Force R&D Center (KETA) began in 1979, and the prototype flew in 1982. Ten systems were produced, Pega-

sus becoming operational by 2003. A redesigned Pegasus II was introduced in 2005, and by 2009 four systems were operational, with another twelve being made. This production may have been intended to meet a December 1995 Greek army request for four UAV systems with an operational radius of 100 km (a modified RFP was released in September 1997). The production of a squadron of Pegasus was announced in August 2001. However, the Hellenic Air Force selected Sperwer in 2002, ordering three systems (delivered beginning late 2004); another two systems were ordered in 2006.

Pegasus I data: span 5 m, length 2.1 m, weight 130 kg, endurance 3.5 hours (maximum speed 160 km/hour, stall speed 75 km/hour).

Pegasus II has improved electronics. Data: span 6.2 m, length 4.3 m, weight 250 kg (payload 50 kg), endurance 15 hours. This is a twin-boom pusher UAV.

In 1986 HAI developed a Telamon jet UAV with Northrop on the basis of the Chukar III target. Maximum speed was 924 km/hour, and range was 740 km, but it was dropped as unaffordable.

India

In 2005 the Indian Aeronautical Development Establishment (ADE of Bangalore) announced plans for three UAVs, in cooperation with IAI Malat: a MALE (Rustom), a tactical UAV (Gagam), and a short-range UAV (Pawan). Rustom is to be developed first under a $100 million program. Gagam is to be derived from the existing (and reportedly troubled) Nishant program, with a 250-

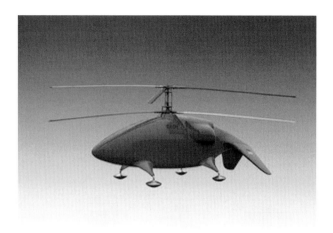

The SHARC helicopter UAV. (EADS)

X-13 developmental flying-wing UAV. (EMT)

km range and 6,000 m ceiling. Pawan (120 kg) is to be similar to the Israeli I-View, Hermes 180, and Silver Arrow. By 2007 the range of UAVs to be developed had extended to HALE and to mini-UAVs, and the Indian navy plans to buy helicopter UAVs for its ships. Also in 2007 the Indian DRDO (Defense Research and Development Organization) announced plans for 100 UCAVs. Design studies were under way, the Indian air force planning a mixture of conventional aircraft and UCAVs. ADE showed unusual configurations, including a tailless aircraft and a B-2-like aircraft, with novel control surfaces and three-axis thrust vector controls (a technology ADE claimed it had mastered). The UCAV was to be capable of high speed and self-defense. It was to be ready by 2020. Also in 2007 the Indian NAL (National Aeronautical Laboratory) was flight-testing micro-UAVs with 30-minute endurance and 2-km flight range, hand-launched (speed over 15 m/second, i.e., 54 km/hour), and with swarm logic.

ADE has been responsible for all Indian drone development. Its first such vehicle was the Ulka air-launched target, seventy-five of which were made beginning in 1975. Work on the Lakshya ground-launched target began in 1986. Lakshya Mk 2 (tested 2009) has a fully digital flight-control system, presumably similar to those in other ADE UAVs. It is fully autonomous. Lakshya has been adapted as a medium-range reconnaissance UAV and, apparently, as a cruise missile (perhaps only in prototype form). The Lakshya UAV was formally inducted into the Indian air force on 17 July 2005, the target version having been delivered in 1999. As of 2007

twenty-seven UAVs were under production by HAL. Of these, twelve were for the Indian Army. Range is 370 miles, ceiling is 29,504 ft, and speed is Mach 0.8. Work on this project reportedly began in 2003.

Nishant is under development by ADE; it has a conventional twin-boom pusher airframe. It first flew in 1995 as a remotely supervised vehicle with waypoint navigation and digital flight control; it made a fully autonomous 4.5-hour flight in 2007. It was considered broadly equivalent to the Israeli Searcher II and could carry either an imaging or an ESM payload. Span is 6.64 m, length is 4.63 m, and takeoff weight is 250 kg (payload 60 kg). Endurance is 4.5 hours (maximum speed 185 km/hour, cruising speed 125–150 km/hour) at 3,600 m, and ceiling is 4,000 m. The power plant is a 52-hp rotary engine. Nishant is credited with a 100-km video downlink and a 160-km command link. As of 2007 mean time between overhauls was 600 hours (200 hours for the engine). A Mk II version is to have 10-hour endurance, the fuel load being increased from 56 to 100 kg by using the wing and booms and by expanding the main fuel tank. This is a wheeled version for conventional takeoff and landing, and it has a new sensor gimbal assembly. The Indian army ordered twelve Nishant systems in October 2005, and in May 2006 it was demonstrated to the Indian coast guard. As of July 2009 Nishant was to have been handed over to the Indian army in the near future.

The original Rustom airframe was derived from ADE's LCRA (Light Canard Research Aircraft) developed in the 1980s by a team led by the late Professor Rustom

Lakshya PTA, 1 November 2008. The underwing objects are targets. (Kaushal Mehta)

Damania, who died in 2001 (after whom it is named); it was apparently a converted Rutan Long-EZ airplane used to develop control technology and subsystems. It was a flying wing with two narrow (long-span) canards at the nose, and with vertical wingtip fins and a pusher propeller. This Rustom-1 offered 12-hour endurance, a ceiling of 20,000 to 25,000 ft, and a 75-kg payload. Rustom-H has a specially designed airframe. Span is 20 m, length is 14 m, and weight is 1,800 kg (payload 350 kg). Maximum speed is 225 km/hour (121 kt), cruising speed is 94 kt, loiter speed is 67 kt, data-link range is 350 km (135 nm), but Rustom is to have a satellite link extending reporting range beyond 1,000 m, and the operating altitude is 30,000 ft (ceiling 35,000 ft). Endurance is more than 24 hours on station at a 1,000-km range from a base. As of 2008 Rustom-H was expected to become operational in 2012. In at least one version, Rustom is to use an Israeli maritime surveillance radar (presumably EL/M-2022) and Israeli optics. India will provide ESM and communications.

At the Aero India 2009 show in Bangalore (February 2009) it was announced that HAL and IAI would cooperate in developing a naval helicopter UAV; the Indian navy had already ordered eight, and a prototype existed. This is probably the NRUAV that IAI displayed at the 2009 Paris Air Show.

In 2007 NPO Saturn of Russia announced that it was supplying India with two hundred miniature turbojet engines (36MT). Possibly in connection with the Saturn program, in 2008 an Indian blog reported that work was proceeding on a jet UAV called Nirbhay (Fearless), which would function both as a fast target and as a reconnaissance UAV with a 130-kg payload for theater-level reconnaissance. The target version would cruise at Mach 0.92 at medium altitude. Span was given as 2.5 m, length as 5.5 m, and takeoff weight as 650 kg. The main reconnaissance sensor is to be an X-band ISAR radar, probably the Israeli EL/M-2060. Plans called for at least thirty UAVs and eighty targets. According to another report, Nirbhay began as an Indo-Israeli feasibility study of an intermediate-range cruise missile, but the Israeli role was later drastically reduced and the project revised from a Tomahawk-like cruise missile (weight about 1,000 kg, speed Mach 0.7, range 300 km greater than that of the Pakistani Babur) to a UAV. It was included in a DRDO presentation, presumably in 2008. The accompanying sketch showed an airframe with a dorsal jet engine, unlike the in-body engine of Lakshya.

Indonesia

In the fall of 2009 Indonesia announced that it would be using a new PUNA (Pesawat Udara Nir-Awak) UAV, made by BPP Teknologi (the government agency for evaluation and application of technology), for surveillance of remote areas; it had already been tested. The main sensor is apparently a camera.

International

France, Germany, and Spain have agreed to fund a joint MALE program beginning in 2010, the first flight to follow in 2013 and the first deliveries in 2015. France and Germany are each to buy six systems, and Spain three; each system includes three air vehicles. The competitors are EADS and Thales. At the 2009 Paris Air Show the German defense minister told his French and Spanish partners that his government was backing out of the project.

EADS displayed a mock-up of its Talarion at the 2009 Paris Air Show. It is apparently derived from the company's twin jet Advanced UAV, initially conceived as a modular UAV with alternative sets of wings for two different missions: long-endurance surveillance and high-speed reconnaissance. The three partners listed above signed an agreement on risk-reduction studies in June 2007. Both versions had a common 10.3 m fuselage; the surveillance version used a 25.25-m span wing (later described as 27.9 m), the fast reconnaissance version a 9.05-m wing. In both cases the power plant was a pair of Williams turbojets. The surveillance version would operate at 46,000 ft with an endurance of 22.5 hours (21 hours over the surveillance zone) and both satellite and line-of-sight communications; speed would be 203 kt.

The alternative fast reconnaissance version would operate at only 1,000 ft, spending 1.75 hours of a total flight time of 2.85 hours over the objective zone, using line-of-sight radio only. Speed would be 361 kt. The difference gives some idea of the performance cost (in endurance) of low-altitude flight, even at what for a jet seems a moderate speed. The shorter-wing version was eventually dropped in favor of the long-endurance MALE, which is now credited with a maximum takeoff weight of 7,000 kg.

Thales leads a team (with Dassault and Indra) offering an Israeli Heron TP airframe with its own electronics. In Paris its representatives argued that neither the Germans nor the Spanish would accept the protracted timetable associated with the EADS airframe.

Neuron (also rendered nEUROn) is a Dassault-led European program to build a high-speed stealthy UAV broadly comparable to the U.S. X-47; the participants are France, Greece, Italy, Spain, Sweden, and Switzerland. The other major airframe manufacturer is Saab. The project was initiated by the French government at the 2003 Paris Air Show, it began formally in 2004, and a mockup appeared at the 2005 Paris Air Show. Formal contracts were let in 2006. The air vehicle is to fly at the end of 2011 (the original target was the first quarter of 2009). Like X-47B, Neuron is to have two internal weapon bays, for weapons up to 500 kg size (e.g., laser-guided bombs). Flight control is to be semiautonomous. Neuron itself is described as a technology demonstrator. Airframe design was frozen in 2009, at which time Dassault claimed that it could enter service in 2020. Flight-control software is based on the fly-by-wire software of the Dassault Falcon 7X business jet. An operational version would be about a third larger, with a newer engine and new electronics. Span 12.5 m, length 9.50 m, takeoff weight 5,000 to 6,500 kg. Endurance is over 12 hours (maximum speed Mach 0.85), and ceiling is 35,000 ft. The power plant is a single Adour 951 turbojet.

Dassault's development effort has produced the AVE-C (Aéronef de Validation Expérimentale) demonstrator and the AVE-D stealth UAV demonstrator. AVE-D (Petit DUC, or little demonstrator) is a cranked delta with two tailfins, angled outboard, powered by a pair of small jet engines. Span is 2.4 m and length is 2.4 m. Takeoff weight is 60 kg (empty weight 35 kg). Radius is about 150 km (speed 600 km/hour). As in other stealthy UAVs, air intakes and exhausts are on top of the wing. The small demonstrators flew in 2000. The follow-ons to AVE-D were a medium (Moyen DUC) and then a large demonstrator. In 2004 DGA made this an official program and awarded a contract to Dassault. It then negotiated the

Talarion at DSEi 2009. (Norman Friedman)

collaborative Neuron project. Moyen DUC made its first autonomous flight on 30 June 2008.

The Neuron team apparently plans a further project: a new European MALE, work on which would begin in 2011–13, leading to a UAV by about 2018–20. Apparently this idea is supported by the European Defense Agency.

Iran

In February 2010 the official Iranian news agency reported that two UAVs, the reconnaissance Nazir (Harbinger) and the bomber Ra'ad (Thunder), had just entered production. The same news release claimed that a radar-evading attack UAV had been tested the previous June. It was described as a one-seventh-scale model of a UAV soon to be produced in full scale. The Iranians also claimed that construction of a factory to mass-produce UAVs had begun in March 2009. Products are to include helicopter UAVs.

According to an Iranian paper published in the 2009 *UAS Yearbook*, a three-man Islamic Revolutionary Guard Corps (IRGC) team demonstrated the value of a UAV to skeptical Pasdaran commanders early in 1984; experience during Operation Khaibar (February 1984) made the need for timely battlefield surveillance more obvious. Presumably deterioration of conventional air reconnaissance assets was an important factor. The reference to the IRGC reflects current Iranian government concentration on that organization rather than on the conventional armed forces; hence it may not be particularly accurate. Operational UAV were first used in July 1984, producing what the authors call surprisingly clear battlefield pictures and current intelligence. The UAV was a simple radio-controlled airplane carrying a Hasselblad camera with a long (135-mm) lens; it overflew Iraqi positions at 50-m altitude. Shown photos of extensive Iraqi fortifications, the Iranian commanders canceled what would have been

Full-scale Neuron mockup at the 2009 Paris Air Show. (Norman Friedman)

a suicidal offensive. Unmanned aircraft flying at higher altitudes and taking oblique as well as vertical photographs figured prominently in later Iranian offensives (March 1985, February 1986, and January 1987). Iran also fielded a rocket-firing version of the same basic UAV, Mohajer-1 (up to six RPG-7 rocket grenades). A photograph shows a twin-boom pusher with tricycle undercarriage. Range is 30 km.

After the war UAVs were developed first in IRGC workshops and then the program was transferred to a new Qods Aviation Industries company. Its first UAV was Talash-1 (Endeavor), used successfully for photo reconnaissance late in the Iran-Iraq War. Talash-2 (also known as Hadaf [Target] 3000) is a target version. Talash has a conventional tractor configuration; Talash-2 has a longer nose and raked wingtips. Each had limited endurance (30 minutes) and limited payload. Span 2.64 m (2.10 m for Talash-2), length 1.70 m (1.90 m for Talash-2), weight 12 kg (11 kg for Talash-2), ceiling 9,000 ft. Maximum speeds were 90 and 120 km/hour (48 and 65 kt, respectively). Radio control range is 500 m.

Qods' Mohajer-2 is a modified version of the earlier Mohajer with a range of 50 km (speed 180 km/hour, ceiling 11,000 ft). Span 3.80 m, length 2.91 m, weight 85 kg, endurance 90 minutes (mission radius 27 nm, speed 108 kt, ceiling 11,000 ft). It is a twin-boom pusher. As dis-

played in 2005, Mohajer-2 had a new rotating camera turret. Mohajer-3 (Dorna [Bluebird]) is an all-weather surveillance/reconnaissance and target UAV similar to the Israeli Pioneer, with a mission radius of 54 nm (100 km) and the same speed as Mohajer-2. It is more capable than Mohajer-3 but lacks the GPS of Mohajer-4. Mohajer-4 (Hodhod) is a twin-boom reconnaissance/surveillance aircraft with an endurance of 5 to 7 hours and a mission radius of 150 km (81 nm). Speed is the same as that of the earlier versions. It is powered by a 38-hp engine rather than the 25-hp engine of Mohajer-2 and -3. Launch weight is 175 kg, and ceiling is 18,000 ft.

Qods' jet UAV is Mohajer-5. Qods also offers Shekarchi (Hunter), which appears to resemble very closely the Israeli Harpy antiradar drone (Israel supplied Harpy to China, which is the primary Iranian arms supplier). Shekarchi is described as in inventory and in service. Qods also offers a hand-launched UAV.

UAVs were also developed by Iran Aircraft Manufacturing Industry (IAMI, or HESA in Persian), which had originally been set up by Bell Textron to make helicopters. Its large UAV is Ababil (a mystical bird). Ababil exists in three versions: target (Ababil B), surveillance (Ababil S), and attack (Ababil T). Ababil B was the initial version, in service in 1993. A short-range Ababil II UAV was reportedly first flown in October 1997, and announced in March 1999. It featured an improved flight-control system and may have been the prototype for Ababil S, announced early in 2000. The attack version (Ababil T) has a 45-kg warhead and is distinguishable by its twin tails (other versions have a single tail). Configuration is canard, with narrow-chord cropped-delta wings and a pusher propeller. Ababil can operate up to 180 km from its ground controller, or it can fly a preset reconnaissance path. Navigation is GPS/inertial. A system comprises two air vehicles, a launcher, and a control vehicle. In 2005 Ababil was shown with a transparent nose camera dome. As a measure of production, an Iranian newspaper stated that fifty-eight Ababil were to be produced between March 2006 and March 2007. Data (for Ababil II/Ababil S): span 3.25 m, length 2.88 m, takeoff weight 83 kg (payload 40 kg). Endurance is 90 minutes (cruising speed 200 kt). Nominal range is 65 nm; ceiling is 10,000 ft.

Ababil T is operated by Hezbollah under the designation Mirsad 1. An Ababil flew down the Israeli Mediterranean coast on 7 November 2004, and another penetrated 30 km into Israel in April 2005, leaving before it could be intercepted. On the first flight the UAV avoided detection by flying low, at under 300 ft. An attack version has a 40-kg (88-lb) warhead. The United Nations arms sales registry shows eight of these UAVs supplied by Iran to Lebanon (presumably to Hezbollah) in 2004. Mirsads were shot down on 7 November 2004 and on 7 August 2006 (and possibly on other occasions).

As of 2009 HESA was developing a jet Ababil and a hand-launched UAV. The jet is called Ababil Jet or Hadaf-1, built around the Toloue mini-engine derived from that of the Chinese C802 missile. Maximum speed is given as 700 km/hour.

In addition HESA advertises three hand-launched electric-powered mini-UAVs, Ababil A, B, and C: endurance is 30 minutes, range is 15 km (10 km for Ababil A), and maximum speed is 60 km/hour. Takeoff weight is 6.5 kg (payload 1 kg for A, 1.5 for the others).

At the low end of the scale, Faraz Asia Technologies Company offers a hand-launched Faraz-2 that can be back-packed; it has 30 minutes endurance and can transmit video over 10-km range. It is a high-wing tractor monoplane.

During 2009 Iranian Deputy Defense Minister BGEN Ahmad Vahidi announced development of a 1,000-km UAV (presumably meaning the beginning of such development).

In addition to these aircraft, the IRGC claims that it has three virtually intact U.S. and British UAVs, which are to be reverse-engineered, including at least one RQ-7 Shadow (crashed 4 July 2008) and a British Hermes 450 (crashed 25 August 2008).

Numerous UAVs have featured in Iranian defense exhibitions, but it is impossible to say whether many (any?) are in full-scale service. The descriptions above are only a sampling.

In 2007 Iran agreed to supply Venezuela with about a dozen Ababil and Mohajer-4 UAVs; they may also be license-produced in Venezuela.

Israel

Israelis in effect invented the modern UAV in the late 1970s, the idea being that what amounted to a large radio-controlled model airplane was a far less expensive form of aerial reconnaissance than a jet fighter. It was also argued that high speed was detrimental in the low-altitude reconnaissance role. The key figure was Alvin Ellis, who worked on autopilots for Teledyne Ryan Firebee drones in the 1960s. He witnessed trials of a Firebee using video cameras for real-time reconnaissance, and became convinced that the drone's high speed reduced its value. Having returned to Israel in 1967, Ellis and a colleague, Jehuda Mamor, began privately developing a mini-RPV—the Owl—which IAI turned down. Tadiran sponsored development after a second prototype was demonstrated in February 1974 using a Sony video camera. The mini-RPV was named Mastiff, and the Israeli Air Force began operations with it in 1980. A few Mastiff 3 UAVs were in service during the 1982 Lebanon War. Although few Mastiffs were sold until the late 1970s, in 1976 IAI began its own RPV program, displaying Scout 2 in 1981; some may have been used during the 1982 war. The Israeli government ordered Tadiran and IAI to consolidate their efforts, which led to the formation of a joint company called Mazlat in September 1984. In 1989 IAI acquired Tadiran's share, and the company became its Malat division.

By 2002 the Israel Defense Force reportedly had accounted for 120,000 UAV flight hours.

Reportedly a major surprise of the 2006 war against Hezbollah in southern Lebanon was the great value of small UAVs, which brigades used as organic surveillance systems they could move with them. In this war the Israel Defense Force used mainly Elbit's Skylark I and Rafael's Skylite B. In 2007 Israeli UAVs operating against terrorists in Gaza accounted for about 24,000 flight hours, indicating their great perceived value. That figure compared to 100 hours for fighters and 1,300 for attack helicopters, indicating the very different kind of surveillance conducted by UAVs; the other aircraft are vectored into place only when the UAVs find targets. On the other hand, in 2008 Israeli officials denied that they would use UAVs in any deep strike against, for example, Iran. That was in the context of a large Aegean exercise, widely reported as a dry run for an Iran strike, in which UAVs were used extensively. There was also speculation that Eitan was the only UAV with sufficient load capacity to be used against Iran (it can carry a ton of weapons, and might be used for stand-off strikes against defensive missiles).

In addition to small numbers of Mastiffs sold to the Israeli military, a few were sold to the U.S. Navy and to Taiwan. Scout was sold to, among others, Singapore, South Africa, and Switzerland, and it was license-produced by Armscor in South Africa (and used in combat over Mozambique in 1983).

In addition to the UAVs described here, note that IAI is developing a UAV version of the Gulfstream business jet for airborne early warning. Israel placed the Gulfstream AEW aircraft, equipped with the Phalcon radar system, into service in 2006, and IAI announced the unmanned project in December 2007. An article describing the project observed that the U.S. Global Hawk had already demonstrated completely autonomous takeoff and landing, the controller merely maneuvering the airplane on the ground. IAI also installed UAV flight-control software on board a maritime patrol G550.

For most of the history of Israeli UAVs the Israel Defense Forces' air force operated them alongside the Israel Intelligence Corps, which might be considered broadly parallel to CIA. Some time about 2006 this duplication was eliminated, at least officially. As of early 2008 the Israeli Air Force was selecting small UAVs to support small ground units directly.

In November 2009 the Israeli Air Force and Ground Forces issued their first joint UAV requirement, for the Low Level UAV System, envisaged as a brigade-level UAV flying at 3,000 ft (i.e., under clouds) for up to 6 hours, deployable by two soldiers. For the Israeli Ground Forces, the new system is a brigade-level complement to the battalion-level Sky Rider. Maximum aircraft weight is 65 kt, including 8 kg of sensors. Each system will include three air vehicles. In contrast to Sky Rider, bids include the sensor and control elements as well as the air vehicle. The requirement had been under study for two years. Proposals were due in March 2010, the winner to be chosen during the summer of 2010.

AEROSTAR/DOMINATOR/PICADOR

A new Aeronautics Defence Systems firm displayed the Aerostar tactical UAV at Paris in 2003; it offers 14-hour endurance with a 50-kg payload. Reportedly this UAV was developed in co-operation with the Israel Intelligence Corps. Users include Greece and Taiwan and, reportedly, the U.S. Navy and Angola. Reportedly, too, the Netherlands bought Searcher in January 2009 to replace its Sperwers in Afghanistan. The company also provides UAV services on a rental basis. In mid-2009 Aeronautics claimed that Aerostar had accumulated more than 50,000 hours of flight time on four continents, for "performance and reliability unprecedented in the UAV industry." Aerostar has the conventional twin-boom pusher configuration, with its data-link radome on a mast above its fuselage. Aeronautics claims that its multichannel and multifrequency link makes it possible to communicate with the UAV using directional antennas at both ends, at ranges up to 200 km, a capacity the company claims is unique. Aeronautics also claims a uniquely high MTBF of 30,000 hours for its flight-control system. Among the features it claims are the best payload-to-weight ratio (presumably in its UAV class) and the best performance-to-platform size ratio. Aerostar is used for antismuggling surveillance of the Gaza Strip. Beginning in August 2003 Aeronautics Defense personnel operated Aerostars to patrol U.S.-owned oil platforms off Angola, and later they covered Angolan platforms as well; by January 2005 the

Aerostar tactical UAV. (Aeronautics Defense Systems)

Dominator MALE aircraft. (Aeronautics Defense Systems)

Aerostars involved had flown more than 6,000 hours. Beginning in September 2004 Aerostars produced by General Dynamics have provided training support to the U.S. Navy strike school at Fallon, Nevada. Nigeria bought three systems for its coast guard.

Data: span 7.50 m, length 4.50 m, takeoff weight 220 kg (maximum payload 50 kg). Endurance is 14 hours (maximum speed 110 kt, loiter speed 60 kt, mission radius 200 km), and ceiling is 18,000 ft. The power plant is a 2-stroke 38-hp Zanzottera 498i piston engine.

An Aerostar at the 2003 Paris Air Show had a new sensor package incorporating Rafael's Top-Scan ESM; a similar aircraft was later sold to Irkut of Russia, presumably as the basis for some of its UAVs.

In February 2010 Poland announced that it was buying eight Aerostars, four for use in Afghanistan. They are considered better than the existing Polish Shadow 200s because they offer greater endurance and can operate at a greater distance from their operators.

This company showed a new Dominator MALE at Bangalore in 2004. It is a flying wing with a pusher-propeller engine, its vertical control surfaces at its wingtips. Span is 8 m, length is 8 m, takeoff weight is 800 kg (payload up to 400 kg). Endurance is 24 hours, speed is 90–150 kt, and ceiling is 25,000 ft. The power plant is a 160-hp Lycoming piston engine. A bulge above the nose carries the data-link and satellite antennas. Launch and recovery are on a retractable wheeled undercarriage. This UAV can carry multiple payloads simultaneously.

The Dominator II (Oz) "strategic" UAV (MALE) was displayed in 2008; it first flew in July 2009. It is based on the twin-engine Diamond DA42 Twinstar and was described as the world's first UAV based on a certified civilian aircraft. Presumably to avoid undue changes to the airplane's aerodynamics, the UAV version incorporates the cockpit shape of the manned version, but completely plated over—and probably suitable for a large satellite dish looking upward. The UAV version is powered by two Thielert diesels, for long endurance—28 hours carrying a 400-kg payload (maximum takeoff weight is 2,000 kg), at an altitude giving a line-of-sight range of 300 km (usable with Aeronautics' unique multichannel multifrequency band link). In addition to the terrestrial link, Dominator 2 carries a satellite antenna. Speed is 190 kt at altitudes up to 30,000 ft; span is 13.5 m. Development took only a year, because the airframe already existed. Photos show winglets at the wingtips and downward-pointing winglets on the horizontal tail, both of which are probably intended to improve stability and to make autonomous flight easier. The prototype has a dummy sensor turret under its nose. Dominator may have been developed for a U.S. customer. Aeronautics claims that its UMAS flight-control system has the remarkable MTBF of 30,000 hours.

The German company Rhinemetall offers OPALE (Optionally Piloted Surveillance and Reconnaissance System) in partnership with Diamond, using the same platform. It claims a speed range of 65 (loiter) to 152 kt; cruising speed is 150 kt (6 hours endurance with 2 hours fuel reserve, 900-nm trip distance). At loiter speed the airplane can remain on station for 18 hours; maximum range exceeds 1,500 nm. The Rhinemetall/Diamond brochure refers to a U-2-like high-aspect–ratio wing.

Dominator II MALE aircraft. (Aeronautics Defense Systems)

Aeronautic Defense also offers a helicopter, Picador, based on a Belgian commercial helicopter (as of July 2009 it had not yet flown). According to a 2009 data sheet, the main rotor diameter is 7.22 m and length is 6.58 m; take-off weight is 720 kg (payload 180 kg). Endurance is 5 to 8 hours (maximum speed 110 kt, range 200 km). Ceiling is 12,000 ft. Here range is communications range, using a multichannel multifrequency data link that Aeronautics uses on its other UAVs. The body of the helicopter is faceted to reduce radar cross section. Drawings on the brochure suggest that Picador is intended for Israeli naval use on board missile corvettes.

Aeronautic Defense also produces Aerolight, the main operator trainer for the IDF's air force; one participated in a 31 March 2003 test in which it was successfully controlled from a U.S. Navy NP-3C Orion ("Hairy Buffalo"). One control station was placed on the ground, another on board the Orion; this was apparently the first air control of a UAV by a U.S. aircraft.

BIRD EYE 400

IAI's third-generation mini-UAV was advertised at the 2009 Paris Air Show. It is intended to supply low-echelon units with imagery. Development was completed in 2005, and it was in production and in service with several unnamed customers by July 2007. It uses a tailless tractor configuration with swept wings (with down-swept end

plates). The EO sensors are in a suspended stabilized turret. When the UAV lands, it flips over so that the turret is on top; it has four landing legs, which are on top in flight and in the appropriate position after the UAV flips over (IAI considers this an important selling point). The entire system fits into two backpacks. Flight modes are auto launch, navigation, return home, and hold. Launch is by bungee catapult, the UAV being slightly too large for hand launch. Propulsion is electric. Data: span 2.2 m, weight 5.6 kg (payload 1.2 kg). Endurance is 60 minutes (maximum speed 50 kt, mission radius 10 km/6.25 miles). Operating altitude is 500 to 1,000 ft.

IAI also offers Bird Eye 600 and Bird Eye 650, improved versions of Bird Eye 400.

BLUE HORIZON 2/BUTTERFLY/DRAGONFLY 2000/MERCURY 3/SPARROW-N (EMIT UAVS)

EMIT was founded in 1986 by Ephraim Menashy, who had been a test pilot for IAI/Malat. It designed, developed, and manufactured the fuselage of the Pioneer UAV and then developed its own UAV. It is apparently primarily an export producer. In September 2003 it and Elbit Silver Arrow lost out to the IAI Searcher in an Israel Defence Force competition. EMIT was responsible for an aerial target system, and about 2005 stated that it had just completed development of a UAV with "unprecedented performance." In 2006 EMIT was convicted of transferring

UAV technology to China via a Southeast Asian cover contract.

EMIT's Blue Horizon 2 was apparently developed specifically for Singapore. It has been used by Sri Lanka; two were lost in a late 2007 attack. According to the UN arms sale registry, the Philippines ordered two in 2001 for use against Abu Saffay and other Muslim rebels. They may have been supplied via Singapore. This is a swept-wing canard whose vertical surfaces are wing end-plates. Data: span 6.5 m, fuselage length 3.2 m, takeoff weight 180 kg (80 kg empty; 37-kg payload, fuel capacity 50 kg). Endurance is 10 hours at 70 kt at 5,000 ft (maximum speed 120 kt, endurance speed 70 kt); ceiling is 18,000 ft. The power plant is a 25-hp 2-stroke engine driving a pusher propeller. Takeoff distance at 150 kg is 250 m; landing distance is 200 m. Blue Horizon was apparently derived from an earlier Sting series, of which Sting I had one or two engines and Sting II (the immediate predecessor of Blue Horizon) was a smaller single-engine version. Blue Horizon was Sting II modified specifically for Singapore.

EMIT's Butterfly uses a body suspended from a para-foil with 50-m² wing area; length is 3.2 m. The payload sensor turret is suspended from the open-frame body. Operating radius, set by the data link, is better than 20 km with an omni antenna and better than 120 km with a directional antenna; speed is 30 kt. Takeoff weight is 450 kg (payload 230 kg). The power plant is a Rotax 582 piston engine. Butterfly takes off or lands in a 50-m space.

EMIT's Dragonfly 2000 is reportedly in current Israeli service. It has a conventional tractor configuration with straight wings and a conventional tail. The company describes it as an affordable UAV with an advanced light airframe. It has automatic and autonomous modes of navigation, and special modes for use with EO payloads. Span is 5 m and length 2.96 m; takeoff weight is 140 kg (payload 16 kg when fully loaded; empty weight 84 kg, fuel capacity 40 kg). Endurance is 14 hours (70 kt, 6,000 ft); speed is 50 to 110 kt at 6,000 ft. Landing distance is 300 m. Ceiling is 15,000 ft. EMIT claims that Dragonfly 2000 is currently in Israeli service. In a series of descriptions of EMIT UAVs, it was given by far the most detailed information, suggesting that it has been tested most thoroughly. EMIT also makes a smaller (80 kg) Dragonfly DF 16B.

Picador at the 2009 Paris Air Show. (Norman Friedman)

EMIT's Mercury 3 is has a conventional configuration and a vee tail. Span is 10 m and takeoff weight is 550 kg (payload 150 kg, 300 liters of fuel). Endurance is about 30 hours (speed 55–140 kt, stall speed 38 kt), and ceiling is 38,000 ft. Takeoff distance is about 250 m. The power plant is an 11-hp 4-cylinder turbocharged piston engine driving a pusher propeller in the tail. Operational range is 200 km either in linked or in autonomous mode.

Sparrow-N is a mini-UAV: span 2.44 m, length 2.14 m, weight 45 kg (12-kg payload), endurance 4–6 hours (speed 60 to 100 kt). Endurance at 60 to 70 kt is over 4 hours. A larger fuel tank can be fitted, extending endurance. Operating radius is 20 km using an omni antenna or over 120 km using a directional antenna. EMIT describes Sparrow-N as a subtactical UAV carrying stabilized day sensors. Its special feature is apparently that it carries software capable of recognizing features on the ground for autonomous operation.

HERMES

Given the success of the first-generation aircraft, another firm, Silver Arrow, began development. IAI attempted unsuccessfully to acquire it in 1997, and instead it merged with Elbit, the Israeli defense electronics company. Elbit

Bird Eye 400 mini-UAV. Note the landing legs atop the fuselage, which flips over to land. (IAI)

Blue Horizon 2 UAV. (EMIT)

Dragonfly 2000 UAV. (EMIT)

Sparrow-N mini-UAV. (EMIT)

showed its first UAV, Hermes 450, at the 1995 Paris Air Show (the 450 indicates takeoff weight). It was followed by Hermes 750 and then Hermes 1500, as well as the smaller Hermes 180. The Hermes 180 is intended to support ground forces at brigade to division level, Hermes 450 from division to corps level. The new Hermes 900 (like the existing Hermes 1500) is designed for corps to national command level.

Hermes 450 was the first drone certified to fly in Israeli civil airspace. Reportedly an Israeli Air Force squadron has operated Hermes 450 since 1997 (also reported as 2000 and 2002) under the name Zik; reportedly fleet strength is 70 to 120–150 air vehicles. In September 2007 Elbit announced that Hermes 450 had exceeded 65,000 air hours on a world basis. Early in 2008 Elbit announced an uprated 69-hp engine for Hermes 450. Hermes can be considered a heavy long-endurance tactical UAV rather than a MALE. Hermes 450 is reportedly used in armed form by the Israel Defense Force. Reported foreign buyers are Botswana, Croatia, Georgia, Mexico, Singapore (one system, twelve aircraft, as of 2007), and the United Kingdom (fifty-four Hermes 450B were bought under the Watchkeeper program). Pending Watchkeeper deliveries, the British army leased ten Hermes 450 for use by the 32nd Regiment Royal Artillery in Iraq and Afghanistan. At least four Georgian Hermes 450s were shot down during the 2008 war with Russia, at least one of them by a MiG-29. Nigeria may operate Hermes 450. Argentina and South Africa reportedly operate Hermes 1500.

In contrast to Hermes 450, the 450B (announced 2007) has a shoulder wing with de-icers, a retractable nose landing gear, and a British engine; it is to be license-produced in the United Kingdom. It will have a Thales Magic ATLS with GPS-based backup and will carry a Thales SAR/GMTI radar plus an Israeli-supplied EO/IR sensor and laser designator. Hermes 450B flew in April 2008, and is to enter service in 2010.

Elbit announced Hermes 900 at the 2007 Paris Air Show to fly by the end of 2008. Hermes 900 has an "independent" ATLS that allows it to use uninstrumented runways. It also offers higher-altitude capability and a larger and more easily replaceable payload. IAI claims

Hermes 90 at the 2009 Paris Air Show. (Norman Friedman)

IAI's model of Hermes 180 at the 2009 Paris Air Show, displaying its configuration, similar to that of Hermes 90. (Norman Friedman)

that it can fly in worse weather than can earlier UAVs, presumably meaning that its flight control system can adapt to more complex contingencies. Hermes 900 first flew on 14 December 2009 (the first flight had been predicted for 2008, when Hermes 900 was announced).

Hermes 90 is the low end of the scale, entered (as Storm) in the U.S. STUAS (Short-Range Tactical UAV System) Tier II competition. It was announced in March 2009, using the Mini-Falcon airframe developed by

Innocon. Like many other UAVs, it has a pusher engine at the after end of its pod fuselage, but in its case the inverted vee tail is supported by a single boom supported by a strut atop the fuselage. For the U.S. competition it is offered by UAV Dynamics, a joint venture of General Dynamics and Elbit. Note that it is considerably larger than the other contenders. In October 2009 Hermes 90 flew for the first time with a heavy-fuel (JP-5/8 rather than gasoline) engine.

Hermes 450 with electronic intelligence pods underwing and additional underbelly antennas. (IAI)

Hermes 450 of the U.S. Customs and Border Patrol. (U.S. Customs and Border Protection Agency)

Hermes 90 data: span 5.5 m, length 4.2 m, weight 150 kg (payload 35 kg). Ceiling is 18,000 ft and endurance is 18 hours (cruising speed 55 kt).

Hermes 180 data: span 6 m, length 4.43 m (fuselage 3.47 m), takeoff weight 195 kg (payload 32 kg). Endurance is more than 10 hours (mission radius 100 nm, speed 105 kt); ceiling is 15,000 ft. The power plant is a 38-hp rotary engine. The UAV has a single tail boom carried back from struts atop its fuselage; it has a pusher propeller below this boom. There are two end-plate tail fins.

Hermes 450 data: span 10.5 m, length 6.1 or 6.8 m, weight 450–580 kg (payload 150–200 kg). Endurance is more than 20 hours (speed 95 kt); ceiling is 18,000 ft. The power plant is a 52/69-hp rotary engine or an 85-hp 4-stroke engine. Unlike Hermes 180, Hermes 450 has a full-length fuselage with a vee tail and a pusher propeller abaft it.

Hermes 900 data: span 15 m, length 8.3 m, takeoff weight 970 kg (payload 300 kg). Endurance is 40 hours, ceiling is 33,000 ft. The power plant is a 100-hp rotary (Rotax) engine. In configuration this is an enlarged Hermes 450.

Hermes 1500 data: span 18 m, length 9.4 m, takeoff weight 1,650 kg (payload 350 or 400 kg). Endurance is more than 40 hours (also given as more than 26 hours; speed is 130 kt); ceiling is 33,000 ft. Unlike most UAVs, this one has twin piston engines (tractors), one on each

Hermes 900 UAV. (IAI)

wing, with what look like drop tanks outboard of them. It has the same vee tail as Hermes 450/900.

HERON/EAGLE/EITAN/HARFANG

IAI's Heron was the step beyond Searcher. It can operate four sensor systems simultaneously, and is advertised as a SIGINT platform. It has two independent ATLS systems, and it uses satellite communications to extend its effective range. This medium-altitude long-endurance (MALE) UAV is the main competitor to General Atomics' Predator series. IAI's Heron (Shoval [Trail] in Israeli service) first flew on 18 October 1994. In 2006 IAI announced that the Israeli Air Force was planning to buy "several dozen" (Shoval officially entered service in March 2007, but it was

Hermes 450 and Hermes 900 compared, in model form, at the 2009 Paris Air Show. (Norman Friedman)

apparently used during the 2006 Lebanon war). The name Machatz (Strike) has also been applied to Heron, presumably in a role other than that of Shoval. An Indian article (2007) identified Machatz with the maritime surveillance mission.

France selected Heron as its SIDM under the designation Harfang (Snow Owl); a ground station and three aircraft began operation in Afghanistan in February 2009 (a fourth was being bought in the fall of 2009). EADS is the prime contractor. The Turkish army ordered ten and leased two pending delivery, but late in 2009 it reported serious problems with the program and was considering cancellation. Canada leased Herons for Afghan service under the Noctua program. India has also bought Heron for all three services. A sale of fifty Herons was reported by Israeli media in August 2005. Heron may be the basis of the Indian Rustom UAV.

Heron 1 has been employed by U.S. antidrug forces in El Salvador and may be based permanently there.

Heron 2 or Heron TP or Eitan (Strength) is a high-altitude UAV about three times the size of Heron; it was first announced in 1994. It is in the weight category of the U.S. Reaper but uses a more powerful engine and has a greater wingspan. It first flew about 2005, and by 2006 it was apparently being armed with Spike and Hellfire antitank missiles. Eitan was displayed at the 2007 Paris Air Show and reportedly entered service in 2008. However, the Israeli Air Force formally announced the "inauguration" of Heron TP in February 2010. At that time

Israeli media described Heron TP as a UAV that could fly as far as Teheran.

The UN register of arms sales shows twenty-five Heron 2 ordered by India in 2001 for delivery in 2002–3 (with fifteen delivered the first year), and another twelve under negotiation in 2004 (these were the Heron Eagle version). The same registry shows unknown numbers of Heron 2, possibly for maritime patrol, under negotiation in 2002–3 for Indonesia. Thales has marketed Heron TP to France, Spain, and Germany, working with Indra in Spain and with Dassault in France. This system could be operational in 2012.

Both Eitan and Heron have been proposed as maritime patrol aircraft, to replace the IAI 1124 Seascans; two Herons (Machatz I?) are operating with Elta EL/M-2022U maritime surveillance radars.

Hermes 1500 UAV. (IAI)

Heron at the 2009 Paris Air Show. (Norman Friedman)

Heron TP is being developed as the basis of a loitering ballistic missile defense system, using a weapon derived from the Python air-to-air missile and a Bluebird sensor developed jointly with Germany. It may initially have been designated HA-10.

Eagle 1 is a modified Heron for France, built by EADS and IAI. It has a bulbous nose similar to that of the U.S. Global Hawk and a belly dome for a radar. It first flew in Israel on 2 June 2003. The follow-on is SIDM (Harfang), which first flew in September 2006. It has ATLS, an EO/IR turret, a laser designator, an Elbit SAR/GMTI radar, and a satellite link. It may be fitted with ELINT receivers and a maritime search radar for a future maritime patrol role. Eagle 2 is a proposed follow-on based on Heron TP, with a turboprop engine; it is intended to meet the EuroMALE requirement. Endurance will be 24 hours at 50,000 ft with a 450-kg payload. EADS is considering weaponizing both Eagle 1 and Eagle 2. The UN arms sale registry shows three Eagles ordered by France in 2001 for delivery in 2003.

IAI and TRW offered a larger longer-endurance UAV for the U.S. Tier II+ competition won by Global Hawk. This entry drew on 1988 design work on a large loitering radar UAV called Hauler (50,000 lbs, 164-ft wingspan).

Heron data: span 16.6 m, length 8.5 m, takeoff weight 1,150 kg (payload 250 kg). Endurance is 20 to 45 hours (maximum speed 120 kt, loiter speed 60 to 80 kt); ceiling is above 30,000 ft. Mission radius is 350 km or more (and satellite communication is available for operation at greater ranges). The power plant is a 100-hp turbocharged 4-cylinder 4-stroke engine. Configuration is twin-boom, with a large underbody radome and a data-link antenna on a dorsal mast. According to an Indian account of UAV maritime surveillance, endurance in this role is 52 hours, the typical mission taking 35 hours.

Heron TP data: span 26 m, length 14 m, takeoff weight 4,650 kg (payload 1,000 kg). Endurance is 36 hours and ceiling is 45,000 ft, permitting operation above commercial traffic. The power plant is a 1,200-hp turboprop.

HUNTER

The Hunter was apparently conceived as Impact, a Scout replacement. The least reliable element of Scout had been its German lightweight motorcycle engine. The solution was a twin-engine configuration (tractor and pusher). Impact was submitted to the U.S. Army as a short-range UAV in 1989 and adopted as Hunter. The German engines were replaced first by British and then by Italian motorcycle engines, and in 1994 a heavy oil engine was tested. IAI's Hunter is also made in the United States by Northrop Grumman as RQ-5/MQ-5 (see separate entry). Note that Hunter was apparently never adopted by the Israeli military.

Data: span 8.90 m, length 6.90 m, takeoff weight 727 kg (payload 114 kg). Endurance is 12 hours (range 100–200 km, maximum speed 110 kt, cruising speed 60 to 80 kt); ceiling is 15,000 ft. The power plant is a pair of engines in push-pull configuration.

The Belgian air force bought three B-Hunter systems (Belgian Hunter, not MQ-5B) in 1998 (delivered 2001). The Belgian army stated a requirement for a division-level system in 1997, the objective being three or four systems, each with four to eight air vehicles. Hunter won over the French Sperwer and the Swiss Ranger. For Belgium the system was produced by the Eagle consortium including Alcatel. Each system consisted of two ground stations and six air vehicles. Range was greater than 100 km, and maximum endurance 11 hours (11.6 hours demonstrated). These UAVs were designed to take off and land on unprepared terrain using an ATLS. Target location error was to be 100 m CEP (circular error probable). Modernization from the U.S. to the Belgian configuration involved new avionics based on the Swiss ADS95 Ranger, a new data link (C-band up- and downlinks with UHF backup), a second-generation TV/FLIR, a new ground-control station (described as fourth-generation), an ATLS based on the Swiss ADS95, and new software. The Belgian army used Hunter in Kosovo in 2005. Beginning in July 2006 Belgian Hunters supported a UN operation in the Congo. One was lost to ground fire on its first flight, and a second crashed (engine failure) on 3 October 2006; it crashed into a house, killing a civilian in what may have been the first civilian death in a UAV-related accident. The system was then withdrawn.

IAI claimed that the B-Hunter had the world's first ATLS to enter service. It employed a tripod-mounted optical sensor (Range Automatic Positioning Sensor, or RAPS), which measured UAV position by reflecting a laser beam from a reflector in the leading edge of the UAV wing. Location data are passed to the ground-control station via a fiber-optic cable. The station calculates the appropriate data and transmits commands to the UAV,

Heron with SIGINT antennas. (Israeli Air Force)

whose flight-control system embodies the relevant flight-control rules and algorithms. For landing the UAV flies into a navigation window, where it links with the RAPS; it then flies down the indicated glide slope. Alternatively, like other UAVs, it could be landed by an external pilot.

Hunter was tested extensively in France but not adopted there. One system with four air vehicles (F-Hunter) was sold to France; France may have used Hunter in Kosovo in 1998–99.

I-VIEW

I-View is IAI's new-generation tactical UAV series: Mk 50, Mk 150, and Mk 250. All have conventional tractor propeller configurations with vee tails on a short boom, and all use parafoils for recovery. The high-end Mk 250 is a medium-range UAV: endurance 8 hours, range 150 km, ceiling 20,000 ft. Span is 7.1 m and length 4.1 m; takeoff weight is 250 kg (payload 60 kg). Mk 150 has an endurance of 7 hours, a range of 100 km, and a ceiling of 17,000 ft. Span is 5.7 m, and length 3.1 m; takeoff weight is 160 kg (payload 20 kg). Mk 50 is the low end of the series, with an endurance of 6 hours, range 50 km, and ceiling 15,000 ft. Span is 4.0 m, length 2.7 m, and takeoff weight 65 kg (payload 10 kg).

IAI's concept of a maritime reconnaissance Heron, with underslung maritime search radar (EL/M-2022) and numerous SIGINT antennas. This model was at the 2009 Paris Air Show. (Norman Friedman)

Heron TP high-altitude UAV. (IAI)

In December 2005 the Australian Army selected Mk 250 to meet its JP 129 requirement. Delivery was to have begun in 2009, but the program was canceled in 2008.

MASTIFF

Mastiff was the first Israeli UAV, used extensively in Lebanon. Development began in the 1970s. The three types are quite different. Mastiff Mk I is a conventional tractor resembling a high-wing model airplane. The standard payload was a remote-control television camera with a zoom lens, capable of being moved up and down and to each side. Span was 4.20 m, length 2.60 m, and weight 80 kg (payload 15 kg). Endurance was 4 hours (level speed 80 kt, cruising speed 40–60 kt, stall speed 35 kt, range 38 nm); ceiling was 10,000 ft. Singapore bought Mastiff in 1979, presumably becoming the first export customer.

Tadiran's Mastiff Mk II introduced the twin-boom pusher layout. It entered production in 1980–81. Span was 4.30 m, length 2.60 m, weight 75 kg (payload 15 kg). Endurance was more than 4 hours (maximum speed

70 kt, cruising speed 40–60 kt, stall speed 30 kt, control range 38 nm but aerodynamic range 75 nm, usable with portable ground station); ceiling was 10,000 ft. The power plant was a 14-hp piston engine.

Mastiff Mk III, the version made by Mazlat, is a twin-boom pusher with its sensor dome underslung. It entered production about 1982. Eight Mk III supplied to the U.S. Navy in 1984–85 were tested by the 1st RPV Platoon of the U.S. Marine Corps, leading to development of the Pioneer for the U.S. Navy. Span is 4.25 m, length 3.30 m, weight 138 kg (payload 37 kg). Endurance is 7 hours 30 minutes (cruising speed 53 kt, maximum 100 kt at sea level [115 mph], stall speed 46 kt), ceiling is 14,700 ft (4480 m). The power plant is a 22-hp piston engine. Sensors are stabilized television cameras supplemented by a small film camera to provide detail. Thus Mastiff III could report in real time, but it also shared the heritage of earlier bringback drones. Scout seems to have been IAI's equivalent UAV, the product lines of Tadiran and IAI being merged in Mazlat's.

MINI-FALCON

Innocon's tactical UAV is reportedly in service (users are not named). Development began in 2002, and it was first shown at Patuxent River in 2003. In 2009 Innocon offered Mini-Falcon to meet a Ugandan border patrol request. It has an unusual pod-and-boom configuration, with the single tail boom extending aft from a pylon atop the trailing edge of the wing, supporting an inverted vee tail. The power plant is a pusher engine. Mini-Falcon I has skid landing gear; the enlarged Mini-Falcon II has wheels. The power plant is a 15- or 26-hp piston engine. Mini-Falcon I data: span 5.00 m, length 3.50 m, weight 90 kg (payload 15 kg), endurance more than 12 hours (maximum speed 90 kt, loiter speed 50 kt). Mini-Falcon II data: span 5.50 m, length 4.20 m, weight 150 kg (payload 35 kg), endurance more than 15 hours (maximum speed 120 kt, loiter speed 55 kt).

MOSQUITO 1.5

Work on the Mosquito micro-UAV began in 2001, a Mosquito 1 prototype flying on 1 January 2003. The current version is Mosquito 1.5. It is a flying wing, nearly semicircular in planform, with a tractor engine and end

I-View Mk 250, with its recovery Rogallo wing. (IAI)

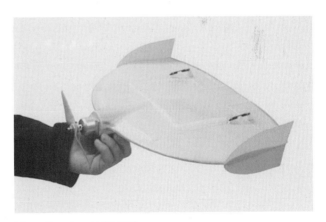

Mosquito micro-UAV. (IAI)

plate vertical fins. Propulsion is electric. Span is 0.34 m, length is 0.3 m, and weight is 0.5 kg; endurance is up to 90 minutes (range 1.5 km), and operating altitude is 50 to 300 ft. Note that a comparative UAV project (2009) gave Mosquito endurance as 40 minutes. However, the broadly comparable U.S. Wasp was credited with 100 minutes.

Mastiff Mk III UAV. (IAI)

NRUAV

IAI has advertised a helicopter converted into a maritime surveillance UAV under the designation NRUAV (Naval Rotary UAV). The helicopter shown is an Alouette, but IAI has offered other airframes as well. IAI claims that NRUAV was developed for a foreign customer. The obvious one is India, which produces the Alouette helicopter under license. See the Indian section.

ORBITER

Aeronautics' mini-UAV was introduced in 2004, for battalion- or company-level use, or for internal security forces. It was ordered by Poland for special forces in 2006, and in July 2007 it was ordered for Polish ground forces (six systems, three air vehicles each). For this order, Orbiter won over eleven other companies, six of which reached the final stage. There have apparently been other buyers (at least Ireland [six air vehicles, one system], another NATO army, and two CIS countries). Orbiter is a flying wing with sharply swept wings and a tail boom carrying a pusher propeller; the sensors are in the semispherical nose. The vertical surfaces are the upswept wingtips. Span is 2.2 m, length 1.0 m, weight 6.5 kg. Endurance is 2 to 3 hours (speed 25 to 75 kt, range 15 km); ceiling is 18,000 ft. An extended-range version with auto-tracking directional communication can enjoy line-of-sight control to 50 km.

PIONEER

Mazlat's successor to Mastiff III and Scout was adopted by the U.S. Navy after a 1985 fly-off against Heron 26, becoming the first modern U.S. operational UAV. According to Mazlat, Pioneer reflected 10,000 hours of operating experience over hostile territory (2,000 sorties) by Mastiff III and Scout. Span is 5.15 m, length 4.26 m, and takeoff weight is 195 kg (payload 45 kg). Endurance is typically 6 to 9 hours (maximum level speed 100 kt, cruising speed 48–70 kt, mission radius 100 nm); ceiling is 15,000 ft. The power plant is a 26-hp piston engine. See also the United States section (below).

SCOUT

IAI's Scout was roughly equivalent to Tadiran's Mastiff III, with a similar twin-boom pusher layout. It entered service in 1977 and was apparently the main platform used in Lebanon in 1982, and it was also supplied to Singapore (replacing Mastiff in 1984), South Africa, and Switzerland (one system for evaluation). Like Mastiff it is equipped mainly with television cameras. Span was 4.96 m, length 3.68 m, weight 159 kg (payload 38 kg). Endurance is 7 hours (maximum speed 95 kt, speed for maximum range 55 kt, stall speed 42 kt, control range 54 nm/100 km/62 miles); ceiling is 15,000 ft (4,575 m). Sri Lanka bought five Super Scout UAVs in 1996.

NRUAV in model form at the 2009 Paris Air Show. Note the SIGINT antennas on the stub wing. (Norman Friedman)

Orbiter mini-UAV. (Aeronautics Defense Systems)

SEARCHER

IAI's third-generation successor to Mastiff was the larger longer-endurance Searcher, work on which began in 1988. It was announced in 1989, and the prototype displayed the following year. Like Scout and Hunter it encountered engine problems, which were solved only with Searcher II, with its more powerful rotary engine. Production began in 1992 (first deliveries July 1992 to the Israeli Air Force). The manufacturer operated Searcher for the IDF until at least 1997; as of 2009 it was operational in No. 200 Squadron at Palmachim, and possibly also Nos. 146 (Radom) and 155 (Hatserim). Searcher II became operational with the IDF in May 1999. In Israeli service Searcher II had the Elta EL/M-2055 maritime reconnaissance radar; it is being or has been replaced by Heron I in this role. Foreign buyers included India (ten delivered from 2001, eight more ordered 2002), Indonesia (plans to acquire four systems announced 2007), Singapore (two systems in service in 2007; forty-two for No. 128 Squadron), South Korea, Spain (four Searcher II-J in 2008 for use in Afghanistan, as a battalion-level system to complement the shorter-range Raven), Sri Lanka (original aircraft lost, then replaced), Taiwan, and Thailand (four ordered in 2000, no longer in service). Colombia may have received Searcher in 2005–6. Total sales reportedly exceed 100 air vehicles and twenty ground stations.

The Indian navy activated 342 Maritime Reconnaissance Squadron in 2006 with eight Searcher II and four Heron UAVs. As of March 2007 India was building a base for these aircraft in the Andaman Islands in the eastern Bay of Bengal. According to the UN arms sale registry, India ordered thirty-two Searchers in 2000. They were delivered in 2001–2 (sixteen each year).

Scout UAV. (IAI)

Searcher Mk II data: span 8.55 m, length 5.85 m, takeoff weight 426 kg (payload 100 kg). Endurance is 15 hours (speed 108 kt), and ceiling is 19,000 ft. The power plant is a 73-hp Wankel engine.

Searcher Mk III was advertised at the 2009 Paris Air Show. A brochure illustrated it in SIGINT configuration, with endplate-type antennas at its wingtips and spaced along its two tail booms (a pair of two near the wing, and a third closer to the tail: eight antennas in all), with a radome on a post above its nose. This is presumably IAI's EL/K-7071 integrated UAV COMINT/DF system (UCOMS). The alternative configurations are for SAR/GMTI and for the usual EO/IR cameras. Features include aerial data relay for beyond line-of-sight operation (not satellite communication), and the same pair of independent automatic takeoff and landing systems that figure in Heron. IAI advertises its integrated 4-stroke engine for minimal audio signature. That matters because increasingly UAVs are vulnerable to ground fire cued by their sound (initially the sound sometimes intimidated troops, but no more). Dimensions apparently match those of Searcher Mk II, except that takeoff weight is 436 kg and payload is more than 120 kg. Endurance is 20 hours (mission radius, presumably based on the data-link range, is

300 km). Maximum speed is 110 kt (loiter speed 60 to 80 kt). Ceiling is over 23,000 ft.

SKYLARK

Elbit's man-portable (backpack) UAV has a conventional configuration (tractor propeller) with its EO turret under its nose, just abaft the propeller. A system comprises three air vehicles plus their ground control, their downlink terminal, and their launcher (the UAV is just too large for hand-launching).

Skylark 1 (originally Skylark IV) was designed to meet a 2002 Israel Defense Force requirement (Sky Rider) for a mini-UAV to support platoons and companies. The entire system weighs 30 to 40 kg (three air vehicles) and can be operated by two soldiers. Skylark was selected in February 2004 for a technology demonstration, but a contract scheduled for late 2005 was delayed as other companies offered alternatives. In November 2005 Skylark was selected for rapid deployment by the Australian army for operation in Iraq, six systems (three air vehicles each, with night and day payloads). It was intended to complement the larger I-View 250 and ScanEagle. At least two more Australian orders followed as of August 2008. An order for French special forces was announced in March

2008. In September 2008 Elbit announced a contract for Skylark and Hermes 450 to Mexico. Skylark 1 was ordered in November 2005 by Canada as an interim UAV for use in Afghanistan. In October 2006 Canada chose it as a standard future mini-UAV, having defeated competitors that included IAI's I-View 50 (parafoil wing) and ScanEagle. In 2007 Sweden acquired six Skylarks (which it calls Falken) for deployment with the Nordic Battle Group. Data: span 2.4 m, length 2.2 m, weight 4.5 kg, endurance 60 to 90 minutes. The French DRAC is comparable, but offers a more mobile sensor turret and has twin engines.

Skylark I LE (long endurance) was selected in December 2008 as the new Israeli battalion UAV (reportedly one hundred systems are involved). It won over entries by Aeronautics Defense Systems (Orbiter), Israel Aeronautics Industries (Birds Eye 400/600), and Rafael (Skylite A/B). Data: span 5.5 m, length 2.2 m, ceiling 6,000 ft, endurance 2 hours. Effective range is 10 km. The power plant is an electric motor. The LE version has a 2.9-m span, 3-hour endurance, and 15-km mission range. The change in endurance is also reported as a doubling, from 90 minutes to 3 hours.

The 43-kg Skylark II is launched by rail rather than by hand. It was announced in June 2006. It is being promoted in the United States by General Dynamics for Tier II, presumably for Special Operations Command rather than the Navy/Marine STUAS. Contract awards were expected in April 2009. Skylark II was selected in December 2007 by South Korea. Skylark II was first shown at Eurosatory 2006. Skylark II is conceived as a battalion-level system. Data: span 4.2 m, weight 35 kg, endurance 6 hours (mission radius 50 km). The power plant is a 4-kW electric motor, the battery pack being slung underbody.

There is also a Skylark II LE with a new configuration, the motor being moved to the tail; endurance is given as 15 hours, and a new data link can operate at 150-km range.

The main alternative in this category is IAI's I-View 50.

Italy

The main Italian system developer is Selex Galileo, formerly Alenia, one of whose components is Meteor (established in 1947). Having built the U.S. MQM-33 and Chukar target drones under license, and having sup-

Searcher III UAV. (IAI)

Skylark "backpack" UAV. (Elbit)

plied about half the value of CL-89s for the Italian army, Meteor developed its own Mirach series both as target drones and as reconnaissance UAVs (it had previously developed Gufone [Owl], a reconnaissance version of the jet Chukar, which did not sell).

In 2000 Italy bought six Predators for the air force (Meteor was the prime Italian contractor). In August 2004 Italy announced plans for five more Predators, but as of 2009 only two had been delivered, one as an attrition spare and one to complete the original plan for six (two more were dropped due to budget limitations in 2005, being shifted to later budgets). In February 2008 the Italian parliament approved procurement of four Predator B (MQ-9) by 2011. In addition, in 2002, Italy also

Molynx civilian UAV. (Alenia)

bought twenty surplus German CL-289s in 2002 to support the Italian component of the EU Rapid Reaction Force (France also bought such drones). By that time the CL-289s were clearly obsolescent. Nibbio (Kite), derived from Mirach-100/-150, is conceived as a CL-289 replacement. See below.

ALENIA MALE/ MOLYNX/BLACK LYNX

Alenia announced the 3,000-kg twin-engine Molynx in October 2006 in the form of a quarter-scale model in Turin. Molynx was a civilian UAV for roles such as border patrol, fire detection, fisheries patrol, communications relay, and powerline and pipeline patrol. Black Lynx was the military version. As of 2007 it was expected to fly in 2009 and to be ready for production in 2010/11. Alenia has also described Molynx as a heavy MALE, or HALE, equipped with the usual EO/IR sensors plus a SAR radar and an ESM system, with satellite communication. Molynx in turn may be used to gain experience for Alenia's projected Black Lynx tailless armed MALE. This twin-engine project was announced in June 2007. The power plant was a pair of diesels, each driving a pusher propeller.

Molynx/Black Lynx data: span 25.00/28.00 m, length 12.27/13.00 m, weight 3,000/3,500 kg (payload 600/800 kg), endurance 30/36 hours, mission radius 2,000 nm (both), cruising speed 220 kt (Molynx), ceiling 45,000 ft (both).

FALCO

Selex Galileo announced the Falco, a MALE UAV, in July 2002 (simultaneously with Nibbio) and first flew it in November 2003; system development was largely complete by late 2004. Falco was conceived for target detection, localization, identification, and designation (as a potential replacement for Mirach-26); it was also intended as a platform for stand-off sensors and/or weapons such as the Multipurpose Air-Launched Payload (MALP) under development by Galileo Avionics. In June 2005 Falco became the first UAV to receive a "permit to fly" from the Italian Civil Aviation Authority, acting for the European Aviation Safety Authority. It has twin tail booms and a pusher propeller. The sensor suite typically includes day and IR cameras and a spotter (presumably a wide-area camera with a real-time link back to the operator). Selex claims that the main features are ATLS (STOL [short takeoff and landing] performance), a fully redundant and fault-tolerant control system, digital buses, automatic surveillance modes, and near-real-time target processing. The launch order for twelve systems was placed by an undisclosed customer in 2005 (delivery of the first tranche was completed about 2006, with a second scheduled for late 2007. Initial production for Pakistan was announced in 2007. Four systems had been delivered by spring 2009, a fifth was being delivered, and license production was being set up; Pakistan uses them in systems each of which includes five air vehicles). Falco was also bought by Bulgaria, and it may have been bought by Libya. In June 2006 Selex Galileo announced that it planned a ship-launched version of Falco by 2008 (it has not yet materialized), combining the usual EO sensor with the Selex Gabbiano X-band maritime radar.

An enlarged evolved version, Falco Evo, is being built in prototype form, to fly in mid-2010. Its stretched wings (about 14 m compared to the original 7.22 m) and tail extend endurance from the current 8 to 14 hours to more than 18 hours (it retains the original 75-hp UEL rotary engine). Maximum takeoff weight increases from 490 to 750 kg (payload increases from 70 to 120 kg). Speed falls from 80 to 60 kt, but ceiling will increase from the current 5,000 m. Existing Falcos can be upgraded to the new version using a kit, which includes new flight-control software to take account of the changed configuration. Planned payloads include the Picosar SAR radar and EW systems.

Data: span 7.20 m, length 5.25 m, takeoff weight 240–320 kg (payload 70 kg). Endurance 8–14 hours (speed 78

Falco MALE UAV. (Selex Galileo)

kt, data-link radius more than 81 nm), ceiling 20,000 ft. The power plant is a 75-hp piston engine.

ASIO/SPYBALL/HUMMINGBIRD

Unmanned Technologies Research Institute of Trieste (UTRI) makes VTOL UAVs in roughly the same class as Bertin's HoverEye, using ducted fans. Development of Hummingbird, the first in the series, began in February 2004, the first hovering flight following in May 2005. Production began in March 2006, and it was expected to enter service (for an undisclosed customer) in November 2006. Like HoverEye the Hummingbird uses two contrarotating fans. Unlike HoverEye it has a conventional body around which the duct for the fans is built. The system is autonomous, with joystick override, and it can be carried in a backpack. A system comprises two air vehicles and a ground station. Duct diameter is 0.5 m, and overall height is 0.75 m; weight is 4.2 kg (payload 0.9 kg). Endurance is 1 hour (mission radius 12 nm, data-link range 8 nm, maximum speed 35 kt, cruising speed 27 kt); ceiling is 10,000 ft. The customer is probably Italian special forces.

UTRI does not list Hummingbird as a current product, but it does list ASIO and Spyball. ASIO diameter is 0.48 m, height 0.75 m, and weight 6 kg (1.5-kg payload). Speed is up to 24 kt. ASIO can hover for 20 minutes (onboard power suffices for perching for over 4 hours in silent mode). The picture is stabilized, and data-link range

ASIO (Selex).

is 12 km. The complete backpack weighs 20 kg, including one ready-to-fly UAV and two camera payloads (the day/night camera automatically switches to night mode when light level falls sufficiently; UTRI also offers an optional X-ray camera). Spyball is a lighter equivalent (less than 2 kg).

UTRI also makes winged mini- or micro-UAVs: Crex-B and Otus-B, the latter capable of water landing.

MIRACH/NIBBIO

Mirach was conceived as a standard ground system that would support any of three types of piston-engine and three types of jet UAVs. Of the piston types, Mirach-10 was described as a small piston-engined delta with twin fins developed for foreign customers, and it was superseded by Mirach-20 in 1980–81. Mirach-20 was a twin-boom pusher powered by a 26-hp piston engine. The design was unusual in that it incorporated a nose radar for target acquisition. About forty Mirach-20 were made beginning in 1987–88 as Condor for the Italian army and Pelican for the navy; there were also versions with pre-programmable autopilots, including Raven and the relay Parrot. Mirach-20 entered Italian army service in 1988. This UAV lost out to Pioneer in the 1985 U.S. Navy competition (it was the Pacific Aerospace Heron 26). Mirach-70 was a conventional tractor aircraft presumably based on earlier Meteor drones ultimately derived from the U.S. MQM-33. The power plant was a 70-hp piston engine.

See Table 2 for data.

The jets differed from the U.S. Chukar (and Gufone) in having their engines over rather than under their fuse-lages. Mirach-100 was apparently successful as a target; it is not clear how well it sold as a UAV. By 1987 more than 150 had been made, for Italy, Iraq, and Libya, and another 15 to 20 were planned for the NATO missile range on Crete. Of 600 Mirach-100 made, about three-quarters were used as targets. The others were fitted with IR linescan sensors. Under a Southern Hawk program they were modified for air launch from Argentine Pucara strike aircraft (the name suggests U.S. sponsorship). Mirach-100 was powered by a 400-lb-thrust NPT 401 turbojet, and used a real-time downlink. Pacific Aerospace offered the extended-range Mirach-100ER for a 1986 U.S. Navy mid-range UAV competition, which was won by the ultimately abortive BQM-124. By 1987 a version of Mirach-100 launched by and recovered by the Agusta A109A helicopter was reported operational. A tactical cruise missile version was also being promoted. Normal one-way penetration range was 485 nm (900 km). As of 2005 90 Mirach-100/2

targets had been delivered to the Italian armed forces; Mirach-100/4 was in service with French, Spanish, Greek, and German forces and was being used at the NATO test range in Crete; Mirach-100/5 was in service (32 ordered by Italy, 39 by the UK); and work was under way on the Nibbio reconnaissance version. Mirach-150 was in service for reconnaissance (Nibbio was apparently a tactical version).

Mirach-300 was powered by an 832-lb-thrust turbojet and had swept rather than straight wings. As of 1987 it was under development. The high end of the series was Mirach-600, powered by two 832-lb-thrust jet engines. In 1987 it was only a proposal.

See Table 3 for data (1987).

Mirach-100/5 serves as a target but is also offered as a UAV for reconnaissance/target acquisition, for damage assessment, for ELINT/SIGINT, as a decoy, and to saturate air defense. Current data: span 2.30 m, length 4.07 m, weight 330 kg (payload 60 kg), endurance 90 minutes (speed Mach 0.85), minimum altitude is 10 ft; maximum is 41,000 ft. One-way penetration range is 800 km (430 nm). Navigation accuracy is 30 m CEP. The jet engine produces 350 lbs of thrust. As a target Mirach-100/5 can weave during a sea-skimming approach to a ship at 4 G and can pull up at 2.5 G with wings level, using a three-axis control system. Configuration: swept supercritical wings, single-piece horizontal tail, two ventral fins, canard rudder.

The Mirach-70 drone was built under license (as a target) in Argentina as MQ-1 Chimango. Mirach-20 may have been made under license in Argentina as MQ-4 Agilucho. The jet Mirach-100 was built under license as MQ-2 Bigua, both as a target and as a reconnaissance UAV (Version 2). Production of the latter reportedly began in 1986; it could be either air or ground launched.

The Italian army bought Mirach UAVs to support its CATRIN (Sistema Campale di Trasmissioni e Informazioni) command and control system, developed by Alenia, the parent company of Meteor SpA, which produces Mirach. It operates up to corps level. It has a communications element (SOTRIN), a surveillance element (Sottosistema di Sorveglianza di Acquisizione Obiettivi, or SORAO), and a tactical air surveillance and command/

TABLE 2

	SPAN	LENGTH	WEIGHT	PAYLOAD	ENDURANCE	SPEED	CEILING
Mirach-10	2.71 m	2.25 m	70 kg	N/A	3 hours	97 kt	N/A
Mirach-20	3.83 m	3.62 m	197 kg	25 kg	3 hours	108 kt	3,000 m (9,850 ft)
Mirach-70	3.57 m	3.66 m	260 kg	20 kg	1 hour	194 kt	N/A

Note: Weight is takeoff weight, including booster. Payload is internal; some can carry external pods.

TABLE 3

	SPAN	LENGTH	WEIGHT	PAYLOAD	ENDURANCE	SPEED
Mirach-100	1.80 m	3.94 m	310 kg	70 kg	1 hour	458 kt (528 mph)
Mirach-300	2.83 m	5.00 m	800 kg	150 kg	2 hours	Mach 0.92
Mirach-600	3.60 m	6.10 m	1,000 kg	300–500 kg	2 hours	Mach 0.92

control element (SOATCC). The concept for such an integrated system seems to date back to 1970; feasibility studies were completed in 1975, and a presentation made to EUROCOM (NATO's European Command) in 1978. The presentation was presumably necessary to ensure that CATRIN was compatible with other NATO corps-level command and control systems. The RFP was issued in November 1984, and in February 1985 a consortium led by Alenia was formed. The Italian army accepted the consortium offer in July 1986; trials were conducted during 1992. Two systems were apparently bought. SORAO used a combination of Mirach-20 and -100 UAVs and CL-89 reconnaissance drones, plus AB 412 helicopters carrying CRESO frequency-agile battlefield surveillance radars. The system includes ground data fusion centers.

The upgraded Mirach-26/150 (derived from, respectively, Mirach-20 and Mirach-100) were intended specifically to support CATRIN, Mirach-20/26 being conceived as a brigade-level system. Each had an upgraded navigation system incorporating GPS, command upgrades, and sensor improvements. Alenia announced a launch order for Mirach-26 in 1995, but no customer has come to light. After the Kosovo campaign, the Italian armed forces decided to buy both aircraft: eight systems of each type were ordered in January 2000 (deliveries began in 2002). In 2002 Selex announced Falco, conceived as a direct replacement for Mirach-26.

Mirach-26 data: span 4.72 m, length 3.78 m, takeoff weight 200 kg. Endurance is 7 hours, and ceiling is 13,000 ft. The power plant is a 28-hp piston engine.

Mirach-150 data: span 2.10 m, length 4.69 m, takeoff weight 345 kg. Endurance is 1.3 hours, and ceiling is 30,000 ft. The power plant is a Mircoturbo TRS 18-1 jet engine.

Selex developed the Nibbio high-speed deep penetrator from Mirach-100/5 as an Italian General Staff demonstration program and as a potential replacement for CL-289. It was first shown at Eurosatory in June 2002 alongside the Falco. At that time it was expected to fly in 2003. The Italian defense ministry study contract was awarded in October 2002. Nibbio was designed to receive new instructions by uplink, but there was no feedback. However, during flight tests begun in May 2005 Nibbio was equipped with a data downlink and a satellite command link; both were successfully tested. Nibbio carries the same payload as Falco but also can carry an IR linescanner in its nose. Speed is Mach 0.85, ceiling is 40,000 ft, and range is 400 km (216 nm). Unlike Mirach-100, Nibbio has its engine underslung. Span is 2.30 m, length is 4.10 m, and weight is 360 kg (payload 70 kg). Endurance is 45 minutes (mission range 400 km). The engine is a Microturbo TRS 18-1. Nibbio was expected to enter service in 2009. The Nibbio brochure also shows the related but different CARAPAS (see the French section).

Mirach-100/5 with Locusta target drones underwing. (Selex Galileo)

Note that the Nibbio UAV made in UAE and exported is an entirely different aircraft, powered by a 45-hp piston engine.

SKY-X

Sky-X development began in January 2003, reportedly to meet an Italian air force requirement for a UCAV to carry two JDAM or their equivalent. A half-scale "integration technology" mockup was rolled out on 13 March 2003, and displayed that year at Paris as the Integrated Technology Vehicle, or ITV. No sensor package was shown, but Sky-X was credited with the ability to carry a 300-kg modular payload. The definition phase began on 16 October 2003, the design was revised in 2003–4, and manufacture of the prototype began in October 2004. It was rolled out on 11 April 2005 and first flew on 29 May. The last of a series of test flights in 2006 demonstrated ATOL (automatic takeoff and landing), the use of auto-throttle, high-load turns, and approach and go-around with a low-altitude fly-by of the runway. A later series of tests included simulated flight refueling. It was the first European-designed UAV with a weight of more than one

Nibbio reconnaissance UAV. (Selex Galileo via UVSI)

metric ton (1,000 kg). As of 2008 flight tests were expected to continue through 2013; at that time Italy was expected to want a UCAV by 2020. In 2006 Alenia stated that full development of a full-scale UCAV could begin in 2007, making possible series production in 2016. Once Italy joined the Neuron project, Sky-X became a technology demonstrator rather than a step toward a full-size UCAV, which would have been twice the size of Sky-X. In 2008 it was planned to remove the tail surfaces and substitute a thrust-vectoring control system.

Sky-X has swept wings and a vee tail, its jet engine above its fuselage between the fins of the vee tail. The fuselage was designed specifically to reduce radar cross section. It incorporates a bay (2.2 m x 80 cm x 48 cm deep) to test various cargoes, including weapons. Span is 5.74 m, length is 6.84 m, and takeoff weight is 1450 kg (fuel 350 kg, payload 150 kg, empty weight 1,000 kg). Endurance 2 hours (mission radius 50 nm, maximum speed 350 kt, cruising speed 260 kt), ceiling 25,000 ft. The power plant is a Microturbo TR160-5 turbojet (990 lbs of thrust).

SKY-Y

Sky-Y is a technology demonstrator for a future surveillance MALE program. It therefore has a typical configuration surveillance UAV configuration, with twin booms and a pusher propeller. To achieve long endurance it is powered by a 200-hp turbocharged Fiat diesel engine, which is to be replaced by a 250-hp Fiat using a two-stage supercharger. Sky-Y was apparently the first European UAV to transmit data via a satellite. It broke a European record by flying for more than 8 hours (design endurance is 14 hours). Like Sky-X it has ATOL. Sky-Y first flew on 20 June 2007. Span is 9.93 m and length is 9.75 m; weight is 1,200 kg (payload 150 kg, fuel 200 kg, empty weight 850 kg). Endurance is 14 hours (cruise speed 140 kt, range 500 nm, mission radius set by data link is 50 nm); cruise altitude is 25,000 ft.

STRIX

Galileo's man-portable UAV was announced in February 2007 and was soon sold to an unspecified NATO country and placed in limited production. It is a flying wing (with only wingtip vertical surfaces) with a pusher propeller.

Sky-X UCAV. (Selex Galileo)

Sky-Y surveillance UAV. (Selex Galileo)

Span 3.00 m, length 1.17 m, payload 1 kg, endurance 2.25 hours when cruising. Speed is 35 kt; altitude is 10,000 ft.

Japan

Japan is currently the world's largest user of UAVs, but for civilian rather than military purposes; they are widely used to help service rice crops. The Japanese Ministry of Agriculture, Forestry, and Fisheries let a contract to Yamaha in 1983 to develop a crop-dusting helicopter UAV based on the firm's earlier work. By 2000 UAVs were dusting about 0.77 of the 1.7 million hectares of Japanese rice land. Yamaha was chosen for this work because of its experience building motorcycle engines, which were likely to be the power plants. It began producing its R-50 in 1987. Yamaha has dominated this market; in 2002, its RMAX accounted for 1,800 of the 2,000 Japanese agricultural UAVs. These UAVs seem to be individually piloted, and they are kept below an altitude of 150 m to prevent interference with manned airspace. Note that Yamaha was *not* chosen to develop a military UAV based on its helicopter; presumably Yamaha has shown no interest in the sort of autonomous control required in a military UAV. Japan is the only country with a significant civil UAV industry.

Both the Japan Air Self-Defense Force (JASDF) and the Japan Ground Self-Defense Force (JGSDF) have UAV development programs. In addition the Japan Maritime Self-Defense Force operated the U.S.-supplied DASH drone and modified it as a reconnaissance platform.

Late in 1988 the JASDF decided to develop a stealthy UAV based on the existing J/AQM-1 target drone, letting a $10.6 million contract to Fuji. The airframe reportedly resembled that of the U.S. space shuttle. It could be air or ground launched, and a prototype was reportedly ready in 1993. The system then evolved into the current Multi-Role UAV, which has been test-launched from F-4EJs at Gifa Air Force Base. There is also a program to convert surplus F-104 fighters into reconnaissance UAVs.

In 1991 the JGSDF asked Fuji to develop a UAV helicopter for artillery spotting (the Flying Forward Observation System, FFOS). Six prototypes were completed in 1993, and trials were conducted between early 1994 and the summer of 1995. The first system was scheduled for delivery in 2004 (two systems may have been bought).

Range is 30 miles; operational altitude is about 2,000 ft. In 1997 Fuji advertised a civil version as RPH2. RPH2A data: length 5.3 m, weight 330 kg (payload 100 kg), endurance 1 hour, ceiling 2,000 m (about 6,500 ft); the power plant is an 83.5-hp 2-stroke engine.

The Japan Defense Agency (equivalent to the U.S. DoD) began a new five-year program to develop a tactical UAV in the fall of 2003. The resulting UAV was to be operational in 2009.

In addition in 2003 the Japanese Joint Staff Office (equivalent to the U.S. Joint Chiefs of Staff) and the U.S. commander in chief, Pacific began a study, NSP (Notional Sensor Platform), to examine the use of a HALE to conduct maritime surveillance in the Sea of Japan (the Japanese Maritime Safety Agency [the Japanese coast guard] had begun a maritime surveillance project in 2000). Japanese work on a HALE began in FY 2003, looking toward tests in 2012. Reportedly Japan is also interested in buying Global Hawk; the Japanese program may ultimately be either a parallel or an effort to develop a Japanese version of Global Hawk.

A militarized version (Mk IIG) of the civil RMAX helicopter was deployed to Iraq in 2005 for surveillance. Compared to RMAX, it has a CCD (charge-coupled device) camera, a thermal imager, and an improved navigation system. The system comprised four air vehicles and a control station. Data are for the civilian version: rotor diameter 3.115 m, length 2.75 m, weight 95 kg (payload 30 kg including fuel), endurance 2 hours 30 minutes with 10-kg payload; mission radius (control range) 2.7 nm; cruising speed 39 kt, ceiling 6,500 ft.

Jordan

In November 2009 an agreement between Selex-Galileo and the King Abdullah Design and Development Bureau was announced, initially for the development of a special forces UAV; however, it also includes licensed production of Falco, which is to become the basis for future Jordanian UAVs.

Jordan Falcon was displayed at IDEX-05 (February 2005), at which time military trials were scheduled. It is a joint venture of the King Abdullah Design and Development Bureau and Jordan Aerospace Industries. It is a small surveillance drone for target acquisition at ranges up to 50 km. The airframe has a high wing and is designed to take off from runways. The power plant is a 15-hp piston engine. Effective range is set by the data-link range; guidance is by GPS. Payloads can include day and night cameras and a communication relay package or jammer. The crew includes both the UAV pilot and the payload operator. Jordan Falcon is a twin-boom pusher with an inverted vee tail between its tail booms. Data: span 4.00 m, length 2.95 m, weight 60 kg (payload 6 kg), endurance 4 hours (maximum range 450 km/243 nm, data-link range 30 nm); maximum speed is 97 kt (cruising speed 65 kt, stall speed 43 kt).

Silent Eye (or Jordan Silent Eye) was announced in 2004, for video surveillance, border patrol, and scouting. It has a full-length fuselage (the part abaft the wing is only a boom) carrying a pusher propeller and an inverted vee tail. The payload is a pair of cameras with different fields of view, carried together in the nose on a platform controlled by the ground station, plus a third (fixed) camera; video reception is switched between the cameras. The system is man-portable. The power plant is a 300-watt electric motor carried near the center of gravity amidship. Span is 2.20 m, length 1.40 m, weight 3.5 kg (payload 0.5 kg), endurance 1 hour (maximum speed 59 kt, loiter speed 38 kt, mission radius 5.4 nm); operating altitude is 1,000 m (3,280 ft).

South Korea

In February 2010 the Korean Agency for Defense Development (ADD) released an RFP for a combat UAV. A scaled demonstrator is to be tested by 2013. Korea Aerospace had already announced plans to build a 20 percent scaled version of its proposed (and internally funded) K-UCAV, which broadly resembles the German Barrakuda, with low swept wings and a vee tail. It flew in 2008 and was first publicly shown at the October 2009 Seoul air show. It has an internal bomb bay and by February 2010 had successfully dropped stores from it. Based on its characteristics, the full-scale UCAV would weigh 4.1 metric tons (8,900 lbs) and would reach a maximum speed of Mach 0.85 and a ceiling of 39,000 ft. Endurance would be 5 hours. A full-scale K-UCAV would be 8.4 m long

Jordan Falcon surveillance drone. (Jordan Aerospace Industry via UVSI)

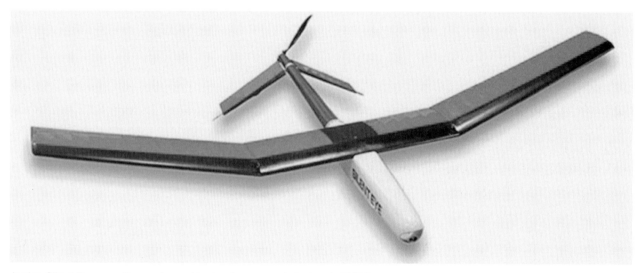

Jordan Silent Eye surveillance drone. (Jordan Aerospace Industry via UVSI)

with a 9.1-m wingspan. Bids were due by 23 March 2010, the winning entry to be chosen in June 2010. The South Korean government will supply radar-absorbing material and one engine each for two prototypes.

As of early 2010 two other South Korean military projects were proceeding: a MALE (15,000 m altitude) to be built by Korean Air Lines (KAL) and a foreign partner (MUAV) and an army battlefield reconnaissance UAV (competition between KAL and Korean Aerospace).

South Korean military interest in UAVs apparently dates from 1982. In December 1995 it was reported that South Korea was about to buy Israeli UAVs; in August 1997 it was reported that it had bought Searcher for delivery early in 1998. This purchase may have been intended mainly to gain experience for the introduction of Korean-built UAVs, beginning with Night Intruder 300 (see below).

Night Intruder 300 reconnaissance and surveillance UAV. (Korean Aerospace Industries via UVSI)

Daewoo began work in 1991 on the Night Intruder 300 strategic reconnaissance and surveillance UAV, under a program initially code-named Bijo (the UAV itself was called Doyosae). The Doyosae prototype flew in 1993, and a fully developed version called XSR-1 was displayed (without data) at the late 1996 Seoul Air Show. At that time it appeared that the UAV would enter service in 1998, but development was not completed until August 2000, the production contract being awarded in 2001. Night Intruder 300 was shown at Seoul in October 2001 as XKRQ-101. Korea Aerospace Industries (KAI) was established in September 1999 under a government consolidation plan and is now associated with this program. Night Intruder 300 entered corps service in the ROK Army. A production contract was awarded in September 2001, first deliveries following in November 2003 (but a South Korean account claims that the system entered service in 2002). Night Intruder became operational in 2004, and as of 2008 about thirty air vehicles were in service. Reportedly the South Korean army bought five Night Intruder systems from 2001 on (deliveries completed December 2004), and the navy bought Night Intruder beginning in 2003. A

system comprises six air vehicles and control vehicles, including a separate ground-control terminal (GCT), which relays commands from the GCS (ground-control station, with mission planning bay) to the UAV. It also relays telemetry and compressed data to the GCS. There is also a separate launch control station. In 2009 KAI claimed that Night Intruder 300 was currently in South Korean service and as of midyear had made 1,800 flights.

The twin-boom pusher Night Intruder 300 is reportedly very similar to the South African Seeker. The successor is Night Intruder 2.

Data: span 6.4 m, length 4.8 m, takeoff weight 300 kg (215 kg empty), payload 45 kg. Endurance is 6 hours (speed 100 kt/180 km/hour, endurance speed 65 to 81 kt, data-link range 65 nm, 194 nm with relay), and ceiling is 15,000 ft. The power plant is a 50-hp Wankel engine.

Roughly parallel with Night Intruder 300 was a program for a TRPV-1 Doyosne (Snipe) mini-UAV, development of which began in 1988 for the South Korean air force. The first flew in 2003; it may have been intended mainly to gain experience with UAV technology. In February 2007 the South Korean army issued a request for information for a short-range UAV. Ucon (see below) has offered its RemoEye 006, roughly comparable to the U.S. Pointer, for platoon and company forward surveillance. The UAE was launch customer for RemoEye 006. Ucon has also developed the smaller RemoEye 002 (used by UAE special forces) and a long-endurance RemoEye 015 for meteorology (comparable to the Australian Aerosonde, not relevant to this survey). Late in 2007 the Koreans bought a single Israeli Skylark 2 system, also for the forward tactical surveillance role.

Shortly after Night Intruder 300 entered service, the Ministry of Science and Technology set up a UAV program. The South Korean government decided to sponsor UAV technology as a key strategic asset. Its industrial plan called for it to seek about 9 percent of the world UAV market by 2012, by which time the Koreans think that there will be a significant civilian market.

KAL became the lead institution in a five-year effort to develop a close-range UAV for maritime patrol and to monitor forest fires. The resulting KUS-7 flew in August 2007; the follow-on is KUS-9. Both have been developed by the Korea Institute of Aerospace Technology, KAL's R&D arm. Both use twin-boom pusher configurations, but KUS-9 has a blended wing and body that presumably reduces radar cross section. KUS-7: span 3.4 m, length 3.1 m, weight 70 kg (payload 7 kg), endurance 2.5 hours (range 45 km); altitude 3,000 m (about 10,000 ft). Speed is 150 km/hour (cruising speed 100 km/hour). KUS-9: span 4.2 m, length 3.4 m, weight 150 kg (payload 20 kg), endurance 8 hours (range 80 km), altitude 4,000 m. Speed is 180 km/hour (cruising speed 140 km/hour).

In 2006 ADD ordered development of a MALE with 24-hour endurance at 45,000 ft. KAL was selected as system integrator. Data: span 25 m, length 12 m, weight 4,000 kg (payload 500 kg), range 500 km. Contrary to reports, this is not KUS-9. Earlier reports, presumably reflecting an alternative KAI design, claimed a takeoff weight of 6,500 kg and a pusher turboprop engine. The MALE program was formally launched in 2008. There may also be a HALE project, as the United States has repeatedly refused to export Global Hawk to South Korea.

SmartUAV is one of a series of "21st Century frontier R&D programs" with ten-year budgets. Objectives in-

RemoEye 006 held by an ROK Marine. (Ucon Industries)

clude the development of innovative UAV technologies, such as ATLS, collision avoidance, fault diagnosis and reconfiguration in flight, and active air flow separation. Development began in July 2002, and a prototype is currently flying. Korea Aerospace Research Institute (KARI) chose a tilt-rotor configuration in preference to a canard rotor-wing and other configurations. The program runs in stages. Stage 1 (completed March 2005) chose the configuration after analysis and tests, stage 2 (completion March 2009) produces a prototype and tests it, and stage 3 (completion March 2012) inserts the new "smart" technologies. Span is 6.8 m (including rotors; wingspan is 4 m), length is 5 m, and weight is 995 kg (payload 90 kg). Maximum speed is 270 kt (cruising speed 238 kt, loiter speed 135 kt); endurance is 5 hours, and range is 108 nm. Ceiling is 16,000 ft.

At the other end of the scale, Uconsystems makes a series of small RemoEye UAVs for small ground units. The UAE became launch customer for RemoEye 006 when it acquired two systems. The later (and smaller) RemoEye 002 is used by UAE special forces. It is hand-launched and has a parasol wing; span is 2.72 m, length 1.55 m, and weight 6.5 kg (payload 0.17 kg); endurance more than 1.5 hours (range 15 km, maximum speed 75 km/hour, speed 50–70 km/hour). RemoEye 002 is a smaller equivalent (span 1.5 m, length 1.3 m, weight 2.7 kg [payload 0.17 kg], maximum speed 80 km/hour, endurance 1 hour, mission radius more than 10 km, speed 50 to 70 km/hour).

In each case a full system employs four air vehicles, and the payload is a color TV camera or an IR imager. Remo Eye 006 can use two remote video terminals as well as its main terminal. The next step up, RemoEye 015, resembles a scaled-down Predator, with cylindrical body, shoulder wing, vee tail, and pusher propeller: span is 3.2 m, length 1.5 m, and weight 15 kg; endurance is 4 hours (range 50 km, speed 170 km/hour). Ucon also makes a series of RemoEye helicopters. H-120 weighs 100 kg (rotor diameter 3.2 m, length 3.5 m, endurance 2 hours, maximum speed 130 km/hour, cruising speed 120 km/hour, range 50 km). Ranges are presumably all set by radio link, not by fuel capacity. H-120 first flew in vertical remote-controlled mode in August 2005. It is not clear to what extent these small UAVs are in current Korean service. In addition to military missions, H-120 can be used for crop dusting (which is an important UAV mission in Japan). As in the other two systems, a full H-120 system includes four air vehicles.

Another firm, MicroAirRobot, is developing military micro-UAVs. Its FM-07 weighs 0.5 kg, with a span of 0.6 m and a length of 0.3 m; endurance is 40 minutes (maximum speed 70 km/hour, cruising speed 40 km/hour, range 5 km).

Malaysia

Aludra (Alliance Unmanned Developmental Research Aircraft) has been chosen by the Malaysian government as a "project of national importance" (as stated on 21 October 2008) to equip the Malaysian armed forces. At least initially it is to be contractor operated from an airfield in Sabah, in east Malaysia. The lead developer, CTRM (Composites Technology Research Malaysia) became involved in UAV development after working on the Eagle 150 aerial reconnaissance vehicle (ARV), an optionally piloted airplane. It developed a small remotely piloted vehicle (EX-01), then teamed with Ikramatic Systems to develop an autopilot. The resulting SR-01 was larger. Another company, System Consultancy Services, meanwhile developed its own Nyamok UAV, and in December 2006 the three companies joined to develop Aludra (SR-02). The prototype (less payload) flew in September 2006, and in fully equipped form on 15 May 2007; it flew with the full Agile sensor suite (intended for the Mk 2 version) shortly before the LIMA (Langkawi International Maritime and Aerospace Exposition) 2007 arms show. Aludra is a twin-boom pusher powered by a 50-hp engine. Data for the Mk 2 version: span 6.10 m, length 4.27 m, weight 250 kg (payload 50 kg), endurance 6 hours (speed 120 kt, loiter speed 55 kt, mission radius 81 nm [150 km]), ceiling 12,000 ft.

The ARV was derived from an Australian-made Eagle 150B two-seat light airplane, modified to conduct maritime surveillance, forest firewatch, and detection of illegal immigration and drug operations. The ARV was proposed in 1999, BAE Systems teaming with CTRM of Malaysia. The airplane flew on 5 June 2001. The payload was an EO/IR combination in an underslung turret. A system includes three air vehicles (three were seen at Labuan in January 2006). Only one system was bought, partly because the Australian manufacturer ceased production of the Eagle in November 2005. The ARV became the first operational Malaysian UAV system. Launch and landing were both automated. Span is 7.16 m, length 6.45 m, weight 648 kg (payload 60 kg), endurance 10 hours (mission radius 135 nm, maximum speed 133 kt, cruising speed 120 kt), ceiling 16,000 ft. As modified the airplane retains its cockpit.

Since November 2008 the Malaysian Unmanned Systems Technology company (UST) has been providing security surveillance and imaging to the Malaysian joint forces command on a private basis using the Aludra Mk 1. This arrangement was expected to lead to the purchase of Aludras, but it has been delayed by the financial crisis.

UST now has a competitor in the form of the Cyber Eye II UAV developed by the Sapura Group and the Australian company Cyber Technology. Cyber Eye was first demonstrated to the Malaysian military in November 2007, and a few have been bought by the Royal Thai Air Force training command. Cyber Shark is a parallel helicopter UAV, which was demonstrated to the Malaysian military in April 2008. Development began in 2006, and an initial demonstrator was shown at the LIMA exhibition late in 2007. The company claims that it is currently working on a MALE comparable to the Israeli Hermes 450. A demonstrator may fly early in 2010.

Cyber Eye data: span 4.5 m, length 2.8 m, weight 50 kg (payload 15 kg; maximum figures 60 kg and 20 kg, respectively), endurance 10 hours (speed 100 km/hour normal, maximum 160 km/hour), ceiling 15,000 ft (normal altitude 1,000 ft), data range 150 km (100 km normal), video range 30 km (20 km normal range). One ground station can control up to six aircraft, each using differential GPS navigation. The standard payload is a Sony 26x pan zoom camera, which is fully stabilized. Configuration: pod and boom (vee tail) with the pusher engine atop a short pylon above the wing.

Cyber Shark data: Rotor diameter 2.1 m, weight 30 kg (normal weight 14 kg, possibly empty weight), payload 5 kg (normal payload 2 kg), endurance 3 hours maximum (normally 1 hour), speed 100 km/hour (maximum 130 km/hour), ceiling 10,000 ft (normal altitude 8,000 ft). Data-link range is 100/150 km as in Cyber Eye. The power plant is either a small piston engine or a micro–gas turbine. The gasoline-engine version has demonstrated an endurance of 3.5 hours and a maximum speed of 70 kt (130 km/hour) and a ceiling of 10,000 ft.

Both UST and Sapura are currently working on small VTOL UAVs to meet a projected long-term Southeast Asian military requirement for close-range surveillance and reconnaissance. UST's Intisar 100 is being offered for aerial photography in Malaysia. It is currently remotely operated rather than autonomous. Development began early in 2008, and flight testing began in mid-2008. Rotor diameter is 1.5 m, length is 1.34 m, and takeoff weight is 13 kg (5-kg payload); cruising speed is 43 kt (endurance 1 hour). Maximum altitude is 800 ft. It is not clear whether Sapura sees CyberShark as equivalent, as it is somewhat larger with higher performance.

Mexico

Hydra Technologies developed the S-4 Ehecatl UAV beginning in 2002 (it first flew in 2006), displaying it for the first time at the 2007 Paris Air Show. One system was delivered to the Mexican national police in February 2008; the second went to the Mexican navy. The primary mission is border surveillance, which would normally mean the Mexican air force for the land border with the United States and the Mexican navy for the sea frontiers. As of 2008 the Dominican Republic was negotiating pur-

chases of S-4 UAVs. The S-4 has also been demonstrated to Panama. Data: span 3.70 m, weight 55 kg (payload 9 kg), endurance 8 hours (maximum speed 90 kt, cruising speed 38 kt, loiter speed 32 kt, mission radius 52 nm), ceiling 15,000 ft.

Pakistan

Pakistan became interested in UAVs in the early 1990s, initially for surveillance in Kashmir. The effort was sponsored by the National Development Complex directed by the Pakistan National Engineering and Scientific Commission. This is the public sector of the Pakistan arms industry, including the Pakistan Aeronautical Complex and Air Weapons Complex (AWC). It makes the Bravo and Vision tactical UAVs for the Pakistani army. Private sector companies developing UAVs are Integrated Dynamics and Surveillance and Target Unmanned Aircraft (SATUMA). In addition East West Infinity makes the Whisper Watch long-range SIGINT system, which can be carried on board its Heliquad micro-UAV (first shown in 2006). Global Industrial Defense Solutions developed Huma-1 and a version of Uqaab. In 2002 it was claimed that Pakistan expected to advance its UAV program as much as a decade by studying an Israeli-made Indian Searcher Mk II that had been shot down.

Pakistan also bought the UAV version of the Meggitt Banshee 400 in 2001. In 2004 Pakistan tried unsuccessfully to buy U.S. Predator A or Shadow 200 UAVs (four Predators may have been supplied in 2008). Given the failure of the Predator request, in April 2006 Pakistan decided instead to buy the German LUNA for its army and the Italian Falco for its air force; Falco is now being manufactured under license in Pakistan. Pakistan (AWC) and Turkey (Turkish Aerospace Industries, or TAI) signed an agreement to develop a data-link system for a MALE at the IDEF 07 show (23 May 2007). Reportedly there is a wider agreement for mutual assistance, probably involving the Turkish TIHA. It was reported in May 2008 that Pakistan was seeking the Boeing ScanEagle for operations along the border with Afghanistan.

Apparently the Pakistani army was the first UAV buyer in the country. The Pakistani air force did not announce a program until 2005, and it first inducted UAVs (Bravo+ and the Italian Falco) into its service in 2009.

Mexican S-4 at the 2009 Paris Air Show. (Norman Friedman)

In May 2009 it was reported that the Pakistani air force and the National Engineering and Scientific Commission were developing the Burraq UCAV, to carry and control laser-designated weapons.

BORDER EAGLE MK II

Introduced in 2003, Border Eagle Mk II is Integrated Dynamics' main export item, and reportedly it was sold to Australia, Libya, South Korea, Spain, and the United States, though it is not certain whether all of them bought Border Eagle. The U.S. customer was the border patrol, operating this UAV near San Diego. By December 2006 about eighteen to twenty airframes had been exported (total $300,000). It is a twin-boom pusher aircraft with a high wing and fixed undercarriage. Endurance is more than 4 hours. The standard system includes four air vehicles. The usual payload is a gyro-stabilized EO platform. Span 3.1 m, length 1.75 m, weight 15 kg (payload 4 kg), endurance over 3 hours (mission radius 16 nm, maximum speed 86 kt, loiter speed 16 kt), ceiling 10,000 ft (typically operates at 1,000 ft).

BRAVO/VISION MK 1

Developed by the Air Weapon Complex, the Bravo battlefield surveillance UAV went into service supporting police and border patrols. One system was delivered to the Pakistani army for operational evaluation late in 2000. Dimensions are not available. Using a 110-kg (loaded)

Border Eagle Mk II UAV. (Integrated Dynamics)

composite airframe, Bravo has a 20-kg payload and a 43-nm radius of action. Endurance is more than 4 hours. Maximum speed is 86 kt (cruising speed 65 kt). Vision-1 is an improved version. AWC also produces the high-altitude Vector.

Vision Mk I/II was developed as an over-the-horizon system. The advertised capability to fly a preprogrammed path suggests that earlier UAVs required continuous control. Effective range is 50 km (120 km for the larger Mk II). Vision Mk II is a pod-and-boom aircraft with a pusher propeller at the trailing edge of the high wing. Span 4.51 m, length 2.9 m, weight 80 kg (payload 15 kg), endurance 4 hours (speed 75–208 km/hour). A system includes four air vehicles. Note that Vision is also credited to Integrated Dynamics.

DESERT HAWK

Integrated Dynamics began work on the Desert Hawk UAV late in 2003 in response to a Pakistani army require-

Uqab UAV. (ISPR)

ment; the prototype flew late in 2004. Desert Hawk entered Pakistani army service about 2006. It was designed for both powered and unpowered flight, using either a gasoline engine or an electric motor. The configuration is pod-and-boom, with a vee tail and a secondary pod on a pylon atop the main (sensor) pod carrying the engine and a two-blade tractor propeller. Presumably the secondary pod carries fuel or, for the electric version, batteries. The nose of the main pod carries the sensor. Because there is no separate stabilized sensor turret, the CCD camera is electronically stabilized. The system includes two air vehicles, allowing communication relay in rough terrain. Span 2.44 m, length 1.83 m, weight 6.8 kg, endurance 2 hours (mission radius approx 0.8 nm; 5.4 nm with autopilot; maximum cruising speed 56 kt, loiter speed 17 kt), typical operating altitude 1,000 ft.

EAGLE EYE PI/PII/UQAAB

Eagle Eye and Uqaab are Integrated Dynamics' runway-launched systems. The PI first flew in 2002, the PII in 2005. PI span is 16.5 ft, takeoff weight 130 kg. PII: 18.9-ft span, 175 kg. Both are twin-boom pushers. At DSEi 2007, Integrated Dynamics and Advanced Computing and Engineering Solutions said that they expected to need another 18 months to complete development of their Eagle Eye PI and PII and Huma-1 UAVs.

Uqab (or Uqaab), tested successfully in 2007–8, is an improved Eagle. Reportedly there are two versions, tactical and strategic, with ranges of 150 and 350 km. Presumably the strategic version uses satellite communication; it

can also change mission during flight. These figures are from a Pakistani Web site, and they contradict the official range figure of 80 to 100 km. Endurance is 5 to 6 hours, and altitude is about 20,000 ft.

FIREFLY

Firefly is a rocket with delta wings (at its tail) and a single vertical tail, fired from a pistol-like hand launcher with an elevation scale. Flying time is 8 sec. Development began late in 2004 in response to a Pakistani army operational requirement for a high-speed short-range observation system usable in the mountainous terrain of northern Pakistan. It uses a commercial miniature solid-fuel rocket, the air vehicle covering 800 to 1,000 m before disintegrating when it hits the ground. The airframe is made of PVC plastic; the fins snap on, and there is no in-flight guidance system. The payload is a fixed focal length disposable CCD camera and a 1.5 GHz data link. The basic system ($3,000) comprises four rockets with their carrying case and a PDA-based ground-control station. Flight tests began in 2005. Integrated Dynamics plans to incorporate some Firefly subsystems in a hand-launched micro-UAV using an 8-in (200-mm) plastic flying wing, with an endurance of about 30 minutes (range 1 km).

HORNET

The Hornet, a short-range adjunct to Vector based on earlier target drones, was developed by Integrated Dynamics. The current Mk V is a conventional tractor airframe with a small piston engine. A system includes four aircraft. Span 3.87 m (also given as 4.25 m), length 2.95 m, weight 60 kg (payload 15 kg), endurance 4 hours minimum (operating range up to 80 km, speed 132–240 km/hour), ceiling 5,000 ft. The normal payload is a daylight television camera; Hornet can carry flares for night work.

HUMA-1

Integrated Dynamics' UAV has a twin-boom pusher configuration similar to that of the Chinese ASN-206. It flew in 2003, and in 2007 Integrated Dynamics stated that it would need another one and a half years of development; it also stated that a larger tactical version was under development. Huma-1 was conceived as a low-cost system,

Hornet Mk 5 short-range UAV. (Integrated Defence Systems via UVSI)

using a GPS-based autopilot with a return-home mode if GPS is lost. It uses a zero-length launcher. Span is 4.40 m, length 3.76 m, weight 130 kg (payload 20 kg). Endurance is 5–6 hours (mission radius 81 nm, maximum range 210 nm [500 km], maximum speed 97 kt [180 km/hour]), and operating altitude is 3,280 ft (1,000 m) to 9,800 ft (3,000 m). The power plant is a 22-bhp 2-cylinder 2-stroke engine.

JASOOS II/FLAMINGO

SATUMA's UAV has the usual twin-boom pusher configuration with wheeled landing gear. Span is 4.92 m, length is 3.59 m, and takeoff weight is 125 kg (payload 20–30 kg). Endurance is 4 to 5 hours, and ceiling is 10,000 ft. The power plant is a 22- to 35-hp 2-stroke engine. It was probably developed as an alternative to Shadow/Vector, offering much the same capabilities in a similar configuration. Another set of specifications claims a takeoff weight of 70 kg (payload 10–15 kg); speeds are given as 130 km/hour maximum, 90 km/hour loiter, and 100 km/hour cruise, with a one-way range of 300 km and an effective live reconnaissance range (set by data link) of 60 km; endurance is given as 3.5 hours. SATUMA calls the air force version of Jasoos II Bravo Plus, stating that it was adopted in 2004.

SATUMA's NB-X2 (also called Jasoos Joined-Wing) UAV is described as a strategic reconnaissance craft, but it falls far short of a MALE or HALE. Span is 3.98 m, and length is 3.72 m; takeoff weight is 180 kg (payload 50 kg).

Endurance is 8 hours (speed 140 km/hour); ceiling is 18,000 ft.

SATUMA also makes a Flamingo medium-range UAV for military and civilian use. Like Jasoos it is a twin-boom airplane with a high wing. The power plant is a 50- to 60-hp 2-stroke gasoline engine. Span 6.61 m, length 5.18 m, weight 245 kg (payload 30–35 kg), endurance 6–8 hours (speed 130 km/hour, range [set by live video link] over 200 km), ceiling 12,000 to 15,000 ft. Flamingo takes off conventionally from a runway.

In 2009 SATUMA announced Stingray, a mini-UAV with flying-wing configuration (span 3 m, length 1.5 m, weight 7.5 kg [1.5-kg payload]) with 1-hour endurance (speed 90 km/hour, range 15 km).

NISHAN MK 1/X-1000

Developed by Integrated Dynamics, Nishan II is a high-speed target/decoy with a canard pusher configuration: two small canards and clipped-delta wings with extensions outboard of the two vertical fins. A complete system includes ten air vehicles. The TJ-1000 version substitutes a mini-turbojet for the pusher piston engine. A system includes six air vehicles. Again, this is a decoy as well as a target. Integrated Dynamics also makes Tornado, a decoy resembling a scale model of the Tornado jet. Nishan X-1000 (Janbaz) is an entirely different HALE using two piston engines, improved IR cameras, and a better data link. About 2008 a Pakistani Web site gave the following data:

Jasoos Joined-Wing UAV. Note that it has both pusher and tractor propellers. (SATUMA via UVSI)

length 25 ft 2 in, weight 200 kg (payload 50–70 kg), endurance 7–9 hours (dash speed 340 mph, loiter speed 170 mph, cruising speed 220 mph); live reconnaissance range 300 miles, one-way range 700 miles. Tests were expected in mid-February 2008, but it is not clear whether that happened.

SHADOW/VECTOR

Integrated Dynamics' twin-boom UAV apparently is painted to resemble a conventional aircraft, presumably in hopes of convincing an enemy tracking it optically that it is far more distant. The design was developed to meet a requirement for a family of modular composite airframes for tactical surveillance at 160 to 200 km; the data link is intended to provide a line-of-sight range of 200 km. As in other Integrated Dynamics systems, in this case a full system includes four air vehicles. Span 5.2 m, length 2.95 m, weight 90 kg (payload 25 kg), endurance 6 hours (mission radius 54 nm [100 km], maximum speed 112 kt, loiter speed 40 kt), ceiling 12,000 ft. Note that an Integrated Dynamics brochure claims that payload is in the "40-kg class," which suggests that these figures may be low. Although Shadow seems to have been developed specifically for the Pakistan military, reportedly two systems were supplied in 2006 to a Spanish government agency for agricultural research. Integrated Dynamics states that Shadow was developed for a specific customer requirement.

Vector was a larger (and earlier) related UAV. Design began 1989–90, Vector first flying in 1995–96; production of Mk 1 began in 2001, and a Mk 2 version was shown in Dubai in 2002. This version was credited with a maximum range of 200 km (108 nm), endurance of 5 hours, and ceiling of 12,000 ft. Note that some illustrations of Vector (presumably Mk 2) show a cylindrical rather than a square-section body. Mk 1 data: span 7.09 m, length 3.54 m, weight 105 kg (25-kg payload, empty weight 66 kg), endurance 4.5 hours (effective range with optical tracking 10 km [5.4 nm], with GPS/autonomous guidance 150 km [81 nm], maximum speed 111 kt, loiter speed 40 kt), ceiling 15,000 ft. The power plant is a 25-hp 2-cylinder engine. The normal payload is a real-time daylight camera, but acoustic sensors and radar are also available.

Poland

In the 1990s Poland began studies of both large tactical UAVs and mini-UAVs; at present both have led mainly to purchases of foreign equipment. The tactical UAV effort began in 1994 under the code name Vektor, funded by the State Committee for Scientific Research. The Polish firm PZL-Mielec approaching SAGEM to discuss possible French assistance with ground stations and avionics. The envisaged payload was 45–50 kg, and PZL-Mielec considered both piston and micro-turbojet power. No UAV seems to have been built, and in 2005 Poland became the first export customer for the U.S. RQ-7 Shadow. Originally at least four systems, to equip four Polish brigades (plus training spares), were desired, but early in 2006 the project was cut to immediate acquisition of two systems (three air vehicles plus one spare each), with four more to be bought through 2010. In October 2008 the Polish Ministry of Defense announced an urgent operational requirement for three tactical UAV systems, the alternatives being the Israeli Aerostar, Hermes 450, and Searcher Mk 2. Presumably all of this means that the original national program was abandoned.

National development of mini-UAVs did go ahead. The Polish air force technical institute studied mini-UAVs in collaboration with the Radwar electronics firm, beginning test flights of HOB-bit in 2005. Meanwhile WB Electronics developed SoFar (see below). Again, foreign UAVs were preferred. Thus when the Polish Grom special forces announced a requirement for a mini-UAV in 2005, the alternatives were SoFar, the Israeli Orbiter and Bird Eye 400, and the U.S. Raven; Orbiter was chosen. One system was ordered in 2006, six more in July 2007, and four more in June 2008, against an objective of twenty-one mini-UAV systems through 2012. Orbiter was deployed with Polish troops to Iraq late in 2007. SoFar and the Israeli Skylark are currently being offered to the Polish armed forces.

SoFar was the result of collaboration between the Polish company WB Electronics and the Israeli company Top-1 Vision. It is hand-launched, with a cylindrical body and a parasol wing carrying its motor and tractor propeller. The fuselage telescopes for easy transport. In December 2006 Hungary bought two systems (three air vehicles each). Sofar had already been used in June 2006 to correct the fire of a battery of 152-mm howitzers; it was said to be the first mini-UAV in the world used for artillery spotting. However, Hungary bought SoFar mainly for deployment to Afghanistan. It was selected in preference to Bird Eye 400 and Skylark. Weight is 4.9 kg, endurance is 2 hours (range 10 km/5.4 nm, maximum speed 49 kt [90 km/hour]).

HOB-bit was used in mid-2005 for a technology demonstration in conjunction with various command and control systems. It was evaluated by the Warsaw police. Unusually for a mini-UAV, it has two electric motors, each driving a tractor propeller on its wing. Span is 1.7 m, length 1.2 m, weight 3.5 to 5 kg, endurance 45 minutes (radius 10.8 nm, cruising speed 22 to 49 kt), and operating altitude is 100 to 600 m (330 to 1970 ft).

Russia

The Soviet Union seems to have been the first country to develop jet reconnaissance drones. All had preset analog control systems, and all brought back their data without any form of data linking. The first to enter service was the La-17R version of the then-standard La-17 target drone (TBR-1 system), development of which was ordered in 1956. This air-launched version proved unsuccessful, so a ground-launched alternative with the same designation was developed. La-17 was radio- and autopilot-controlled and used conventional film. The autopilot was programmed to switch off periodically so that course corrections could be ordered on the basis of radar tracking. Tracking in turn precluded very low altitude operation. Development began in 1958, and tests were completed in 1962.

Combat radius was about 400 km (250 miles). At its minimum altitude (600 m) the La-17 could overfly targets 60 to 80 km beyond the front line; at its maximum altitude (5,000 to 7,000 m, i.e., up to 23,000 ft) that increased to 150 to 200 km (i.e., up to 100 nm). Production continued through 1974, when La-17R was superseded by the Tupolev VR-3 Reys system. The system was withdrawn from service in the early 1980s. Because development of the original La-17 was completed before the Sino-Soviet split, the target version was supplied to China, where it entered production in modified form as CK-1. The Chinese apparently did not develop a reconnaissance version.

Tupolev began developing a much faster reconnaissance drone, based on abortive cruise missiles, at about the same time. Because the new drone was not based on an existing airframe, development was presumably expected to be protracted (in fact, the new system was tested alongside La-17R). Tupolev's Tu-121 ground-launched cruise missile was canceled in 1960 in favor of the R-5 ballistic missile; its airframe was modified into the Tu-123 Yastreb reconnaissance drone (DBR-1 system, D indicating Dalny, long range). Initially the Tu-123 designation referred to a longer-range follow-on to the Tu-121 cruise missile. Yastreb (Hawk) development using the Tu-121 airframe was ordered in 1960, six months after cancellation of the cruise missile. Unlike La-17R, Tu-123 carried electronic as well as photographic intelligence equipment. At this stage the airframe was not expected to be recoverable, data being recovered in a nose section that parachuted to earth. Because the airframe already existed, tests began soon after the order for development, but they continued into 1963. Each Yastreb squadron had six launchers, each with twelve aircraft; presumably this combination was the complement of a single DBR-1 system. References to the production of fifty-two aircraft in 1964–72 presumably mean fifty-two systems (it is not clear to what extent squadrons had replacement aircraft). The system was retired about 1979 in favor of the MiG-25R supersonic reconnaissance aircraft. Abortive projects included a manned version and a version powered by a nuclear turbojet.

A Tupolev proposal for a reusable version, Tu-123P, was rejected at the outset of the project. However, in 1964

Tu-243 and other elements of the Reys-D (VR-3D) UAV reconnaissance system. (Steven Zaloga)

Tupolev began work on a reusable reconnaissance drone system it called DBR-2 (Tu-139 aircraft), which was tested successfully beginning in the late 1960s. Although work on supersonic long-range drones was canceled (presumably as satellites began to enter service), in 1968 Tupolev received approval for a shorter-range subsonic system, VR-3, or Reys (Flight). Tupolev's development of a drone that could be used at least ten times proved crucial. The initial version was limited to photographic reconnaissance, with planned versions carrying a television camera (i.e., providing real-time intelligence) and ESM. The air vehicle was Tu-143; when production ended in 1989, 950 aircraft and about 152 full systems had been built. Range was 170 to 180 km, compared to 3,200 km for Tu-123, and Tu-143 was subsonic (Tu-123 flew at 1,680 mph). Each VR-3 squadron had four launchers and twelve Tu-143s. The system was exported to Czechoslovakia (1984), Romania, Syria, and probably Iraq. Syria used it in 1982 to observe Israeli forces in southern Lebanon. The Soviets used Tu-143 in Afghanistan and apparently it was

well liked. The improved Reys-D (Tu-243 aircraft derived from Tu-143, D for longer range, 360 km) began development in 1983 and began flight tests in 1987, and soon entered production, the system being designated VR-3D. Tu-243 was stretched by 25 cm to add fuel capacity, and it had a new engine and an entirely new equipment suite, including alternative day and IR cameras with a data link. The air vehicle follows a preset path, transmitting its pictures once it has cleared the target area (typically 12–14 minutes after taking them). VR-3D remains operational in 2009. Data (Tu-243): span 2.2 m, length 8.3 m, weight 1,600 kg (payload 130 kg), speed 850–940 km/hour, altitude 50–5,000 m, radius of action 360 km. In 2004 about thirty Reys-D systems were reportedly in service. A modernization program began in 2008, the first two Tu-143s arriving at the plant that November.

A parallel development was VR-2 (Tu-141 aircraft) Strizh (Swift, the bird) system for tactical reconnaissance within a few hundred km of the front line (in effect replacing the La-17 system). Given its greater range, Tu-141 was effectively a scaled-up Tu-143. The prototype flew in February 1974, and production began in 1979, 152 (including prototypes) being built. Tu-141 might be considered more or less equivalent to the U.S. Firebee reconnaissance drones used extensively during the Vietnam War, and the date of the approved requirement suggests that it was at least partly inspired by that example. At about the same time the Tu-143 project was approved, a U.S. Tagboard (D-21) supersonic reconnaissance drone fell into Soviet hands, its autopilot having failed during a mission over China. The Tupolev design bureau designed an equivalent that it called Voron (Raven), but it was not built. Strizh remains operational in small numbers in 2009.

A follow-on Orel (also given as Oryol) program was to offer 24-hour endurance and 20,000-m (65,000-ft) altitude, with a takeoff weight of about 4,000 kg. The aircraft would have carried synthetic aperture radar. Competitive designs were solicited from Tupolev, Myasischev, and Yakovlev, but no funds were available in the 1990s, and the program died.

Early in 1982 the Soviet Ministry of Defence developed a requirement for a UAV to support airborne units, which would be inserted behind enemy lines and would not have access to the usual front reconnaissance assets. Presumably they were part of the evolving concept of deep battle in which these units would disrupt NATO formations in support of a non-nuclear assault. A formal directive followed in July 1982. This development roughly coincided with the Israeli use of UAVs during the 1982 Lebanon War but probably preceded it. Outside of airborne troops, the Soviets did not then have the sort of independent units that would have required their own reconnaissance assets. Because so much depended on the sensors and the control system, overall responsibility went to the Kulon design bureau of the Ministry of the Electronics Industry; the design of the UAV was assigned to the Yakovlev aircraft design bureau. The UAV was designated Izdeliye 60 (Item 60) or DPLA-60 (literally, remote-controlled vehicle 60) or Pchela (Bee)-1.

The 1982 requirement demanded that tests begin in February 1983; Pchela actually made its first successful flight on 17 June 1983. An initial batch of 50 Pchela-1M was ordered in September 1985. This version was sometimes designated Pchela-1TM for its television (data-link)

system, to differentiate it from a later ECM version, Pchela-1PM. Meanwhile, in June 1984 Pchela was assigned experimental status because a much-improved follow-on, Shmel' (Bumblebee), entered development. This air vehicle had much the same configuration as Pchela but differed considerably in detail. It flew in April 1986. Shmel' at least was a fully digital UAV in the Western sense, operating autonomously beginning slightly before launch. To confuse matters, by 1992 Shmel' was being called Pchela-1T.

Meanwhile the Soviet General Staff, impressed by the achievements of Israeli UAVs during the 1982 Lebanon War, decided to extend the use of these systems throughout its army. It conceived a system called Stroy (Formation) to operate at different levels: Stroy-P (Polk: Regiment), Stroy-A (Army), and Stroy-F (Front, corresponding to an army group). In Stroy-P, Pchela would interact with new long-range weapons: multiple rocket launchers, self-propelled howitzers, and attack helicopters. Presumably this kind of operation was connected with the attempt to evolve the Soviet army toward a more mobile dispersed force whose weapons would often fire beyond its horizon. The Stroy-P system was offered for export as Sterkh, and the export version of Pchela-1T was, again confusingly, called Shmel' for export. Five production Stroy-P systems (ten Pchela each) were delivered by the end of 1991, and the system was formally accepted for service in 1997. By that time the system had seen combat in Chechnya. Production was suspended after 36 Pchela-1T for three Stroy-P units were built in 1991–92; one unit went to North Korea in 1993 before any had been delivered to the Russian military. Five Pchelas conducted eight combat sorties during the Chechnyan war of April to May 1995; these operations were considered experimental, although their ability to support target indication for rockets and to attack helicopters was considered unique.

Production was reportedly resumed in the late 1990s due to the needs of the war in Chechnya (one report has it resumed only in 2002, and then on so small a scale that the UAVs were made in the Yakovlev prototype shop). The estimated Russian requirement was ten systems (100 to 120 Pchela). Chechnyan experience convinced the Russians to provide an alternative IR sensor for night operations (Pchela-1I, with an IR linescanner). The system was later modified to provide it with real-time artillery spotting capability. Pchela was also used in Georgia in 2008, at least one falling into Georgian hands. Other versions of Pchela envisaged in 2004 were -1P, with a communications jammer, a signals intelligence version, and a laser target designator version.

Pchela-1T data: span 3.25 m, length 2.78 m, take-off weight 138 kg (payload 70 kg). Endurance is 2 hours (mission radius 60 km, speed 97 kt); ceiling is 3,000 m. The power plant is a 32-hp Samara P-032 piston engine. Configuration: shoulder wing with ducted-fan propeller; there is an EO turret under the nose.

A shorter-range Stroy-BP (Blizhniy, "short range") uses the 25-kg Osa air vehicle, a canard with delta wings and twin tail fins using a piston engine. Endurance is 2.5 hours (cruising speed 120 km/hour); altitude is 150 to 8,200 ft. The payload is a wide-angle TV or IR camera, an NBC dosimeter, or a gas analyzer. The BP version operates out to a range of 20 km, rather than the 60 km of the Stroy-P system. Each unit operates two air vehicles.

A follow-on Stroy-PD using Pchela-1K (Kruglo-sutochnyi: round the clock, i.e., the IR version) began tests in 2004. This version had a slightly increased span, with straight rather than bent-down wingtips and better maneuverability using new control surfaces; ceiling increased to 13,000 ft. The control system was also upgraded. Effective range was given as 60 km. A new twin-engine Yulia air vehicle for Stroy-PD was advertised in 2007. This twin-engine UAV offers quadrupled (400 vs. 100 km) endurance and range and a greater variety of sensors. Yulia uses an airborne relay to communicate with a ground station beyond the horizon. Given its extended range, Yulia is promoted as a way of targeting the Iskander precision tactical ballistic missile.

At the 2005 Moscow Air Show Vega Radio and Luch aviation design announced a new tactical UAV, Tipchuk or Tipchak (9M62). The air vehicle is a twin-boom pusher with slightly tapered wings. The associated reconnaissance system is designated 1K133. Tipchuk has a real-time digital data link to pass its information and to conduct laser target designation. Sensors are EO and IR. Vega produced the sensor. Following acceptance trials in 2006–7, the system was accepted into service late in 2008. The Russian Ministry of Defense ordered ten systems (each with six air vehicles) in 2007, for delivery in 2008 (the industrial number 9M62 implies official status). The rate was later cut to one system per year over three years beginning in 2010. Plans originally called for one Tipchuk unit for each artillery brigade (with three or four gun or rocket batteries), but later Tipchuk was considered a general-purpose UAV. The Russians began negotiations with Israel to obtain what they considered more satisfactory UAVs. Data: span 3.4 m, length 2.4 m, weight 60 kg (payload 14.5 kg), endurance 3 hours (radius, probably set by communications, 40 km; maximum mission range 70 km [38 nm]), ceiling 10,000 ft, maximum speed 108 kt (loiter speed 49 kt). The power plant is a 13-hp engine. According to the manufacturer, the system takes no more than 30 seconds to present a formal report (presumably a system readout) after recovery. Two UAVs can be controlled simultaneously. Tipchuk was used unsuccessfully during the 2008 Georgian war. Reportedly the Russians are developing a larger version that can fire missiles in the Hellfire class. The figures above refer to an air vehicle internally designated BLA-05; as of 2009, Vega/Luch was working on a smaller BLA-07 with folding wings.

Stroy-A and Stroy-P each had their own air vehicles: Dyatel for Stroy-A (Sokol and Yakovlev alternatives) and Korshun (Tupolev) for Stroy-F. Note that the name Korshun has been applied to the Tu-300 UCAV described below. None of these vehicles became operational. In 2004 Stroy-F was being revived using the Tu-300, and an export version was being offered as Malakhit-F.

At the 2003 Moscow Air Show Sukhoi showed models of a new-generation endurance UAV called Zond-1, -2, and -3, of which Zond-3 was the smallest, roughly analogous to the Predator. Like Predator it has a pusher propeller and a stabilized EO platform under its nose. It also has a nose dielectric panel, which may be for either satellite communication or for a radar. Zond-2 is broadly analogous to Global Hawk, with turbojet power and a vee tail; its large dielectric panel is presumably for a satellite link. Zond-3 is similar to Zond-2 but has a large triangular radar antenna over its body, possibly for the airborne early warning role. All three seemed to be no more than design studies, but they suggest interest in Western-type

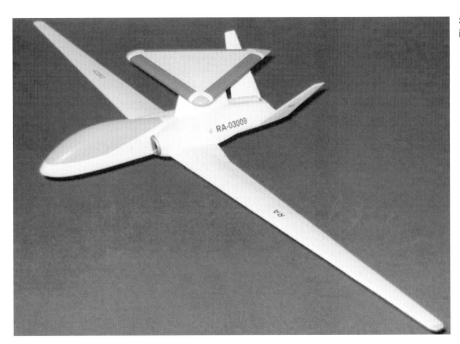

Sukhoi Zond-1 UAV project, showing its phased-array AEW radar. (UVSI)

long-endurance UAVs. Sukhoi had previously designed a HALE called S-62, development of which was canceled after the completion of the concept design.

In 1999 Irkut Corporation began a long-term UAV program; in 2003 it bought Israeli Aerostar UAV components and technology. The company is primarily interested in civil applications; its program is to develop three classes of UAVs of different sizes. Irkut-800: span 23 m, length 8.42 m, weight 860 kg (payload 200 kg), speed 165–270 km/hour, ceiling about 9,000 m, radius 200 km (endurance 12 hours). There is also a larger Irkut-850 in the same MALE class. Irkut-60 and -200 use Aeronautics (Israel) airframes, and -800 uses a German Stemme airframe.

The Kronstadt defense company has developed a series of Dozor ("patrol," "watch," or "picket") UAVs, apparently beginning with Dozor-2, a twin-boom pusher of conventional UAV design (it was shown at the 2007 Moscow Air Show, and tests were announced in February 2008). A test batch of twelve Dozor-2s was announced; if tests were successful the UAV would be adopted by the Russian border guards. The series includes Dozor-3, announced in April 2008 but probably not yet flown. It can be armed. Takeoff weight is 600 kg (payload 100 kg). A drawing published in 2008 showed a Predator-like airframe with a bulbous nose carrying, presumably, a satellite antenna, and a pusher propeller with an inverted vee

tail. Dozor-3 was shown with a tricycle undercarriage. Endurance was given as 6 hours. The Dozor-600 displayed at the 2009 Moscow Air Show (to fly in 2010) is probably Dozor-3 renamed. Length was given as 7 m, and maximum range as 3,500 km (1,890 nm); payload is the 100 kg listed for Dozor-3.

Dozor-4 was demonstrated for five days in the fall of 2008 for border guards in Daghestan in the North Caucasus. It is a high-wing airframe (span 4.8 m) weighing 90 kg at takeoff (payload 10 kg), powered by a 19.2-hp piston engine (pusher propeller). Endurance is 8 hours; range is 1,200 km. Ceiling is 10,000 ft. Positioning accuracy is 15 m. Note that Dozor-4 is sometimes credited to TransAS, which is apparently a related organization. Dozor-4 is an evolved version of Dozor-2 with a conventional instead of inverted vee tail. Dozor-5, to fly in 2009, is enlarged to a maximum takeoff weight of about 100 kg, and has greater endurance.

Dozor-2 data: span 4 m, length 2.6 m, weight 50 kg (payload 8 kg), ceiling 13,000 ft, endurance 10 hours (range 750 mi, cruising speed 60–80 kt). Takeoff run is 330 ft, landing run 200 ft.

Dozor-4 data: span 4.8 m, length 2.8 m, weight 60 kg (payload 10 kg), ceiling 10,000 ft, endurance 10 hours (range 750 miles, cruising speed 65–80 kt). Takeoff and landing runs as above.

Dozor-3 data: span 12 m, length 6.7 m, weight 500 kg (payload 115 kg [with 1-hour fuel], fuel up to 160 kg), ceiling 4,500 m, endurance 8 hours with maximum fuel (maximum range 900 km, cruising speed 120–150 km/hour). Takeoff and landing runs are 300 m (about 1,000 ft). The power plant is a 115-hp pusher engine. These data are from the Kronstadt data sheet, which predicts a first flight in 2009. Note that the weight and payload differ from those in the company's announcement. Kronstadt pointed out that the arrangement allowed for a parabolic antenna with a radius of 50 cm (it may be in the sphere shown in the nose of the UAV in the 2008 announcement).

Other recent projects included in a UAV list on a Russian Web site are Colibri, Aist, and Irkut-800.

Colibri data: span 5.9 m, length 4.25 m, weight 380 kg, speed 120 to 150 km/hour, ceiling up to 3,500 m, radius of action 70 to 80 km, endurance 8 hours.

Aist (Stork) is under development by NII Kulon (as BLA-06), having been authorized by the Russian Ministry of Defense in 2005; it was announced at the 2007 Moscow Air Show. BLA is an internal designation indicating *bespilotnyi letatebryi apparat*, literally "pilotless aerial vehicle." The system within which Aist is intended to work may be code-named Yulia. As of January 2009, Aist prototypes were beginning a two-year test program, in which they would be evaluated as target designators for the Iskander-M surface-to-surface missile system. Aist is a low-wing aircraft with two small piston tractor engines, one above each wing, and a vee tail. Span is 8 m, length 4.7 m, weight 500 to 550 kg (payload 100 kg), endurance 12 hours (maximum speed 135 kt, loiter speed 70 kt, mission radius 125 nm); ceiling is 20,000 ft (operating altitude is 100–6,000 m [330–19,000 ft]). This UAV is in the same class as Dozor-3 and Dan-Baruk (see below).

Nart (A-03) is apparently also in the MALE class.

About 1975–80 the Soviet Ministry of Defense reportedly became fascinated by a U.S. RAND publication that stated that by 2000 manned military aircraft would no longer be affordable; the future would belong to UAVs (presumably to high-performance UCAVs). All the major design bureaus were ordered to begin UAV research. The Sukhoi version was Korshun, which was to carry a 500-kg bomb under the control of a modified

Su-24 designated PUN-24 (*punkt upravleniya navigatziye*, "navigation control point"). Work began in 1982 but was stopped in 1983.

The effort was then transferred to Tupolev, which designed a Tu-300 air vehicle similar in layout to Tu-141/143; it was flight-tested in 1991, and displayed at the 1995 and 1997 Moscow Air Shows (no details were provided). This system may have been designed particularly to attack carrier battle groups. Photos show what appears to be a radar nose flanked by an IR or EO sensor fairing below and probably by an ESM radome above. There was an internal weapons bay and a centerline pylon that could carry a standard KMGU-1 cluster munition dispenser or a sensor package. Tu-300 was to have been part of the Reys-F (presumably F for Frontovaya, the standard designation for Soviet or Russian tactical strike aviation) unmanned strike system. A Russian Web site gave a speed of 950 km/hour at an altitude of 50 to 6,000 m, with an endurance of 2 hours (radius given as 200 to 300 km). Takeoff weight was given as 3,000 kg, but no dimensions were given. There are apparently two versions, Tu-300R (reconnaissance) and Tu-300U (strike). The Tu-300 program seems to have been revived in 2007, when major modernization (implying that the aircraft had been produced and made operational) was announced.

Sokol (of Kazan) displayed its Dan-Baruk hunter-killer UAV (like Predator) at the 2007 Moscow Air Show. It is a conventional pusher-propeller design, the only unusual feature being that its EO sensors are in its nose behind an angled panel rather than in an underslung turret. It also has a small nose radar. Dan-Baruk has hard points for submunition pods; at the Moscow show the pods contained Motiv submunitions equivalent to the U.S. Sensor Fuzed Weapon. Note that there was apparently no interest in using Dan-Baruk like Predator, to guide precision weapons toward a target the UAV detects. Dan itself is a target aircraft intended as an La-17 successor, but it may have originated in the Stroy-A program. Data: span 5.63 m, length 4.6 m, weight 500 kg (payload 90 kg external, 30 kg internal, also given as 100 kg total). Radius of action 150 km (range given as 2,400 km), altitude 50 m to 6,000 m, endurance 15 hours. Speed is 120 to 240 km/hour. Dan-M, a modernized jet target with unswept

Tu-300, with VR-3D/Tu-243 system in the background. (Steven Zaloga)

wings, has also been proposed as a UAV, equipped with sensors such as side-looking radar, a multichannel radiometer, and a broadband link; it may also be equipped with jammers. Speed is 300 to 750 km/hour, altitude 50 to 9,000 m.

The MiG design bureau displayed a mockup of a Skat (Skate, stingray) UCAV at the 2007 Moscow Air Show. Development reportedly began in 2005. It is similar in outline to the U.S. X-47, powered by a Klimov RD-5000B turbojet (about 11,000 lbs of thrust). An internal bomb bay is to accommodate two air-to-surface missiles or two 250- or 500-kg bombs. Claimed performance is a speed of 800 km/hour (432 kt), range up to 2,000 km (1,078 nm), and ceiling of 12,000 m (39,000 ft). Span is 11.5 m, length 10.25 m; weight is 10,000 kg (payload 2,000 kg). It is not clear just how real this project is, particularly since the MiG design bureau is reportedly close to collapse due to poor funding.

In addition to Skat, the Yakovlev design bureau is developing the Yak-131 Proryv (Breakthrough) UCAV, reportedly in cooperation with Alenia/Selex. Proryv was first shown in 2006. It envisaged a common fuselage (with the same AI-222 engine, sensors, and flight controls) and at least three alternative wings, two for subsonic surveillance (Proryv-R for reconnaissance and Proryv-BLD for SIGINT, with a large dorsal radome) and a Proryv-U UCAV using swept wings. Data published on a Russian

Web site: weight 10,000 kg (payload 1,000 to 3,000 kg), speed 1,100 km/hour, ceiling up to 16,000 m. Note that there is also a Yak-133BR based on the Yak-130 trainer, with 40 percent parts commonality. It does not resemble the trainer at all, having a delta wing without vertical surfaces.

There is reportedly also a Sukhoi design, details of which are not available.

In 2008 the Russians turned to Israel for UAVs, on the ground that their own manufacturers had failed to produce satisfactory ones. The initial purchases were the Bird Eye 400, I-View Mk 150, and Search Mk II; there was speculation in Israeli newspapers that the Russians would go on to buy advanced UAVs such as Hermes.

Perhaps the most ingenious current Russian UAV has been developed by Splav, which makes multiple rocket launchers including the 300-mm Smerch. Splav produced an R-90 UAV to be launched from a Smerch tube to indicate targets. To fit the rocket tube, it has folding wings and tail surfaces: tandem wings and two vertical tails. Weight is reportedly 92 lbs; the UAV can loiter over a target area for half an hour at 600 to 1,800 ft. The power plant is apparently a pulse jet. Downlink range is 70 km. Splav claimed that trials showed that the UAV reduced the number of rockets that had to be fired to hit a target by 25 percent. The sensor is a television camera in a dome in the nose of the UAV. R-90 was being described publicly

The R-90 tube-launched UAV in flight. (Steven Zaloga)

by early 2002, and it was shown at the August 2006 Russian ground forces exhibition, but it seems not to have entered Russian service. The UAV would become more significant if, as a Splav publication suggested, the rockets themselves were modified into precision weapons.

The current mini-UAV is apparently ZALA 421-08, a flying wing: span 0.8 m, length 0.41 m, weight 1.9 kg, endurance 90 minutes (speed 65–150 km/hour, ceiling 4,000 m/13,000 ft, radio link range 25 km). The complete system includes two air vehicles and weighs 8 kg; ZALA can be prepared for flight in 3 minutes. Sensors (presumably alternatives) are video and still and IR cameras. ZALA 421-12 is a slightly larger successor: span 1.6 m, length 0.62 m, weight 3.9 kg, endurance 2 hours, speed 65 to 120 km/hour (maximum limited by software). The ZALA 421-06 is a helicopter UAV for the Ministry of the Interior.

Ka-137 is a follow-on to the Ka-37, the first Russian unmanned helicopter, flown in 1993 and developed by Kamov with its own funds. Like the bureau's manned helicopters, Ka-37 had two coaxial contrarotating rotors; each had twin blades. Ka-37 was described as an agricultural UAV, but the redesigned Ka-137 has military applications. It is reported in service with Russian border guards and possibly on board Russian coast guard boats.

Data: rotor diameter 5.3 m, body diameter 1.22 m, takeoff weight 280 kg. Endurance is 4 hours (speed 175 km/hour), and ceiling is 11,500 ft. The power plant is a 65-hp piston engine.

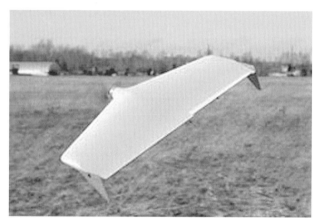

ZALA 421-08 mini-UAV. (Bespipotnye Sistemiye)

Singapore

Singapore bought the Israeli Mastiff in 1979, replacing it in 1984 with Scout (operated by 128 Squadron). A large order for Scout, in the 1990s, was reportedly canceled when the first batch proved unsatisfactory. However, in 1998 Singapore signed a $14 million technology transfer deal with the Israelis. In May 2006 Singapore's air force created a triservice UAV command, under which are the 128 Squadron as well as 119 Squadron (Searcher) and a new 116 Squadron (Hermes 450). Under the 1998 agreement, Singapore Technologies Aerospace produced the Israeli EMIT Blue Horizon, which was displayed in 2000.

The Singapore ground forces are to adopt a locally developed (Singapore Technologies Aerospace, or STA) series of Skyblade mini-UAVs. It was ordered in 2004 for

Skyblade IV mini-UAV. (STA)

delivery in 2005. Each system includes three air vehicles. Skyblade II (reportedly first flown 2003, used in trials in November 2003, announced April 2005, first delivered January 2006) has an interchangeable sensor pod and other improvements requested by the Singapore army. Late in 2005 Singapore announced plans to buy seven systems in 2005, and ultimately to buy twenty by 2008. Skyblade III (2006) replaced the gasoline engine of the earlier types with an electric motor. Skyblade IV is somewhat larger and is rail-launched; it is similar to the Israeli EMIT Sparrow and may be a license-produced derivative. Skyblade II data: span 1.83 m, length 1.22 m, weight 5 kg, endurance 2 hours with piston engine, 1 hour with electric motor (maximum speed 70 kt, cruising speed 30 kt, stall speed 18 kt), operating altitude 1,500 ft. Skyblade III data: span 2.6 m, length 1.4 m, weight 5 kg, endurance more than 1 hour (speed 70 kt, range 8 km). Skyblade IV is an entirely different UAV, with a pusher propeller in its tail, powered by a gasoline engine: span 3.51 m, length 1.98 m, weight 50 kg (payload 12 kg), endurance 6–12 hours (speed 50–80 kt, range 100 km [54 nm]), ceiling 15,000

ft. Apparently it was radically redesigned between 2006, when a version with a cylindrical body was shown, and 2008, when the version shown had a more conventionally tapered and streamlined body. In both cases the UAV carried an underslung sensor turret.

In 2001 Singapore announced plans to award a contract to the U.S. Rutan company to assist in development of a LALE UAV for ocean surveillance; Singapore may buy Global Hawk instead.

STA announced a jet tactical UAV, MAV-1 (Multi-role Air Vehicle), in February 2004; development had begun about a year earlier. STA then claimed that a first flight was imminent, but it did not occur until the second half of 2005, and was very short; as of February 2006 MAV-1 had not flown again. MAV-1 was the first entirely indigenous UAV developed by STA, and it may have been intended mainly as a means of demonstrating STA's technological capabilities. However, STA has indicated that it may develop a UCAV based on MAV-1. In 2006 it was reported that MAV-1 would be part of a program to develop swarming air vehicles, the Smart Warfighting

MAV-1 jet tactical UAV. (STA via USVI)

Fantail 5000 ducted-fan VTOL UAV. (STA)

Array of Reconfigurable Modules (SWARM). In configuration MAV-1 is reminiscent of the German Barrakuda and the Swedish SHARC, with a broad fairly flat body, short swept wings, and a vee tail. There is an internal bay. Span is approximately 3 m, and length approximately 2.50 m; weight is 80 kg (payload 20 kg). Maximum speed is probably low subsonic.

STA (with SAGEM) developed the small Fantail ducted-fan VTOL UAV, flight tests of which began in May 2005. The configuration is much like that of the Bertin HoverEye. Fantail takes off and lands vertically but normally flies horizontally. It has a cylindrical body protruding from its midbody ducted fan; the power plant is a 3.5-hp gasoline engine. Rotor diameter is 30 cm, and height is 65 cm; weight is 2.5 kg (payload 0.2 kg). Endurance is 0.5 hours when hovering; range 8 km, maximum speed 54 kt. Range in urban conditions is 1 km. France has expressed interest.

At the February 2004 Asian Aerospace show Cradance Services displayed Golden Eagle, a micro-UAV in the same class as the Israeli Mosquito, with a similar configuration (semicircular or heart planform, tractor propeller driven by an electric motor) and endplate fins and rudders. Golden Eagle is considerably larger than the Israeli UAV: span 0.65 m, length 0.77 m, weight 0.85 kg (payload 0.08 kg). Endurance is 2 hours (mission radius [data-link range] 5.4 nm, maximum speed 39 kt, minimum speed 16 kt, typical altitude 500 m/1,640 ft). The UAV was described as stable at high angles of attack (5 to 45 degrees), which might particularly suit it for an urban environment. It may have competed with the Fantail (above).

South Africa

South Africa benefitted from a close relationship with Israel and hence adopted Israeli UAVs, which became the basis of further developments. It bought two Israeli Scout systems and reportedly operates Hermes 1500. South Africa reportedly sold Seeker UAVs to Algeria (permission for export was granted in 1997, and by 2000 these UAVs were apparently operational).

BATELEUR

Denel (formerly Kentron) advertised the Bateleur (named after an African eagle) MALE in mock-up form late in

Golden Eagle micro-UAV. (UVSI)

2004; one account stated that the company decided to begin development that April. Bateleur was an entirely private venture project, without official backing. Denel hoped to minimize costs by using existing systems from its Seeker II UAV and Skua high-speed target drone, as well as commercial off-the-shelf equipment. Bateleur was intended to use the same ground station as Seeker II. Span was set by the requirement that Bateleur fit a standard shipping container (6 m ISO container). Construction is modular, the payload contained in the separate nose module. A flat circular radome above the center section carries the data link (there may be a satellite dish). Roles include ELINT and COMINT as well as the usual photo reconnaissance (Bateleur can also carry a laser designator and a laser rangefinder). Denel also envisages a SAR radar payload. An unnamed overseas partner contributed to development. Bateleur is a pusher airframe reminiscent of Predator but with upswept wingtips. A small radome abreast the wing is presumably for a satellite link. As of 2004 the first flight was expected in 2007, with initial operating capability following in 2010. However, as of 2009 development had not proceeded any further because no foreign partner had been found. Denel reported contacts with several potential buyers, including Brazil (2008). The contact with Brazil may be connected with the existing cooperative agreement with Brazil to co-develop the South African A-Darter air-to-air missile.

Bateleur MALE UAV, 23 September 2004. (Darren Olivier)

Data: span 15.0 m, length about 10 m, takeoff weight 1,000 kg (maximum 1,400 kg), payload 200 kg (maximum 500 kg). Endurance is 18 to 24 hours (operating radius 750 km [405 nm], maximum range 3,500 km [1,900 nm]). and ceiling is 25,000 ft. Nominal cruise speed is 135 kt (250 km/hour); loiter speed is 65 kt (120 km/hour). The power plant is a single piston engine.

KIWIT

Advanced Technologies' mini-UAV completed development by October 2006, low-rate production beginning early in 2007. Kiwit is very similar externally to Israeli mini-UAVs, with a cylindrical body carrying a tractor propeller and an underslung pod for sensors and batteries. Span is 2.5 m, length 1.2 m, weight 3 kg. Endurance is 45 to 60 minutes (operating radius 2.7 nm, maximum cruising speed 27 kt). It is not clear whether the South African defense forces have adopted Kiwit.

SEEKER

The South African Kentron (now Denel) company developed Seeker as a derivative of the Israeli Scout. It became operational in 1986 (it was made public in 1988). It was first used in 1987 during Operation Modular in Angola, but the Seeker squadron (three systems, ten aircraft) was disbanded in 1991. At least two systems were exported to unnamed clients (reportedly Abu Dhabi and Algeria for Seeker I, Algeria and an undisclosed customer for Seeker II). The standard system comprises four to six air vehicles and three ground vehicles. Denel began to advertise the

upgraded Seeker II or Seeker 400 in 2004; the company claimed in 2008 that the South African military plans to buy this system. Seeker II is digital, with a 250-km range and day and night capability, presumably beyond that offered by Seeker. Denel's Seeker II is operated by the South African air force for the South African Police Service (ten systems reported in service beginning about 2000), and a larger Seeker 400 (100-kg payload) was announced in 2008. Both use the same twin-boom pusher configuration. Seeker 400 uses the same avionics and ground station, but in contrast to Seeker II it can carry more than one sensor payload at a time. It is also to be powered by an aviation-certified reduced-noise engine made in South Africa.

Austria tentatively chose Seeker as the 1997 winner of a 1996 UAV competition, but the Austrian government refused to buy, preferring a European UAV. In June 2009 it was reported that Denel had sold seven Seeker II systems to four countries, but not to the South African military. Algeria bought one Seeker I system in 1998 and one Seeker II system about 2000. The UAE reportedly obtained five Seekers (probably full systems) in 2003.

Seeker IIE data: span 7.00 m, length 4.43 m, takeoff weight 240 kg (payload 40 kg standard, 50 kg maximum; empty weight 165 kg), endurance 15 hours with standard payload/12 hours with maximum payload (maximum speed 120 kt, cruising speed 70 kt, operational radius 135 nm without TGS, 216 nm [400 km] with TGS; time over target 5 hours at 135-nm radius, 4 hours at 54 nm), ceiling 18,000 ft. The power plant is a 4-cylinder 2-stroke 50-hp piston engine.

Seeker 400 data: span 15.0 m, length 10.0 m, takeoff weight not given (100-kg payload). Endurance is 16 hours, and ceiling is 8,000 ft.

SERAPH

Kentron announced the Seraph stealthy deep-penetrating UAV in 2002 (Mach 0.85, endurance 100 minutes). It is apparently an outgrowth of an earlier black program, Flowchart, which may not have progressed beyond the wind tunnel model stage. In 2005 Denel displayed the Seraph II UCAV armed with a Mokopa antitank missile. An illustration shows a pair of air intakes flanking a narrow

Seeker II UAV. Note the ESM antennas around the nose wheel; the electro-optic turret is under the fuselage, as in Seeker I. (Denel via UVSI)

pointed nose tipped with what appears to be a radome. The wings are cranked deltas reminiscent of the Swedish Draken fighter, with a pair of inward-sloping vertical tail planes. A Denel drawing of Seraph itself shows only the cranked delta, without the air intakes or the nose body. A full system would employ three to six air vehicles.

Data: span 3 m, length 5.7 m; maximum payload 80 kg. Endurance 1.4 hours (maximum speed Mach 0.85 at 30,000 ft; maximum range 1,300 km [700 nm]), ceiling 30,000 to 40,000 ft); the guidance/tracking link range is 250 km. It can also fly a preset mission profile.

VULTURE

The Vulture, a tactical and artillery support UAV, was developed based on experience in Angola. The configuration is unusual for a UAV: a more or less conventional airframe with its pusher piston engine mounted above the shoulder wing. Unlike other South African UAVs, this one was developed by Advanced Technologies and Engineering. Vulture was developed to meet a South African military requirement for a small system to support self-propelled artillery, part of a larger AS2000 program

intended to field an integrated artillery C3I system. The UAV flew in March 1995, the year government funding began. Procurement was scheduled for 1997, but that year the South African forces began considering a new Super Vulture instead. The production decision for Vulture was deferred to 2000 but then deferred again to consider its replacement by the improved Super Vulture. However, a single Vulture system was sold to an undisclosed client in 2008, perhaps China, where it may be license-produced. The current brochure claims that it is owned and operated by South African Army artillery. The manufacturer currently offers a family of systems: Vulture, Night Vulture, Endurance Vulture (endurance 8 to 9 rather than 3 to 4 hours), and Civil Vulture.

Data: span 5.2 m, length 3.1 m, weight 125 kg (payload 35 kg). Endurance is over 3 hours (mission radius 60–200 km [32.4–108 nm], maximum cruising speed 86 kt, loiter speed 65 kt, stall speed 48 kt); ceiling is 16,000 ft. Claimed target acquisition accuracy is within 30 m in 30 seconds. Launch, flight, and recovery are all automated. The flight computer is derived from fighter and helicopter mission computers, and Vulture incorporates a new

Vulture. (Denel Aerospace via UVSI)

South African secure video data link. Navigation is by a combination of an inertial reference system and differential GPS. The UAV returns home automatically if it suffers a mission critical failure.

Spain

Despite efforts to develop military UAVs in Spain (see below), the Spanish government has opted for foreign systems to support its troops in Afghanistan: one Searcher II system (four UAVs, announced April 2007) and twenty-seven Ravens (2007), some of the latter going to Afghanistan in 2008. The system itself (Plataforma Autonoma Sensorizada de Inteligencia, or PASI) was developed by a consortium comprising EADS/CASA, Indra, and IAI. Spain has been negotiating to buy up to five Global Hawks, receiving a U.S. State Department waiver in the summer of 2008. Presumably this is not the Euro Hawk program.

ALO

The Spanish Army adopted the mini-UAV ALO (Avion Ligero de Observacion) in 2000; sometime after 2005 it may have been superseded by Raven and Searcher II. It was developed by the Instituto Nacional de Técnica Aeroespacial (INTA) and evaluated by the Spanish military in 1995–96. ALO has a conventional tractor configuration with a high wing and a vee tail, and it uses a small piston engine. Span is 3.03 m, length 1.75 m, weight 20 kg (payload 6 kg); endurance is 2 hours (normal range 27 nm, maximum speed 108 kt, loiter speed 27 kt); ceiling is 1,000 to 1,500 m (3,280 to 4,920 ft).

ATLANTE/MILANO

CASA (Construcciones Aeronáuticas, SA), EADS' Spanish arm, designed the long-endurance ATLANTE (Avión Táctico de Largo Alcance No Tripulado Español) for the Spanish army for target detection, shoot correction, and damage evaluation, among other missions. Other planned roles are coastal and maritime surveillance and route reconnaissance, as in Afghanistan. The larger goal is to provide Spanish industry with UAV experience. EADS received the contract for this system in 2008, and apparently the UAV had not yet flown as of the fall of 2009. Each system can operate four or more air vehicles. The air vehicle is a tractor with a high wing and a vee tail, the sensor turret being suspended under the belly roughly under the wings. Span is 8 m, takeoff weight is 380 kg (payload 60 kg), and endurance is 12 hours. The payload is an EO/IR sensor turret.

Milano is a related or parallel INTA MALE project, a model of which was displayed at the 2009 Paris Air Show. Work began in September 2006, and the first flight was expected in mid-2009. Endurance was to be better

ALO mini-UAV. (INTA via UVSI)

than 25 hours (the same display also showed an endurance of 20 hours), maximum speed 230 km/hour, and ceiling 7,000 m (23,000 ft), and the design was intended for low radar cross section. Weight was given as 900 kg, but no dimensions were stated. Takeoff and landing are automatic. A poster showed Milano flying a pattern with 1,000-km legs.

SIVA

Instituto Nacional de Técnica Aeronautica developed the tactical UAV SIVA (Sistema Integrado de Vigilancia Aerea) in cooperation with CESELSA of Spain (ground control) and Dornier of Germany (flight navigation system). It has a tractor propeller, a vee tail, and folding outer wing panels. SIVA was first shown at the 1993 Paris Air Show, and flight tests of six prototypes began late in 1995. One prototype system was delivered to the Spanish army for operational evaluation in July 2003 after contractor trials were completed; a production version was delivered to the Spanish army (for training) in September 2006. A SIVA system displayed in Madrid in 2008 was assigned to the Target Identification and Acquisition Group of the Spanish army 63rd Field Artillery Regiment. Span is 5.81 m, length is 4.025 m, and weight is 300 kg (payload 40 kg). Endurance is 10 hours (6 hours with maximum payload); maximum speed is 92 kt (170 km/hour), cruising speed is

76 kt; mission radius is 81 nm (150 km). Ceiling is 20,000 ft. The power plant is a 48-hp 4-cylinder 2-stroke engine.

Sweden

The Swedish defense research agency FOA (Försvarets forskningsanstalt) began studies of a very small reconnaissance UAV, Skatan (Magpie), in 1979, but the program was dropped about 1983 because it duplicated existing equipment.

The Swedish army bought its first tactical UAV late in 1997: three Sperwer systems. A standing requirement for a system for the brigade or battalion level was to have

ATLANTE long-endurance UAV. (EADS)

A model of Milano at the 2009 Paris Air Show. The blister atop the fuselage carries a satellite communication dish. Milano is designed to carry wing pods (near its wingtips) housing SAR radar antennas; they were shown in drawings but were not incorporated in the model. (Norman Friedman)

been filled in 2002–4, but it was not bought, and it became the TUMAV (Tactical Unmanned Multirole Air Vehicle), a 500-kg replacement for Sperwer (Ugglan in Swedish service). Saab began work on its own approach to TUMAV in 2006 (see below), but in 2007 it sought partners, and its attention shifted to modifying an existing air vehicle. It saw the vehicle as support for the EU Rapid Reaction Force Nordic Battle Group II, which was expected to need such vehicles in 2009–10.

The Swedish defense development agency FMV (Försvarets Materielverk) began studies of endurance UAVs in 2000, looking at Predator, Altus, Hermes 1500, and Eagle, but the acquisition is planned for 2012, when other alternatives will become available.

Cybaero's APID (Autonomous Probe for Industrial Data-acquisition) 55 is a helicopter UAV. Despite its name it has military roles; it is used by the Swedish armed forces and by the UAE (seven systems, deliveries completed 2009). Rotor diameter is 3.3 m, length is 3.2 m, and weight is 150 kg (95 kg empty; payload 55 kg including fuel). Endurance is 3 to 6 hours (mission radius 27 nm, maximum speed 48 kt, endurance speed 32 kt), and ceiling (depending on payload) is up to 9,800 ft. The power plant is a 55-hp Hirth gasoline engine.

Saab's Skeldar V-150 is based on APID 55. Design began late in 2004, and a Skeldar 5 prototype flew in May 2006 (Saab expected the craft to become operational in 2007). Skeldar was tested on board a ship and thus under consideration by the Royal Swedish Navy. In May 2009 Saab signed a strategic partnership agreement with Swiss UAV (SUAV) to develop further VTOL UAVs. SUAV introduced the 75 kg Neo S-300 in 2008. Under the agreement, both companies will use Saab's ground station technology. Rotor diameter is 3.3 m, length is 4 m (including rotors), and takeoff weight is 200 kg. Endurance is 4 to 5 hours (mission radius 100 km [54 nm]). A new heavy-fuel engine will give the follow-on V-250 version an extended range (180 km) and a heavier payload. This 250-kg helicopter is also called Skeldar M.

As of late 2007 Saab was seeking a naval partner (Skeldar had been tested on board Swedish warships). At that time the Swedish armed forces did not have a funded requirement for a VTOL UAV. Saab was still pursuing this idea in 2009, envisaging integration of Skeldar into its 9LV shipboard combat system. As of 2009, Saab expected first Skeldar sales in 2010. Integration with the C4I system of a *Visby*-class corvette was demonstrated in 2009; given the modular character of the corvette's 9 LV

Skeldar, with the Neo S-300 helicopter UAV in the background, on the Saab stand at DSEi 2009. (Norman Friedman)

command system, it was necessary only to add a module incorporating the helicopter flight-control software. A new rotor system increased takeoff weight to 200 kg, and as of 2009 Saab was integrating the Italian Selex Galileo PicoSAR radar with its helicopter. It is also integrating a Saab ESM suite.

Skeldar was part of a larger UAV program, the other element being a long-endurance medium-range system with an enhanced payload, with a weight of about 400 kg. A 2006 presentation showed a canard with broad swept wings and a ducted-fan propulsor at its tail. Operating radius was given as 250 km. Further data: span 4 m, total length 3.9 m (body 2.7 m), weight 400 kg (payload 60 kg), endurance 12 hours (maximum speed 250 km/hour, loiter speed 150 km/hour). As of 2006 Saab expected to fly this fourth-generation UAV in 2010.

Cybaero also developed the Vantage helicopter UAV in cooperation with the U.S. Naval Research Laboratory (NRL). It uses differential GPS navigation. Rotor diameter is 2.77 m (109 in.), body length 2.84 m (112 in.), weight 174 kg (380 lbs); payload is 15.9 kg (35 lbs).

Saab has built two small-scale UCAV demonstrators, SHARC (Swedish Highly Advanced Research Configuration) and FILUR (Flying Innovative Low-Observable Unmanned Research). Announced in 2001 and flown in February 2002, SHARC has a swept-wing configuration with a conventional horizontal tail and twin canted vertical fins, with an air intake above the tail. SHARC first

flew in 2002. It was intended to test autonomous UAV behavior (including ATLS), Saab's rapid-development process, and to test the airworthiness certification process. SHARC was described as a quarter-scale model of a possible 5-ton UCAV. SHARC data: span 2.1 m, length 2.5 m, weight 60 kg, speed 320 km/hour (172 kt). The engine is an AMT Olympus jet (45 lbs of thrust) burning JP-8 fuel.

FILUR was a half-scale stealth demonstrator using the same navigation and control systems and the same engines as SHARC. It was intended to demonstrate the effect of signature management for future reconnaissance systems. FILUR is a flying wing with a diamond center section and swept wings outboard, and with two inboard-canted vertical fins. The air intake is above the body. It first flew on 10 October 2005. Data: span 2.5 m, length 2.2 m, weight 55 kg, maximum speed 300 km/hour (162 kt).

Plans call for a new tactical UAV system to replace the current Ugglan (Sperwer); this program is led by Saab. Apparently an off-the-shelf UAV will be combined with Saab's new Sensor Source Intelligence Center. Given the UAV, the system is to become operational in 2011 and to be deployable overseas in 2012.

Castor is a Saab demonstration project to qualify UAVs to operate in controlled airspace. UAVs currently operate in segregated airspace or in spaces without restrictions. Saab wanted to demonstrate autonomous operation in current Class 1 (flight within visual sight

SHARC small-scale UCAV. (Saab via UVSI)

of the operator) and Class 2 (segregated airspace with restricted ground vision) conditions. That entails an autonomous sense/avoid system on board the UAV, which follows an automatically generated flight plan. It also entails interoperability with the commercial Mode 4 aircraft reporting system. The Saab sense-and-avoid system envisages sensing within 110 degrees of dead ahead in azimuth and within 15 degrees in elevation/depression.

In June 2009 Saab became coordinator of a European project, MidCAS, to make it possible for UAVs to fly in nonsegregated airspace. The consortium involves Sweden, France, Germany, Italy, and Spain.

Switzerland

Ranger is a joint program between Contraves-Oerlikon and IAI/Malat. It began in 1986, the Swiss army having tested four Israeli Scouts in 1985–86. The prototype flew in December 1988, six preproduction aircraft following in 1989, and this ADS 90 (Auflkarungs Drohnen System, or reconnaissance drone system) being tested in 1990. Further developmental versions were tested in 1993. Ranger was adopted as part of the ADS 95 system. The main procurement contract was awarded in April 1995, for twenty-eight air vehicles (probably five systems), with deliveries in 1998–2000. More are planned under the Swiss Army XXI plan. Raug Aerospace showed a Super Ranger in-

tended for this project at the 2007 Paris Air Show. RUAG describes it as intermediate between a MALE and a tactical UAV, offering MALE performance at a cost below that of a current tactical UAV. RUAG claims that Super Ranger is the first UAV to meet the new international USAR (UAV Systems Airworthiness Requirements) standards. However, a first flight scheduled for 2008 did not occur, and by 2009 the project may have been dropped.

Finland bought Ranger, apparently from Israel. The first shipment was reported as having been agreed in 1999, with UAVs delivered in 2001; a second deal, for Ranger-2, went via a Swiss company. It involved six air vehicles (total $20 million) ordered in 2003 for delivery in 2005.

Data: span 5.708 m, length 4.611 m, weight 280 kg (payload 45 kg). Endurance 9 hours (command link range 97 nm [180 km], speed 130 kt, cruising speed 97 kt, loiter speed 70 kt, stall speed 49 kt), ceiling 18,000 ft. The power plant is a Goebler-Hirth 38-hp piston engine.

Super Ranger: span 9.48 m, length 6.74 m, takeoff weight 500 kg. Endurance is up to 20 hours (mission radius 180 km, speed 130 kt), and ceiling is 20,000 ft. The power plant is a 4-cylinder 4-stroke engine.

Taiwan

In 2005 the ROC government announced that it planned to acquire three battalions of UAVs in 2005–10. The

Ranger 2 at Zurich Air Museum, January 2009. (South Wales Aviation Group)

Chang Shan Institute of Science and Technology (CSIST) government military development agency began work on UAVs in 1994, building two Kestrel I (20-kg payload) and then six Kestrel 2 since 1998. Kestrel II was announced at the February 2000 Singapore air show, having flown in May 1998; it may have been derived from a smaller UAV shown in 1995. Kestrel 2 has been offered for export at air shows. Kestrel 2 and the larger Chung Hsiung were used in May 2003 war games. Span is 5.00 m, length 4.00 m, weight 120 kg (payload 30 kg); endurance is 6 hours (operating radius more than 54 nm/100 km, maximum speed 100 kt, cruising speed 70 kt); ceiling is 12,000 ft. The power plant is a Limbach L275E gasoline engine.

In 2009 it was reported that CSIST had finally acquired sufficient technology to develop its desired army UAV; this project is to be completed in 2011. Work reportedly began in 2002, the result being the Chung Shyang II revealed in August 2005 (but also reportedly revealed at the February 2002 Singapore air show). Chung Shyang IIC (2006) has a better engine, improved aerodynamics, improved payloads, and a revised ground-control station. A version shown in mid-2009 flew in prototype form in 2007, and by mid-2009 CSIST had five operational prototypes, and hoped for an order for twenty in 2010. Endurance is 8 hours (range 100 km, cruising speed 60 kt). Chung Shyang II is currently equipped for surveillance and targeting, but an armed version is planned,

and as of 2009 the ROC military planned three battalions of UCAVs. Reportedly they would carry an 800-kg payload, including Hellfires and possibly also Hsiung Feng IIE cruise missiles. For example, it might be possible for Taiwan to place long-range ground-attack missiles on board long-endurance UAVs that would be invulnerable to PRC missile attack. The payload involved is far heavier than that of the reported Kestrel 2 test vehicle. Weight is 450 kg, endurance is 10 hours, and speed is 150 km/hour (81 kt).

In mid-2009 CSIST displayed its hand-launched Cardinal and Magpie mini-UAVs. Cardinal development began in 2007, and as of mid-2009 ten were in production for further tests. Range is 15–20 km (speed 30 kt, endurance 1.5 hours, maximum altitude 15,000 ft). Cardinal may be bought by the Taiwan military, but it has shown no interest in the even smaller Magpie, in development since 2006. Weight is 1 kg, range 3 km (endurance 1 hour, cruising speed 25 kt); maximum altitude is 5,000 ft (1.5 km).

Turkey

Turkey received some German CL-89 reconnaissance drones in 1991; presumably they were the first Turkish UAVs. Late in 1992 Turkey planned to test Gnat-700, Falcon 600 (AAI Corporation), and Searcher (six UAVs for each of the two U.S. systems). Plans were modified due to funding problems, and in 1994 Turkey received two ground-control stations and six Gnat-750s (two more UAVs were ordered in 1998 as attrition spares). Meanwhile TUSAS, which had been set up to manage coproduction of F-16 fighters in Turkey, developed its own UAV-X1 in 1989–92; however, it never entered production. A further UAV-X2 became the Baykus described below, which flew in 2003 but had not yet been ordered as of 2009.

Turkey seems first to have stated requirements for a UAV force in 1998: fourteen short-range systems, eight medium-range, and five endurance (HALE). For a short time about 1999, the longer-range systems were dropped in favor of buying only nineteen short-range ones. Then the short-range systems were dropped from the list of potential projects for collaboration; that is probably when plans to develop a domestic short-range UAV took shape. In 2001 plans called for six medium-range and five endurance systems, and by 2004 that had changed to six medium-range and three endurance systems. This total would provide fifty-four UAVs. In 2001 plans called for four systems for the army, three long-range for the navy, and two long-range for the air force. The 1998 statement was part of a call for proposals, the short list of competitors (to work with a Turkish partner) being Elbit/Silver Arrow/IAI, General Atomics, and CATIC of China. When competition was reopened in 2001, foreign bidders included General Atomics and an Israeli consortium consisting of IAI and Elbit. The 2002 program (twenty-eight tactical and twelve strategic UAVs) was canceled in May 2004 but resurrected that October. At that time Turkey planned to buy three off the shelf MALE systems for the army, air force, and navy (respectively, four, four, and two air vehicles) and six tactical systems from TUAS. The MALE competitors were Predator and Heron, Turkey selecting Heron (ten systems). Meanwhile TUSAS has developed the TIHA MALE described below.

The six TUAV systems envisaged in 2005 would employ eighteen aircraft. Initially it seemed that this would be a short-range UAV, but later it emerged that it would be a MALE, presumably TIHA. In 2005 plans called for a first flight within thirty-nine months, with delivery of the first system complete within fifty-one months, then delivery of the remaining five systems by 2010. To further complicate matters, in July 2006 Turkey announced plans to acquire tactical UAVs jointly with Pakistan, using Pakistani airframes with Turkish electronics. At that time plans called for six to seven systems.

Also, in August 2005 the Turkish Defense Industries Undersecretariat released an RFP for nineteen mini-UAV systems, the choice being the Bayraktar, which was already under development.

Turkey is reportedly seeking a UCAV, preferably Predator or Reaper.

BAYRAKTAR/GLOBIHA

A mini-UAV, the Bayraktar was the first to be operational with the Turkish army. Development began about 2003, and it flew in October 2005. Developed by Baykar Machine, it is hand-launched. Bayraktar (Standard-Bearer) is a high-wing pod-and-boom monoplane with a pusher propeller. The B version appeared in 2006, and as of early 2009 was credited with more than 4,000 flight hours. This is a fully autonomous UAV with waypoint control and the ability to return to the launch site. The manufacturer claims that it can estimate target coordinates with better than 10 m accuracy. These mini-UAVs are electrically powered. In August 2006 the Turkish army awarded the Kalebaykar UAV joint venture a contract for nineteen systems (four air vehicles each), for delivery from mid-2007. Note that a preproduction prototype shown at Farnborough in 2006 and a brochure showed a twin-boom twin-propeller layout with an inverted vee tail. This is probably Bayraktar A. Other photographs show the single-tail pod-and-boom layout. A 2009 Turkish catalog credits Bayraktar with two electric motors, but a photograph shows the single-tail pod-and-boom layout with a vee tail.

Bayraktar A data: span 1.6 m, length 1.2 m, weight 5 kg (payload 1 kg), endurance 60 minutes (communication range 20 km); ceiling is 12,000 ft (operational altitude 2,000 ft). Cruising speed is 70 km/hour (maximum 90 km/hour).

Bayraktar B data: span 1.9 m, length 1.2 m, weight 4.5 kg, endurance 60 minutes (communication range 15 km); ceiling is 12,000 ft. Cruising speed is 55 km/hour.

Bayraktar mini-UAV. (Bayhaluk)

A Turkish equipment catalog distributed at DSEi in September 2009 featured Bayraktar. It also showed the broadly equivalent GlobIHA by Global Teknik, which was credited with 15-km range and 1.5-hour endurance using a unique software interface and Real Time Control hardware. Like Bayraktar it automatically returns to the launch point. Span is 1.51 m, length 1.4 m, weight 3.1 kg, endurance 75 minutes (data transmission range 15 km). Maximum speed is 110 km/hour (cruising speed 65 km/hour), and mission altitude is 150 to 1,500 ft.

BAYKUS

Turkish Aerospace Industries' Baykus uses an unusual tractor-pusher configuration with twin tail booms. Span is 7 m, length 6 m, takeoff weight 250 kg (100 kg empty; 80-kg payload). Endurance is 12 hours (mission radius 27 nm to maintain line-of-sight radio contact; endurance speed 110 kt); ceiling is 15,000 ft. The power plant is two 2-cylinder 2-stroke gasoline engines.

EFE/ARI

Vestel's EFE was included in the Turkish arms catalogue distributed at DSEi in September 2009. It is an electric mini-UAV similar in concept to the Israeli Skylark and to many others. A system comprises a single air vehicle, a ground station, a ground data terminal, and alternative day and night payloads. The entire system is backpackable, an advance on Bayraktar. The absence of concrete data suggests that the program is just beginning. Endurance is

given as 1.5 hours, and data range as 12 km. To complicate matters, the airframe shown in Vestel's EFE brochure looks like that of Bayraktar, with a pod and boom and a vee tail. Figures in the brochure are 2.5-hour endurance, maximum speed 160 km/hour (86 kt), cruising speed 80 km/hour (43 kt), and data range 15 km. Maximum altitude is given as 15,000 ft. No dimensions are given.

Vestel also offers the Ari micro-UAV, which was not advertised at DSEi. Vestel advertises it as "the ultimate solution for C4ISR 'over the hill' reconnaissance, surveillance, and target acquisition." Ari appears to be a molded-plastic airplane of conventional configuration, with a pusher propeller in its tail. It is backpackable; span is 1 m, weight about 1 kg (payload 0.2 kg), with an endurance of 30 minutes (mission radius 1 km); maximum speed is 120 km/hour (65 kt); cruising speed is 60 km/hour (32 kt). Maximum altitude is 10,000 ft. The UAV is hand-launched and electrically powered, offering stabilized day/night sensors.

KAYAREL

Vestel's MALE was included in the Turkish arms catalog distributed at DSEi in September 2009 in the form of side and front view drawings, which suggest an optionally piloted light airplane with a tractor propeller, retractable tricycle landing gear, and a vee tail. Dimensions were not given. Endurance is 10 hours and operational altitude 18,000 ft; video data transfer range is 150 km. The stabilized turret carries day and night sensors and a laser target designator (plus, according to the description, a laser pointer, but that would seem to be the same as the designator). Takeoff and landing are automatic, and the description emphasizes capability in rough terrain.

MALAZGIRT

The Malazgirt, a helicopter UAV, is operated by the Turkish armed forces. The manufacturer is Kale and Bakhtar, which also makes Bayraktar. It claims that much of the performance is embodied in software, so the hardware of the UAV is relatively inexpensive. Software-based capabilities include ATLS and autonomous hover, autonomous waypoint navigation, autonomous hover with or without holding a set heading, autonomous waypoint tracking with GPS/INS support, and autopilot-assisted joystick control. The manufacturer claims that this was the first operational mini-UAV helicopter, placed in service about 2007 or earlier. Rotor diameter 1.8 m, length 1.2 m, payload 1 kg. Endurance is 35 minutes with an electric motor or 90 minutes with gasoline; range is 20 km, and ceiling is 12,000 ft (operational altitude 3,600 ft).

TIHA

Turkish Aerospace Industries' 1,500-kg TIHA-A MALE is to fly in 2009. It is to be the basis for the 3,500-kg (500-kg payload) TIHA-B, designed to meet a Turkish air force requirement. The configuration is similar to that of the U.S. Predator, with a pusher propeller at the after end of a conventional fuselage and a vee tail. TIHA is a Turkish acronym for Türk İnsansız Hava Aracı (Turkish Unmanned Aerial Vehicle). The development contract, calling for three prototypes, was let on 24 December 2004. Development is to be completed by 2011. Plans call for at least six systems (three air vehicles each). An armed version may be developed.

Data: span 17 m, length 10 m; weight 1,500 kg (payload 200 kg, maximum fuel 250 kg). Endurance is 24 hours (mission radius 200 km [108 nm] to remain within line of sight for data transmission; endurance speed 200 kt, cruise speed to be more than 75 kt). The power plant is a single turboprop. The wing and tail (span 4.5 m) are both to be detachable. Ceiling is to be about 30,000 ft.

TIHA-B will be capable of carrying laser-guided missiles and JDAMS (Joint Direct-Attack Munition System) bombs.

Ukraine

It is not clear to what extent, if any, the Ukrainian military has bought the small UAVs described below. The Ukrainian army may have bought Remez-3 beginning in 2005, and other Ukrainian services may now operate the Albatros-4. Both systems were developed by the Vzlet Design Bureau of Kiev, which began UAV work in the 1990s; it received a design award in Bulgaria in 1998 and showed its UAVs at Eurosatory in June 2000. The UAVs are made by Scientific Industrial Systems, a division of Vzlet founded in 1996 specifically to produce UAVs. Work on the Remez series began in June 1997. Remez-1 and -2 differed in the sophistication of their

Malazgirt helicopter UAV. (Bayhaluk)

payloads, Remez-3T can carry two disposable payloads (1 kg each), and Remez-3U (tested 2005) is a "universal" version presumably usable for both military and civilian tasks. The standard version is Remez-3. Remez has a canard airframe with a ducted pusher propeller and fins and rudders mounted on the wings. It is powered by a 2.5-hp piston engine. Span is 2.00 m, length 0.78 m, weight 10 kg (payload 3 kg). Endurance is 2 hours (control range 2.7 nm, maximum speed 57 kt, minimum speed 31 kt).

Albatros (A-4) is a pod-and-boom UAV with a shrouded pusher propeller on the trailing edge of its wing. The prototype flew on 5 June 2000, a catapult-launched Albatros-4K version beginning flight tests on 12 December 2001. Albatros-4B is intended for hot and high conditions. The power plant is a 3.1-hp piston engine. Span is 2.475 m, length 1.425 m, weight 18.3 kg. Endurance is 2 hours (control range 10.8 nm, flight speed 32 to 67 kt). This may be a civil rather than a military UAV.

United Kingdom

The main current tactical program is the British army's Watchkeeper, in theory a replacement for Phoenix but in fact far more capable. The single Watchkeeper program supersedes two planned programs, for a short-range or unit-level (30 km) Sender and for the division- or formation-level (150 km) Spectator. A slide prepared in November 1998 showed the distinctions involved. The unit-level UAV would operate over a space 60 km in diameter (weapon reach 30 km), up to an altitude of 400 ft. The formation-level UAV would operate over a space 150 km in diameter (weapons reach 150 km), up to 10,000

TIHA in model form, 2009 Paris Air Show. (Norman Friedman)

ft. Several units would operate within this space. The next level up, force level, would see several formations operating together in a space more than 250 km across (weapons reach 250 km), at an altitude of up to 70,000 ft.

Thales UK won the competition in August 2004 (the contract was formally signed in July 2005), and its system is to enter service in 2010. This £800 million program is to buy, among other things, fifty-four air vehicles, each to cost £15 million. The air vehicle is a heavily modified Hermes 450 called WK-450; major partners are Boeing, Cubic, and Qinetiq. Compared to Hermes 450, WK-450 has a slightly larger body, new separate flight-control and mission computers, a new parasol wing, piezo-electric de-icers, and landing gear adapted to semiprepared airfields. The main payloads are a Thales Eye Master SAR/GMTI radar in the nose and an Israeli Compass IV EO/IR aft. The data link is the U.S. Tactical Common Data Link, and the UAV uses a Thales ATLS (Magic). Although in theory WK-450 is not to be armed, it seems likely that, as in the case of the nearly identical Hermes 450B, weapons will be added. Thales UK claims an endurance of 16 hours, making it possible for two UAVs to maintain continuous surveillance. Watchkeeper is the largest single European UAV program, its base contract worth £800 million (awarded in 2005 by taking funds from other programs). Apparently Watchkeeper was bought partly because of

deficiencies in the earlier Phoenix program that became evident in Iraq, including problems in "hot and high" environments. Phoenix could not operate in the summer in Iraq, and it could never be deployed to Afghanistan.

Watchkeeper was described as a fast-track program, but it has been badly delayed. Initial Watchkeeper operating capability is now to be achieved in 2011. Given that date the British Ministry of Defence bought off-the-shelf UAVs to fill urgent operational requirements (UORs): Desert Hawk, Tarantula, Predator, and Reaper. Two Hermes 450 systems were leased from Elbit (by March 2009 they had flown 18,000 hours). Beginning late in 2007 video imagery from the Hermes 450s was downloaded to laptop-size L-3 Remote Optical Video Enhanced Receiver (ROVER) used by troops in forward areas. In 2004 the RAF sent a detachment of forty personnel to Creech Air Base in the United States to operate Predators remotely over Iraq via satellite links. Predators were bought in the summer of 2006; the first RAF Predators flew over Afghanistan in October 2007, and the first strike mission followed in May 2008. During 2008 RAF Predators fired twenty Hellfire missiles (AGM-114P) and dropped thirteen 500-lb laser-guided bombs, but during the first three months of 2009 that dropped to a single Hellfire. At that time the RAF operated two Reapers and planned to buy three more. The Reaper experience convinced

Watchkeeper is the most important current British program close to operational use. This Watchkeeper was displayed at the 2009 Paris Air Show. (Norman Friedman)

the RAF that UCAVs should be a permanent part of its armory, and it sought more Reapers in the 2009 budget. Reportedly BAE Systems successfully argued that the capability should be filled by a British-built system such as its Mantis, due to fly by the middle of 2009 (but delayed). In any case it appears that plans to field British UCAVs are being accelerated: When the contract for Taranis (to fly in 2010) was let in 2006, it was assumed that UCAVs would replace the current Tornado bombers from about 2025 on, but apparently plans are now much more urgent.

After many years of slow progress, in 2005 the UK's Defense Industrial Strategy White Paper advocated concentrating resources on UAVs in hopes that Britain could become a world leader. In particular UAVs promised results from local industry, which had been forced to collaborate with Europeans in manned combat aircraft programs. Hence the decision that Britain would not join the European Neuron UCAV program. BAE Systems claims that it has achieved unique results in attempts to develop fully autonomous UAVs, which would connect back to base only when decisions were required or when assignments were changed.

The Engineering and Physical Sciences Research Council and BAE Systems awarded a £6.5 million, five-year advanced technology UAV development contract to Cranfield University (leading a British university consortium) in June 2004. It apparently focused on a configuration—Flapless Air Vehicle Integrated Industrial Research, or FLAVIIR—which was to fly in 2008 using the Demon demonstrator UAV. The flapless concept uses fluidic thrust vectoring to control pitch and roll: air blown from the trailing edge of the wing entrains the normal flow over the wing and thus increases lift. A flapless UAV should be significantly less expensive because it should be simpler; BAE Systems hoped that such a UAV could be maintenance-free. Stealth might be improved by reducing edges and gaps in the airplane. The Eclipse UAV was apparently the beginning of this project.

As of late 2009 the British Ministry of Defence was promoting a "Novel Air Capability Vision" involving a new UAV that might provide an experimental operational capability by 2015. The objective is to drive innovation in survivability, maneuverability, payload integration, and transit speed. Target range is 600 km, and the vehicle is to be launchable from and recoverable by a frigate (suggesting vertical takeoff and landing). The UAV is to loiter in the target area to conduct battle damage assessment after it strikes and to reengage if need be; it is also to be able to operate in an urban environment. Payloads are described as novel, which suggests RF and laser packages. (The British have been working on high-powered microwave [EMP] warheads for about two decades, and have studied a payload suitable for cruise missile delivery, which would also be suitable for a UAV.) Survivability presumably means low observability, which is already the case with Taranis. The novel air capability is part of a larger UK defense technology plan announced in February 2009. Proposals were submitted by BAE Systems, MBDA (Matra BAE Dynamics Alenia, the European missile manufacturer), and Cranfield. MBDA is teamed with Selex Galileo and GKN for a proposal it calls Black Shadow.

In the early 1980s the British AEL (RPV) firm developed a range of small targets, from which it derived the AEL 4800 Sparrowhawk reconnaissance vehicle. Sparrowhawk was sold to the French Army in 1986 after trials in which it was launched from Gazelle helicopters. The airframe was a simple high-wing tractor carrying a television camera and a downlink. Data: span 3.21 m, length 2.77 m, weight 59 kg, endurance 1 hour, range 16 nm (maximum speed 162 kt).

In 1983–84 prototypes were ordered for a Ministry of Defence Phoenix competition, which envisaged a low-observable UAV launched by catapult and recovered by parachute. The payload was a thermal imager for day/night surveillance.

BAE Systems developed a family of Stabileye UAVs for the Ministry of Defence specifically to test sensors and payloads; as the name implied, the goal of the airframe design was such inherent stability that the payloads themselves would not have to be stabilized. Mk 1 flew on 24 October 1974, and the twelve built remained in service through 1981. Mk 2 (flown 20 December 1979) was strengthened to take payloads twice as heavy (15 kg). As an indication of what the British were then expecting, endurance was 30 minutes and 1 hour, respectively. Mk 3 adopted the now-familiar twin-boom layout and could lift a 25-kg payload (total weight 80 kg). Mk 4 adopted the pusher configuration of UAVs such as Predator, with the usual underslung sensor pod. It was a candidate for the Phoenix UAV requirement. Data give some idea of what was expected for the Phoenix: span 3.66 m, length 3.40 m, weight 131.5 kg (payload 50 kg), endurance 4 to 7 hours (speed 68–87 kt), ceiling 13,000 ft.

Ferranti, at the time another leading British defense technology company, offered an alternative, which it marketed as Firebird after failing to win the Phoenix competition. It was a conventional tractor airframe (span 3.50 m,

length 2.83 m, weight 137 kg [payload 44 kg]), with an endurance of more than 5 hours (maximum speed 93 kt, cruising speed 68 kt, range 340 nm).

GEC Avionics won the contract (see below).

There is also apparent interest in ultra-long-endurance UAVs. BAE Systems has flown the Zephyr demonstrator powered by solar cells (with lithium batteries for backup) driving a propeller on each wing. Span is 12 m and takeoff weight is 27 kg. Test flights began late in 2005, and in 2007 Zephyr stayed airborne for 54 hours (the flight was cut short by a system failure). In 2008 Zephyr remained aloft for three days, and by 2010 BAE Systems hopes to demonstrate flights lasting weeks or months.

HERTI

BAE Systems' HERTI (High-Endurance Rapid Technology Insertion) was conceived as a fully autonomous unmanned aircraft under a black Australian program. It was announced in 2006, and a prototype shown at Dubai in 2007. Fully autonomous flight is intended for stealth, and the artificial intelligence in the aircraft is also used to identify points of interest and to select the appropriate sensors. The UAV emits bursts of sensor data as required. It can reportedly detect people walking across a border, and can fly a surveillance pattern at 80 kt at 9,000 ft using a fixed EOI sensor, switching to a higher-resolution turreted sensor to provide a ground operator with identifiable images. The HERTI first flew in 2004 and is to be built by Slingsby, a British glider manufacturer. It is based on a motor-glider designed by the Polish firm J&S Aero Design. HERTI reportedly successfully flew fully autonomous missions in Afghanistan as part of the UK UAV Battle Laboratory Project Morrigan. In 2008 BAE Systems showed an attack version, Fury, armed with twin Thales LMM missiles (derived from the Short Javelin/Blowpipe series). As of mid-2009, about twenty HERTI had been built, apparently for BAE Systems itself. The first production-standard HERTI was shown in 2008; it was the first of three built by Slingsby Aviation. Apparently BAE Systems built its production aircraft in hopes of receiving an Urgent Operational Requirement to repeat previous operations over Afghanistan, but that did not materialize.

HERTI fully autonomous UAV. (BAE Systems)

The HERTI flew the first fully autonomous UK UAV mission on 18 August 2005. In this flight the UAV took off from Campbeltown Airport in Scotland, flew a fully autonomous mission over Machrihanish Bay, and returned autonomously to Campbeltown, landing autonomously. HERTI successfully completed fully autonomous flight trials at Woomera in November and December 2006.

The HERTI D concept demonstrator used the common systems, power plant, and ground station of the Corax and Raven programs, with the J&S Aero airframe. Concept design was completed in June 2004; it flew in Australia that December. HERTI A (or 1-A) is a larger version with greater payload capacity and endurance; this was the vehicle that carried out the August 2005 mission. In September 2006 a two-year program (Project Morrigan) was announced, to integrate HERTI into UK military exercises. This included deployment to Afghanistan in the summer of 2007. The first two production aircraft were delivered in November 2007 and in February 2008.

Data: span 12.6 m, length 5.1 m, takeoff weight 500 kg (payload 150 kg). Endurance 24 hours (speed 120 kt, mission radius 1,500 km); ceiling is over 20,000 ft. The power plant is a 115-hp Rotax 914 engine. The production version has a takeoff weight of 750 kg.

MANTIS

BAE Systems' demonstrator MALE was first shown at Aero India 2009 (February 2009). In July 2008 BAE Systems announced a cooperative agreement with the Ministry of Defence to develop the Mantis Unmanned Autonomous System (UAS) as an advanced concept demonstrator. Presumably it shares the autonomous control techniques developed for HERTI, but it has much higher performance. UK industrial partners include Rolls-

Mantis on its first flight, 21 October 2009. (BAE Systems)

Royce, QinetiQ, GE Aviation, Selex Galileo, and Meggitt. A mockup was displayed at Farnborough 2008, at which time the first flight was expected early in 2009 (Mantis first flew at Woomera in October 2009). The model shown at Farnborough had six underwing hard points; it was shown with four GBU-12 laser-guided bombs and two Brimstone missiles. It had an electro-optical turret and a radar under its body, and the usual satellite antenna in a bulge over its nose. In February 2009 BAE Systems published photos of Mantis in final assembly. This version is described as Spiral 1. BAE hopes that the Ministry of Defence will finance a Spiral 2 version (Spiral 1 was funded on a fifty-fifty basis beginning late in 2007). This version would take off at about 8.5 to 9 t, twice as much as Reaper.

BAE Systems sees Mantis as a domestically produced alternative to the U.S. Reaper acquired under an urgent operational requirement. A British decision not to buy more Reapers may indicate interest in buying Mantis instead. Mantis was originally funded under the Ministry of Defence strategic UAV program, which was later merged with the tactical UAV program. Mantis first flew on 21 October 2009, slightly delayed but still only nineteen months from program start.

Data: Mantis has a 22-m wingspan and an endurance of 24 hours, with a ceiling of 50,000 ft. It is powered by two small (250-hp) Rolls-Royce RB250B-17 turboprops in pods on struts atop its rear fuselage.

PHOENIX

GEC Marconi/BAE Systems' Phoenix first flew in 1986 in response to a 1982 requirement for a UAV to work with the new Battlefield Artillery Target Engagement System (BATES). It was conceived to replace an earlier canceled Supervisor program. At this point it was expected to enter service in 1989. The long delay between first flight and entry into service presumably reflects difficulties in meeting the major requirements of a UAV system, control and integration (the airframe is relatively easy to design and build). The project was reviewed in March 1995 and the contract renegotiated (limited production had begun in 1994). A new in-service date (December 1998) was approved in September 1996 (Phoenix entered service the following year). The 1995 review concluded that although there were off-the-shelf systems that approached the stated requirement, Phoenix came closest and thus was still worth buying. Phoenix in turn replaced the Canadair 501 Midge, which had been in service with 94 Locating Regiment Royal Artillery and 22 Battery Royal Artillery since 1972. Midge used "wet film," and its data were not available until it returned; Phoenix had a live video downlink.

The ground-control station communicated to artillery batteries via the British BATES. Phoenix was part of 32 Regiment Royal Artillery, which had three Phoenix batteries, a total of twenty-seven UAVs; each battery could support seventy-two sorties. A ground station could control two aircraft, the second launched eight minutes after the first.

Initial purchase was 198 aircraft. Phoenix was deployed beginning in 1999 in Kosovo: 12 of the 27 air vehicles were lost. It was deployed beginning in 2003 to Iraq (as part of Operation Telic) by the 22 (Gibraltar) Battery of 32 Regiment Royal Artillery. During Operation Telic (Iraq, 2003), Phoenix conducted 138 sorties, but 23 air vehicles were destroyed and 13 others were damaged but repairable. Only about 15 percent of these losses were attributed to enemy action. Performance in hot weather was considered unacceptable. Reports of excessive radio interference suggest that the system command data link is not digital. Even so, the operations demonstrated the value of a UAV, beyond the artillery support role. Reportedly some of the losses in Iraq were deliberate sacrifices, the UAV being kept on station beyond the point of recovery in order to maintain coverage of important targets. The final operational flight was in May 2006, and Phoenix was retired on 20 March 2008. Phoenix was to have remained in service through 2013, but in 2002 the British held an international competition for the follow-on Watchkeeper (the Israeli Hermes 180 won). Probably high attrition caused the premature retirement of Phoenix, as Watchkeeper did not begin operational trials in Iraq until 2007. As of 2008 it was to enter service in 2010; in the interim Hermes 450 was deployed to Afghanistan. The unit deployed to Afghanistan, 56 (Bhurtpore) Battery, also has the Desert Hawk mini-UAV.

Phoenix may survive as a test-bed to develop UAV and UCAV operating concepts pending introduction of Watchkeeper. Configuration: twin-boom tractor with underslung pod (radomes fore and aft) from which an EO turret is slung. There was no undercarriage. Instead, Phoenix was recovered by parachute, flipped on its back (to preserve the sensor), its fall cushioned by a crushable dorsal "hump."

Data: span 5.50 m, length 3.76 m, takeoff weight 209.2 kg (payload 52 kg, empty weight 157.2 kg). Endurance is more than 4 hours (mission radius 50 km, speed 86 kt); ceiling is 9,000 ft. The power plant is a 25-hp, 2-stroke, flat twin-piston engine.

RELIANT MAUSER

BAE Systems' modular UAV concept envisages a common fuselage with alternative wings and even power plants. A sketch shows a simple UAV with a tractor propeller and a vee tail, and an alternative jet version (engine above the after fuselage) with longer wings. Alternatively two fuselages could be joined together with either type of propulsion. All would have common flight processors, which could adapt automatically to the configuration chosen.

TARANIS/CORAX/KESTREL/RAVEN

The Ministry of Defence announced the award of a contract for the Taranis demonstrator UCAV program to BAE Systems in December 2006. The first flight date was given as 2010. First steel was cut in September 2007, and assembly of the first vehicle began in February 2008. Taranis won the UK's Strategic UAV contract, in a program announced in March 2005; on this basis the United Kingdom did not join the European Neuron program. SUAV in turn reflects a statement in the UK's December 2005 Defence Industrial Strategy White Paper that Britain should engage in targeted investment in the UAV market. The associated air vehicles are Corax (estimated span 9.1 m), Kestrel (span 5.5 m, fixed landing gear), and Raven (span 5.5 m, retractable landing gear). Corax is apparently the full-scale demonstrator vehicle. Taranis may be conceived as the basis for an unmanned follow-on to current British attack aircraft such as Tornado. It is described as stealthy and about the size of a Hawk trainer (span 9.94 m). Estimated weight is 8,000 kg. Based on released video of this stealthy UCAV, estimated Corax span is 9.1 m, and estimated length is 5.5 m. Kestrel uses a pair of AMT turbojets (65 lbs of thrust each). The full Taranis is powered by an Adour 951 (6,480 lbs of thrust) turbofan. Span is 9.94 m, and length is 12.43 m. The fully developed air vehicle is described as capable of delivering weapons to another continent with substantial auton-

Taranis in model form, at the 2009 DSEi exhibition. (Norman Friedman)

omy, and thus resembles in concept some long-range un-manned hypersonic bombers proposed by the U.S. Air Force. Taranis and the associated aircraft are described as fully autonomous from takeoff to landing.

Kestrel is a blended-wing UAV developed by BAE Systems with Cranfield University. It was the first jet UAV to receive British CAA permission to fly in civil air-space (March 2003). Kestrel flew seven months after the project began.

Raven is a delta-wing demonstrator developed by BAE Systems in 2003–4; it took ten months from concept to flight, and it tested key Taranis technology, includ-ing autonomous flight control. It flew in 2003 and has been described as the only finless UAV to fly outside the United States.

Corax uses the Raven centerbody with new compos-ite wings.

Stealth features of Taranis were developed under the Replica program, which produced a full-scale model of a low-observable airplane. One objective was to achieve low observables in a low-cost paperless design and produc-tion environment.

BAE Systems and Cranfield University produced the smaller low-observable demonstrator Eclipse, which flew about 2000. It uses a diamond wing and a single vertical tail (no horizontal tail) and has a jet air intake over the center of the wing. The nose protrudes forward, a photo suggesting strakes leading from the wing. Eclipse seems to have been part of a FLAVIIR project to develop a flapless UAV, which would have inherently lower cost.

Taranis is named after the Celtic god of thunder. BAE Systems claimed about 2008 that the program re-flected ten years of efforts to develop fully autonomous aircraft, related programs including those listed above plus HERTI and Nightjar I and II. BAE Systems Australia is to have a 5 percent workshare. As of mid-2009 Taranis was in final assembly and was expected to fly in 2010. Weight is about 6 tons (6,000 kg).

ZEPHYR

Qinetiq's Zephyr may be the first solar-powered UAV to be deployed, either in Iraq or in Afghanistan by the U.S. Department of Defense. It would be used to collect signals intelligence at long range. Although Qinetiq is a British

Corax, a control test vehicle in the Taranis program. (BAE Systems)

Zephyr solar-powered UAV. (QinetiQ)

company, Zephyr is apparently intended for U.S. service. Zephyr 6 set an endurance record of 82 hours 37 minutes, and a contract has been awarded for Zephyr 7. The U.S. Navy has bought Zephyr. In May 2009 Qinetiq received a U.S. contract for seven air vehicles and a ground station. The record flight (28–31 July 2008) was cosponsored by the British Ministry of Defence and the U.S. DoD under the Joint Capability Technology Demonstrator program cosponsored by United States Central Command, the Office of the Secretary of Defense for Advanced Systems and Concepts, and the U.S. Army Space and Missile Defense Command.

Data: span 18.2 m, length 5 m, weight 45 kg (payload 3 kg). Ceiling is 60,000 ft and cruising speed is 50 kt.

United States

Largely because of extensive employment of UAVs in combat in Iraq and in Afghanistan, and against terrorists elsewhere, the United States is now by far the world's largest user of military UAVs. The U.S. Navy's use of Israeli Pioneer UAVs during the 1991 Gulf War may have been the first combat use of such aircraft with real-time data transmission. Reportedly the U.S. Marine Corps bought the Israeli Pioneer, the first operational U.S. UAV, after the October 1983 Beirut massacre, in which the Marine barracks was blown up by a truck bomb. Afterward the Israelis showed Gen. P. X. Kelley of the Marine Corps UAV video of him walking through Tel Aviv; Kelley wanted that capability. In March 1984 the Israelis demonstrated their Mastiff to the U.S. Navy, landing it on the helicopter carrier *Guam*, and that September the Marines had a Mastiff at Camp Lejeune. Meanwhile Secretary of the Navy John F. Lehman ordered a UAV competition; he wanted something faster, with better range and endurance, and with a secure data link. The competition was announced in August 1985, and it was won by Mazlat (later IAI Mazlat) working with the U.S. AAI corporation. This Pioneer UAV was an improved version of the Israeli Scout. Deliveries began in 1986.

Initially U.S. UAVs were designated in the missile (M) series, with the prefix Q, which in the past had been applied to drone versions of manned aircraft (e.g., QF-4 for an F-4 drone). In 1997 they were designated in their own Q (UAV) series, with prefix R for reconnaissance or M for multipurpose, meaning reconnaissance and combat.

After many false starts, in 1987 Congress froze all U.S. UAV/RPV funding pending development of a coherent joint-service program (among others, this killed the Army's Aquila). In June 1988 the DoD submitted a seven-year $2.3 billion master plan envisaging four categories: close range, short range, medium range, and endurance. Close range was defined as 50 km, and short range as 200 km. The program was to be administered by a Joint Program Office within the Naval Air Systems Command but funded directly by the secretary of defense. Later the close- and short-range categories were combined and a new shipboard category added. The Hunter (RQ-5) emerged from this program. Another product was the RQ-6 Outrider, which for a short time was to have been bought by both the Army and Marine Corps. It was an Advanced Concept Technology Demonstration, and plans called for competing the contract for a standard biservice tactical UAV in December 1999. That never happened because the Army and Navy had radically different requirements. Problems in the Outrider program prompted the Joint Requirements Oversight Council (JROC) to approve separate service systems (November 1998). In the Army's case, that led to the quick development of the RQ-7 Shadow, its current brigade-level UAV.

In 1994 a Defense Airborne Reconnaissance Organization (DARO) analogous to the National Reconnaissance Office (NRO), responsible for space reconnaissance, was created to manage wide-area manned and unmanned airborne reconnaissance systems. It took over much of the power of the earlier Joint Program Office and seems to have been responsible for the concept of Tiers endurance UAV coverage. The endurance end of the scale produced Global Hawk and the abortive Tier III Dark Star.

In 2009 DARPA continued to seek energy sources that would make it possible for a relatively heavy HALE to remain aloft for longer. In March 2009 it awarded a contract to Eltron R&D of Colorado to develop metal hydrides, the agency's preferred solution for long-term energy storage in a thin, cold atmosphere. Eltron envisaged a battery in which the metal hydride would serve both as fuel source and as anode.

The Air Force also became interested in a tactical UAV, the Boeing Robotic Air Vehicle (BRAVE 200), which could be used as a loitering antiradar missile or a jammer. Boeing received a development contract in 1983 and flew fourteen prototypes in 1983–84, but the program was canceled late in 1984. At that time it was designated YQM-121A Pave Tiger. The air vehicle had a span of 2.57 m and a length of 2.12 m and weighed 120 kg at launch; the power plant was a 28-hp piston engine driving a pusher propeller. In 1987 the Air Force revived the project as YQM-121B Seek Spinner, a loitering antiradar drone; another version was the CEM-138 jammer (the designation is probably garbled). These versions weighed 200 kg. The configuration was flying wing with wingtip vertical surfaces. Both revived programs died in 1989, presumably due to the Congressional freeze on UAV funding.

After 2000 the U.S. Army sought to create a transformational lightweight (hence more deployable) Future Combat System (FCS), which would rely more heavily than past formations on information, which in turn meant largely information gathered by UAVs. Boeing/SAIC received the overall FCS system contract, so this private contractor chose the final contenders for the various classes of UAV. The reorganized Army would be built around brigade-size Units of Action rather than divisions. The Army split the UAV mission into classes. Each of the thirty-three Units of Action would operate about 200 UAVs: 108 Class 1, 36 Class 2, and 48 Class 3/Class 4A/B. Class 1 was a platoon UAV (16-km range, 1-lb payload, endurance 90 minutes). Class 2 was a company-level Organic Air Vehicle (30-km range, 10-lb payload, 5-hour endurance, 1,000-ft altitude). Later Class 2 was redefined as a 112-lb UAV with 2-hour endurance and 10-km operational range. Class 3 was the battalion-level UAV. Class 4 was a brigade- or division-level UAV (ultimately 4A was the brigade UAV and 4B the divisional or corps UAV). Only Classes 3 and 4 are covered by this appendix.

Classes 1 and 2 were too close to remain separate. Honeywell received the System Demonstration Contract for Phase 1 (twelve systems) late in May 2006. This is a hand-launched mini-UAV. Class 2 attracted ducted-fan VTOL UAVs. However, Class 2 was dropped from the FY 2008 budget in February 2006.

In August 2005 Boeing/SAIC chose three finalists for Class 3: Pieseki's Air Guard, AAI's Shadow II, and Prospector (a license-built German KZO). Like Class 2, Class 3 was dropped from the budget in February 2006, no System Development Demonstrator having been chosen. The previous year the Army had called Classes 2 and 3 its highest priority.

The U.S. Army bought three Gnat UAVs from General Atomics in May 2003 to help define UAV requirements. They were deployed to Iraq in 2004. The Army then split Class 4 in two. Class 4B was also defined as the Extended Range Multi-Purpose UAV (ERMP-UAV). The two ERMP competitors were General Atomics/AAI with a modified Predator (Warrior) and Northrop-Grumman with a modified Israeli Heron, Hunter II. General Atomics was selected on 8 August 2006.

Fire Scout, which was already being developed under a Navy program, was selected as the Class 4A UAV in preference to unmanned versions of the Boeing AH-6 and the Bell 407X (which won the armed reconnaissance helicopter competition). The Army cancelled the Class 4 program in February 2010.

The U.S. Marine Corps operates air-ground task forces in three sizes: the Marine Expeditionary Unit (MEU), the Marine Expeditionary Brigade (MEB), and the Marine Expeditionary Force (MEF). The ground components of each correspond broadly to the Army's battalion, brigade, and division. In 2003 the Marines assigned a type of UAV (a "Tier") to each unit level. Each corresponds to the area of interest of the unit. As of 2005 the existing Tier I UAV was the hand-launched Dragon Eye. It was owned by the battalion, and it supported the battalion, company, and platoon. Projected upgrades (as of 2005) included a communications relay payload, because in urban areas Marine Corps line-of-sight radios often could not reach far enough. As of 2005 the Marines hoped for a joint program with the Army and Special Forces. The range for Tier I was set at about 10 km. It would have day and night imaging capability to allow the using unit to detect, classify, and identify man-sized objects from an altitude of 300 to 500 ft.

Tier II was intended to fill an intelligence/surveillance/reconnaissance gap identified during Operation Iraqi Freedom. These short-range tactical UAVs have an endurance of less than 12 hours and an operational altitude of about 12,000 ft. The interim Tier II was the contractor-provided ScanEagle mini-UAV; as of 2005 the Marines hoped for a more permanent solution. Tier II was to be low-observable, easily transportable, and compatible with shipboard use. It would have a laser pointer/rangefinder in addition to its EO/IR sensor, and its ground station would be interoperable with those for Tiers I and III. It would be owned by the regiment/division to support the division, the MEU once ashore, and the regiment and battalion.

Tier III is the MEF UAV, owned by the MEF and operated by its Marine Air Wing. It was the only Tier expected to be suitable for weaponization. In 2005 it was the Pioneer. A new craft was needed because in 2003 retirement of Pioneer was approved. However, Pioneer retirement was then extended to 2013–15 because the expected successor, the tilt rotor Eagle Eye (which would be developed mainly by the Coast Guard) was in trouble (which proved fatal). The current Tier III UAV is the RQ-7 Shadow, which is also operated by the Marines.

Note that the U.S. Navy is responsible for Marine Corps aircraft, and there is always an attempt to provide aircraft that both services can use. Thus the naval UAV plan includes Marine Corps aircraft. The Navy calls the Tier II Marine UAV the Small Tactical UAV (STUAV). As of 2000 plans called for retaining Pioneer (which was then used on board ships) until a suitable vertical take-off UAV (VTUAV) could be developed. At this time the other Navy programs were the MRE (Multi-Role Endurance) UAV and a future UCAV-N (UCAV-Navy). The Navy operated six Pioneer systems (each with five air vehicles) in FY 1999 and planned to reduce that to two contingency systems in FY 2000. They would be retained until the VTUAV entered service. At this time the Fire Scout was the projected VTUAV; after some hesitation, it was adopted.

A FY 2004 program, DUSTER (Deployable Unmanned System for Targeting, Exploitation, and Reconnaissance) examined a UAV system to replace current airplane reconnaissance systems. It is ironic; the Navy had funded a joint reconnaissance UAV program only to cancel it and much later move its digital ATARS sensor to manned aircraft. Presumably something like DUSTER will become a modular payload for the X-47B UCAS or a later aircraft of that type.

There has been interest in submarine-launched UAVs, particularly in connection with the conversion of four strategic submarines to SSGNs assigned to support Special Forces. Early in 2003 Northrop Grumman received a contract to develop an expendable launch capsule, the stealthy affordable capsule system (SACS); in May 2003 DARPA funded the Cormorant submarine UAV (see entry below); it was eventually canceled. The recovery technique involved was tested in 2006.

UCAVs have interested both the U.S. Navy and the U.S. Air Force, but currently this is a Navy-only program, using the X-47B described below. The idea predates mod-

ern UCAVs. In 1964 Ryan, which made the standard U.S. jet target (Firebee), proposed a bomb-carrying version under Project Cee Bee. The drone was given two underwing hard points. Cee Bee attracted only limited interest because it was unlikely that the bombs could be dropped very precisely. At that time, too, the Air Force had not yet experienced the brutal attrition of the Vietnam War. In 1971, however, the Air Force ran Project Have Lemon, in which a Firebee was provided with a television, two Maverick missiles or television-guided bombs, and a data link. Have Lemon was intended specifically for defense suppression, and the remote operator could lock the missiles onto a target visible on his television screen, just as pilots could lock them on in flight. A Firebee thus modified launched a Maverick on 14 December 1971. Firebees also carried Shrike antiradar missiles. New versions of the Firebee were developed in 1973–74 specifically for the strike mission, but the Air Force lost interest after the end of the war (cynics suggested that it did not want unpiloted aircraft). The test squadron was disbanded in 1979.

By the late 1990s there was again interest in UCAVs, both services starting limited programs. Note that UCAVs were *not* included in the original unified UAV program but that a UCAV-N certainly was included in the DoD's year 2000 UAV *Road Map*. Ideas raised at this time included "air occupation," in which long-endurance UAVs would orbit in enemy airspace to inhibit an enemy by threatening to strike moving targets (an idea reportedly inspired by the use of air patrols during the Balkan wars). The U.S. Navy considered VTOL and STOVL (short take-off and vertical landing) UCAVs. In March 1999 DARPA awarded Boeing a contract for two X-45A UCAV demonstrators, the first flying on 22 May 2002. During the summer of 2000 the U.S. Navy awarded fifteen-month concept exploration studies to Boeing and to Northrop Grumman. At this point the naval mission was mainly reconnaissance in the face of enemy air defenses. Early in 2001 Northrop Grumman won this competition with its X-47A Pegasus. It flew on 30 July 2003. Among other things, Pegasus demonstrated a stealthy airframe without any vertical surface.

It must have seemed that the Air Force and the Navy were developing parallel UCAVs, so a joint UCAS office

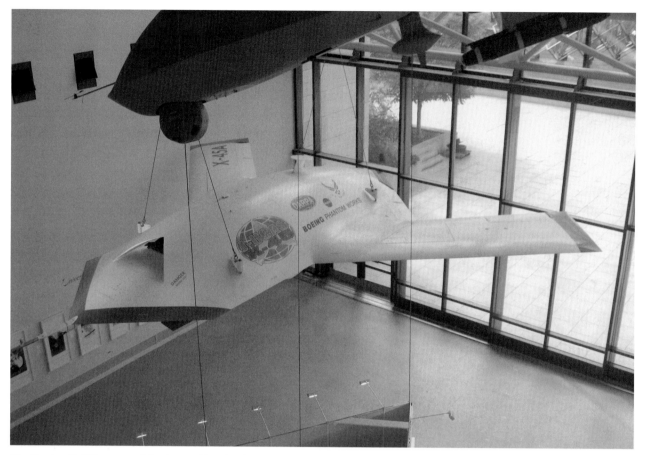

The Boeing X-45A successfully dropped bombs. It was conceived as an Air Force UCAV, but the Air Force dropped out of the program, and Northrop Grumman won the follow-on Navy program. This X-45A is on display at the National Air and Space Museum. (Norman Friedman)

under DARPA direction was formed in October 2003. DARPA and Boeing were then developing the X-45B for flight in 2008. Before metal was cut, the Air Force redirected the program to a more capable X-45C. Meanwhile Northrop Grumman and Lockheed teamed to produce the alternative X-47A Pegasus. They were interested in a modular configuration. Late in 2004 the Air Force took over the joint program, but early in 2006 it canceled X-45C and dropped out, citing the need to rethink requirements. There has been speculation that the Air Force took its program black at this point. The Navy retained interest, so early in 2007 it ran a competition between the two teams (Boeing and Northrop Grumman), which Northrop Grumman won in August 2007 with the X-47B.

At the lower end of the scale, in the summer of 2005 DARPA proposed a three-year program (Peregrine) to develop a UAV killer in the form of a small low-cost high-endurance UAV with high dash speed. The program

justification mentioned the proliferation of UAVs (at that time more than 250 types were under development or in service) and the rapidly declining cost of guidance systems such as GPS receivers. DARPA therefore expected more expendable UAVs. It is not clear how such craft could be distinguished from small cruise missiles. DARPA envisaged a UAV that would use long, narrow wings to extend its loitering endurance, flying at 30 to 40 mph on a small diesel engine. Once a target was detected, the UAV would dash to it on jet power (DARPA suggested a pulsejet, but small turbojets of the requisite size existed). At this point the long high-endurance wings would be jettisoned to reduce drag. The February 2007 DARPA submission for the FY 2008 budget showed funding beginning in FY 2006 and continuing through FY 2009 (the end of the period covered in the budget submission, not necessarily the end of the program). No contractors were mentioned. However, DARPA awarded a contract in April 2009 for the UAV sensor to a team consisting of Aerophysics, Raytheon Missile Systems, and Michigan Tech Research Institute. Their system, also called Peregrine, was a radar-cued active/passive IR device based on Raytheon's Quiet Eyes electro-optic turret. It apparently identifies the object detected as a UAV based on doppler from its propeller. A laser in the turret provides range and geometry information and may also be used to neutralize the sensors of the target UAV. DARPA also awarded contracts for high-powered, presumably ground-based, lasers to be used against UAVs and for electro-optical (including LIDAR) sensors to control them.

In January 2009 DARPA awarded a contract to Two Lights Technology LLC to develop a close air support system (presumably UAV-based) specifically for special forces and other small units. It would be available 24/7, and it could be controlled from a hand-held unit that, presumably, would not give away the user's existence. Weapons would be visually guided. Phase I was system engineering, Phase II would be prototype development, and Phase III would be partnering with manufacturers.

DARPA is currently interested in very small UAVs under a program for stealthy, persistent, perch-and-stare (SP2S) craft. This effort apparently funds AeroVironment's birdlike Mercury (10 grams), which flew in December 2008 and a version of the same company's more conventional Wasp (430 grams). This device is intended to launch vertically, tip over into conventional flight, and land vertically to perch in position to acquire data over a sustained (ultimately 24-hour) period. Such vehicles might well be launched by a larger UAV; they have some of the characteristics of unattended ground sensors but are more mobile and can be targeted more precisely. DARPA has also funded what it calls morphing air-land vehicles (MALVs), which can both fly and crawl; one such vehicle with a 28-in. span flew at Eglin Air Force Base in 2004.

The step below is DARPA's nano–air vehicle, under development by both AeroVironment and Lockheed Martin. It is defined as weighing less than 10 grams and carrying a 2-gram payload, to place a sensor at a range of 1,000 m. No dimension is to be greater than 75 mm (3 in.). These are effectively small mechanical birds or large mechanical insects.

The U.S. Ballistic Missile Defense Organization (BMDO), now the Missile Defense Agency (MDA), has tested UAVs for boost-phase interception under the program name RAPTOR (Responsive Aircraft Program for Theater Operations). RAPTOR envisaged a long-endurance detector cueing a more conventional UAV that would fire hypervelocity air-to-air missiles. The reference to theater operations meant operations at the edge of a battle area to defeat short-range tactical missiles.

The missile-carrier prototype was Talon, designed by Scaled Composites; it is a conventional-looking low-wing tractor piston airplane with twin vertical tails. Armament was two 50-lb kinetic-kill hypervelocity missiles with 100-km range. Span was 20 m, length was 7.6 m, and weight was 815 kg (370 kg empty). In addition to missiles, Talon carried 68 kg of IR search and track sensors. Endurance was 50 hours (maximum speed 450 km/hour), and ceiling was 65,000 ft.

The cueing aircraft was the flying-wing Pathfinder, which was an existing AeroVironment solar-cell aircraft (see Helios). Span was 30.5 m, length 2.4 m, weight 245 kg (payload 41 kg). In theory endurance was indefinite; cruising speed was 57 km/hour, and service ceiling was 68,900 ft. In 1997 Pathfinder broke the world record for altitude by a propeller driven airplane by reaching 71,000 ft.

The BMDO dropped this program in the late 1990s, but the aircraft were passed to NASA for extreme-altitude tests. As of 2010 interest in boost-phase interception is reviving. While operating it, NASA upgraded Pathfinder to Pathfinder Plus, stretching its wing to a 36.3-m (also given as 37-m) span and adding two more electric motors (total of ten) and improving the solar cells. Takeoff weight increased to 340 kg (maximum payload 45 kg). The power plant is two 8-hp brushless electric motors driving two-blade wide-chord laminar flow propellers designed for high altitudes. Endurance is 15 hours (endurance speed 15–18 kt). Payload varies with altitude: approximately 100 lbs to 65,000 ft and 50 lbs to 80,000 ft. In August 1998 Pathfinder Plus reached 80,000 ft. The next step was the scaled-up Centurion, also built by AeroVironment; it flew at the NASA Dryden research center in November 1998. Span is 62.8 m (206 ft), and there are twelve propellers

Peregrine UAV killer. (DARPA)

AeroVironment's nano-UAV, camouflaged to look like a local bird. (AeroVironment)

and four gondolas instead of two. It weighs 630 kg and is intended to reach 100,000 ft. Centurion was conceived as a prototype for the ultimate long-endurance Helios, with a span of 75.3 m (247 ft), fourteen propellers, and five gondolas. Its solar cells generate 37 kW, of which 10 kW drives the fourteen propellers. It is intended to reach 100,000 ft and to sustain flight at 50,000 ft for at least four days. Helios first flew (at low altitude) on 8 September 1999, and on 13 August 2001 it achieved a record of 96,863 ft altitude, exceeding the previous world record of 85,068 ft (for horizontal flight) set by an SR-71 in July 1976. The U.S. Navy is reportedly considering Helios as a communications relay; for some years it has seen aircraft, manned and unmanned, as "poor man's satellites." The use of a UAV would dramatically reduce the fleet's vulnerability to detection via the satellite downlink, without requiring the fleet to use expensive specialized satellites with steerable down-beams.

Note that AeroVironment's Global Observer (see below) does *not* rely on solar power for long endurance.

The U.S. Navy and U.S. Marine Corps currently plan a new STUAS to replace the ScanEagles bought off the shelf for service in Afghanistan and Iraq beginning in 2004. They want a UAV at least triple the size of ScanEagle. Work on requirement formulation began in August 2007, and the RFP was issued in June 2009. Of at least twelve suppliers who expressed interest, four offered proposals: AAI's Aerosonde Mk 4.7, Boeing/Insitu's Integrator, UAV Dynamics's Storm (a version of the Elbit Hermes 90), and

Raytheon/Swift Engineering's KillerBee 4. STUAS Tier II is to replace the Boeing ScanEagle. The current requirement is to operate at least 4 km (2 nm) from a ship or land control station, with at least 10-hour endurance (24 hours desired), providing the ground station with full-motion video. The system is to be capable of sustained 12 hours/day operation for thirty days and one surge (24 hours per day) for a ten-day period during any thirty-day cycle. It must be transportable by HMMWV (Humvee); no individual component is to require more than a two-Marine lift. Although the RFP initially called for initial operating capability in 2012, early in June the RFP was modified to allow a contractor to offer five systems by the third quarter of 2010. The reported expected production run is 250 systems, with three or four air vehicles per system (initial plans are apparently for fifty-four systems). As of early August 2009, the STUAS competition was set to conclude that month or in September 2009, but as of January 2010 it had been extended to that March.

As of mid-2009 the U.S. Air Force had completed work on the MQ-X initial capabilities document; work may have begun as early as 2004. It is not clear to what extent the Air Force envisages a fast attack bomber such as the X-47B UCAS or something more like a Predator or Reaper. Both of the UCAS competitors, Boeing and Northrop Grumman, are reportedly interested in MQ-X. Raytheon has announced its own interest in MQ-X, using either a new vehicle with two aft-mounted jets or a scaled-up KillerBee. It is not clear whether Lockheed

Martin intends to compete (see below). Apparently General Atomics sees its new Predator C as a possible MQ-X, assuming that the initial intent is simply to replace Predator and Reaper with something of higher performance (some have interpreted the stealth and speed of Predator C as a response to the vulnerability of the earlier aircraft). The Air Force has released a road map looking out to 2047 (its centennial) and envisaging successive stages of UAV development: MQ-Ma, -Mb, and so on—but without specific timing. MQ-Mc would be capable of air-to-air combat.

Also in mid-2010 the Air Force was apparently seeking a small tube-launched UAV that could be carried by an airplane or even by another UAV. The existence of the program was revealed in August 2008 when L3 Geneva Aerospace, apparently one of four bidders, mentioned its Tube Launched Expendable UAV, up to 3 ft long, weighing 15 lbs, with about 1-hour endurance, transmitting data either to a pilot or to a ground commander. The Army and Navy are also reportedly working on such UAVs, perhaps under a single triservice program. L3 Geneva Aerospace claimed it could have a UAV flying within eighteen months. It offers a maximum speed of 85 kt and a cruising speed of 55 to 65 kt, using a piston engine driving a propeller with flip-out blades. Projected unit price would be $2,000 to $50,000. This UAV would fly until it crashed into the ground. Note the Navy's sonobuoy tube–launched UAV described below, which appears to be similar.

On 29 January 2010 DARPA issued an RFP for a close air support UCAV. It can be either a specially built UCAV or a version of an existing drone aircraft; DARPA specifically mentioned the QF-4, QF-16, and UA-10. The latter is the two-seat version of the A-10 ground-attack aircraft. A new UCAV would have to equal the persistence of existing UCAVs (MQ-1 and MQ-9); a converted manned airplane would match the persistence of that airplane. The new features sought are high subsonic speed (better than Mach 0.65) and maneuverability (more than 3 G), presumably to ensure survivability in the face of antiaircraft weapons. Payload is to be 2,000 to 5,000 lbs. Compared to the existing Reaper, the new airplane would be significantly faster and more agile. Unlike existing UAVs, it would in effect replace a segment of the manned Air Force. It is not clear why this is a DARPA program, given that vehicles such as the X-47B already offer higher performance to much the same end. DARPA normally tries to drive development in directions not yet covered by existing programs. That suggests some further feature of the program, such as greater autonomy linked to artificial intelligence.

The U.S. UAV program structure deserves special comment. In theory U.S. procurement operates under a relatively slow cycle in which requirements are formulated and contracts are then competed. However, UAV development has been so explosive and combat need so urgent that many systems have been bought on an ad hoc basis. The normal procurement cycle was circumvented by classing the UAVs and their systems as ACTDs (Advanced Concept Tactical Demonstrations) or JCTDs (Joint Concept Tactical Demonstrations). In theory an ACTD or JCTD tests some new technology in sufficient quantity to assess its tactical value; the ACTD or JCTD leaves the test articles with the using command. In theory the next step is insertion into the long-term program. However, the usual next step was to buy more of the UAVs, the ACTD or JCTD approach having been chosen simply because the standard cycle was far too slow.

This approach has had some unexpected consequences. An ACTD or JCTD does not require standardization with other systems; that is part of the way that it produces quick results. Past attempts to standardize UAV ground stations and data links have had mixed results (the Navy seems to have been more successful than the Army and Air Force in this respect). In February 2009 the services were ordered to develop a single all-service control system architecture for all UAVs (presumably not for the very small ones). Open architecture suggested a plug-and-play concept, special software accommodating different aircraft. However, the single architecture also suggests that UAVs that have been considered parts of separate systems may be used for much the same missions. For example, the Air Force was ordered to assess the ability of the Army's Sky Warrior One to fly the Air Force Predator mission (the two aircraft are essentially identical). One advantage of a common ground station approach would be to encourage different companies to offer competing ground station software tools, for tasks such as visualization, auto-tracking, and data archiving and tagging. The U.S. Army is to be lead service in this project. One immediate consequence was that the Air Force cut back a project developing an advanced cockpit for Reaper and Predator. It would have provided displays simulating those in the cockpit of a manned airplane, with a 120-degree view. Presumably the project reflected the Air Force's strong preference to treat individual UAVs as aircraft each requiring its own full-time pilot, a view not shared by the other services.

As UAV technology has apparently matured, it has become possible to return to the standard model. The first such procurement after the run of ad hoc systems seems to have been the Army's 2005 award of a contract for its Extended Range/Multipurpose (ER/MP) UAV, which went to General Atomics for its MQ-1C Sky Warrior. However, DoD policy continued to favor ad hoc contracting, because the need for numbers of UAVs in Iraq and Afghanistan was so urgent. The next two formal requirements were formulated only recently, for STUAS/Tier II and MQ-X (the Air Force follow-on to Predator).

Because of the way they were procured, many U.S. UAVs were designed with gasoline engines. By 2009 the U.S. Defense Department wanted to standardize on heavy fuel, which offers survivability advantages; too, limiting the Army to a single fuel greatly simplifies logistics. Hence the interest in converting various UAVs.

Note: In the list of systems below, those with official designations (Q series) are given first, followed by two with other official designations (X-47B and MQ-X), followed by systems without current Q-series designations in alphabetical order.

RQ-1/MQ-1 PREDATOR/SKY WARRIOR/GNAT 750

Predator, which uses the General Atomics Gnat 750 air vehicle, was the first U.S. Air Force medium-endurance (MALE) UAV, derived from earlier Tier I and Tier II medium-endurance programs (Tier I was funded mainly by the CIA, which first deployed Predator over the former Yugoslavia in 1993–94). The upgraded Gnat 750TE won the DoD Tier II competition in January 1994, and

became RQ-1A (deployed over Bosnia in the summer of 1995). This is now an Air Force program. Air Force budgets between FY 2000 and FY 2008 bought 199 Predators (including earlier budgets, the total was apparently 268; another 38 were requested in FY 2009). The FY 2009 budget shows an objective of 413 aircraft at the end of the FY 2013 program. Predator B became MQ-9 Reaper (see below).

In September 2009 General Atomics announced that Predators had flown more than 500,000 hours and nearly 50,000 missions, 85 percent in combat; the 500,000th hour was flown by P-131 on 26 July on an armed reconnaissance mission. This particular Predator A had flown more than 300 combat missions (more than 6,000 hours of flight) in two and a half years. Predators are now flying an average of 20,000 hours each month both in combat and in support of homeland security.

By 1993 there were two customers, Turkey (one system, six aircraft) and the CIA, the latter needing a surveillance platform to monitor the expanding war in Bosnia. Gnat video (visual and IR) would be relayed through a manned Schweizer sailplane to a ground station. Operations were based in Albania after it was discovered that the data link interfered with Italian television; a Gnat-750 team deployed there in February–March 1994 and then to the Croatian coast the following winter. Five such two- to three-month deployments had been completed by July 1996. The system proved effective but was limited by Balkan weather.

In July 1993 the DoD announced the Tier II UAV requirements: a payload of 400–500 lbs (to provide images with 1-ft resolution) and 24-hour loiter endurance 500 miles from a base. General Atomics already had plans for an enlarged Gnat-750 it called Predator, which won the Tier II competition to receive a Navy contract on 7 January 1994. Predator first flew on 3 July 1994, just meeting the six-month requirement in the contract. It soon demonstrated an endurance of 40 hours 17 minutes. In the Roving Sand exercise that spring it flew on twenty-five of twenty-six exercise days, provided 85 percent of the images used, and imaged more than two hundred targets. Predator then deployed to Europe for the kind of video surveillance that had been pioneered by Gnat-750.

An RQ-1L Predator rolls toward its hangar after a flight over Afghanistan, February 2002, 57th Wing Operations Group. (U.S. Marine Corps photo by CWO William D. Crow)

It first operated in Europe in July 1994, the initial 60-day operation (Nomad Vigil, from Gjader, Albania) being extended to 120 days, and it was brought back to enforce the 1996 Dayton peace agreement (Nomad Endeavor, flying from Taszar Air Base, Hungary). In August 1997 Predator became the first UAV system to graduate from an advanced development program (ACTD) to a conventional acquisition program.

Operations with Predator over Kosovo highlighted a problem, the time lag between spotting a target via UAV and attacking it. The Air Force's solution was to place a laser designator in the usual gimballed sensor turret and to arm the UAV with Hellfire missiles that would attack targets thus designated. This combination was tested at China Lake in February 2001. The designation was changed from RQ-1 to MQ-1 when Predator was armed. The MQ-1B version carries two Hellfires.

By 2000 CIA Predators were operational over Afghanistan, presumably using bases in Pakistan. A Predator reportedly spotted Osama bin Laden after 11 September 2001 but could not attack him. It is not clear to what extent the CIA was aware of the Air Force program to arm Predator. Reportedly the CIA decided to arm Predators with Hellfire missiles, and these aircraft were used extensively during the war in Afghanistan and later against terrorists elsewhere, including one strike in Yemen. The first strikes may have been mounted in October 2001.

In 2007 the U.S. Air Force formed its first UAV wing, the 432nd Wing comprising six operational squadrons and a maintenance squadron; the goal was a total of fifteen MALE squadrons (Reaper and Predator), most of which would be assigned to the Air National Guard. British Predators were operated by British personnel seconded to the U.S. 15th UAV Squadron. At this time the Air Force estimated that a wing could conduct 5,000 hours of operations in a year, 85 percent of them operational. This force seems to have been in addition to at least one Predator A squadron assigned to the Air Force Special Operations Command. In 2007 the Air Force maintained twelve Predators constantly airborne (on 24-hour flights) over Iraq and Afghanistan. In 2008 the Air Force announced that, given an expanding force, it could now maintain twenty-one Predator patrols each day. As of June 2007, since their entry into service, Predators had accounted for 250,000 flight hours.

Predator was heavily used and it took heavy losses. A third of the 65 built by early 2002 crashed; in May 2002 it was reported that 9 had been shot down, 8 were lost to mechanical problems or bad weather, and 6 were lost to human error. In all, between 1991 and 2003 the U.S. military lost 185 UAVs. In 2004–6 Predator crashes amounted to 32 per 100,000 flight hours.

In June 2008 Raytheon announced that an undisclosed customer (probably the UK) was using its privately developed Griffin missile on Predators. Griffin is a tube-launched rocket with a laser seeker; three can be carried in place of each Hellfire. Including its launcher, the missile weighs 45 lbs (it is 42 in. long).

The U.S. Air Force was expected to receive its 200th MQ-1 in April 2009; at that time plans called for sufficient aircraft to maintain thirty-one "orbits" by late 2009. In 2010 the Air Force was ordered to provide enough Reapers (see below) to make sixty-five CAPs (combat air patrols) over Afghanistan (presumably a CAP was the same as the old "orbit"). A CAP was defined as 95 percent assurance that the UAV would be available in a particular area. The Air Force in turn estimated that it needed 2.5 UAVs for each CAP, and that in turn was increased to a factor of four to take into account spares and wastage; the sixty-five CAPs translated into 260 Reapers.

Predator data: span 14.8 m, length 8.1 m, weight 1,134 kg (payload 204 kg/450 lbs). Endurance is about 35 hours (radius of action 400 nm). Ceiling is 25,000 ft (operating altitude 15,000 ft); maximum speed is 110–115 kt (cruise speed 65–70 kt, loiter speed 60–65 kt). The power plant is a 105-hp Rotax 912/Rotax 914 4-cylinder fuel-injected piston engine.

In August 2006 the U.S. Army selected the Predator air vehicle (MQ-1C) as its Extended-Range Multi-Purpose UAV (replacing the RQ-5 Hunter), using the same AAI One System ground system as the smaller RQ-7A Shadow rather than the dedicated system used by Predator. The system is called Sky Warrior (in February 2010 it was reported that it would soon be renamed Gray Eagle). The losing UAV was Heron II, offered by Northrop Grumman and IAI. General Atomics credits Sky Warrior with a triple-redundant flight-control system, presumably absent from other versions of Predator, and with the Army's favored heavy-fuel engine. The company claims that the system was ready for deployment two years earlier than expected. The first Block 0 aircraft flew on 6 June 2007, and Block 0 aircraft soon deployed to Iraq. Each system consists of five ground stations and twelve to eighteen aircraft; current plans call for one system for each of the ten divisions, for a total of 132 Block I air vehicles. MQ-1C is an improved MQ-1 with a heavy-fuel (Thielert diesel) engine (burning JP-8), ATLS, a Raytheon EO/IR

Common Sensor payload, and a Tactical Common Data Link. Later aircraft will have the Northrop Grumman SAR-GMTI Starlite radar, and a tactical SIGINT package is to be added by 2011. The aircraft has two 227-kg and two 113-kg hard points. Thus it can carry four Hellfires rather than the two typically carried by a Predator. Endurance is up to 40 hours, compared to 24 for MQ-1B. Full operational test and evaluation is expected in 2013. Under a Quick Reaction Capability (QRC) program, weapon tests with Hellfire P+ missiles were completed in January 2010, and fast-tracked units were already in Iraq and in Afghanistan. Formal troop release of an updated software package was planned for May 2010; units using it would deploy in July.

The U.S. Army has gained experience with this airframe by operating five Gnat-ER in Iraq since March 2004; another sixteen, called Warrior Alpha, began deployment to Iraq in April 2008, and as of the spring of 2009 nine were reportedly in Iraq and another three in Afghanistan. The Army is currently buying eleven Warrior Block 0 with C-band data links and dedicated General Atomics ground-control stations, without ATLS and without hard points or de-icing. Four were in Iraq as of early 2009.

The planned Warrior System Demonstration involved seventeen Block 1, but eight more were later added; the first flew in April 2008. Plans originally called for eleven production systems (one per division), each with twelve airframes, but more recent Army statements envisage thirty-five to forty-five systems. Presumably the increase reflects the reality that the Army is more likely to fight in dispersed brigades than in divisions. The Army also is interested in an "Enhanced Warrior" with greater range and with a 225-kg hard point added under its body.

In 2008 the U.S. Army announced that between 2005 and 2007 the crash rate per 100,000 flight hours had fallen by 80 percent although the number of flight hours had grown by 380 percent (absolute figures were not given), suggesting that much of any initial problem had been poor maintenance. In a mid-2009 brochure General Atomics claimed that Predator-series UAVs had logged over 700,000 flight hours, 65 percent of them in combat, with over forty aircraft airborne worldwide at any moment. A single airframe surpassed 14,000 flight hours.

A version of Predator lost out to Global Hawk in the Navy Broad Area Maritime Surveillance (BAMS) competition. In December 2006 the Navy bought one MQ-9A for an undisclosed role, explicitly not in connection with BAMS and hence probably in support of special operations in Iraq or Afghanistan. It is also possible that it was intended for tests of an armed UAV launchable from shipboard, to reach terrorists in areas in which the United States cannot obtain basing rights. As of 2009 General Atomics was still advertising the marinized version of Predator B, which carries a multimode marine radar in a large ventral pod, suspended under a pylon. Claimed endurance is over 30 hours. Data: span 20 m (66 ft), length 11 m (36 ft), altitude over 50,000 ft, speed over 240 kt. The marinized Predator B retains the under-nose EO/IR turret and has a receiver for the commercial Automatic Identification System (for ships). It is not clear whether an ESM/SIGINT package and a Lynx SAR/GMTI radar are alternative payloads.

Predator was bought by Italy in 2000 (six MQ-1B, with five more ordered later), and leased by Britain for operations in Iraq early in 2004. It is also used by the U.S. Border Patrol and by NASA. Turkey bought two ground stations and six Gnat 750 air vehicles in 1994, plus two more air vehicles (to make up for attrition) in 1998.

Early in 2009 the United States refused to supply Predators to Pakistan, apparently for fear that the Pakistanis would provide access to the Chinese.

SAGEM considered teaming with General Atomics to offer a Predator derivative, Horus, for the EuroMALE requirement but abandoned the idea.

In addition to military applications, U.S. Customs and Border Patrol has been building up a Predator force. It opened an operations center in Grand Forks, North Dakota, on 16 February 2009, to support Predators patrolling the U.S.-Canadian border.

General Atomics announced the jet (rather than propeller) Predator C (formerly Avenger, and sometimes called Predator B) in 2009; it flew on 4 April. It offers better performance and increased weapons capacity, and it is described as lower-observable, with a shaped fuselage and a diffuser for its jet exhaust (to reduce IR signature). Span is 20 m and length is 12.5 m; ceiling is 60,000 ft. Speed exceeds 400 kt. Illustrations of Predator C displayed at the 2009 Navy League Show had a tail hook and folding wings. Reported maximum speed is 740 km/hour (399 kt) and reported ceiling is 60,000 ft. Reported endurance is 20 hours, presumably at low speed. The engine is a P&W Canada PW545B turbofan. An internal weapon bay can accommodate 120-kg-class weapons, presumably the Small Diameter Bomb, and its doors can be removed to provide a field of view for a reconnaissance package. In February 2010 it was announced that Avenger had attracted its first (unnamed) customer.

RQ-2 PIONEER

AAI produced the Pioneer UAV under license from IAI (it is RQ-2 because the designation was applied retroactively). Pioneer was the first modern UAV used by U.S. forces. The U.S. Navy bought the AAI-IAI Pioneer on an expedited basis beginning in 1985, having been impressed by the Israeli use of such aircraft during the Lebanon War of 1982. It entered service in 1986, and within a decade had amassed about 14,000 flight hours. The 7 January 1986 contract called for three systems and twenty-one air vehicles: two systems for ships and one for the Marines. Deliveries began in June 1986. The contract included 1987 options for two more systems (exercised in February 1987) and for four in 1988. USS *Iowa* deployed its UAVs during a Central American cruise in January 1987. Pioneer was intended both to provide spotting for the recommissioned battleships and overall imagery intelligence and as a land-based Marine Corps UAV. It flew from both the battleships and large-deck amphibious ships, and was typically recovered in a net. It flew more than 300 combat missions during the 1991 Gulf War. Later it was used in Bosnia, Haiti, and Somalia. Nine systems (each with eight air vehicles) were bought. Initial problems included electromagnetic interference and recovery on board ship. Despite problems, Pioneer was retained in service well beyond its expected lifetime, thirty air vehicles being acquired in 1994 to make up for losses. Sixteen Pioneers supported the 1st Marine Division during the 2003 invasion of Iraq. They were used extensively around Falujah.

After the end of Pioneer use in Iraq, the Marines stated that during its last 1,045 flight hours the UAV had

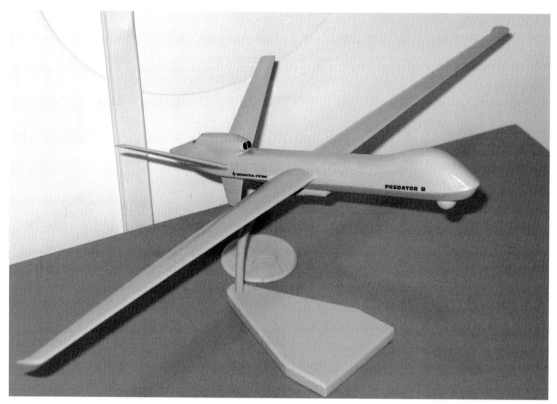

General Atomics' model of the jet version of Predator at the 2009 Navy League show. (Norman Friedman)

suffered only a single incident; during the 62,373 hours of initial use in Iraq, they suffered one incident for every 123 flight hours and one crash for every 472 flight hours.

Data: span 5.12 m, length 4.24 m, takeoff weight 210 kg. Endurance is 6.5 hours; ceiling is 15,000 ft. The power plant is a 27-hp Sachs SF2-350 piston engine. Maximum (dash) speed is 110 kt, cruising speed is 65 kt, and stall speed is 52 kt. Endurance is 3.5 to 4 hours. Ceiling is 15,000 ft. The payload is either a daylight camera (CCD) or a FLIR. A replacement payload was approved in August 1998. It included a new FLIR and a color camera.

RQ-3 DARK STAR/POLECAT/RQ-170 SENTINEL

Lockheed Martin's Tier III Minus HALE was sponsored for DARO by the DARPA joint UAV program office. Dark Star was a joint product of the Lockheed's Skunk Works and Boeing. It was canceled in February 1999, but it is included here because it provides some idea of what a stealthy reconnaissance UAV looks like. Dark Star was the first DARPA project executed under a prototyping program that dramatically cut detailed specifications;

the one-page Dark Star specification reportedly specified only best altitude, endurance, signature, and unit cost ($10 million in FY 1994 dollars) for production aircraft 11 through 20. In FY 1999 the estimate was about $13.7 million for Dark Star and $14.8 million for Global Hawk. The Dark Star name indicates the emphasis on reduced observability; it had a tailless configuration. The complementary Tier II Plus UAV was optimized for range and endurance in a more benign environment; the Common Ground Segment was intended to handle both UAVs. The sensor system was to have been similar to that in Global Hawk, but Dark Star would carry only one of the two payloads that Global Hawk carries simultaneously (EO or radar). Dark Star flew in March 1996, but a second flight crashed in April 1996 due to problems with its fly-by-wire software. A redesigned RQ-3A flew early in the summer of 1998, but the program died in January 1999 due to budget problems.

The Tier III Minus designation for Dark Star indicated that it had come out of a black Tier III program for a much larger unmanned Advanced Aerial Reconnais-

This RQ-2A Pioneer operated from the battleship USS *Wisconsin* during the 1991 Gulf War. While it was assessing battleship gun damage to targets on Faylaka Island, several Iraqi soldiers signaled their intention to surrender—to this unmanned aircraft—during a low pass. This RQ-2A is shown in the National Air and Space Museum, 2009. (Norman Friedman)

Dark Star is shown at the National Air and Space Museum, 2009. (Norman Friedman)

sance System (AARS). Reportedly this Lockheed Martin Quartz stealth UAV was abandoned at the end of the Cold War, after about $1 million had been spent. Skeptics have suggested that Quartz was never canceled, or that it was revived after Dark Star was canceled.

In the summer of 2003 Air Force officials announced that the Lockheed Martin Skunk Works had developed a larger successor. Reportedly it was used over Iraq during the 2003 invasion. The new UAV was said to have less

than the payload of a U-2 and less than the range of a Global Hawk, although it was several times as expensive. This was probably Polecat, revealed at the Paris Air Show on 19 June 2006. Unlike Dark Star, Polecat resembles a B-2. It may be used for strike as well as for reconnaissance operations. Lockheed Martin described Polecat as a demonstrator, not an operational aircraft. It crashed in December 2006 after three flights. No successor was reported. However, in 2007 the French magazine *Air &*

Cosmos published a photograph of a flying-wing UAV taken that year in Kandahar, Afghanistan. It may be Polecat or a derivative. A drawing based on a photograph of the UAV taxiing showed two bumps above the wing, presumably for engines, and a single exhaust. A very poor photograph suggests a central body protruding well above the wing. There were no vertical surfaces. The craft was sometimes called the "Beast of Kandahar." Reported shoulder patches referring to Desert Prowler may be related to this aircraft.

In December 2009 the Air Force admitted the existence of this airplane under the designation RQ-170 Sentinel (the designation RS-170 was also reported). No details were released. RQ- or RS-170 fits into neither the standard aircraft nor the standard missile designation series; like F-117, it seems to be part of a series of more or less random designations applied to black programs. There was speculation that this stealthy UAV was being used for covert surveillance of Iran and Pakistan from Afghan bases.

According to a 1997 DoD UAV report, Dark Star had much the same data links as Global Hawk, although in one case at a lower data rate: UHF satellite (4.8/1.2 and 2.4 kbps), X-band (Common Data Link: up to 137 Mbps [84 used] downlink, 200 kbps control link), and Ku-band satellite (1.54 Mbps downlink). In the UHF satellite mode, in which all users in one hemisphere must share all UHF satellites, the 1.2 kbps mode would have been shared by three air vehicles, with a single vehicle using the 2.4 kbps mode for air traffic control. By way of contrast, as listed in 1997, Global Hawk used 48 rather than 84 Mbps of the Common Data Link (downlink for data). However, it could use 9.6 kbps on a UHF satellite channel and up to 48 Mbps on a Ku-band downlink. Presumably the higher data rates are due to its larger satellite dish antenna.

Dark Star data: span was 69 ft and length 15 ft, the UAV consisting of a long, straight wing with a 12-ft-wide (3.5-ft-deep) fuselage and without any vertical control surfaces. Takeoff weight was 8,600 lbs (4,360 lbs empty); payload was 1,000 lbs (in comparison, Global Hawk was credited with a 1,960-lb payload in 1997). Sensors were carried in pallets inserted into the bottom of the fuselage: an avionics pallet on one side, a sensor pallet on the other. Maximum (and cruising speed) was 345 mph (300

kt); loiter speed was 130 kt. Comparable figures for Global Hawk are better than 345 kt maximum, 345 kt cruising, and 300 kt loiter speed. Endurance was 12 hours (8 hours at 500-nm range); radius of action was more than 500 nm. Comparable figures given in 1997 for Global Hawk were 3,000-nm range, 38-hour endurance (20 hours at 3,000 nm). Ceiling (and operating altitude) was 50,000 ft, compared to 65,000 ft for Global Hawk. The power plant was one Williams Research FJ-44-1A turbofan (1,900-lb thrust). As described in 1997, Global Hawk used a 7,050-lb-thrust Allison AE3007H turbofan. Dark Star required a 4,000-ft runway; by way of comparison, Global Hawk requires 5,000 ft. Relatively short range required that Dark Star be deployed into theater on board multiple cargo aircraft, whereas Global Hawk is self-deploying, given its range.

Polecat (P-175) data: span 90 ft and takeoff weight 9,000 lbs (maximum payload is 1,000 lbs); ceiling is 65,000 ft. The power plant is a pair of 3,000-lb-thrust Williams International FJ-44-3E engines.

Note that beginning in 2004 American media also reported a secret (black) fast reconnaissance UAV capable of remaining for a sustained period in an area but also capable of high speed. This presumably corresponds to the accounts of a fast armed UAV mentioned above. According to these reports, the U.S. Air Force has two vehicles and a ground station; the UAV has an endurance of 8 hours, during which it can operate over a heavily defended area 1,000 nm from its base. This aircraft reportedly incorporates lessons of the Iraq and Afghan wars.

No code word has been associated with these reports.

RQ-4 GLOBAL HAWK/EURO HAWK

The U.S. Air Force expects Global Hawk to replace the current U-2, though it would operate in a somewhat different mode. A U-2 uses wet film cameras to capture wide-area (synoptic images), and at least as of a decade ago, electronic media could not yet compete (that was several generations of sensors and computers ago, however). The U-2 captures images that become available only when it lands, whereas Global Hawk will transmit back its imagery (or at least a great deal of it) as it is collected. Initial arguments that Global Hawk would lack

Global Hawk, with men to provide scale. (Northrop Grumman)

non-optical sensors are no longer valid because advances in electronics, and the huge capacity of the aircraft, have solved the problem.

Development of this high-altitude long-endurance UAV began in spring 1995 when a Ryan/E-Systems team was selected for what was then called the Tier II Plus requirement. Later these companies merged into Northrop Grumman. The prototype flew in February 1998. The U.S. Air Force was the initial customer, series production beginning in the FY 2002 program. As of the spring of 2009, the U.S. Air Force planned seventy-eight Global Hawks. In 2009 Global Hawk became the first UAV the FAA allowed to fly an autonomous flight plan in U.S. air space. The Air Force reportedly sees Global Hawk as the direct successor to the current U-2 reconnaissance airplane. Global Hawk first flew in an exercise in May 2000 (Linked Seas 00), flying across the Atlantic the previous month. Because it was linked to its controller by satellite, it was controlled from the United States while operating over Europe. Operations at this time included direct support of naval units in a littoral exercise. In April 2001 a Global Hawk flew 7,500 nm to Australia to demonstrate its value for Australian defense (Australia later decided to

order Global Hawk). During Operation Enduring Freedom (Afghanistan), Global Hawks flew more than 60 missions (1,200 hours). During Operation Iraqi Freedom, Global Hawk accounted for 5 percent of Air Force high-altitude reconnaissance sorties but provided more than 55 percent of the time-sensitive targeting images used to support strikes. It located more than thirteen full surface-to-air missile batteries, fifty surface-to-air missile sites, three hundred missile canisters, three hundred tanks (38 percent of all known Iraqi armor), and seventy surface-to-air missile transporters. Note that sortie numbers are deceptive because the unmanned Global Hawk remains in the air for much longer than a manned reconnaissance airplane, so each of its sorties is equivalent to several manned ones.

The U.S. Air Force has a program to develop air-to-air refueling for Global Hawk using a manned Learjet as a surrogate. At the 2010 Singapore air show it was announced that the Learjet had successfully brought itself into position for refueling and that its automated approach was more accurate than the usual manned approach. Since this project is being conducted by Northrop Grumman, presumably it is also significant for that company's attempt to demonstrate air-to-air fueling with its X-47B UCAS air vehicle.

The U.S. Navy chose Global Hawk in April 2008 for its BAMS program. It also is being bought by the U.S. Coast Guard as part of its roughly parallel program, Deepwater. Australia became a BAMS partner in 2007 but later reduced its participation due to budgetary problems. Global Hawk won the BAMS competition against a Boeing proposal to use an unmanned version of the Gulfstream G550 (Gulfstream proposed an optionally piloted version of this aircraft in July 2003), which it called RQ-37 or Boeing BAMS 550. Boeing offered a scaled-down version of the APY-10 radar the U.S. Navy was already buying for its P-8A patrol aircraft. As initially proposed the aircraft would have been far more massive than Global Hawk: span 28.5 m, length 29.4 m, weight 41,277 kg; but its endurance was given as only 15 hours. Israel Aircraft Industries later installed the Phalcon airborne early warning radar in a Gulfstream, and it is modifying this aircraft as a UAV (aircraft endurance would greatly exceed the endurance of the pilots, and there was little internal space for substitutes). The Boeing aircraft would have cost more than $35 million, compared to $24–25 million for Global Hawk/BAMS.

Germany and NATO have selected Global Hawk as Euro Hawk, Spain has been cleared to buy it, and South Korea has recently been cleared to buy it. The first Euro Hawk was rolled out at Palmdale on 8 October 2009.

RQ-4A is Block 10. Of nine production aircraft, three operate from a U.S. base in the UAE, two are used for the U.S. Navy Global Hawk Maritime Demonstration (for BAMS), and two NASA aircraft are being modified as tanker and receiver for aerial refueling trials. Block 10 has a 35.4 m wingspan and a length of 13.5 m; takeoff weight is 12,110 kg. Payload is 2,000 lbs (907 kg). Maximum range is 12,000 nm (endurance up to 35 hours; 31.5 demonstrated); loiter speed is 343 kt; maximum altitude is 65,000 ft.

RQ-4B is a stretched Block 20 (14,638 kg) with a Raytheon sensor suite. Span is 39.9 m and length is 14.5 m. Loiter speed is 310 kt. Maximum endurance is 36 hours. Germany has bought five aircraft (with EADS sensor suites) under the Euro Hawk program; the first aircraft is due for delivery in 2012. Internal payload is 3,000 lbs,

and onboard electrical power is two and a half times that of Block 10. This version has an open ("plug and play") system architecture. Takeoff weight is about 32,250 lbs (14,628 kg). The first Block 20 flew on 1 March 2007.

Block 30 has a heavier payload and was designed for the Airborne Signals Intelligence Payload. Operational testing and evaluation of Block 20/30 was to have been completed by the end of 2009. Spain is expected to buy five Block 30s.

Block 40 carries the Northrop Grumman MP-RTIP (Multi-Platform Radar Technology Improvement Program) sensor (twelve ordered). Eight Block 40s are to be bought by seventeen NATO countries under the AGS. Operations are to begin from Signella in 2012.

RQ-4N is the U.S. Navy BAMS version; the projected sixty-eight-aircraft fleet includes the initial six system development aircraft. The first is to fly in FY 2012, the system is to become operational in FY 2016, and all aircraft are to be in service by FY 2019.

RQ-4B data: span 39.9 m, length 14.5 m, takeoff weight 14,628 kg (payload 1,360 kg). Endurance is 36 hours (endurance speed 310 kt); ceiling is 60,000 ft. The engine is a Rolls Royce AE3007H turbofan.

Euro Hawk is the European (NATO) version, built by a consortium of that name, a joint venture between EADS and Northrop Grumman. The span of this version is 39.9 m, and length is 14.5 m; takeoff weight is 14,640 kg (maximum payload 1,360 kg). Endurance is more than 30 hours, maximum speed is 630 km/hour, and ceiling is 65,000 ft. Euro Hawk is the first international version of Global Hawk.

RQ-5 HUNTER (EX-BQM-155)/MQ-5B

The U.S. version of the Israeli Hunter, the RQ-5 Hunter is made by Northrop Grumman. It was developed as the Short Range UAV by the Joint Project Office set up to administer the joint UAV program in 1988. In 1990 Hunter won over the Developmental Sciences/McDonnell Sky-Eye. It first flew in 1991. Plans originally called for fifty systems (four air vehicles each). However, the Army objected that range was inadequate, the data link was unsatisfactory, and the air vehicles did not fit the transport aircraft. However, an LRIP (low-rate initial production) contract was placed in 1993 for seven systems,

Hunter on board the USS *Essex* (LHD-2) for tests. (U.S. Navy)

giving a total of eight. Further tests revealed further problems, and procurement was canceled in 1996, when another fifty-two systems would have been ordered. By that time twenty had crashed. However, Hunter did see operational service, not only with the Army but also with the Navy and Air Force, and it was used to evaluate the use of UAVs as communications relays and in electronic warfare. Eight Hunters were sent to Albania in the spring of 1999 to support Operation Allied Force (the air war against Serbia); they were based in Macedonia. They flew 281 missions; two UAVs were damaged badly enough to be sent back to the United States. In 2002 the U.S. Army experimented with Hunters dropping the acoustically guided BAT (Brilliant Anti-Tank munition); in October 2002 a Hunter hit three armored vehicles, in one case blowing the turret off a tank. Hunters were also deployed during the 2003 invasion of Iraq, and by the summer of 2004 they had amassed 30,000 flight hours in Army service. As of October 2009 Hunters in U.S. service had exceeded 80,000 flight hours, 53,000 of them combat related. At that time it was deployed in both Afghanistan and Iraq.

The MQ-5B flew in August 2005. It has a diesel engine, more fuel, and updated avionics including ATLS, plus weapon pylons in each wing (maximum load 60 kg). MQ-5B was bought by the U.S. Army and by Belgium. In September 2007 an MQ-5B struck a target in Iraq using the Northrop Grumman GBU-44/B Viper Strike weapon. The U.S. Army bought twelve MQ-5B in November 2008, plus six Block II ground-control stations and eight tactical common data-link systems.

In 2005 the Army decided to replace this Northrop Grumman UAV with the larger MQ-1C, retaining fifteen Hunters to carry the Greendart SIGINT system.

In October 2009 Northrop Grumman announced that the U.S. version of Hunter has now been equipped with an ATLS, replacing the earlier External Pilot (EP) for takeoffs and landings (note the earlier use of an ATLS on board Belgian Hunters in the Israeli entry above).

Data (MQ-5B): span 10.44 m, length 6.90 m, takeoff weight 885 kg (payload, including fuel, is 226.8 kg; payload alone is 100 kg). Endurance is 21.3 hours (mission radius over 250 km in relay mode, dash speed 110 kt, endurance speed 60 to 80 kt), and ceiling is 20,000 ft. The power plant is a pair of 55-hp 3-cylinder engine burning JP-8 fuel in tractor/pusher configuration. February 2006 flight tests demonstrated a 21-hour endurance. Effective control range can be extended by transmitting video from one Hunter through another.

A new version called Endurance Hunter (E-Hunter) or MQ-5C flew on 17 March 2005 as part of a continuing cooperative program between the Army and Northrop Grumman to extend Hunter range. It combines the Hunter fuselage with a new 54.5-ft wing and tail to extend endurance to 30 hours and maximum altitude to more than 20,000 ft. Using a kit, Hunter can be converted into E-Hunter in 3 hours. The wing and tail are those Northrop Grumman offered the Army for its next-generation Hunter II (the Army bought Sky Warrior instead). With a heavy-fuel engine, E-Hunter endurance was increased to 40 hours and ceiling to 25,000 ft. Note that in August 1996 IAI and TRW announced an improved Hunter they also called E-Hunter, combining the Hunter body with the Heron long-endurance wing, tail, and booms. Characteristics of this UAV: span 15.24 m, length 7.52 m, take-off weight 954 kg (payload 114 kg). Endurance is 25 hours (range 200 km, speed 106 kt), and ceiling is 6,000 m. The power plant is a 68-hp piston engine.

Hunter II data: span 16.8 m (54.5 ft), length 9.3 m, takeoff weight 1,497 kg (payload 136 kg internal, 318 kg external). Loiter time at 300-km range is 29 hours (maximum speed 160 kt, loiter speed 60–80 kt), ceiling 28,000 ft. Hunter II has wing hard points and pylons for external stores, including Aviation Class 5 munitions and weapons.

According to a mid-2009 IAI brochure for MQ-5B, by that time Hunter had accumulated over 60,000 flight hours. IAI claimed that Hunter is relatively quiet, presumably as a design feature. It pointed out that in addition to the usual stabilized optronic sensors, Hunter could support COMINT and ESM sensors and a communications relay package. It incorporates a direct line-of-sight data link, but it can also use either an airborne (UAV) or a ground relay to extend effective range.

RQ-6A OUTRIDER

An Army/Marine TUAV, also called the Maneuver UAV, the Outrider was intended for brigades and Marine air/ground task forces. This was an Advanced Concept Technology Demonstration sponsored by PEO Cruise Missiles and Unmanned Aerial Vehicles. The relevant acquisition decision memorandum was signed on 21 December 1995. It called for a range of 200 km, use of GPS for navigation and target reporting, and electro-optical and IR sensors. The entire system was to be contained on board two Humvees and transportable in a single C-130. In May 1996 Alliant Techsystems received a contract for six systems for Army, Marine, and Navy users. The air vehicle was based on the Mission Technologies Hellfox flown in 1995. In effect Outrider was an attempted replacement for Hunter. It was hoped that the attrition rate would be 7 percent per year, about half that of the Pioneer then in service.

Data: span 4.0 m, length 3.3 m, maximum gross take-off weight over 227 kg (payload 27 kg). Maximum (dash) speed was over 120 kt (cruising speed 90 kt, loiter speed 60–75 kt, stall speed 32 kt). Radius of action was more than 200 km (over 108 nm); endurance was 3.6 hours at 100 km or 2.0 at 200 km. Maximum altitude was 15,000 ft. The power plant was a 4-cylinder heavy-fuel McCulloch 4318F engine. Requirements included the ability to return home automatically if the data link were lost. Initial tests showed that a TUAV was indeed useful, but also that the different services required different vehicles, the Navy in particular wanting a vertically launched UAV. Outrider itself never entered mass production. It was canceled in 1999. However, its joined-wing technology reappeared in the current Buster.

RQ-7 SHADOW

AAI's RQ-7 is the U.S. Army's brigade-level UAV. In December 1999, having received permission to go ahead with a tactical UAV, the Army awarded a contract to AAI Defense Systems for their Shadow 200. It was, in effect, an improved Pioneer. The Army requirement called for a gasoline engine, an EO/IR imaging sensor turret, and a minimum range of 50 km with 4-hour endurance at that range. An LRIP contract for four systems was let on 30 March 2001, and another in March 2002; Milestone III (approval for full production) followed on 25 September 2002, and the full-rate production contract was let on 27 December 2002. RQ-7 was first deployed with the 4th In-

Outrider, the unsuccessful joint UAV. A few UAVs have adopted the same unusual tandem-wing configuration. (Alliant Techsystems)

fantry Division (Fort Hood) in 2002 and was deployed to Iraq in 2003. The Marines decided to buy the system in 2006, their objective being six systems (to replace existing RQ-2s). Their first RQ-7s deployed with VMU-1 on 5 October 2007.

Each system includes four air vehicles. In 2008 the Army approved an upgrade including a shift to a heavy-fuel (JP-8) engine and increased fuel capacity, with extended wings and tail booms. Payload increases to 45 kg and endurance to 9 hours. A high-resolution IAI EO turret is to be installed. Some aircraft will be given the Tactical Common Data Link. These aircraft will be able to carry and drop a 9-kg medical payload.

The current RQ-7B, in production since August 2004, has a 36-in. longer "wet" (i.e., contains fuel) wing, which increases range (endurance increases to 6 hours), and payload increases to 45 kg. Avionics is improved, and the new wing accommodates the high-capacity Tactical Common Data Link.

According to the FY 2009 budget, the Army objective is a total of eighty-three systems, and the Marines plan another eight (to replace old RQ-2s). Army objectives fluctuated from sixty (FY 2000–2003) to thirty-nine (FY 2005) to seventy-four in FY 2007 (as submitted February 2006), to seventy-nine in FY 2008 and now to

A Shadow 200 being prepared for launch at Forward Operating Base Warhorse, Iraq, 24 September 2004. (U.S. Army by SPC James B. Smith Jr.)

eighty-three, partly because of competition with the RQ-8 Fire Scout program.

Poland became the first export customer in 2006. According to the UN arms sale registry, it was allocated thirty under U.S. military aid. These may be Shadow 600s.

Shadow 600 has been sold to Turkey and Romania (which has deployed three to Iraq). Romania ordered sixty in 1997 (delivered 1998–2000) and five in 2000 (delivered 2001). In January 2010 Defense Secretary Robert Gates announced that twelve Shadows would be supplied to Pakistan.

AAI also offers a Shadow 1200 Guardian UAV.

Shadow 200 (RQ-7A) data: span 3.89 m, length 3.41 m, takeoff weight 149 kg (payload 27.2 kg). Endurance is better than 5 hours (speed 225 km/hour), and ceiling is 15,000 ft. RQ-7B: span 4.27 m, length 3.75 m, takeoff weight 170 kg, payload 45 kg. Endurance 5–7 hours (speed 110 kt, loiter speed 60–70 kt), and ceiling is 15,000 ft. Data-link range is 125 km. The power plant is a 38-hp piston engine.

Shadow 400 data: span 5.15 m, length 3.82 m, takeoff weight 211 kg (payload 30 kg, empty weight 147 kg). Endurance is 5 hours (speed 110 kt), and ceiling is 12,000 ft. Data-link range is 200 km. The power plant is the same 38-hp engine as in Shadow 200.

Shadow 600 data: span 6.83 m, length 4.8 m, takeoff weight 265 kg (payload 41 kg, empty weight 207 kg). Endurance is 12–14 hours (speed 108 kt, loiter speed 75 kt), and ceiling is 17,000 ft. Data-link range is 200 km. The power plant is a 52-hp Wankel engine.

A current Marine Corps program (Group Four, formerly Tier III) envisages a larger replacement UAV to be bought about 2016, capable of carrying weapons, with a higher speed (over 450 km/hour) and a much larger payload (725 kg). Reportedly this UAV may be required to carry cargo and to have VTOL or STOL performance, and it may take over some electronic attack missions from the EA-6B Prowler.

RQ-8/MQ-8 FIRE SCOUT/XM-157

The Navy originally bought Fire Scout as a direct replacement for Pioneer, its first UAV. It demanded vertical takeoff and landing, a payload of 90 kg, a range of 200 km (125 miles), an endurance of 3 hours on station at 20,000 ft, and the ability to land in a 29-mph wind, plus 190 hours between maintenance. The three finalists were Bell, Sikorsky, and a Ryan-Schweizer Helicopters team. The latter (later taken over by Northrop Grumman) was selected in the spring of 2000, RQ-8A being a derivative of a Schweizer three-person helicopter (330SP), itself derived from the Hughes 300 light helicopter. It had a new fuselage and fuel system and UAV electronics. The prototype first flew autonomously in January 2000. Although progress was considered satisfactory, production funding was cut in December 2001 due to budget problems. Devel-

opment continued, and the Army awarded a contract for seven evaluation helicopters late in 2003 (MQ-8B). This version replaced the original three-blade rotor with a four-blade rotor, which reduced noise but increased load capacity. Navy interest then revived, with an order for eight MQ-8B for evaluation and then commitment to full production.

This unmanned helicopter was selected by the U.S. Navy for operation from a littoral combat ship (LCS). Current concepts of littoral ASW envisage fairly precise location of submarines, which in turn makes attack with the new ultralight torpedo viable. These weapons would probably be delivered by unmanned helicopters (MQ-8). Initial sea tests on board USS *Nashville* included the first autonomous deck landings by a U.S. Navy drone. Successful tests on board the frigate *McInerney* followed, and the ship deployed with an MQ-8 for counternarcotics operations in October 2009. The U.S. Army has selected MQ-8B for its Future Combat System, envisaging procurement of 480 to 560 aircraft (which are to enter service beginning in 2014).

RQ-8 is also the likely candidate for the U.S. Coast Guard unmanned helicopter, following the failure of the tilt-wing Bell Eagle Eye previously favored.

XM-157 is the Army designation. Current plans call for thirty-two per brigade combat team. Fire Scout (RQ-8B) was Class 4 UAV within the Army's Future Combat System. In January 2010 the Class 4 program was terminated.

Data: rotor diameter 8.4 m, length 7 m, takeoff weight 3,150 lbs (payload 600 lbs). Endurance exceeds 8 hours with baseline payload (speed over 125 kt, mission radius 150 nm); ceiling is 20,000 ft. The power plant is a 420-hp turboshaft.

MQ-9 REAPER

The Reaper, formerly Predator B, is described as a hunter-killer UAV. It has four times the gross weight of the earlier Predator and a payload of 1,700 kg; it was conceived as an attack aircraft. U.S. Air Force Reaper operations in Afghanistan began in October 2007, and operations in Iraq began in July 2008. A noteworthy feature of these operations (and of RAF Reaper operations) is that the UAVs are controlled not from the forward area but from a base

A Fire Scout (RQ-8) helicopter fires 2.75-in. rockets at Yuma Proving Ground, 25 July 2005. The UAV had just fired its first rocket. (Northrop Grumman)

An Air Force Reaper, newly arrived in Afghanistan, October 2007. (U.S. Air Force)

in Nevada. Apparently, however, imagery from the UAVs is handled directly in forward areas; it is not clear whether long-distance piloting is affected. U.S. Air Force upgrades included a Northrop Grumman airborne signals intelligence payload (mainly to deal with low-band radio) and a projected Gorgon Stare wide-area airborne surveillance sensor that simultaneously will provide twelve streams of full-motion video. Plans call for increased takeoff weight, ice detection capacity, and Mode 5 IFF.

Through FY 2008 the U.S. Air Force funded eighteen aircraft (it requested another nine in FY2009), but in FY 2008 it stated that it hoped to buy fifty-one through FY 2013. Reaper entered service in both Afghanistan and in Iraq in 2007. The U.S. Navy bought a single MQ-9A in December 2005, probably to support riverine operations in Iraq. The Royal Air Force acquired three Reapers, delivered to Afghanistan between September 2007 and July 2008; one was lost in April 2008. Others were obtained on an Urgent Operational Requirement basis, but an RAF request for ten more was apparently turned down. Italy bought two Reapers and two ground stations and later requested three stations and four aircraft; Germany has requested four stations and five aircraft. Reaper is also operated by the U.S. Customs and Border Patrol service.

Data: span 20.1 m, length 11 m, weight 4,760 kg (payload 1,700 kg). Ceiling is 50,000 ft, endurance is 28 hours, and cruising speed is 200 kt. Claimed payload is 850 lbs (360 kg) internally and 3,000 lbs (1,361 kg) externally. A General Atomics sketch shows Reaper with three hard points under each wing and carrying Sidewinders on the outer pylons, quad-packed Hellfires on the middle pylons, and Paveway laser-guided bombs on the inboard pylons (it is not clear how the Sidewinders would be cued, but presumably they indicate the carrying capacity of the pylons). General Atomics claims that Predator B normally carries GBU-12 and -38 precision bombs.

CQ-10A SNOW GOOSE

The Snow Goose cargo delivery UAV is produced by Canadian Mist Mobility Integrated Systems Technology. It employs the company's Sherpa GPS-guided parafoil delivery system. CG-10A first flew in April 2001, and it entered Special Forces service in July 2005. Maximum cargo weight is 600 lbs (272 kg). Length is 2.90 m and maximum weight is 635 kg (1,400 lbs); empty weight is 270 kg. The UAV cruises at 60 mph, and the ceiling is about 18,000 ft. Range is 300 km (160 nm) with a 34-kg payload. The power plant is a turbocharged flat-four engine. Four air vehicles can be launched by a C-130 cargo airplane. This UAV can also be ground-launched. The configuration is unique: a body suspended from an inflatable parafoil wing. The payload can be a reconnaissance camera.

RQ-11B RAVEN

AeroVironment's tiny hand-launched Raven, derived from its earlier Pointer, is the most numerous of U.S. UAVs. After a 1999 Pointer demonstration of UAV use in urban areas, the U.S. Army asked AeroVironment to develop a smaller UAV initially called Flashlight; the Army then bought Raven under an ACTD called Pathfinder, the SUAV (Small UAV). Special Forces Command was the first large-scale purchaser, for 5 systems with options for 10 more. Army experience in Iraq led to acquisition of 185 systems in FY 2003–4 (the 100th system was delivered late in 2004). Each system (about $25,000) included three air vehicles. As of mid-2009 Raven was expected to remain in production for at least the next five years, with formal block upgrades keeping it current. As of that time more than nine thousand had been delivered worldwide.

Raven is essentially a model airplane with analog electronics (to be converted to digital over the next two fiscal years, to increase control and data-link range). It can operate either under operator control or autonomously, and its Kevlar bottom can withstand about 200 belly landings. Initially it was tested by Special Forces (179 systems, three air vehicles each). The U.S. Army then bought it on an accelerated basis (twenty weeks from funding to service) to support operations in Iraq and in Afghanistan; each combat battalion in these areas operates it. The Army's RQ-11B (announced November 2005) entered service in 2006, Army orders including systems for the Marines and Special Forces. The Marines use it as an interim replacement for their 2.04 kg RQ-14A Dragon Eye; Special Forces use it to replace Pointer. Raven-B is also used by the armies of Britain, Denmark, Italy, and Spain. The U.S. Army requirement alone is 2,200 Raven systems, of which about the first 1,300 are analog (later ones are delivered with digital avionics). The full system, which is transported in two suitcases, comprises three air vehicles, three sets of sensors (high-resolution day camera, high-resolution night camera, and side-view IR imager), and the control station. Raven is conceived as a company- and platoon-level system.

Raven was the interim solution to one of the UAV requirements of the U.S. Army's FCS; in June 2005 the Army had 185 systems in service, with 270 on order. Production reportedly peaked at 702 aircraft in FY 2008, and as of mid-2009 about 5,000 had been produced for the Army, 1,000 of which were in Afghanistan and Iraq.

As an indication of its significance, during 2007 Raven conducted 150,000 combat hours of flight in the two theaters, and the figure was expected to double in 2008. According to the DoD's 2009 *Unmanned Systems Road Map*, the goal for U.S. Raven procurement was 3,333 systems (three aircraft each).

Raven B data: span 1.37 m, length 0.9 m, takeoff weight 1.9 kg (payload 184 grams [6.5 oz]). Raven uses battery power; endurance is 60 to 90 minutes using a rechargeable battery or 80 to 110 minutes using a one-use battery; range (probably set by data link) is 10 km (5.4 nm). Cruising speed is 17–44 kt, and maximum altitude is 14,000 ft (operating altitude 100 to 500 ft). Payloads are dual forward and side-looking EO cameras in the nose, using electronic pan/tilt and stabilization, or forward and side-looking nose IR cameras.

YMQ-12A

The YMQ-12A designation was rejected in favor of YMQ-1C. No Q-13 designation was assigned.

RQ-14 DRAGON EYE/SEA ALL/ SWIFT/EVOLUTION

AeroVironment's mini-UAV was designed and built early in 2001 by the Naval Research Laboratory and the Marine Corps Warfighting Laboratory to meet the Marine Corps I-SURSS (Interim Small Unit Remote Scouting System) requirement. Initial tests were conducted in June 2001, and in July development and preproduction contracts went to BAI and to AeroVironment for a fly-off to select a manufacturer for the production version. Like other mini-UAVs the Dragon Eye was a backpack system, in this case with three air vehicles. In this case the air vehicle uses two electric motors, each driving a propeller mounted on its wing. Endurance was 60 minutes, and effective radius was 10 km. The UAV could operate autonomously, or it could be updated periodically by its operator, in contrast to Pointer, which was continuously controlled by its operator (like a radio-controlled model airplane). Dragon Eye was supplied to Marine Corps units in 2002 for operational evaluation, and it served for the first time during Operation Iraqi Freedom for reconnaissance and battle damage evaluation. The main problem encountered was lack of zoom capability, which made it difficult to do quick

Raven on display at the 2009 Paris Air Show. (Norman Friedman)

and reliable identification of what it saw. It also lacked an IR camera for night operation. The prime contract was awarded to AeroVironment in November 2003, the Marine Corps planning 467 Dragon Eye systems (three aircraft each). The mass production RQ-14B (Swift) uses the same standardized ground-control equipment as the company's other mini-UAVs: the Pointer, Raven, PUMA, and Wasp, which provides full manual control. At least 6 systems were supplied to Special Forces. According to the DoD's 2009 *Unmanned Systems Road Map*, planned inventory is 194 Dragon Eye systems (three aircraft each) and 33 Swift (four aircraft each).

A block upgrade, which AeroVironment calls X-63, has a larger span (1.6 m) and an improved battery, giving greater endurance, more precise navigation and new payloads (IR and zoom cameras), and a new communications system with twice the number of channels (eight rather than four, presumably meaning that more UAVs can feed the same unit).

RQ-14B production version data: span 1.10 m, length 0.91 m, weight 2.8 kg, maximum speed 52 mph (cruising speed 31 mph), ceiling probably 1,000 ft, endurance 80 minutes (60 in RQ-14A). RQ-14A had a 1.14-m span and weighed 2.7 kg.

Dragon Eyes on display at the National Air and Space Museum, 2009. The two laptops are its ground-control and output devices. This example was operated by the Third Marine Division in Afghanistan in 2005 for surveillance of Nangarhar and Kunar provinces, the city of Jalalabad, and the Korengal Valley. (Norman Friedman)

The U.S. Navy version of RQ-14A is Sea ALL (Sea Airborne Lead Line), an Office of Naval Research (ONR) initiative.

L-3's Evolution is an offshoot of Dragon Eye, due to BAI's involvement in the early stages of the NRL program. It has a similar configuration, with the two electric motors. BAI is now part of L-3, hence the attribution. Evolution appeared in 2003. By 2005 it was in U.S. service in unspecified parts of the world, presumably supporting special forces. Span is 1.14 m, length 0.89 m, weight 2.95 kg (payload 0.45 kg); endurance is 45 minutes (a wide-body version has endurance increased to 2.5

hours); maximum speed is 43 kt (minimum 22 kt); range is 5.4 nm, and typical operating altitude is 300 ft. The 2009 *Unmanned Systems Road Map* described Evolution as an export version of Dragon Eye.

RQ-15 NEPTUNE

DRS developed Neptune as a maritime UAV. It first flew in January 2002, and the U.S. Navy awarded its first production contract in March 2002 for fifteen UAVs; however, the designation was not officially applied until 2007. Neptune can land on and take off from the water, unlike other UAVs, but it also can have a land undercarriage.

The power plant is a pusher piston engine mounted (for dryness) above the fuselage, which is blended into the wings; there are twin tail booms. Optimization for water operation extends to the UHF data link, which has provision to overcome multipath due to reflection off water. The autopilot uses GPS for autonomous waypoint navigation. Neptune is used by naval special forces (the SEALs). As of late 2005 at least fifteen of the planned twenty-seven systems had been delivered. This procurement may be separate from that for U.S. Special Forces Command, which bought two Neptune systems in each of FY 2008 and FY 2009.

Data: span 2.1 m, length 1.8 m, weight 36 kg, speed 84 kt (loiters at 60 kt), ceiling 8,000 ft, range 40 nm, endurance 4 hours. The power plant is a 2-stroke 15-hp piston engine.

RQ-16 T-HAWK/XM-156 CLASS I

Honeywell's ducted-rotor VTOL micro-UAV or MAV (micro–air vehicle) was developed under DARPA funding (as an ACTD) beginning in 2003. T-Hawk was selected as the Army's FCS Class I platoon-level UAV and designated RQ-16A; it is to enter Army service in 2015 with a heavy-fuel engine. Requirements included an operational radius of 16 km, payload of 1 lb, and endurance of 90 minutes. In January 2008 the test schedule was accelerated; eleven Block 0 systems were due for delivery within the following six months. T-Hawk survived the demise of the FCS program and as of mid-2009 was to equip all seventy-three Army active and Reserve brigades by 2025, priority going to units engaged in Afghanistan (there is Congressional interest in accelerating this program). The U.S. Navy was the initial customer. It deployed the Block 1 version to Iraq and Afghanistan in 2007. Block 2 (2009) has a gimballed sensor and electronic engine control. Some of the twenty-five systems ordered for assessment went to the Navy-led EOD (explosive ordnance disposal) Joint Task Force in Iraq; they were designated G-MAV, indicating gasoline fuel. Given the urgency of EOD in Iraq, in November 2008 Honeywell received a Navy order for ninety Block 2 systems, each with two air vehicles. This was apparently the first production order. T-Hawk has also been bought by the British army for stand-off inspection of improvised explosive devices. The first contract for six systems

Neptune on display at Patuxent River, 27 June 2005. (U.S. Navy by PH Daniel J. McLain)

T-Hawk shown on 14 November 2006. (U.S. Navy by MC3 Kenneth G. Takada)

was let in February 2009. The first British training exercise is scheduled for November 2009, with deployment to Afghanistan planned for 2010. As of mid-2009 another export contract was imminent.

Data: Rotor diameter 0.33 m, height 0.61 m, weight 7.7 kg (dry); payload 0.680 kg. Maximum altitude is 10,000 ft, cruising speed 40 kt, and endurance 50 minutes. Weight wet is 8.6 kg.

The T stands for Tarantula.

The DoD's 2009 *Unmanned Systems Road Map* lists a gasoline MAV (G-MAV), which is probably the Army version of RQ-16. Inventory: 83 air vehicles/41 systems delivered, 166 additional systems planned. This was part of the MAV ACTD; G-MAV was transferred to the Army after a successful military utility assessment in FY 2005–6 and deployed with the 25th Infantry Division. An upgrade to Block II (FCS Class I Block 0) includes gimballed sensor and upgraded radio. Block III includes an engine control unit, electric starter, and electric fueler, and is under development for deployment. A modified version under test incorporates the software-controlled JTRS radio, which would link the UAV into the Army FCS network. As described in the *Road Map*, G-MAV weighs 16.5 lb (payload 3 lb [EO or IR]), with a 14-in.-diameter ducted propeller. Endurance is about 45 minutes, radius is about 8 nm, and ceiling is about 10,000 ft. These figures are slightly different from those for RQ-16.

The 2009 DoD *Unmanned Systems Road Map* includes Honeywell's XM-156 Class I, which seems to be a derivative of RQ-16; plans call for ninety systems per FCS brigade combat team. Class I is intended to provide ground troops with reconnaissance and situational awareness using autonomous flight and navigation and operating on the FCS network. Soldiers can dynamically update routes and target information using data from the UAS. It is intended to provide dedicated support and early warning to platoons and companies. The UAV is man packable, with an integrated EO/IR/LD/LRF sensor and a 10-hp silenced heavy-fuel engine. The system comprises a single air vehicle and a centralized controller (CC) to navigate it; the CC is to be a single hand-held device connected to the FCS network. The first risk reduction flight is scheduled for the first quarter of FY 2010 (i.e., the fall of 2009), a critical design review following in the fourth quarter of FY 2010. The system should become operational in the third quarter of FY 2015. Preliminary data: diameter (from landing gear tips, outboard of the ducted fan) 36 in., duct diameter 18 in. (46 cm), weight 32.5 lbs (payload 8.5 lbs); endurance about 60 minutes (radius about 8 km, ceiling about 11,000 ft). A prototype apparently already exists, as the data sheet in the *Road Map* is illustrated by a photograph.

XMQ-17A SPY HAWK/T-20

Spy Hawk was a failed Marine Corps attempt to develop a Tier II successor to the interim ScanEagle; MTC Technologies (which became part of BAE Systems in 2008)

received a November 2006 contract from the Marine Corps Warfighting Laboratory. Unusual features included a retractable belly sensor turret, allowing a combination of better sensing and belly landing; and a control station based on the commercial PlayStation. The enlarged turret was apparently attractive for functions such as hyperspectral imaging and synthetic aperture radar. The ground-control system incorporated 3-D mapping software for navigation and had a dual screen for simultaneous evaluation of imagery and vehicle operational status and position. All of these features may figure in future Tier II UAVs bought under the STUAS program. Spy Hawk was launched from a pneumatic catapult. Data: span 3.89 m, weight 39 kg, speed 103 mph (cruising speed 52 mph), ceiling 10,000 ft, range about 50 nm, endurance 16 hours. The power plant was a Honda GX-57 piston engine.

The airframe, presumably the least important part of the system, was that of the Arcturus T-15/T-16 family. California-based Arcturus UAV LLC produces a range of UAVs using hollow molded airframes. It received its first defense contract in 2008, probably for a military version of its large T-20. Most fuel is carried in the large wing, so the body offers considerable payload capacity. Data: span 207 in., length 113 in., takeoff weight over 150 lbs (empty 80 lbs, payload up to 65 lbs), endurance over 16 hours. The power plant is a 10-hp 4-stroke engine. T-20 completed its first mission at the U.S. Army Dugway Proving Ground on 14 May 2009; it had been completed in 2008 and had previously flown at Edwards Air Force Base. The 2009 flight was the first of several data collection missions. Note that Dugway is a chemical warfare proving ground, suggesting that the missions were air sampling to test contamination or to monitor actual chemical tests.

YMQ-18A (A160T HUMMINGBIRD)

The A160 began as a DARPA AAV (Advanced Air Vehicle) project (ONR was later involved) to demonstrate a rigid-rotor helicopter configuration under the Hummingbird Warrior program. The object was to produce a VTOL MALE, with great endurance (30 to 40 hours) and radius of action (3,000 nm). In a conventional helicopter, the blades are articulated so that they maintain lift as they rotate while the helicopter moves forward. In theory such operation limits helicopter speed, since at some speed the

Boeing's Hummingbird VTOL UAV in model form at the 2009 Navy League show. (Norman Friedman)

blades can no longer maintain the necessary angle of attack. A rigid rotor is more like a wing, with large diameter so that it is more lightly loaded than a classical rotor. It is lighter weight because its blades are not articulated. It operates at optimum rotational speed, for minimum noise (which may be the most important characteristic, as A160 has evolved). In theory a rigid rotor helicopter offers greater range, endurance, and altitude. DARPA became interested in rigid rotors because they can be used at higher speeds, at which the rotor tips are supersonic.

A160 was designed by Predator inventor Abe Karem. It is about the size of that aircraft. The T in A160T indicates replacement of the original piston engine by a turboshaft. This program began early in 1998 with the modification of a Robinson R.22 helicopter to test control systems. Special Forces bought two of these modified helicopters, called Maverick. The prototype Maverick crashed in 2002, but the A160 flew on 29 January 2002. Boeing bought Frontier Systems in 2004 and continued the DARPA program, building demonstrators at its Phantom Works. The U.S. Army and Special Forces have been very interested in the program, roles including extracting troops from behind enemy lines. There is interest in a UHF synthetic aperture radar for foliage penetration, ultimately with its receiving antennas integrated into the rotor blades and its transmitting antennas mounted conformally on the fuselage (the Foliage Penetration Reconnaissance Surveil-

lance Tracking and Engagement Radar, or FORESTER) and in a wide-area visual surveillance sensor (ARGUS-IS, Autonomous Realtime Ground Ubiquitous Surveillance Imaging System). Other possible developments are a 450-kg cargo pod and Hellfire missiles for a UCAV version (Boeing showed a model of a Hummingbird with EO turret and eight Hellfires).

The A160 first flew on 29 January 2002, the Army testing it in FY 2003–5. After that DARPA continued to fund the program; it was extended beyond its planned end date of 2007. In 2008 the U.S. Army Special Forces Command began to acquire A160s to meet an urgent operational requirement, presumably in Afghanistan. In May 2009 the U.S. Special Operations Command announced that it wanted to buy about twenty A160s in FY 2010, and as of mid-2009 the U.S. Marine Corps was evaluating A160 as an "immediate cargo UAS" for delivery as early as February 2010, to carry up to 910 kg (1,000 lbs) of cargo to forward bases. However, it was also reported that unless orders were forthcoming the A160 production line could shut down by October 2009.

In August 2005 the U.S. Navy acquired three Hummingbirds for a flight demonstration program. Between August and October 2009 Hummingbird successfully tested a DARPA Forester (Foliage Penetration Reconnaissance, Surveillance, Tracking, and Engagement Radar). Also in 2009 A160T was selected to participate in the

Immediate Cargo UAS Demonstration Program of the U.S. Marine Corps Warfighting Laboratory. According to the 2009 *Unmanned Systems Road Map*, six of the turboshaft version have been delivered, with seven more planned; three of the gasoline version have been delivered.

Data: Rotor diameter 10.67 m; takeoff weight 5,000 lbs (payload over 300 lbs), endurance over 24 hours (speed 140 kt), ceiling 30,000 ft. Payload is 300 kg (given as 300 to 1,000 lbs in the DoD's 2009 *Unmanned Systems Road Map*). The original power plant was a 390-hp 6-cylinder engine. According to the 2009 *Road Map*, maximum/loiter speeds are 140/50 kt; radius is greater than 1,000 nm; endurance is 20 hours at 500 nm with a 300-lb payload. Ceiling is given as 30,000 ft when cruising and as better than 15,000 ft when hovering. The objective, which is beyond the current helicopter, is more than 24-hour endurance, 160-mph (260-km/hour) speed, 2,875-mile (4,625-km) range, and a ceiling of 30,000 ft with a payload of 454 kg (or 20-hour endurance with 136 kg). The figures here seem to reflect those plans rather than actual performance. The A160 made a record-breaking 18-hour flight in 2008.

X-47B UCAS-D

Northrop Grumman's X-47B is conceived as an attack UAV, effectively an unmanned equivalent to a carrier attack aircraft such as the F/A-18. It is the successor to X-47A, developed for the abortive Joint UCAS program. After the U.S. Air Force dropped out, the U.S. Navy continued the program, Northrop Grumman winning on 8 August 2007 with its X-47B. X-47B is the culmination of a process that began with competitive awards by DARPA to Boeing and Northrop Grumman on 30 June 2000 for feasibility studies of a carrier-capable UCAV, UCAV-N. DARPA decided in April 2003 that UCAV should be a joint Air Force–Navy program (J-UCAS); by that time Lockheed Martin had joined Northrop Grumman's team. At this time the selected airplane was to enter the engineering manufacturing design phase in 2008–10. Northrop Grumman rolled out its X-47A Pegasus on 30 July 2001 (it flew on 23 February 2003).

Pegasus was intended to establish carrier feasibility, using a simulated carrier flight deck at China Lake. In fact X-47A demonstrated the feasibility of its tailless

configuration but not carrier landings. Changes in the FY 2005 budget limited Northrop Grumman to two X-47B prototypes, the first to be non-stealthy, with limited mission equipment, mainly for carrier suitability trials. Plans called for a third-phase X-47C, substantially larger than X-47A and -47B. However, the entire J-UCAS program was terminated in February 2006 (money was reallocated to a program for a carrier-based persistent ISR program). The program then reverted to the Navy-only UCAS, X-47B winning the contract as noted above. The first prototype was rolled out on 16 December 2008 and was due to fly on 11 November 2009; that flight was postponed until 2010. First carrier launches and recoveries are expected in 2011. The key issue is to demonstrate carrier suitability, including carrier landing capability and (at Northrop Grumman's initiative) the ability to extend endurance by air-to-air refueling (an initiative approved by the Navy in 2008; autonomous in-flight refueling is to be demonstrated in 2015). The X-47B is designed both for Navy-type probe and drogue refueling and for Air Force type boom refueling.

Data: span 18.9 m, length 11.6 m, endurance up to 100 hours with in-flight refueling. Range exceeds 2,100 nm (combat radius exceeds 1,500 nm; ferry range exceeds 3,500 nm). Speed is given as high subsonic. Ceiling exceeds 40,000 ft. Each of two weapon bays can accommodate up to six Small Diameter Bombs, and the bays can also be plumbed for extra fuel tankage. Maximum weapon capacity is 4,500 lbs. The engine is a Pratt & Whitney F100-PW-220U. X-47A data: span 8.47 m, length 8.50 m, engine P&W Canada JT15D-5C turbofan. The objectives of the original J-UCAS included a combat radius of 1,300 nm and a payload of 2,041 kg (4,500 lbs), with the ability to loiter for 2 hours over a target up to 1,000 nm from base.

Data given in the DoD's 2009 *Unmanned Systems Road Map*: span 62 ft, length 38 ft, gross weight 46,000 lbs, payload 4,500 lbs; endurance 9 hours, maximum speed 460 kt, radius 1,600 nm, ceiling 40,000 ft.

MQ-X

The MQ-X is the tentative designation of the next-generation Air Force UAV. It is to be released in 2010. The winner will probably have to provide initial operat-

X-47B UCAS soon after rollout, December 2008. (Northrop Grumman)

ing capability within 24 months of winning the contract. Lockheed Martin's Skunk Works showed its approach to the evolving MQ-X requirement at the September 2009 Air Force Association show. A placard stated that the Air Force would acquire 200 to 250 such aircraft, plus more to replace Predator and Reaper attrition. Characteristics included 24-hour endurance, a dash speed of Mach 0.8, and "survivability in contested airspace," which latter means a stealthy airframe. A photograph showed a chined fuselage (for low observability on radar), moderately swept wings, and a vertical tail fin carrying a pod for a pusher propeller between vee fins. There were two air intakes at the base of the tail. Reportedly the UAV has a hybrid power plant, using its propeller and a turbo-diesel for long endurance and a jet engine for high-speed dash. Both would be used together for maximum altitude. The modular wing can be installed in different spans for different roles, for example, short for attack and long for high-altitude reconnaissance. It is not clear how such a hybrid airplane would limit the

drag due to the propeller, but it might fold at high speed. Presumably the air intakes can serve either engine.

Apparently the General Atomics Predator C is aimed at the same requirement. Boeing seems likely to offer a variant of its abortive X-46 carrier attack airplane.

AD-150

American Dynamics Flight Systems expects this VTOL UAV to compete for the Marine Corps Tier III Shadow replacement, which should be able to operate with aircraft like the MV-22 Osprey. AD-150 uses a pair of tilting ducted fans. It is intended to meet a U.S. Navy specification demanding a speed of at least 200 kt, with 240 kt preferred (American Dynamics claims that the craft can make 300 kt). Takeoff weight is 2,250 lbs (payload 500 lbs). The power plant is a P&W Canada PW200 turboshaft. An early full-scale model was displayed at the August 2007 Washington meeting of the Association for Unmanned Vehicle Systems International.

American Dynamics Flight Systems' AD-150 VTOL UAV. (American Dynamics Flight Systems)

AEROSONDE MK 4

As its name implies, Aerosonde began as a very long endurance low-cost mini-UAV for meteorology (which uses "sondes"). The initial version was developed in Australia in 1995–98 by two Australian companies, the Australian Bureau of Meteorology, and the U.S. Insitu Group; the ONR was a cosponsor. In August 1998 an Aerosonde was the first UAV to cross the Atlantic (more than 2,000 miles in a flight of 26 hours 45 minutes). Two companies, Aerosonde Pty. Ltd. of Australia and Aerosonde North America, were formed in 1999 to market Aerosonde.

As of 2009 Aerosonde was employed in noncombat roles, for example, at Wallops Island (NASA) and at Barrow, Alaska. Aerosonde also flies from Guam under the Air Force Weather Scout Cooperative Test program.

AAI's contender for STUAS Tier II uses a twin-boom configuration with a pusher engine. Span is 2.9 m, length 2.1 m, and weight is 15.20 kg (payload 5 kg). Ceiling is 15,000 ft, and endurance is 30 hours. Aerosonde Mk 5 flew in January 2009.

BROADSWORD (MQM-171)

Broadsword is used by the U.S. Army to evaluate UAV components, including sensors, payloads, and propulsion; it is sometimes described as a UAV-T, a generic version of the tactical UAV the Army hopes to use. In 2006 UAV-T requirements were described: span within 5 percent of 5 m, length within 5 percent of 4 m, max-

imum cruise speed 115 kt (132 mph) with a goal of 200 mph, minimum cruise speed 60 kt (69 mph) with a goal of 50 mph, minimum ceiling of 12,000 ft (goal 23,000 ft), minimum operating altitude less than 1,000 ft, minimum slant control range 25 km (goal 50 km), and loiter endurance 1 hour on station.

It is an enlarged version of Griffin Aerospace's MQM-170 Outlaw target, with the same pusher configuration (conventional wing, vee tail). Griffon announced a 2-hour April 2007 flight as the first in a series of spiral development flights that would help mature Broadsword. It expected Broadsword to enter Army service during FY 2008. In 2007 the company was promoting an XL version as an observation platform or, like Broadsword, as a test/evaluation platform. The data below apply to the XL version rather than to Broadsword itself.

Data: span 6.86 m, length 4.51 m, weight 250 kg (maximum payload 54 kg), ceiling 14,000 ft, endurance 4–6 hours (speed 126 mph; cruising speed 68 to 103 mph).

BUSTER/BLACKLIGHT

The configuration of Mission Technologies' tandem (linked)-wing mini-UAV recalls that of the unsuccessful Outrider UAV (the company seems to market Outrider) and has patented that UAV's wing configuration. The U.S. Army ordered its first Buster in August 2003; as of 2009 it had nine systems (four air vehicles each). Since 2007 Buster has been involved in numerous C4ISR exercises at Fort Dix and airborne assault exercises at Fort Benning; it also has been used by the Army's Night Vision Laboratory and in U.S. Navy exercises at Dahlgren (as an "enabler" in coalition warfare). According to the DoD's 2009 *Unmanned Systems Road Map*, the current planned inventory is five systems (four aircraft each). This document states that nine systems were delivered in 2007 and that other contracts are with the British Ministry of Defence Joint UAS Experimentation Programme, Buster training being conducted for the Royal Artillery, RAF, and SOF. Two systems were delivered to the Ministry of Defence. Status is given as "under evaluation" for the U.S. Army and SOCOM (Special Operations Command). At present Buster is primarily a sensor testbed for the Army Night Vision Laboratories. The current E-Buster has a pusher

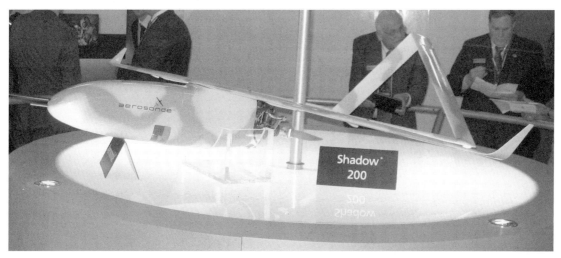

Aerosonde on the AAI stand at the 2009 Paris Air Show (the sign refers to the Shadow 200 shown nearby). (Norman Friedman)

A Royal Artillery Buster Mk 1 at the 4 July 2009 Waddington Air Show. (South Wales Aviation Group)

propeller rather than the tractor shown. Mission Technologies also produces a vehicle called Blacklight, which it equipped with a NanoSAR radar in August 2009. Note that the British call a Raven variant BUSTER (Backpack Unmanned Surveillance Targeting and Enhanced Reconnaissance).

Data: span 1.26 m, length 1.04 m, weight 4.5 kg, ceiling 10,000 ft, endurance better than 4 hours (range 10 km/6 miles, speed 35 kt).

CORMORANT/MORPHING UAV

Lockheed Martin's developmental jet gull-wing (flying-wing) UAV is intended for launch and recovery by the U.S. *Ohio*-class strategic submarines converted for special forces operation. To that end it is made of titanium (to resist corrosion). It is guided out of a converted missile launch tube by a docking "saddle" and floats to the surface, where its boosters fire. On completing a mission it lands in the sea at a designated rendezvous, and the submarine sends out another unmanned craft to meet it. DARPA let this contract to Lockheed Martin late in 2005, envisaging transition to the Navy in 2010, if tests succeeded. Initial tests were funded by DARPA, which was to decide in September 2006 whether to fund a flying version. The program was apparently canceled in the fall of 2007. A Lockheed Martin video released at that time showed Cormorant deploying LOCAAS (Low Cost Autonomous Attack System) intelligence loitering submunitions. The

Cormorant gull-wing UAV in action. (Lockheed Martin)

UAV folded up for stowage; it had large delta wings and an underbody delta vertical fin. The booster fired it vertically out of the sea, like a missile. Recovery was in two stages: by parachute to the sea surface, then recovery into the submarine using an underwater vehicle.

Cormorant has also been referred to as the Morphing UAV, because it changes shape in the sea. The Lockheed Martin patent application for the idea showed the UAV floating vertically up from a Trident missile tube, then unfolding (morphing) in the water, to be powered out of the water by a rocket. The patent application envisages a lead (reconnaissance) UAV that would identify time-sensitive targets for attack by follow-on UAVs. In the patent, the UAV is buoyant, water being kept out by nitrogen gas pressurization. It could float to the surface, to start engines there, or it could be fired through the water and out by a rocket. The morphing UAV seems to have begun as part of a DARPA Morphing Aircraft Structures program; morphing would make it possible for the same aircraft to carry out radically different missions during the same flight, for example, loitering surveillance and high-speed attack. A subscale version was set for a first flight in 2004 but was damaged in high-speed taxi tests; repaired, it was ready for a first flight in August 2005. Cormorant seems to have been an application of this technology (the "buckle wing") rather than the initial effort. Lockheed Martin let a flight-control system contract for the morphing UAV in April 2006.

This entry is retained despite cancellation because U.S. Navy interest in submarine-launched UAVs remains strong.

Data: span is 16 ft, length is 19 ft, and takeoff weight is 9,000 lbs (payload is 1,000 lbs). Endurance is 3 hours (mission radius 400 to 500 miles), and ceiling is 35,000 ft. The power plant is a 3,000-lb-thrust jet engine.

DP-5X WASP/DP-5XT GATOR/ DP-12 RHINO

Dragonfly Pictures is a small UAV manufacturer based in Essington, Pennsylvania, formed in 1991. Its main products are helicopter UAVs, all of which are designated in a DP series. It received its first substantial Defense Department contract ($1.06 million) in 2008. In 2009 it received an additional $2.9 million increment (out of $5.4 million) to expand vertical takeoff capability, which presumably applies to the VTOL aircraft described below. Dragonfly considers the helicopters suitable for commercial and military missions. DP-4X Dependable has a takeoff weight of 64 kg (29-kg payload) and so is outside the scope of this appendix.

DP-5X has a conventional single-rotor configuration with a horizontal propeller at the tail. Rotor diameter is 10.5 ft (length 11 ft); takeoff weight is 475 lbs (payload 75 lbs). Endurance is 5.5 hours (speed 100 kt); ceiling is 10,000 ft. The power plant is a 97-hp heavy-fuel engine. DP-5X was used on behalf of DARPA for 27–28 September 2006 live fire tests of the Metal Storm gun at the U.S. Air National Guard Warren Grove bombing range.

By way of contrast, DP-5XT Gator is a two-rotor helicopter resembling a miniature CH-46. Four can be carried in a single 20-ft container, or two on one UH-60, four on one CH-47, or eight on one C-130. The craft has an EO turret under its nose, and it has an ATLS. Width (presumably rotor diameter) is 2.33 ft, and length is 12.5 ft; weight is 872 lbs (payload 215 lbs for 6 hours). Endurance is 6 hours (dash speed 162 kt, range 530 nm).

The electrically powered DP-6 Whisper is a much smaller two-rotor helicopter with a similar configuration (50 lbs takeoff).

DP-7 BAT /DP-10X BOOMERANG/ DP-11 BAYONET

Dragonfly Pictures' flying-wing UAVs have twin three-bladed propellers on its leading edge and two vertical tails. They are intended for vertical launch and recovery

Bat UAV. (Dragonfly Pictures)

and for horizontal flight; the configuration is reminiscent of the abortive Vought "Pancake" of the 1940s (the F5U). They are described as shipboard compatible; six can be carried in a UH-60 hangar. This combination of data suggests that DP-7 was offered in the LCS support UAV competition. It has an ATLS system, and Dragonfly claims that it is compatible with all air-capable ships, as well as with unprepared shore sites.

Data: span 19.5 ft (9-ft wings folded), length 6.8 ft, takeoff weight 600 lbs (payload 100 lbs for 12 hours at 110-nm radius of action). Dragonfly gives "rotor diameter" as 6 ft, suggesting that it envisages vertical launch with the propellers acting as rotors. Endurance is 12 hours (dash speed 207 kt, 110-nm mission range), and ceiling is 30,000 ft. The UAV carries a SAR radar and a TCS data link; the latter is a small-ship alternative to the CEC link used by Aegis ships.

DP-10X data: span 24 ft (12 ft folded), length 7.5 ft, propeller diameter 8 ft, takeoff weight 1,900 lbs (300-lb payload for 21 hours mission at sea level at 110-nm mission radius); ceiling is 35,000 ft. Dash speed is 295 kt, range is 3,859 nm (maximum endurance is 23 hours). This UAV can carry Spike (China Lake's, not the Israeli type) missiles. It can carry mine detection gear, presumably the Navy's laser, and it has a SAR radar and the TCS data link.

The DP-11 is a smaller version of these craft, with a takeoff weight of 125 lbs (479-nm maximum range, 112-kt dash speed, 68-kt cruising speed), and thus is outside the scope of this appendix. Dragonfly promotes it for naval for protection (in port) and for the Marines. The company offered modular payloads in 2008.

DAKOTA

Geneva Aerospace of Addison, Texas, developed UAV-control technology rather than UAVs. Presumably the Dakota described below was its system demonstrator. DARPA sponsored tests of its variable autonomy control system (VACS), which was intended to allow operators with no piloting skills to control UAVs; it also allows one operator to control several UAVs simultaneously. VACS was used for the Navy's abortive Affordable Weapon (a low-cost cruise missile) and for an ONR project on "sense and avoid" anticollision self-control for UAVs operating in civilian airspace. The company was founded in 1997 by six Texas Instruments engineers, initially funded by the Air Force Research Laboratories specifically to develop UAV control and related technologies. In July 1998 the U.S. Navy demonstrated simultaneous control of four Dakotas by a single operator using the Northrop Grumman CAMMS (Cooperative Aggregate Mission Management System). Geneva is now a unit of L-3 Communications. An L-3 brochure adds work on ultraprecise course following and networked high-bandwidth communications.

Geneva Aerospace's UAV (presumably its control demonstrator) uses a high-wing tractor configuration. Span is 15 ft and takeoff weight is 180 kg (payload 40 kg). Endurance is more than 2 hours (mission radius 60 nm). The power plant is a 22-hp engine. The Naval Research Laboratory uses Dakota to develop and demonstrate advanced UAV control technologies. Dakota first flew in August 1994, and the main buyer seems to have been the U.S. Naval Research Laboratory.

DESERT HAWK III

Lockheed Martin's micro-UAV is used by the U.S. Air Force for air base security (i.e., surveillance) in Afghanistan, but it is being superseded by the more capable Raven. Lockheed Martin currently describes Desert Hawk as designed specifically for high-altitude operation in high winds and extreme temperatures. Delivery of eighteen Desert Hawk I systems (ninety-six air vehicles) began in 2002 (however, the procurement goal was twenty-one systems). Desert Hawk was offered to the U.S. Air Force in response to a 2001 request for information on a very small man-portable UAV for the FPASS requirement. The production contract was awarded in February 2002, and

Desert Hawk micro-UAV at DSEi 2009. (Norman Friedman)

the first two complete systems (six air vehicles each) were delivered early that July. By mid-November 2002 Desert Hawk was operational in Afghanistan. Later it was deployed to Iraq. In February 2006 the USAF had twenty-one systems (126 air vehicles), and in December 2006 it had another forty-eight systems on order. Replacement by RQ-11B Ravens began in October 2007, at which time the DoD's UAV *Road Map* showed an eventual goal of eighteen Desert Hawk systems (108 aircraft). Lockheed Martin had previously participated in a DARPA program to develop a micro–air vehicle (no dimension greater than 15 cm), concluding that anything with a wingspan of less than 60 cm would be too unstable (due to gusts) to be useful for surveillance. An unusual feature is the ability to circle over a specified place and keep the camera pointed at it; the spot can be preprogrammed or selected on the fly. The aircraft can fly autonomously, so the operator can concentrate on the video it produces. Desert Hawk I was upgraded to I+ status, and a redesigned Desert Hawk III (with a more robust and less bulky fuselage) was introduced in 2006 and entered service in 2007.

Another fifteen systems were bought for the British 47 Regiment Royal Artillery for service in both Iraq and Afghanistan; they entered service in 2007. Upgraded communications introduced in 2008 ended interference with mobile phones, so gunners could be trained in the United Kingdom. All Desert Hawk I/I+ were out of British service by 2008. They were replaced by Desert Hawk III, which became operational in June 2007; as of August 2008 the British Ministry of Defence reported 187 Desert Hawk III ordered or in service. A total of twenty-seven had been lost in Afghanistan as of early 2008.

Recently the UAVs were upgraded with the Icarus control system, which enables one operator to handle several air vehicles by increasing their autonomy. In May 2009 Lockheed Martin completed flight trials with a new wing and with a SIGINT payload, the first on so small a UAV. In 2009 Lockheed Martin demonstrated a turret-mounted IR sensor that could scan through 360 degrees on board Desert Hawk.

Data: span 1.32 m, length 0.86 m, weight 3.2 kg; ceiling is 1,000 ft, and endurance is 1 hour (speed 57 mph). The power plant is an electric motor.

EAGLE EYE

Bell's tilt-wing Eagle Eye was considered a UAV equivalent to the MV-22 Osprey, and for a time it seemed destined to be the standard Coast Guard shipboard UAV, a very important role within that service's Project Deepwater. It first flew in January 2006 but crashed that April, and in February 2008 the Coast Guard decided to abandon it. It is retained here because of its earlier prominence and the possibility that this configuration (as in the Korean KARI SMART) may ultimately be adopted. Bell and SAGEM promoted Eagle Eye in France and in Germany as Euro Eagle Eye, without visible success.

Data: span 4.63 m, length 5.46 m, takeoff weight 1,500 kg, endurance 8 hours, ceiling 20,000 ft. The power plant was a single Pratt & Whitney turboshaft engine geared to both propellers.

EXCALIBUR

Aurora Flight Sciences is developing Excalibur, a VTOL close air support UAV, under contract to the Army Aviation Applied Technology Directorate. The initial project is a 325-kg proof-of-concept vehicle using a tilting turbine at the center of gravity plus battery-driven fans in the wings and nose. The ultimate 1,815-kg Excalibur would carry four Hellfire missiles with a maximum speed of 560 km/hour at low altitude. The weapons stowage is unique. Weapons are loaded on the ground on top of the wings to protect them from dust or sand. In flight Excalibur flips over to place them in the conventional position. The technology demonstrator was scheduled to fly in 2007, but that slipped to 24 June 2009.

Data (planned vehicle): span 21 ft, length 23 ft, takeoff weight 2600 lbs (payload 400 lbs, empty weight 700 lbs). Endurance is 3 hours (speed 460 kt, loiter speed 100 kt); ceiling is 40,000 ft. The power plant is a single Williams International turbofan. Excalibur is to be compatible with lightweight missiles such as Hellfire, APKWS II, Viper-Strike, and Spike (China Lake, not the Israeli antitank missile). The test vehicle has a span of 10 ft and length of 13 ft. Note that in both cases span does *not* include sizable wing-tip fans with the same diameter as the nose fan.

Note that Aurora produces about a third of the exterior structure of the Global Hawk.

EXDRONE (BQM-147)

With Pointer, Exdrone was the first U.S. operational mini-UAV. It was developed by the Johns Hopkins University Applied Physics Laboratory as a low-cost expendable (hence the name) communications jammer, flying in that form in 1986. The U.S. Army ordered 14 of them from BAI (now part of L3) in 1988, receiving them early in 1989 and awarding a production contract to RPV Industries of Canada that August. When the Canadian contract was canceled in 1990 due to quality control problems, a contract was awarded to BAI; by that time the Marines were interested in Exdrone for reconnais-

Eagle Eye tilt-wing UAV. (U.S. Coast Guard)

sance. During Operation Desert Storm (1991) they used Exdrone for day surveillance of Iraqi barriers and minefields. In 1998 the Marines upgraded about 40 Exdrones to Dragon Drone configuration, with new autopilots and improved sensors. Total production amounted to about four hundred.

Bahrain has one Exdrone system.

Exdrone is a delta flying wing with a tractor propeller driven by a single-cylinder 2-stroke 8.5-hp engine. An auxiliary fuel tank can increase its range from 65 nm to 195 nm (i.e., from 120 to 360 km). The normal sensor is a forward/downward looking television camera, but Exdrone could also accommodate a laser rangefinder, IR camera, jammers, or a communications relay. Its autopilot can be programmed before or during flight. Presumably the real-time sensor readout was initially analog. The autopilot includes a GPS receiver. Data: span 2.5 m, length 1.62 m, weight 41 kg, ceiling 10,000 ft, endurance 2.5 hours (range 65 nm, speed 100 kt; loiter speed 65 kt).

FINDER

Finder, the Naval Research Laboratory's small UAV, is designed for air launch and operation. It began as an ACTD for the U.S. Defense Threat Reduction Agency Counterproliferation II activity, which seeks to detect chemical warfare agents. Finder means Flight-Inserted Detection Expendable for Reconnaissance. NRL received a three-year development contract in May 1998, and Finder flew on 22 March 2000.

Finder has a conventional configuration with a pusher propeller in its tail, something like that of Predator.

Excalibur VTOL close-air support UAV. (Aurora Flight Sciences)

The original payload was a point ionizing spectrometer, which would analyze gas taken in by Finder as it flew. In 2007 the Army flew two Finders fitted with shortwave IR cameras integrated with a laser pointer (designator). Finder is intended to be carried aloft by a Predator, which can carry one on each underwing hard point. Power is electric. For carriage the wing turns 90 degrees to lie flat on the fuselage. Span is 2.62 m, length 1.60 m, weight 26.8 kg (payload 6.1 kg), endurance typically 6.5 hours (maximum 10 hours); maximum speed 87 kt (cruising speed 70 kt, loiter speed 61 kt); mission radius with 2 hours loiter is 43 nm (maximum range 521 nm/600 statute miles). Ceiling is 15,000 ft. At the end of the ACTD (2004), eight Finder systems (sixteen air vehicles) were to be retained. An AC-130 gunship was adapted to launch Finders during 2007.

GLOBAL OBSERVER (GO-1)

A DARPA-sponsored electric UAV, the Global Observer is the first approach to the desired ultra-long-endurance surveillance aircraft. The manufacturer, AeroVironment, is usually associated with micro-UAVs such as the RQ-11 Raven. The company has proposed developments of the initial Global Observer. AeroVironment's internally funded Global Observer (Odyssey) flew in 2005; it was the world's first hydrogen-powered UAV. Six propellers were distributed along its wings. Overall configuration was conventional, with a pod-and-boom layout. The company points out that the specific energy of hydrogen is three times that of petroleum-based fuels and hence should be key to longer endurance and higher operating altitude (it claims that a conventional UAV cannot operate at 30,000 ft for more than two days). GO was approved in 2007 as a new-start JCTD, the first stage being GO-1. Late in 2007 AeroVironment received a contract to provide three Global Observers for evaluation. GO-1 is to have a span of 53.4 m (175 ft), takeoff weight of 1,800 kg (payload 160 kg [352 lbs; payload is sometimes given as 400 lbs]), and 168 hours endurance. GO-1 is to fly in FY 2010.

Exdrone mini-UAV. (NASA Langley)

Data for GO-2: span 78.94 m (258.9 ft), length 25.4 m, takeoff weight 4,127 kg, payload 450 kg. Endurance is to be over 168 hours (i.e., a full week in the air; sometimes as much as 400 hours is claimed), and ceiling is to be 65,000 ft. Maximum loiter speed is to be 110 kt and radius 10,750 nm. The power plant is eight electric motors (each driving a propeller) powered by fuel cells. This is apparently the limit a more or less conventional craft driven by fuel can reach; the step beyond is a solar-powered aircraft.

GOLDENEYE 80/50

Aurora Flight Sciences' ducted-fan VTOL was built for the DARPA Organic Air Vehicle Class II (OAV II) competition, its team (Aurora, General Dynamics, Robotic Systems, and Northrop Grumman) being selected as semifinalists to compete with a Honeywell team; it was selected for Phase III in June 2006. Although it appears that Honeywell won with its T-Hawk, GoldenEye has continued development. The first of the series, Golden-Eye 100, flew on 8 September 2003; it was a proof of concept vehicle for the DARPA Clandestine UAV project. The next version was GoldenEye 50, which has two tilting wings protruding from its barrel-shaped body (plans call for similar modification of GoldenEye 80, and they are shown on its current fact sheet). Twelve prototypes were built, the first flying in July 2004. It may be in current production for an unspecified customer.

It is 0.85 m high, with a body diameter of 0.46 m and a wingspan of 1.37 m; takeoff weight is 7.7 kg (payload 0.9 kg [also given as 1.4 kg]), and endurance is 0.75 hour (speed 60 kt); ceiling is 5,000 ft. GoldenEye 80 first flew on 6 November 2006 and made its first public demonstration flight on 10 August 2009. It had been demonstrated for potential customers the previous March. It is consider-

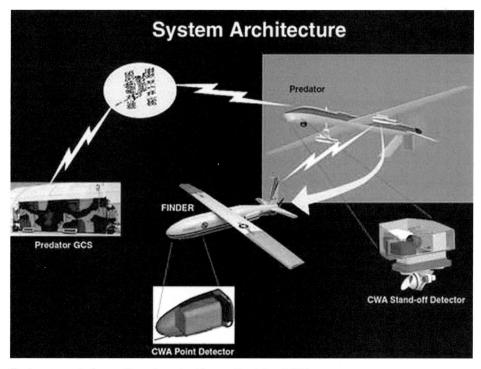

Finder concept of operations, launched from a Predator. (NRL)

GO-1 long-endurance UAV. (AeroVironment)

ably larger than ducted-fan VTOLs such as those made by STA, Bertin, and Selex Galileo; it is about the height of a man, and its payload sits on top. Aurora's video shows it flying at an angle rather than tipping all the way over for flight. GoldenEye 80 features acoustic damping to quiet its hover, and it can carry a laser ranger/designator in addition to the usual electro-optical sensors. It is powered by a derivative of the Army Shadow heavy-fuel engine. DARPA is the current sponsor. Height is 1.65 m, body diameter 0.91 m, planned span 2.92 m, weight 81.7 kg (payload 11.3 kg); endurance is 3 hours at 60 kt (maximum speed 90 kt); ceiling is 15,000 ft.

HAA

Lockheed Martin's High Altitude Airship is a Missile Defense Agency project intended to provide persistent long-range missile warning. It began as an ACTD in the third quarter of 2002; Lockheed Martin won the contract on 29 September 2003. Requirements included the ability to loiter with a 4,000-lb payload in quasi-geostationary orbit at 65,000 ft altitude. The critical design review was completed in October 2004, but the program was restructured in July 2005. The payload requirement in particular was drastically reduced. On this basis Lockheed Martin received a contract that expires on 30 November 2010. Solar panels are intended to provide an excess of 3 kW (10 kW in the production version) to operate sensors including radars. The airship is to have two electric motors

(driving large-diameter propellers) on each side, driven by lithium batteries to propel and steer the airship.

Data given in September 2007 for prototype/production version: length 122/152 m, diameter 36.5/45.7 m, propeller diameter 7.62 m, maximum payload 227/907 kg (500/2,000 lbs); endurance 1 month/1 year; maximum speed 70 kt (prototype), ceiling 60,000/65,000 ft.

HUAV/PERSIUS

Hybrid Unmanned Aircraft Vehicle/Persistent Elevated Reconnaissance Surveillance Intelligence Unmanned System is a hybrid airship/airplane being built by Lockheed Martin for prototype delivery in December 2009. It is conceived as a 250-ft device with a 110-ft tail span, capable of carrying a 2,500-lb payload at 20,000 ft for twenty-one days. The expectation is that it will provide an affordable and easily relocatable ISR platform, using a flexible payload gondola. Hybrid lift means a combination of buoyancy and aerodynamic lift. PERSIUS is a 2009 JCTD.

HUNTER-KILLER

During the summer of 2004 the U.S. Air Force issued a specification for a hunter-killer UCAV to carry a warload of 1,360 kg (six 225-kg bombs) with an endurance of 16 to 30 hours and a ceiling of 35,000 to 50,000 ft. It would have the usual sensors (SAR/GMTI or EO/IR) and a laser target designator. This was not too far from what Reaper offered.

GoldenEye 80 ducted-fan VTOL UAV. (Aurora Flight Sciences by Kurt Lengfield)

HAA airship. (Lockheed Martin)

Northrop Grumman offered Model 395, a militarized UAV version of Scaled Composites' twin-boom Proteus, with a sensor pod under its nose and a bomb bay. Because it used a bomb bay rather than wing hard points, it could also carry a single unitary weapon, such as a 5,000-lb "bunker buster." The alternative Model 396 was a half-scale Global Hawk. Other submissions were by Lockheed Martin (no details), Aurora Flight Sciences/IAI (armed Heron 2), and General Atomics (Predator B). Predator B was chosen, renamed Reaper.

KILLERBEE/BAT

This low-altitude long-endurance scalable UAV was developed by Swift Engineering, then sold in May 2009 to Northrop Grumman (as Bat). The design was then licensed to Raytheon (for STUAS Tier II) as KillerBee-4 (meaning the fourth version of the design). Raytheon claims that it has the right to scale this aircraft up or down, but Northrop Grumman rejects that claim. It apparently considers Bat the name for the entire Swift Engineering product line and KillerBee the version licensed to Raytheon. The original intent seems to have been to dispense the UAV in swarms of three, five, or ten from an airplane. As initially

envisaged, span was 6.5 to 17.5 ft (takeoff weight 43–360 lbs, payload 7–120 lbs). Endurance was 12–14 hours (endurance speed 67 mph), ceiling 18,000 to 20,000 ft. The demonstrator had a span of 6 ft 6 in. and is powered by a small piston engine; it carries a 7-lb payload for 30 hours or a 20-lb payload for 8 hours, cruising at about 110 km/hour (60 kt) at 15,000 ft. Demonstrators with spans of 18 in. and 5 ft have flown.

KillerBee-4 is a contender for STUAS Tier II. Data: span 3.1 m (also given as 3.04 m), length 1.92 m (also given as 1.8 m), weight 74.4 kg (payload 22.3 kg). Weight and payload have also been given as 77 and 30 kg, the latter including fuel. Ceiling is 10,000 ft, endurance 15 hours (cruising speed 55 kt). The current engine develops 17 hp, but Raytheon is apparently working on a replacement, which may employ a patented two-stage vaporization technique with a special igniter, so as to burn heavy fuel without using the high compression ratio of a diesel. That should make for a lighter engine. Payload volume is 95 liters; Raytheon points out that a conventional airframe of the same size would have a payload volume of only 15 liters. The company claims that the design has considerable growth potential and that its blended wing-fuselage

KillerBee as displayed by Raytheon at the 2009 Paris Air Show. (Norman Friedman)

design makes for low drag and hence long endurance. Growth potential apparently includes arming the UAV with 5-kg-class weapons.

KINGFISHER II

Vought's UAV can take off or land on skids in the water; hence, it was offered for the U.S. Navy LCS support role won by Fire Scout. The name recalls the original Kingfisher shipboard reconnaissance floatplane used during World War II; there is no Kingfisher I UAV. The UAV is designed to fold into the space normally occupied by an 11-m rigid inflatable boat. The UAV has a twin-boom configuration with an air intake atop its body.

Data: span is 41 ft, length 38 ft, takeoff weight 9,500 lb (payload 2,500 lbs, empty weight 4,360 lbs). Ceiling is 45,000 ft. Maximum speed is 345 kt; endurance speed is 250 kt at 25,000 ft. The power plant is a 4,100-lb-thrust PW545B jet engine.

INTEGRATOR

The Boeing/Insitu submission for the STUAS Tier II competition, announced in August 2007, is a twin-boom pusher aircraft. Data: span 4.8 m, length 2.1 m, takeoff weight 59 kg (payload 23 kg). Ceiling is 20,000 ft. Endurance is about 24 hours and cruising speed is 60 kt.

ISIS

DARPA initiated the Integrated Sensor in Structure program in 2004. It is intended to create an electrically powered long-endurance airship carrying a massive UHF SAR/GMTI radar, capable of floating at 70,000 ft and therefore of seeing troop movements 180 miles away and cruise missiles about 370 miles away. Expected operational lifetime would be ten years. The key technologies are the lightweight antenna and the means of energy storage. As of 2009 DARPA already had the necessary radar array (UHF and X-band) in the form of a 40-X-46-m cylinder, which would be carried vertically in the body of the airship. Much effort went into cutting array weight by about 90 percent, from 20 to 2 kg per square meter.

For power, the airship uses solar cells to create enough energy to break down water into oxygen and hydrogen, which are stored and then recombined (the energy recovered) in a fuel cell. As of 2009, this technology was being demonstrated. Lockheed Martin was expected to assemble a prototype for tests beginning in the late fall of 2012.

L15

Airship Surveillance announced the successful flight of this autonomous airship in March 2008. It has no gondola, only a propeller at its tail and three tail fins. The L15 is the company's first airship optimized for surveillance missions; it is intended to operate at 15,000 ft with payloads up to 1,000 lbs, with an endurance of 50 hours and a speed of up to 50 kt. The company claims that the design provides laminar flow for minimal drag.

LEMV

The Long-Endurance Multi-Intelligence Vehicle (LEMV) is a conceptual persistent intelligence platform, the contract for which is to be awarded by the end of 2009. It is intended to remain aloft for three weeks at 20,000 ft carrying a 2,500-lb wide-area sensor payload combining a signals intelligence system, multiple electro-optical/IR sensors, and a synthetic aperture array/ground moving target indicator radar. Apparently LEMV is justified particularly for an ability to detect the improvised explosive devices that are proving effective in Afghanistan. That generally means detecting changes on the ground by constantly comparing photographs of the same area. The airship would be optionally manned (for self-deployment to theater). A single demonstrator is to be fielded to Afghanistan within eighteen months of contract signature. The FY 2010 budget includes $80 million for LEMV. A consortium was to have been created by early October 2009, with an RFP to follow in November and a contract by the end of December 2009 (it was deferred to at least January 2010).

As of early October 2009, potential platform providers included Lockheed Martin's Skunk Works and the UK's Hybrid Air Vehicles. Lockheed Martin offers a 250-ft craft deriving 80 percent of its lift from helium bouyancy and the rest from aerodynamics, a feature making it possible to launch and recover without the usual airship infrastructure. It has a three-lobe non-rigid envelope. The underslung gondola is 40 ft long, 15 ft wide,

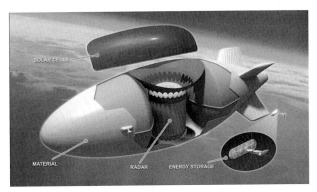

ISIS electrically powered long-endurance airship. (DARPA)

LEMV long-endurance vehicle. Note the gondola (the airship is optionally piloted). (Lockheed Martin)

and 6 to 8 ft high, and there are three thrusters. They are driven by turbo-diesels during takeoff and climb and then from a single turbo-generator during loiter.

MAKO (XPV-2)

The Mako, a low-cost long-endurance mini-UAV, was developed by Navmar Applied Sciences; the designation suggests some relationship with Tern. Navmar describes this UAV as Mako II. Thirty Makos were procured by U.S. Special Operations Command and used successfully during Operation Iraqi Freedom. The Navmar Web site suggests that customers for Mako include the Air Force, NAVAIR (Naval Air Systems Command), NAVSEA (Naval Sea Systems Command), ONR, NGA, and SPA-WAR (Space and Electronic Warfare Systems Command) (it does not give details). Mako has a twin-boom pusher configuration and can be launched from the roof of a vehicle.

Data: span 3.86 m, length 3.02 m, weight 64 kg (payload 13.6 kg); ceiling is 10,000 ft, range 40 nm (endurance more than 7 hours, speed 70 kt, cruising speed 45 kt). The power plant is a 10.5-hp piston engine.

MAVERIC

Prioria Robotics' bird-like mini-UAV may be in Special Operations service. Production began in February 2008. The bendable wings (presumably inflatable for strength) can be wrapped around the fuselage for storage in a 6-in. diameter tube. Propulsion is by a tractor electric motor with foldable propeller blades. The payload is nose- and side-mounted cameras. Span 0.75 m, length 0.67 m, weight 1.13 kg (payload 100 or 300 g), endurance more than 50 minutes (data-link limit 2.7 nm); maximum speed 56 kt (cruising speed 26 kt, stall speed 18 kt); ceiling is 16,000 ft (theoretically 25,000 ft).

This is probably the Tactical Mini-UAV (TAC-MAV) described in the DoD's 2009 *Unmanned Systems Road Map*. Late in 2004 the Army's Rapid Equipping Force (REF) leveraged an Air Force contract to acquire TACMAVs. After evaluating six Spiral 1 systems, the REF bought another seventy-eight as Spiral 2 in support of operations in Afghanistan and Iraq; each system cost $36,000 (no more are being bought). This account mentions a 5- rather than 6-in. container (22 in. long). The ground control uses a standard Air Force Portable Flight Planning System for mission planning, in-flight updates, and manual control. TACMAV is used by platoons, squads, and fire teams. Production ceased because soldiers complained of poor images and lack of stability, grid coordinates, and IR capabilities; TACMAV is very weather-dependent. Newer configurations added an IR camera and lengthened flight time.

MINION

In September 2003 the Lockheed Martin "Skunk Works" announced that it was developing this air-launched UCAV, two of which could be carried underwing by a fighter such as an F-22. The configuration recalls the somewhat stealthy Anglo-French Storm Shadow cruise missile. Launch weight is 3,400 kg and range is 1,850 km. Minion apparently has bays (like those of Storm Shadow)

Maveric mini-UAV. (Prioria Robotics)

that can accommodate a reconnaissance payload, a microwave jammer, or four 100-kg GPS-guided Small Diameter Bombs. In theory they would be launched by a pair of aircraft, one pilot dealing with threats while the other guided the four missiles. After attacking they would return under their own power and land conventionally. Minion may have some commonality with Lockheed Martin's AGM-158 JASSM missile.

The status of this program is unclear. Rumors of a cruise missile–like UCAV under development at the Skunk Works had circulated for some time before 2003, and there were rumors that it was used during the invasion of Iraq in 2003.

ODYSSEUS

Aurora Flight Sciences' ultra-long-endurance UAV under development for DARA uses a modular "Z" wing and brushless electric motors supplied with power by solar panels. Each wing module carries a pair of motors driving pusher propellers. The wing can change shape during flight to optimize solar power output (e.g., to capture light when the sun is not directly overhead). A cruciform set of control surfaces is carried on a boom extending from the midpoint of each constant-chord wing module. Plans call for launching the vehicle as three separate UAVs, which dock in flight to constitute the full vehicle. Total wingspan is 500 ft; the length is 80 ft. Takeoff weight is 6,800 lbs (payload 1,000 lbs). Endurance is to be 44,000 hours (five years) at a ceiling of 70,000 ft. Cruising speed would be 226 km/hour in daytime and 155 km/hour at night. A subscale demonstrator is to prove ninety-day endurance by 2012.

Odysseus is part of a larger DARPA Vulture program to develop an ultra-long-endurance UAV. In April 2008 DARPA awarded $4 million design contracts to Aurora, Boeing, and Lockheed Martin. The goal is to maintain a continuous high-resolution view of a battlefield over a 750 mile diameter (i.e., from 60,000 ft). Boeing and Lockheed Martin both offered launch-once ultrareliable aircraft with wingspans greater than 300 ft. Reported goals are five years on station with a 450-kg payload served by 5 kW of onboard power. The UAV must remain on station for 99 percent of the time in the face of winds at 60,000 to 90,000 ft. Phase 1 (2008–9) is Concept Definition; Phase 2 (2009–12) is risk reduction. Phase 1 concluded with a successful System Requirements Review, confirming that Vulture had a reasonable prospect of success. Phase 2 is to include tests of subscale demonstrators capable of remaining aloft for 3 months, ending with an uninterrupted 3-month flight. Phase 3 would involve construction of a full-scale prototype capable of remaining aloft for 12 months, leading to system design and development as a program of record.

Boeing's entry is Zephyr, with a 30-m wingspan (weight only 30 kg). Lockheed Martin offers a much larger vehicle (said to be 300 ft long, launched from a blimp) with rotating tails intended to collect maximum sunlight as well as a means of capturing sunlight reflected from the earth. Zephyr apparently has other sponsors, since partner Qinetiq announced a U.S. (not DARPA) contract in May 2009 for seven UAVs and a ground station.

A California start-up company, AC Propulsion, began flight tests of a solar-powered SoLong during the summer of 2005. SoLong combines solar cells with lithium batteries for night power. An early flight lasted 48 hours. This very small UAV (span 4.76 m, weight 12.8 kg, 1-hp motor) is intended as a technology demonstrator for a much larger one.

As complement to Vulture, DARPA conceived Rapid Eye, a surveillance UAV carried to its operating area on board a ballistic missile. Rapid Eye would permit quick response to a sudden crisis. The payload would have to be packaged to fit the missile re-entry vehicle, yet it would need the long high-aspect ratio wings required to fly at 65,000 ft for 7–15 hours. Its engine would have to start instantly at this oxygen-starved altitude.

ORION HALL

Aurora Flight Sciences' HALE has a conventional tractor configuration. HALL means High Altitude, Long Loiter. It is currently in development for the U.S. Army and U.S. Air Force. Its special feature is its liquid-hydrogen internal-combustion engine. Aurora claimed improved reliability through the use of off-the-shelf parts and systems. Design and two vehicles were sponsored by the U.S. Army Space and Missile Defense Command; production of the two vehicles began in 2006. The first flight was expected late in 2009 or early in 2010 (the original target was 2008).

Data: span 40.2 m, length 17.4 m, takeoff weight 3,175 kg (payload 181 kg). Endurance is 100 hours at 65,000 ft (speed 54–74 kt) or 160 hours at 45,000 ft.

Boeing acted as partner in this project. Aurora's description of Orion HALL includes the statement that it is partnered with Boeing in the concept study of a larger twin-engine UAV with greater endurance. This may be Condor NG, based on the much earlier Boeing Condor long-endurance twin-engine UAV. Condor itself was the first U.S. HALE, built mainly with Boeing funds but with some DoD support. To achieve long endurance and high altitude, Condor had the now-familiar extremely long high-aspect wings (span 200 ft, like that of a Boeing 747); length was 68 ft. The fuselage was a box-section structure (4.33 X 2.83 ft) suspended from the wing by a short pylon. The tail was conventional. Takeoff weight was 20,000 lbs, about 60 percent of it fuel, and Condor could carry 1,800 lbs of instrumentation, not including flight control. There were two 175-hp 2-stage turbocharged Continental piston engines driving 16-ft diameter propellers. The aircraft was designed so that it could be dismantled for carriage by a C-5 cargo plane. Attention to weight saving is shown by the fact that the wing weighed 2 lbs/sq ft, compared to 20 for an airliner. Given its limited power, Condor took 2 to 3 hours to reach its 60,000-ft operating altitude; it cruised at about 200 kt. Condor first flew on 9 October 1988, and it set world records for altitude (67,028 ft) for a piston aircraft and for endurance (58 hours 11 minutes). Estimated maximum range was 19,000 nm. In effect Condor inspired later HALE projects. It had the first satellite antenna on board an unmanned U.S. aircraft. DARPA supported Condor flight tests and presumably looked at

Orion HALL high-altitude, long-endurance aircraft. (Aurora Flight Sciences)

Amber as a less expensive approach to the same sort of performance.

As of mid-2009 Boeing and Aurora hoped to demonstrate 48-hour endurance in the third quarter of 2010. The power plant is a Ford liquid hydrogen fuel cell feeding a pair of electric motors driving propellers. Reported payload is 910 kg for 168 hours or 225 kg for 240 hours. Maximum altitude would be 65,000 ft.

PAWS

In November 2009 the Air Force Research Laboratory announced the Precision (Target) Acquisition Weapon System, or PAWS, a JCTD it was conducting for Special Operations Command. It employs a micro–air vehicle (MAV) from CLMax Engineering of Fort Walton Beach, Florida. That company's Web site shows a flying-wing MAV that can be carried by a larger UAV and in turn carries small munitions. The object of the JCTD is to provide Special Forces UAVs with multiple-target attack capability using munitions that will generate little collateral damage or threat of fratricide. Guidance is described as visual, meaning that the attack will be based on an image produced by the MAV. The laboratory announcement stated that hardware would be received in December 2009, with tests to follow in 2010.

PHANTOM RAY

On 8 May 2009 Boeing announced the Phantom Ray, an internally funded UCAV using the X-45 airframe it had already built for the abortive J-UCAS program. It was expected to fly in December 2010; Boeing planned ten flights over a six-month period, presumably as part of its MQ-X bid. X-45A was completed in September 2000, flying in May 2002 after extensive ground tests including taxi tests. X-45A dropped a weapon for the first time in March 2004, and in April it hit a target with an inert GPS-guided bomb. The test program was completed in July 2005 after 64 flights, the final test including detecting and avoiding multiple simulated threats, choosing one of several targets to attack, replanning after the operator changed attack priorities, and then conducting the attack with one or two aircraft (there were two prototypes). X-45A was conceived as a technology demonstrator, leading to an X-45B, which in turn was superseded by the X-45C offered for the Joint UCAS (which was won by Northrop Grumman's X-47). Boeing also developed X-46A for the follow-on carrier UCAS program. The single released photograph of Phantom Ray (presumably of a mockup) suggests it follows the full flying-wing design proposed for X-46 rather than the body and swept wing design offered for X-45A. This aircraft was superseded by X-45C, which had the same sort of flying-wing configuration.

Given Boeing's announcement that Phantom Ray is an X-45 derivative, the data below seem relevant.

X-45A data: span 10.3 m, length 8.08 m, weight 5,530 kg, speed Mach 0.75, ceiling 35,000 ft, mission radius 500 nm. The power plant was a Honeywell F124-GA-100 turbofan (6,300 lbs of thrust).

X-45C data: span 14.9 m, length 11.9 m, weight 16,600 kg, speed Mach 0.85, ceiling 40,000 ft, mission radius 1,300 nm. The power plant was a GE F404-GE102D turbofan (7,000 lbs of thrust).

POINTER (FQM-151A)/PUMA

AeroVironment's Pointer was the first practical hand-launched UAV. AeroVironment began development on a private venture basis in 1986. Four were delivered to the U.S. Army in 1988 for test and evaluation, and another twenty-four air vehicles plus associated equipment were ordered in 1989 for extended evaluation by the Army and the Marine Corps. The first was delivered early in 1990. About fifty air vehicles were delivered, and the Army and Marines both used Pointer during Operation Desert Storm (1991). It was initially used to check whether U.S. forces were effectively concealed, and later for damage assessment and battlefield surveillance. Pointer is hand-launched and lands on its belly. Configuration is conventional, with a tractor propeller and a parasol wing; the power plant is a battery-powered 350 W electric motor. The major upgrade during service was GPS-based auto-navigation, which greatly reduced operator workload. Raven uses many Pointer components.

Data: span 2.74 m, length 1.83 m, weight 4.3 kg, speed 43 kt, ceiling 1,000 ft, endurance 1 hour on primary batteries, 20 minutes on rechargeable batteries.

AeroVironment's Pointer Upgraded Mission Ability was intended to replace the company's widely used FQM-151A Pointer. It weighs 6.35 kg rather than the 3.76 kg of Pointer. Initially separate land and water versions (Terra Puma and Aqua Puma) were tested, but in 2008 Puma-AE (All Environments) was adopted as the standard U.S. SOCOM Small UAS.

Data: span 2.6 m, length 1.8 m, weight 4.5 kg, speed 60 mph (cruising speed 15–31 mph); ceiling 12,500 ft, range 9 miles, endurance 4 hours on primary battery or 3 hours on rechargeable battery. The power plant is a 600-W motor.

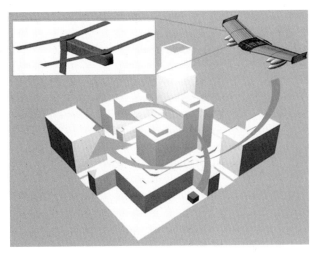

The CLMax PAWS operating concept, taken from the company's Web site. (CLMax)

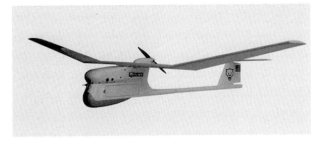

Phantom Ray, using the mockup of the earlier Boeing X-45C. (Boeing)

Puma, a modified Pointer. (AeroVironment)

Puma-AE is a different UAV, with a new configuration. Here it is being hand-launched. (AeroVironment)

SCANEAGLE/INSIGHT/NIGHTEAGLE

In February 2002 the U.S. Navy awarded a fifteen-month contract to Boeing and Insitu for work on their small ScanEagle, a hand-launched flying wing. ScanEagle first flew autonomously on 19 June 2002. It was derived from Insitu's SeaScan tuna fishing boat scout (under development from the late 1990s) but adapted by the Marines to operate in Afghanistan and Iraq from 2004 onward. Scan-Eagle in turn was derived from Insitu's Insight, which was also the basis for Fugro's GeoRanger. ScanEagle provided communications relay (as a "poor man's satellite") during the Navy's Giant Shadow exercise, in which special forces UUV (Unmanned Underwater Vehicle) functions were demonstrated. The July 2004 Marine Corps contract to Boeing called for two mobile units, each with eight air vehicles. Navy operation from ships began in 2005. By mid-2009 ScanEagle had completed 15,000 shipboard operations. In April 2009 one operating from USS *Bainbridge* monitored activity on board the freighter *Maersk*

Alabama after its seizure by Somali pirates. That month Insitu received a Canadian contract for UAV services in Afghanistan.

The DoD's 2009 *Unmanned Systems Road Map* shows an inventory of two systems (eight aircraft each). However, it also states that six systems are deployed to Iraq under contracts to the Marines (for force protection), twelve have been deployed on Navy ships, four for support ground operations, and two have been acquired by the Air Force.

ScanEagle is tailless, its slightly swept wing terminating in two end plates. It has a pusher engine. The sensor is an integrated camera on an inertially stabilized pan/tilt nose turret (pan for wide-area search at operator command). The recovery technique is unusual, involving a "sky hook" that catches the approaching UAV in a near-vertical posture.

The 0.9-kg NanoSAR radar was tested on board a ScanEagle.

A ScanEagle being mounted on its catapult at Marine Corps Yuma during exercise Desert Talon 2006. (U.S. Marine Corps by Cpl. Michael P. Snody)

In 2003 Boeing offered a ScanEagle family of UAVs: ScanEagle A was the 15-hour endurance version, available immediately; B was a stretched 48-hour version (offered for 2004), ScanEagle II was a version with more payload using a heavy-fuel engine to achieve 24-hour surveillance, ScanEagle XL was a much larger version with a 60-lb payload and 24-hour endurance, and ScanEagle XS was a canister-deployable 12-hour version. It is not clear whether any of the proposed versions was produced. A brochure suggested that maximum attainable endurance, presumably with an ultralight payload, was 60 hours. Another brochure credited ScanEagle A with a maximum speed of 66 kt (cruising speed 49 kt, loiter speed 41 kt) and 16-hour still-air endurance; unit cost in modest numbers was given as $60,000. The airframe weighed 8.1 lbs, the avionics (presumably including sensors) another 7.0 lbs, and the power plant 5.3 lbs, for an empty weight of 24.2 lbs; fuel added another 15.4 lbs. Another brochure gave a maximum speed of 70 kt.

Data: span 3.05 m (also given as 3.1 m), length 1.19 m, weight 18 kg, ceiling 19,000 ft, endurance 20 hours (speed 75 mph). The power plant is a 2-stroke 1.5-hp piston engine. However, Insitu figures for Insight are span 3.11 m, length 1.22 m, weight 20 kg (fuel and payload 6.58 kg), endurance over 20 hours (maximum speed 75 kt, cruising speed 48 kt), ceiling 19,500 ft.

Late in 2009 Boeing announced ScanEagle Compressed Carriage (SECC), which it hoped to fly by December. This company-funded project drew on work Boeing had done under the Air Force's Air Dominator project. This version is intended to be launched in the air, from a UAV or a fighter or tactical transport; it may also be carried internally by an F-22 or a P-8A. It will be recovered by Skyhook or conventionally, on the ground or on a ship. The UAV will not resemble ScanEagle externally, but it will use many of the same systems (as well as systems developed for Boeing's Small Diameter Bomb). Prior to launch the wings, canards, and propeller will all be folded. Span is to be 3.7 m and length 1.2 m. Cruising speed is 80 kt (dash speed 115 kt), and endurance is 14 hours (24 hours if space planned for munitions is not used). The planned load is three self-forging smart munitions (BLU-108 Skeets), but alternatives now planned include smart weapons and rockets. The combined IR/EO sensor is larger than that currently carried by ScanEagle. Alternatives are a synthetic-aperture radar, a laser designator, and a biological/chemical/nuclear detector. As of November 2009, Boeing claimed that the technology would be mature enough for a concept demonstration within six months and for deployment eighteen months after that.

Also late in 2009 Insitu announced NightEagle, a modified ScanEagle carrying a mid-wave IR payload. As modified, the UAV could carry both an EO and an IR camera simultaneously in its new bulbous nose (the UAV also has a third, centerline, fin).

Insitu develops long-endurance UAVs; it was responsible for Aerosonde, the first UAV to cross the Atlantic (27 hours on 1.5 gallons of gasoline). Insitu claims that as of mid-2007 its UAVs had completed more than 40,000 combat hours of operation; in their first year of operation ScanEagles flew about 5,000 hours in theater.

SCARAB (MODEL 324)

Teledyne Ryan (now the UAV division of Northrop Grumman) developed the Scarab reconnaissance UAV for Egypt; the Egyptians reportedly bought it because they were impressed by the success of Israeli unmanned vehicles during the 1982 war in Lebanon. Given the date of development, Scarab used a preset analog control system and it brought back its data. It was a fast jet reconnaissance aircraft comparable in concept to reconnaissance versions of Ryan's Firebee. A total of fifty-six (two squadrons) was supplied; by 2008 Scarabs were being flown about once a month to maintain proficiency. In 2005 Egypt approached Northrop Grumman with a request to modernize the system.

Data: span 3.66 m, length 6.10 m, weight 1,134 kg (payload 113.4 kg), cruising range 1,700 nm (speed Mach 0.85, maximum altitude 45,000 ft). Fifty-two were supplied. The abortive U.S. BQM-145A was derived from Scarab.

SENTRY

For some time DRS has been offering Sentry, a lightweight UCAV that would be armed with the compact Spike missile developed by China Lake (not to be confused with the Israeli Spike antitank missile). It has four underwing hard points, each with a capacity of 25 lbs (but note that rated payload is considerably less than 100 lbs). DRS claims that the UAV's modular design makes for unusually quick assembly, modification, or upgrade. Unusually for a UAV, Sentry has a tractor configuration.

Data: span 1.90 m, length 2.57 m, takeoff weight 150 kg, payload 35 kg. Endurance is 6 hours, and ceiling is 10,000 ft. The power plant is a 28-hp 2-stroke piston engine.

Sentry HP data: span 12.8 ft, length 11 ft, takeoff weight 420 lbs (payload 75 lbs, empty weight 180 lbs). Endurance is over 6 hours (endurance speed 75 kt), and ceiling is 100,000 ft. The power plant is a 38-hp engine. The uplink operates at S-band and the downlink at L-band.

SILENT EYES

Raytheon has been developing Silent Eyes, a gliding air-launched UAV derived from its earlier Microglider (eight prototypes built under Air Force contract let in April 1999). Microglider was successfully tested in September 1999, transmitting target video to an RC-135 and other platforms. In 2002 the glider was rethought as a much smaller vehicle that could be launched by UAVs, particularly to descend through cloud blocking their sensors. At that time Raytheon thought that unit price (June 2004) would be $15,000. This is a continuing Raytheon program without current support, but it is interesting as an indication of a likely line of development (see also NRL's Finder). Silent Eyes would be dropped from a container similar to that used for the current towed decoy. Dropped from 60,000 ft, it could glide for about 90 nm. It was test-launched by a Predator B at Edwards Air Force Base in May and June 2004; its data were transmitted via the Predator data link. Typical dimensions (the configuration has varied) are: span 0.7 m, length 0.5 m, weight 3 kg. Gliding speed would be 80 to 100 kt.

SILVER FOX/MANTA

Advanced Ceramics' mini-UAV has deployed with U.S. Navy riverine boats in Iraq. BAE Systems acquired

The U.S. BQM-145A medium-range reconnaissance UAV was derived from the Scarab (Model 324) built for Egypt, with much the same configuration. This BQM-145 was photographed on 1 October 1991. (Teledyne Ryan [now Northrop Grumman])

Sentry HP is shown at Patuxent River, June 2005. Note the miniature rockets underwing. (U.S. Navy by PH2 Daniel J. McLain)

Advanced Ceramics in mid-2009, so this is now a BAE Systems product. It is a small gas/electric UAV developed in cooperation with ONR and NAVAIR, offering 8- to 10-hour endurance, a payload of 5–8 lbs, and autonomous takeoff and landing. Wingspan is 2.4 m (94 in.). A typical system includes three air vehicles. Silver Fox was designed and built in 2001 to meet a U.S. Navy requirement to search for and monitor the movement of whales, in response to a legal requirement not to operate very-low-frequency, high-powered active sonars in their vicinity. In January 2003 the Marine Corps asked ONR to build Silver Foxes rapidly for tactical reconnaissance/surveillance (RISTA: Reconnaissance, Intelligence, Surveillance, and Target Acquisition). Several systems were delivered in support of Operation Iraqi Freedom in 2003 (the first six UAVs were delivered within two months). That year a heavy-fuel version with an extended fuel tank set an endurance record of 21.5 hours. Multivehicle flight and autonomous convoy station keeping were demonstrated. In 2004 some were delivered to the Canadian Department of National Defense, and the Marines began an extended evaluation. By 2005 the evolved Block 4 version offered the endurance quoted above and a mission communications range of 20 miles. This version was designed for belly landing. In 2005 the U.S. Army Transportation School completed an evaluation of Silver Fox in the road convoy protection role. In 2006 Silver Fox was fitted with inertially stabilized gimbal-mounted sensors, enhanced tracking/targeting capability, upgraded software, a heavy-fuel engine, an onboard power generator, and other improvements.

According to the DoD's 2009 *Unmanned Systems Road Map*, plans call for seventeen Silver Fox systems (a total of fifty-four aircraft).

Advanced Ceramics designed Manta in 2002 to provide a larger payload (6.8 to 8.2 kg, compared to 2.3–3.6 kg for Silver Fox) by using much the same wingspan with a larger lifting area and fuselage. The Navy Special Clearance Team (NSCT) became interested in Manta due to its ability to carry a hyperspectral imaging unit and other advanced cameras. Access through the top of the fuselage was also attractive. The NSCT was established in October 2002 from the earlier Very Shallow Water Detachment, which in turn combines elements from Navy Special War-

Silver Fox mini-UAV. (Advanced Ceramics)

fare, Marine Reconnaissance, and EOD. It has four platoons: marine mammals, UUV, UAV, and divers. During Operation Iraqi Freedom, NSCT cleared the Iraqi port of Umm Qasr. Silver Fox has operated from 36-ft rigid inflatable boats of the NSCT, landing on the water.

The design is modular, with straight wings of various sizes that make it possible to trade off duration and payload for speed.

Silver Fox data: span (maximum) 2.39 m, length 1.47 m, weight 12 kg (maximum payload 1.8 kg), ceiling 12,000 ft (normal operating altitude 500 to 1,200 ft), endurance 10 hours (cruising speed 70 kt). The UAV can fly a preprogrammed mission of 180 miles. In its autonomous "convoy reconnaissance" mode it flies automatically ahead of a control vehicle in the convoy. A modified heavy-fuel engine doubles endurance to 20 hours.

SKY SERIES

Proxy Aviation systems offers three versions of an autonomous UAV (optionally piloted vehicle) with canard configuration (with pusher propeller) whose vertical surfaces are at the ends of its wing: Skyforce, Skyraider, and Skywatcher. Proxy Aviation offers a Skyforce Distributed Management System (DMS), which can support cooperative flight and ATLS. A single point of management and control can handle 12 vehicles simultaneously and up to 20 ground stations working cooperatively. Span is 32 ft and length is 20 ft; takeoff weight is 4,000 lbs (payload 330 to 1,000 lbs). Endurance is 20 to 30 hours (dash speed 175 kt, endurance speed 110 kt, mission radius 100 nm). Ceiling is 24,000 ft. The power plant is a 250-hp Lycoming engine. Skywatcher is credited with a takeoff weight of 2,900 lbs and a payload of 330–650 lbs; endurance is 8 to 15 hours (dash speed 150 kt), but it has the same dimensions as the others.

SKYEYE

BAE Systems' R4E-50 and -100 have twin booms and pusher propellers. This is a U.S. design developed beginning in 1980 by Developmental Sciences Corporation, then a division of Lear Astronics, which in turn was later acquired by BAE Systems. The U.S. Army evaluated R4E-30 as a battlefield UAV carrying unguided rockets. A squadron of six aircraft was supplied to the Royal Thai Air Force in 1982. R4E-40 had a more powerful engine and more fuel. About 1984–86 some were bought by the U.S. Army Central Command for reconnaissance of the Honduras/Nicaragua border in Central America, flying from Honduras. They had day television, low-light-level television, FLIR, and panoramic cameras. Missions included night launch and recovery. R4E-50 flew in 1986; it added GPS and had a heavier payload. It entered production in 1988 and was exported to several countries, including Egypt (forty-eight air vehicles) and Morocco, for battlefield surveillance. In 1989 McDonnell Douglas offered an improved version, Sky Owl, for the Army/Navy short-range UAV competition won by Hunter. The designations PQM-149 and -150 seem to have been reserved for this competition, but they were not used (Hunter became BQM-155). Sky Owl first flew in June 1991.

In 2005 Egypt approached BAE Systems to modernize the SkyEye system; it rejected that company's suggestion that it buy an additional squadron of these UAVs but wanted to keep existing ones operational.

SkyEye has also been used for crop spraying.

R4E-50 data: span 7.3 m, length 4.1 m, weight 566 kg. Endurance more than 12 hours (speed 110 kt), ceiling 16,000 ft. The power plant is a 98-hp twin-rotary engine.

Developmental Sciences used the SkyEye designation for several earlier flying-wing (swept-wing) UAVs with ducted propellers similar to Lockheed's Aquila (Developmental Sciences was involved in the Aquila program). The SkyEye series began with the design of the RPA (remotely piloted aircraft) on 12 February 1973, a date suggesting that it was part of the DARPA ground combat drone program. SkyEye 1-A flew on 26 April 1973. The enlarged R4D flew in 1978, and some were sold to an unnamed foreign customer. Their configuration matched that of Aquila. Span was 3.78 m, length 2.12 m, weight 99.3 kg (payload 36.3 kg). Endurance was 6 hours (8 hours with auxiliary fuel); maximum speed was 130 kt (stall speed 39 kt); ceiling was 20,000 ft. The power plant was a 16- or 22-hp piston engine.

SKYLYNX II

BAE Systems offered the Skylynx II UAV for the STUAS Tier II requirement. Initial tests were completed at Yuma Proving Ground in August 2006. This UAV has twin booms and a pusher propeller. It is smaller than R4E: span 18.4 ft, length 13.9 ft, takeoff weight 330 lbs (payload 70 lbs, empty 205 lbs). Endurance is 16 hours (mission radius 120 nm, speed 45–110 kt), ceiling 18,000 ft. The power plant is a 38-hp AR741 engine.

SL-UAV (COYOTE/VOYEUR)

These Sonobuoy-Launcher UAVs were developed to meet a 2004 ONR request for an SL-UAV (SL means Sonobuoy Launch), envisaged as an expendable (i.e., very cheap) UAV that could be deployed by P-3s and other ASW aircraft. Presumably it was inspired by the use of P-3s for surveillance in Iraq and in Afghanistan. NAVAIR let the contracts. The sonobuoy chute set air vehicle dimensions, and weight was set by maximum sonobuoy weight (39 lbs). The air vehicle would drop vertically out of the sonobuoy tube, suspended from a parachute, deploy its wings and propeller blades and tail, and its autopilot would pop it up into flying position. In parallel the Navy is developing a low-cost Expendable Ad Hoc Networked Data Link System to connect the SL-UAV with the launch platform. Existing ad hoc networks were rejected as too expensive, too massive, too limited in range, limited to commercial frequencies, and lacking in encryption (as did sonobuoy communications links). The goal is bidirectional linkage and control at a distance of 20 nm between airplane and SL-UAV, with an objective of 50 nm. Initial concepts of operation called for an airplane to operate six SL-UAVs simultaneously.

Initially the P-3 was to provide centralized control and data handling. As a near-term goal, it should be possible to extend that control and data receipt to other air-

R4E-50 as advertised July 1990 as a new short-range UAV. (McDonnell Douglas)

borne platforms and to ground units. The long-term (be-yond five years) goal was for the UAVs to communicate with each other so that they could operate as a swarm, that is, as a group that would be controlled as such, with-out reference (from outside) to specific units. Specified performance included maximum altitude of 25,000 ft (i.e., the altitude at which the SL-UAV could be launched without losing it), a range objective of 50 nm, and an en-durance of 1.5 hours. The SL-UAV would typically fly 300 to 500 ft above a boat to decide whether it was friend or foe (sufficient resolution was needed to determine wheth-er the boat was carrying a weapon). It would have alterna-tive EO and IR payloads.

The first SL-UAV to fly was Advanced Ceramics' Coyote, which has tandem wings and two vertical tail sur-faces, with a pusher propeller and its sensor in its trans-parent nose dome. It can be programmed by either the pilot or the tactical officer via the airplane's normal sono-buoy interfaces.

Data: span 1.47 m, length 0.79 m, weight 6.4 kg, ceiling 20,000 ft (nominal mission altitude 500 to 1,200 ft), command and control range 20 nm (endurance 1.5 hours), speed was 80 kt (cruising speed 55 kt). The power plant is an electric motor driving a pusher propeller. Data describe Block A2. Originally testing from a sonobuoy chute was planned for the spring of 2006, but in mid-2008 it was reported that a test from a P-3C would be con-ducted in the third quarter of the year. Coyote had been launched from a representative sonobuoy chute on board a Raytheon C-12 in April 2007. Note that BAE Systems acquired Advanced Ceramics in mid-2009.

NAVAIR also tested Lite Machines' Voyeur. Unlike Coyote, it is a mini-helicopter using folding counter-rotating rotors with an unfolded diameter of 76.2 cm (30

Coyote shown with a typical sonobuoy (SSQ-53E DIFAR) and its container. (Advanced Ceramics)

in.); it weighs 3 lbs (originally 4 lbs). Length was given as 27 in. The configuration allows it to "hover and stare." It is electrically powered and can hover at up to 7,000 ft. At least initially Voyeur was described as canisterized rather than as sonobuoy launched; it could be launched from a backpack. In 2008 it was credited with an endurance of 30 minutes and a speed of 30 kt. In mid-2008 Lite Machines received a $10.5 million Small Business contract for a Phase III transfer program titled Sonobuoy Tube Launched UAV, presumably referring to Voyeur. Up to that point Lite Machines had concentrated on building radio-controlled helicopters for hobbyists.

By 2008 there was a third SL-UAV, an unidentified L3 device.

A somewhat analogous idea was a wingless UAV that a helicopter could fire from the standard M260 rocket tube to obtain information about a situation. This UAV would be expendable. It was sponsored by the U.S. Army's Aviation Applied Technology Directorate. By 2005 this project was slowing.

STALKER

Lockheed Martin's hand-launched UAV was announced at a Washington show in August 2007; it is currently in low-rate production for a classified U.S. customer, report-

edly Special Operations, to replace Raven. Development began in 2006, and Stalker first flew in mid-2006. Stalker was developed by Lockheed Martin's Skunk Works. At 6.4 kg it is somewhat heavier than most hand-launched UAVs. The sensor module fits into a two-axis gimballed turret, and it has a "plug and play" interface for easy interchange of sensors; for landing, the turret retracts into the body of the UAV. Unusually, Stalker has a tractor propeller; it has a pod-and-boom configuration with a high wing. It uses a "hush drive," which combines a low-noise electric motor with a quiet propeller. Reportedly the configuration was chosen to provide sound buffering between motor and propeller. The UAV autonomously returns to within 50 ft of the launch point, going into a steep stall and crash-landing on its shock-absorbing belly. Span is about 3 m, weight is 6.4 kg (payload up to 1.4 kg), ceiling is 15,000 ft (normal operating altitude 400 ft), and endurance is 2 hours.

TALON LASH

Global Aerial Surveillance's Light Attack and Surveillance Helicopter (LASH) has a maximum payload of 800 lbs (empty weight is 780 lbs). It uses a conventional single-rotor helicopter configuration with a rotor diameter of 25 ft and a fuselage length of 22 ft. Endurance is 6 to 8 hours (speed 130 mph, endurance speed 110 mph); ceiling is 15,000 ft.

TERN (XPV-1)

BAI's mini-UAV was begun by H-Cubed, which BAI acquired in 1993. It was used by the U.S. military in the late 1990s for research; for example, two were modified by the Army with fiber-optical guidance as surrogate fiber-optic guided missiles. Tern was modified into the XPV-1 tactical UAV in 2001 for special operations. A total of sixty-five were acquired by the U.S. services. Tern means Tactical Expendable Remote Navigator. It was conceived as a peacetime trainer cheap enough to be expendable in combat. XPV-1 is the company designation, meaning Expendable Payload Vehicle. Note that BAI was acquired by L-3 in December 2004. U.S. Navy Fleet Composite Squadron 6 (VC-6) operated some Terns in Afghanistan in 2001. They were used to drop unattended ground sensors.

Data: span 3.45 m, length 2.71 m, weight 59 kg. Ceiling 10,000 ft, range 40 nm (endurance 4 hours, speed 78 mph, cruising speed 52 mph). The power plant is a 12-hp piston engine.

TIGERSHARK/FOXCAR

This twin-boom UAV was designed specifically for Special Operations Command; developed in less than sixty days, it was delivered between 2002 and 2005 (and announced in 2004). The officers of the manufacturer, BTC (Brandebury Tool Company), had founded Aerosystems (now part of L-3), which produced Exdrone. In addition to SOCOM, a "significant number" were sold to Navmar Applied Sciences Corporation, presumably as UAV demonstrators. The power plant is a 13-hp piston engine. Span is 5.33 m, length 4.72 m, weight 136 kg (payload 22.7 kg); endurance is 10 hours (cruising speed 65 kt). TigerShark was apparently conceived as a part-scale version of a larger UAV with a payload of at least 100 lb (45.4 kg). The reference to SOCOM suggests that the larger UAV lost out to L-3's Viking 400. FoxCar combines the TigerShark fuselage with enlarged tailbooms and enlarged wing and tail surfaces (span 6.40 m, endurance 9.5 hours).

VIGILANTE 502

SAIC's single-rotor UAV has a rotor diameter of 23 ft and a fuselage length of 19.9 ft. Takeoff weight is 1,100 lbs (payload 230 lbs, empty 650 lbs). Endurance is 7 hours (mission radius 210 nm, dash speed 117 kt, endurance speed 50 kt), and ceiling is 12,000 ft. The power plant is a 115-hp Rotax 914 avgas engine. The U.S. Army used this UAV for tests, including those of the guided 2.75-in. rocket (APKWS) in early 2005 at Yuma.

VIKING 400

In September 2009 Special Operations Command let a five-year contract to Geneva Aerospace, an arm of L-3 Communications, for expeditionary UAV systems employing this all-composite aircraft. Viking 400 marks the entry of L-3 into the UAV market. L-3 sees Viking 400 as intermediate between the Army's Shadow and the larger Predator. L-3 sees it as a "truck" with a 100-lb payload. SOCOM apparently likes the way in which the UAV can

Tern mini-UAV. (UVSI)

be disassembled into a small container for easy transport; a C-130 can lift six UAVs and two ground-control stations. SOCOM requirements included silencing; Viking 400 has mufflers and specially designed quiet propellers.

Span is 6.1 m, length is 4.5 m, takeoff weight is 530 lbs (payload 75 to 100 lbs), and endurance 8 to 12 hours (range over 70 nm at a speed of 60 to 90 kt). The UAV is designed to operate conventionally from unimproved expeditionary runways. It is assembled in the field like a model airplane. The power plant is a 38-hp piston engine driving a pusher propeller (Viking employs the usual twin-boom layout). Mission control is via GPS waypoints that can be reassigned in flight; Viking uses Geneva's flightTEK ATOL technology. Payloads include the usual cameras plus a LIDAR, which it is hoped can see through trees and other cover, SIGINT, ELINT, and NBR (nuclear-biological-radiological) detection devices. There is a prominent window in one side of the nose, plus the usual underslung turret. According to Geneva/L-3, embedded sensor processing makes it possible for the UAV automatically to focus multiple sensors on a target it detects.

In addition to Viking 400, L-3 offers the 100-lb Viking 100 and the 300-lb Viking 300.

WASP/BATMAV

DARPA supported the development of AeroVironment's Wasp as the first true micro-UAV (MAV), exploiting advances in electronic miniaturization and batteries. The battery is integral with its wing. Development began in 1998 based on an earlier Black Widow project. Wasp weighs 340 grams (0.34 kg) but carries two color video cameras and has a nominal endurance of 60 minutes (it has demonstrated 107-minute endurance). Range is 3.7

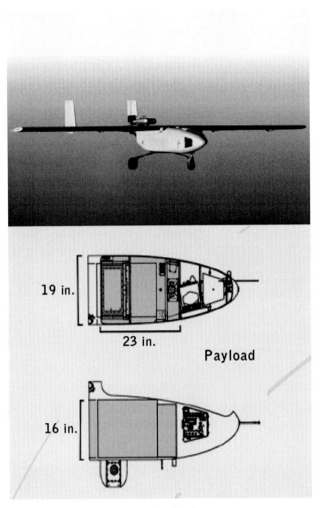

Viking 400 UAV. (L-3 Communications)

A Wasp is hand-launched by slingshot, August 2007. The UAV is upside down when launched. (U.S. Navy by MC3 Daisy Abonza)

km, sufficient to look beyond a hill. In November 2007 the Marine Corps ordered Wasp to complement the larger Raven-B; ultimately it wants twenty-one systems (four air vehicles each). Block I was the developmental version with a 30.5-cm wing. Block II is the heavier operational version with a longer wing and a more powerful version. Block III has 72-cm span and FLIR. Wasp can fly autonomously or it can be manually controlled by Aero-Vironment's standard system, which controls its other mini-UAVs, such as Raven.

In 2006 the U.S. Air Force adopted Wasp III as its BATMAV (Battlefield Air Targeting MAV); full-rate production was approved in January 2008 (314 systems). The U.S. Army is buying one hundred systems for evaluation. There is at least one export customer. AeroVironment's SP2S is based on Wasp. The Marines describe Wasp as "one-third of a Raven" in package size and thus operate it at platoon level (Raven is a battalion asset). The U.S. Special Operations Command adopted Wasp as its Rucksack UAV. According to the DoD's 2009 *Unmanned Systems Road Map*, plans called for one Wasp per team, or a total of at least two hundred such aircraft. It is intended to provide Air Force Special Operations Command Battlefield Airmen with situational awareness; the BATMAV project was designed to meet combat needs felt by Combat Controllers and Tactical Air Control Party Airmen for engagement and self-protection.

In addition to the Air Force, Wasp is used by the Marine Corps and the Navy.

Block II data: span 41 cm (also given as 35.5 cm), length 15 cm, weigh 275 grams. Endurance is 40–60 minutes and range is 2.5 miles (4 km); speed is 25–37 mph.

Owl UAV. (Acuity Technologies)

Block III data: span 72 cm, length 38 cm, weight 430 grams. Endurance is 45 minutes and range is 3.1 miles (5 km); speed is 25–40 mph.

WBBL-UAV (OWL/TURAIS)

Under its Wing and Bomb Bay Launched UAV (WBBL-UAV) program the U.S. Navy let small business innovation research contracts to Pieseki (Turais) and to Acuity Technologies (AT-3 Owl). These UAVs can weigh up to 1,000 lbs, can carry multiple payloads (including ten sonobuoys), may have 8-hour endurance, and are designed for recovery to a land base. Turais is turbojet powered with a scissor wing and parachute recovery. Payload is 200 lbs. Maximum speed is 200 kt, and endurance is over 6 hours. Owl has a large weapon bay and is driven by a 36-hp rotary engine driving a ducted fan. Span is 13.7 ft, length 7.43 ft, weight 411 lbs (payload 200 lbs or ten sonobuoys; empty weight 150 lbs); endurance is 8 hours (range 700

nm). It is a tailless vehicle with swept wings and a ducted-fan pusher propeller. Phase II contracts, including tests of full-scale prototypes, were awarded in May 2008. Turais was reportedly about to fly as of mid-2009.

Turais UAV, with its deployment sequence in the background. (Piaseki)

Notes

Chapter 1. Introduction: An Unmanned Combat Air System

1. The swarm concept is already being tested in other (related) contexts. In November 2009 *Aviation Week and Space Technology* reported that the U.S. Navy had tested autonomous operations by a swarm of UAVs, unmanned ground vehicles, and unattended sensors using the EdgeFrontier networking middleware and swarming algorithms developed by the Australian Vector Research Center. The swarm acted in accord with rules and policies inserted into the software. This kind of state-based decision making could be seen decades earlier in the Aegis air defense system, which uses rules to decide what targets to display and (in automatic mode) what targets constitute urgent threats.

2. For a more detailed discussion of network-centric warfare, see the author's *Network-Centric Warfare: How Navies Learned to Fight Smarter in Three World Wars* (Annapolis: Naval Institute Press, 2008).

3. This kind of distributed control was envisaged for Aegis ships in the Cooperative Engagement Capability, which incorporates a Force Threat Evaluation and Weapon Assignment element. This potential was never completely realized because individual commanders rejected the idea that the system as a whole might decide automatically to fire the weapons on a particular ship. No such problem would of course arise with a group of unmanned attack aircraft.

4. Fighters and surface-to-air missiles clearly work together, but fighters are area weapons that can deny attackers the space between zones covered by missiles, preventing them from using standoff weapons to overcome missile defenses. Once the attackers can use standoff weapons, fighters become the main remaining barrier to air attack. That became obvious in the first Gulf War (1991), when the destruction of the main Iraqi air defense center made it impossible for the Iraqis to coordinate their fighters and their missiles and thus to operate fighters freely without fear of losing them to friendly missiles.

5. The UCAVs would benefit from the changing character of air-to-air weapons. In the past, for anything but short-range missiles, fighters needed onboard fire-control systems including dedicated radars. The UCAS air vehicle is likely to have its own radar, and modern technology makes it possible for such a sensor to function in both air-to-air and air-to-ground (e.g., surveillance) modes; that was demonstrated as long ago as the first Gulf War, when a pair of F/A-18s on a bombing mission shifted to deal with approaching Iraqi MiGs and then shifted back to bombing mode. Now it is possible to fire a missile, such as an AMRAAM, toward the indicated and predicted position of an enemy aircraft, as expressed by its coordinates, course, and speed; the missile turns on its seeker as it approaches the estimated position. The coordinates can be provided by an early warning airplane or by some other source external to the individual UCAS air vehicle. If there were sufficient warning, the attack on enemy aircraft would be handled much like an assigned attack on a surface target. Sensors on individual aircraft would provide backup. The UCAS self-defense capability becomes an important fleet asset, because it can be used to grind down the enemy fighter force (which is finite) and thus to gain the air equivalent of sea control. This is a new version of a classic idea. In 1944 U.S. bombers were escorted over Germany by long-range P-51 fighters. The bombers had very limited

bomb capacity (largely because their designers had provided so much defensive firepower, which turned out not to be terribly effective). They became, in effect, the lure that brought the German fighters into contact with the P-51s, which destroyed them. The level of demand on the German fighters, and the limited German supply of fuel, dramatically limited training, so that many German fighters that survived these encounters crashed on landing or takeoff. Given a degree of air superiority, the P-51s also caught many German fighters on the ground. However, the Germans always had more fighters than pilots, so the key battle, to destroy the German fighter pilot corps, was fought in the air. UCAS turns a very potent surface attack capability into a potent means of gaining air control. It also, of course, offers the possibility of catching many enemy fighters on the ground—and given the cost of modern aircraft, now there generally are not many more airplanes than pilots.

6. This is one (though not the only) aspect of carrier or fleet design: presenting a threat an enemy must counter, hence triggering a decisive battle victory in which one gains sea control. The U.S. maritime strategy of the 1980s looked at carrier operations in just this way—as a means of securing sea control, which the carriers would then help exploit. This was much the view the U.S. Navy had taken until about 1970, that sea control and power projection were two sides of the same coin (the two were explicitly separated in the 1970s). See the author's *Seapower as Strategy* (Annapolis: Naval Institute Press, 2003).

7. The *Vincennes* incident is applicable because it involved a missile system; in the air-to-air role, UCAS is essentially an automated part of a two-stage missile system. The *Vincennes* shot down the Iranian Airbus over the Strait of Hormuz because the system operator (the ship's commanding officer) had insufficient information. A fighter pilot would have done better because he would have followed standard operating procedures to visually identify the target before firing. A human pilot does not of course guarantee against such tragedies; Soviet pilots shot down two airliners (both Korean Air, one near Leningrad and one near Petropavlovsk) that had strayed into forbidden areas, as did an Israeli pilot, who shot down a Libyan airliner near the Dimona nuclear plant. During the Cold War U.S. naval fighter pilots often intercepted Soviet bombers near or over the fleet, escorting them away without firing; there was no thought that the fleet could become a no-fly zone. That did create a problem—that the Soviets might do exactly the same thing to support

a surprise attack, in accordance with their doctrine of fighting for the "first salvo." In a war game a solution was found: As tensions increased, the president told the Soviets over the hot line that any flight within fifty miles of task group center would be considered an act of war. That did not work, but it illustrates just how ambiguous air-to-air encounters can be in situations short of war. Such situations are all different from the sort of air-to-air action U.S. fighters encountered over Iraq, because in that case all aircraft were either friendly or enemy, never of ambiguous or civilian status.

8. In the late 1950s the threat that most worried U.S. air defense planners was possible Soviet use of large numbers of ground-launched decoys to accompany their bombers. They knew that their resources, though large, were finite; mass use of inexpensive decoys would exhaust them. The United States developed a ground-launched decoy of its own but did not field it. Ground launching was important because it prevented the air defense system from distinguishing decoys from ground-launched aircraft (it was presumably expected that future over-the-horizon or even space-borne radars would see enemy bombers as soon as they became airborne).

9. The combination of high capability (against high aircraft performance and stealth) and wide-area coverage is expensive, and world production rates of such systems are limited. When the Cold War ended, it was surprising how many earlier systems the Soviets had felt compelled to retain. The Russians are now the main suppliers of high-end systems to countries likely to be hostile to the United States; system production rates are typically fewer than ten per year to supply all customers. Shorter-range systems, the sort that would be used to protect a brigade on the move, are far more numerous, but presumably an airplane or UCAV could release missiles outside their range. It is often forgotten that our potential enemies must pay for high-end systems at rising prices using increasingly scarce resources.

10. That is a considerable advantage, as a human pilot operating at a distance is under a distinct disadvantage. Flight commands are inevitably slightly delayed, and the human pilot lacks the feel of the airplane. In one case a pilot crashed a Predator that was in trouble because the corrective action he took was appropriate not to the slow Predator but to the fast fighters he had previously flown. Obviously there will be cases of system failure in which human intervention would be essential, as in manned aircraft. However, experience with long-endurance UAVs such as Global Hawk sug-

gests that they will be few, and the cost of such failures will have to be accepted as a trade-off against the great advantages of the UAV. Human pilots do crash their own aircraft, of course, and in that case the cost of a crash is far less acceptable. UAV crash rates are still considerably higher than those of manned aircraft, but they are declining much as manned aircraft rates have declined. It seems likely that they will soon be either equivalent to those of manned aircraft or substantially lower. Moreover, because UAVs fly only as needed, and never for pilot training, the total hours involved (hence the total number of accidents per UAV per year) are far lower.

11. Aircraft, manned or unmanned, have some subtle but vital advantages. It is extremely difficult to replenish shipboard vertical missile launchers at sea, but it is relatively easy to transfer weapons horizontally to a carrier. Surface missile stowage is also relatively inefficient: Ton for ton an aircraft carrier accommodates much more ammunition—about 2,000 tons for a 100,000-ton carrier but only about 50 tons of warheads on board a 10,000-ton cruiser (missile propulsion, equivalent to the carrier's aircraft, adds about another 150 tons for the cruiser). The proportion of weapons is about the same, but if the carrier's aircraft are considered part of the weapon system, the proportion tilts dramatically against the cruiser. That is why, in recent years, cruisers have fired their Tomahawks and then retired (to be relieved by other cruisers), whereas carriers have conducted sustained operations. Replacement of manned by unmanned aircraft would not change this equation. In air defense the fighters had the additional advantage over shipboard missiles that they could fly beyond the carrier's horizon, in what the Cold War U.S. Navy called the "Outer Air Battle." Alternative schemes in which an airplane controlled the missiles foundered because that airplane could not fight beyond the horizon over more than a single narrow sector, leaving other sectors open to attack. Sufficient numbers of fighters could cover multiple sectors. The strike equivalent of saturation by enemy aircraft coming from various directions is the need to protect scattered groups of ground troops against more or less simultaneous enemy ground threats. For more than a decade the Marine Corps requirement has been to receive support within ten minutes of a request—a considerable problem for a shipboard missile two hundred miles away, as Mach 1 is ten nautical miles per minute. The alternatives are either hypersonic missiles (which offer very limited payloads, if they are ever successful at all) and aircraft orbiting near the ground units.

Chapter 2. A Changing Tactical Environment

1. This perception lasted until 1994, when one of Saddam Hussein's sons-in-law defected and described nuclear facilities in places the coalition air forces had never been ordered to strike. They were identified by weapons inspectors and the Iraqis were forced to destroy them. The prewar failure of intelligence explains why, during the run-up to 2003 war, so many intelligence agencies around the world assumed that Saddam really had a nuclear program, that he was not bluffing. In effect his nuclear program had been the most valuable thing in his country, and he had previously managed to hide it effectively. In 1991 the problem was that the supporting United Nations resolution called simply for ejecting Iraqi forces from Kuwait, not for disarming Iraq or eliminating its nuclear programs. However, from a U.S. point of view, it was essential that Saddam be denied the dominance of the Persian Gulf a successful nuclear program would have supplied. To this extent the initial strategic bombing phase cannot be evaluated in terms of its effect on the subsequent ground war to liberate Kuwait.

2. We are familiar with mass wars with well-defined front lines because from the nineteenth century on a combination of mechanized food production and mechanized transport supported mass armies. Prior to the American Civil War, mass armies were difficult or impossible to field (even Napoleon, who benefitted from a large-scale draft, typically maneuvered around Europe rather than occupying an extended World War I–style front line).

3. It is arguable that even had the United States overrun North Vietnam, Communists there would have continued to fight from a sanctuary in China. It is not clear whether the North Vietnamese population would have supported such a fight, had it felt that unification with South Vietnam was at hand on favorable terms. Communist governments that seemed secure (as in East Germany) turned out in 1989 to enjoy remarkably little popular support; the collapse of the Soviet state was also surprisingly quick.

4. We now know that in 1967 some North Vietnamese seriously considered abandoning the war in the south. They were dissuaded by the Chinese, roughly as the Soviets had dissuaded the Chinese from abandoning the war in Korea in 1951. At this time the Soviets were less than enthusiastic backers of the North Vietnamese out of a fear (which seems grossly misplaced to us) that the war could somehow escalate to nuclear combat; a well-connected Soviet journalist said at the time that the Soviet Union put up 80 percent of the weapons

used by North Vietnam but had only 20 percent influence. After the Paris peace talks began in 1968, the Soviets decided that the war was safe to fight. After President Nixon opened relations with the Chinese, the Chinese tried to restrain the North Vietnamese. The Russians now saw a North Vietnamese victory as a way to gain a position outflanking China in the south. In 1975 the Russians promised the North Vietnamese that they would replace whatever the North Vietnamese lost if they carried out their planned conventional attack on South Vietnam, and that made the attack a reasonable proposition.

5. Enemy forces in South Vietnam were a mixture of regular North Vietnamese troops and Viet Cong units raised in the south as a kind of auxiliary force. Both depended on North Vietnam as a logistical base.

6. Unfortunately U.S. success during Tet was masked by ineptitude; the U.S. Army presented Tet not as a victory but as a disaster justifying more troops.

7. The Saudi government, which provided the logistical base for the war, also had strong reasons for not wanting to destroy the Sunni-led Iraqi state, and that in itself may have been decisive.

8. The historical precedent is the situation in the Ukraine in 1941, when the Germans invaded. The Germans were warmly welcomed as conquerors of the Bolsheviks, who had massacred Ukrainians in the 1930s. They ruined their welcome by their racist attacks on the local population.

9. The Pakistani government supported the Taliban in hopes that they would reciprocate by recognizing the border. Even though dependent on the Pakistani government for their finances, the Taliban refused to do so. The situation is even more complicated because Pakistan regards a friendly Afghanistan as a valuable rear area in its continuing fight against the Indians over Kashmir, an issue too close to the center of Pakistani national values to be truly negotiable. Thus the Pakistani intelligence agencies that first financed the Taliban undoubtedly wish to preserve a portion of the Taliban they regard as friendly. Many Pakistanis apparently fear that losing part of their territory (Waziristan) to Afghanistan will unravel the rest.

10. The situation became far more confused as many Shi'ites armed themselves to deal with the Sunnis and, naturally, with each other. The central government has only limited legitimacy.

11. Land lines might obviate the problem, but few Third World countries are adequately wired; they usually depend on cell phones and wireless networks, all subject to intercept. This is one reason that electronic intelligence has become so important in both Iraq and Afghanistan.

Chapter 3. A New Way of War: The New Technology

1. I have made this argument in greater detail in *The Fifty-Year War: Conflict and Strategy in the Cold War* (Annapolis: Naval Institute Press, 2000). That the book was taken seriously is suggested by the fact that in 2001 it won the Westminster Medal of the Royal United Services Institute as the best military history book published the previous year (a senior British Foreign Office specialist in Soviet affairs was among the jurists). Ogarkov's repeated calls for reconnaissance-strike complexes will be familiar to anyone reading the mass of translated Soviet military writings of the early 1980s (he was dismissed in 1985, when Gorbachev came to power). It seems fairly clear that Americans were unaware of just how few small computers the Soviets were then producing or of just how integral such computers were to U.S. military systems. Usually the Strategic Defense Initiative (Star Wars) program is credited with Gorbachev's industrial crisis, but Star Wars was only one of several applications of microcomputers (it took masses of small computers to produce either more missile killers [like "Brilliant Pebbles"] or the missiles and decoys to overcome them). There were of course other factors, such as the naïve belief among Soviet leaders that the United States could accomplish whatever technical miracles its leaders could describe. In effect Gorbachev sought a truce in the arms competition to allow the Soviet Union time to catch up. The Reagan administration was happy to agree, provided Gorbachev told his own people (as he was telling Reagan) that the struggle had been suspended. Gorbachev found it impossible to motivate Soviet workers without that claim of struggle (this motivation may have worn out anyway) and found himself offering liberalization as an alternative. The path from reconnaissance-strike complexes to perestroika and then to the downfall of the Soviet Union was lengthy and indirect, but it seems clear in retrospect.

2. Land bases may be provided much closer to the battle zone, as in Vietnam. In that war they proved quite vulnerable to insurgent attacks (destroying many aircraft, not the bases themselves). Presumably much the same would apply to future air campaigns against insurgents. Land bases are also subject to political attack, causing their withdrawal, as has happened in countries neighboring Afghanistan.

3. From the point of view of maximum air effort, it would be preferable to keep the carrier as close as possible to

the targets. After the Cold War the U.S. Navy accepted the short-range F/A-18 Hornet as its sole attack aircraft because it doubted that it would have to hit targets more than about two hundred miles from the carrier. Efforts by countries such as China to develop effective anti-access weapons make it likelier that future carrier operations will be conducted, at least initially, at maximum range—at which persistence near the targets becomes a real issue. Afghanistan demonstrated the need for carrier air range because the carriers in the Arabian Sea were so far from their targets. They were still the only nearby tactical air bases, as the closest friendly country, Pakistan, could not accept U.S. combat aircraft on its territory. Thus the war in southeast Afghanistan—Taliban home country—was fought mainly by carrier attack aircraft, heavily refueled in flight. The tankers were based elsewhere in the region.

Chapter 4. The Need for Transformation

1. The Chinese, for example, have advertised the guided version of their DF-21 ballistic missile as a way of neutralizing U.S. aircraft carriers that otherwise might intervene in a future Taiwan Strait crisis. It is by no means obvious that the system in which DF-21 is embedded suffices to guide it effectively. However, it is obvious that a DF-21 system trying to intercept a carrier at much greater range, providing effective air cover for Taiwan despite its range thanks to UCAS, would present the Chinese with a far more difficult targeting problem and us with much more potential for decoying. Moreover, much of what would happen in the Strait would be, in effect, a poker game. The Chinese hope that their DF-21 move causes us to fold; we would hope that something that appeared to neutralize DF-21 would cause them to fold. A combination of UCAS and fleet missile defense (SM-3) would seem to fill that bill.

2. In the early 1980s the author studied fighter costs for Grumman, specifically comparing the Hellcat to the F-14, taking into account lifetime and inflation since 1945. The F-14 was still far more expensive; the increase in cost could be justified only by the fact that a much smaller number of F-14s could execute the same fleet air defense mission that required a cloud of Hellcats in 1945.

3. Production runs declined through the Cold War, as individual airplanes became more expensive. World War II–style area bombing became impossible, despite claims from time to time that places had been carpet-bombed by B-52s. Strategic bombing survived as a concept only because the immense increase in firepower due to nuclear weapons balanced off the decline in numbers. The World War II B-29 could deliver ten tons of bombs, so a thousand-bomber raid delivered 10 kilotons of TNT. A single B-52 probably can deliver about 25 tons, so a carpet raid by fifty such aircraft (which would be a remarkably large raid) could deliver 750 tons, an eighth of a very large World War II raid. The B-52 in turn has a large capacity because it was designed to deliver 10,000-pound nuclear weapons; later strategic bombers were designed for much smaller weapons.

4. Adm. William Frederick Halsey seems to have had this point in mind when he explained that he could not split his battleships from his carrier force when he went north in pursuit of the Japanese carrier force (which turned out to be a decoy). The issue arose because there had been a contingency plan for Halsey to form his battleships into a separate force, Task Force 34, specifically to cover the invasion area against a Japanese surface force. When the Japanese surface force actually appeared, Adm. Chester W. Nimitz, the naval commander for the Pacific theater, famously signaled Halsey to ask, "Where is Task Force 34?" as the Japanese seemed to be on the brink of overrunning the transports off the beach at Leyte Gulf. They were defeated by the heroic action of a light force intended to support the landing, in the Battle off Samar.

5. This was the late Col. William S. Boyd, USAF, who used the Battle of France as a prime example of his OODA-loop analysis of combat. Boyd pointed out how puzzling the French defeat was at the time; the French had adequate forces (in total). Despite claims to the contrary, they fought well (inflicting considerable casualties on the Germans) and their generals were willing to fight (despite claims that they hated the Third Republic). To Boyd the key was that the French decision cycle was so slow; the French could not anticipate what the Germans were doing and hence could not react. Strong evidence supporting Boyd is that contemporary accounts have the Germans popping up unexpectedly again and again. In Boyd's view the French government in effect suffered a nervous breakdown because it could not imagine any effective counterstroke. French belief that breakthroughs were impossible may explain the famous lack of a mass of reserves in 1940. When the French premier told Winston Churchill that France had been defeated, Churchill asked where the reserves were and was told they did not exist.

6. However, command and control practices were rad-

ically different, the Soviets insisting on rigid control from above, whereas American doctrine envisaged far more initiative at lower levels. The comparison between a Soviet offensive and a British defensive came from the British, who very long ago had trained the Iraqis. An important factor in Iraqi performance was that Saddam Hussein feared that aggressive ground commanders might try to overthrow him. He much preferred inventive fortifiers. The U.S. AirLand doctrine used in Iraq was actually modeled on German World War II doctrine, in particular on the idea that orders should be about objectives and not about how they were to be reached, what the Germans called Auftragstaktik. The offensive flavor of AirLand battle came from the perception that defensive depth was needed but that the necessary depth should be gained on the other side of the inter-German border. That in turn might encourage Central Europeans to help, because they might feel that NATO could liberate them. Presumably the Soviets found all of this profoundly threatening once Poland became unstable (from 1980 on).

7. Col. William Glantz, USA (Ret.), seems to have been the first to realize this. He found that, contrary to what the Germans always said, given very heavy Soviet losses, by 1944 both sides on the eastern front had about the same overall strength. It was deception that gave the Soviets their vital local superiority. Later a former KGB agent, Pavel Sudoplatov, claimed in his memoirs that he had been the case officer for the single Russian who had sent the vital deceptive messages. Under his guidance Rudolf Abel (who was arrested as a Soviet spy in New York in 1957) presented himself to the Nazis during the period of the Soviet-German Pact as a disaffected officer eager to provide secret intelligence. The Germans failed to infiltrate the Soviet general staff, so they regarded Abel as their star agent. It seems remarkable that the Germans fell for disinformation in both their Eastern and Western theaters, the latter to the British Double-Cross System. The earliest success of Soviet deception, according to Glantz, was to distort the German picture of Soviet deployments in June 1941, obscuring the existence of large armored units. Tactical incompetence made this success pointless, but as the Soviet army became more competent deception became effective.

8. The ASW (antisubmarine warfare) transformation using SOSUS, HF/DF (high frequency direction finder), and aircraft is described in detail in Cross Associates, *Sea-Based Airborne Antisubmarine Warfare 1940–1977*, published in 1977 at the secret level and

declassified on 31 December 1990. A copy is in the U.S. Navy Operational Archives, Naval Heritage and Historical Center.

Chapter 5. What Pilots Do—and Need Not Do

1. This flexibility may be somewhat illusory. During World War II many fighters were described as fighter-bombers. However, their pilots were apparently generally trained mainly for one role or the other. My source is the memoirs of a British naval fighter pilot who was retrained specifically as a Corsair attack pilot and no longer considered himself effective in air-to-air combat. For the U.S. Navy much the same distinction applied to scout and dive bomber pilots, who flew the same airplanes (for much of the war, SBD Dauntlesses) but were organized into separate scout and bomber squadrons. The ability of modern pilots to be dual-roled may reflect a reduced need to understand the details of air-to-surface attack, since the airplane's mission computer conducts much of the attack once the target has been designated.

2. Rules of engagement (ROE) should be distinguished from whoever is decision maker. Some ROEs empower the pilot as primary decision maker. In other cases the targeter is the decision maker; in the past that has been the case in strikes against fixed targets. The case of a target struck on the basis of imagery provided by the airplane to a distant interpreter working with a distant command authority is particularly complex.

3. This refers to the OODA-loop idea, in which it is assumed that military operations are cyclical: observation, orientation (interpretation of observation), decision, and action, after which the cycle begins anew. An enemy whose OODA loop is significantly slower than ours falls out of phase and finds himself reacting to actions several cycles back. The Taliban collapse in Afghanistan seems to have been an OODA-loop victory. Of course hardware cannot guarantee a fast OODA cycle, but without the right equipment the cycle cannot be fast enough.

4. The situation is different when there is a well-defined front line (FEBA, or forward edge of battle area), in which case the area beyond the FEBA may be (in effect) a free-fire zone. However, in recent cases from the former Yugoslavia on, there have been few or no free-fire zones, because friendlies or neutrals have always been mixed with combatants.

5. About 1912 the Royal Navy had to choose between two fire-control computer systems, the Dreyer Table (which was part of a semimanual system) and the more automated Argo Clock developed by Pollen.

Dreyer's was largely a means of smoothing data and making predictions from the smoothed data. It was somewhat simplistic in operation and its solutions were likely not to be correct for long. Dreyer's view was that all inputs were faulty, and the human operator would make the crucial difference. Pollen was a lawyer; in his experience people *were* the problem. He sought the maximum degree of automation. Many British gunnery officers regarded Pollen as a genius who alone truly understood gunnery, and they regarded his clock as the future of scientific fire control. The Admiralty bought Dreyer's device, probably mainly because it made possible a new short-range tactic. Pollen made little provision for human correction of his fire-control solution, and in its initial form it might not have been very successful (a Pollen ship, HMS *Queen Mary*, does seem to have made excellent shooting at Jutland before being destroyed). However, it contained the seeds of all later fire-control systems (which did take corrections very much into account). One irony of the story is that the Admiralty apparently dumped Pollen because he refused to cut his prices; at the same time the Admiralty was encouraging Barr & Stroud, who made their rangefinders, to develop an analogous system even though they had granted Pollen a monopoly contract. The outbreak of World War I badly slowed the efforts of Barr & Stroud, so that they completed their design only after the Admiralty had derived one it preferred, using some elements of Pollen's clock. Barr & Stroud obtained permission to export its system, the Admiralty having rejected it. Ultimately it formed the basis of Italian and Japanese fire-control systems, and apparently the Italian system in turn was the basis of the one on board the German battleship *Bismarck* when it sank HMS *Hood*, which had a Dreyer Table. One advantage of the Pollen and Barr & Stroud systems was that their degree of automation made it easier for a partly trained crew to make hits; the Dreyer Table required far more elaborate teamwork. The *Bismarck* had had little time for training, so without an automated computer system it probably would not have sunk *Hood*. HMS *Prince of Wales*, which made an ultimately fatal hit on *Bismarck*, also had an automated system and a raw crew. For a more detailed account, see this author's *Naval Firepower: Battleship Gunnery in the Dreadnought Era* (Annapolis: Naval Institute Press, 2008).

6. It can, however, become an issue when the situation is ambiguous, for example, when the vehicle on a targeted bridge may be either a bus or a personnel carrier. How serious the issue is depends on how intense the war is. Errors that might be dismissed as minor misfortunes in a war like World War II or even Vietnam become major disasters in a much smaller and more ambiguous war such as in Kosovo.

7. Automatic target recognition does not in itself increase attack range, but it increases the range at which a pilot may feel that he can lock on his missile. It also reduces communication; the pilot can simply say that he has locked onto the planned target instead of sending back his sensor data.

8. The current ROE calls for the fighter to fly at a minimum of 1,500 feet, and fighter pilots say that they can distinguish, say, a bus from an armored personnel carrier (APC) painted in school bus color. Pilots are trained to default to safe—*not* to attack unless they are sure the target is legitimate. In the Kosovo war the combination of enemy hand-held surface-to-air missiles and fear (by political authorities) of NATO casualties caused pilots to be restricted to much higher altitudes, and Serbian decoys proved quite effective; it appears, for example, that no Serbian tanks at all were hit.

9. The problem was not automation so much as an attempt by the ship's combat decision crew to understand what was happening. The *Vincennes* and the frigate *Sides* were both conducting surveillance of the Iranian airfield at Bandar Abbas when the Airbus took off. Each ship's combat system assigned the new target a track number. Because the *Sides* detected the Airbus first, it assigned a lower number. The two ships passed data back and forth, their combat systems trying to create a common picture by eliminating double counts. Thus the track on board the *Vincennes* received the number *Sides* had assigned, but those on board the *Vincennes* did not know that because the system was not rigged to display these numbers. The display was two-dimensional, so in order to find out whether this airplane was climbing or diving, those in the combat direction center had to key in the track number. Unfortunately another group of ships using (illegally) the same block of track numbers was operating nearby at the same time. Because ships passed their data by HF radio, the two groups inadvertently merged their data. Worse, the track number the *Vincennes* had assigned to the Airbus was assigned by this group to an A-6 Intruder landing on a carrier. Thus when an officer on board the vessel keyed in what he (wrongly) thought was the Airbus track number, he saw, to his horror, that this airplane was diving—as it should have been to land on the carrier. It seems clear that an overly pessimistic intelligence briefing had already

convinced the ship's commander that the Iranians were likely to make a kamikaze attack that weekend (July Fourth weekend). It also happened that the *Vincennes* had an early version of the Aegis system whose display computer could show only the centerline of the air corridor Iranian airliners could safely fly. The Airbus track was off the centerline but inside the corridor—and that was not at all obvious. Probably no one could imagine so elaborate an application of Murphy's law. The disaster can be traced in part to a design assumption, long forgotten, that there would never be more than one data link net (Link 11 net) operating in proximity. Ironically the *Vincennes* had been sent to the Persian Gulf specifically to clean up Link 11 practice (the problem was that two groups were using the same block of track numbers).

Index

Ababil UAVs, 100, 128–29

Abu Dhabi UAVs, 96, 174

AD-150 UAVs, 221–22

Advanced UAVs, 119

Aegis air defense system, 1, 10, 249n1, 249n2

Aequare UAVs, 79

Aerolight UAVs, 132

Aerosonde UAVs, 222, 223

Aerostar UAVs, 130–31, 162, 167

Afghanistan: air presence over, 7; aircraft carrier basing of aircraft, 252–53n3; base facilities for operations in, 6; insurgency warfare, 15, 18, 19–21, 22–23; Kandahar, 47, 48; mass strikes against, 31; Predators over, 9; resistance movements, 19; Taliban, 20–21, 47, 48, 252n9, 254n3; target recognition by pilots, 15–16, 30, 54; UAV use in, 95; warfare in, 15, 44; zone divisions for air support over, 5

African Eagle UAVs, 100

Agile UAVs, 119, 120

air defenses: decapitation of, 64; decoys and mass attacks, 7, 250n8; fighter use versus shipboard missiles, 251n11; high-quality wide-area systems, 8, 250n9; mass strikes against, 31; swarm of UAVs and, 6–8

Air Force, U.S.: air tasking order (ATO) technique, 26; interservice cooperation, 79; interservice rivalries, 1; pilots for UAVs, 66, 71, 200; propeller-driven versus jet aircraft, 36; target assignment and engagement, 64; UAV wing, 201

Air Guard UAVs, 194

aircraft: advantages of UCAS over, 1–2, 5–6, 11, 29, 45, 47–48, 55–59; affordability of manned aircraft, 168; air coverage, importance of, 5–6; air presence with, 6–7, 12, 251n11; airframe materials, 57; attrition, 56, 57, 58; base facilities for, 6; bomber force, 39; cost of, 34–35, 36, 37, 57, 58–59, 253nn2–3; landings,

takeoffs, stress, and fatigue, 55–56, 58; maintenance and spares, 55–56, 58; manned reconnaissance, retirement and replacement of, 12–13, 81–87; Marine Corps aircraft, 195; mass and dispersed precision attacks with, 25; mass strikes by, 12; missile use against, 253n1; mission computers, 48–49; obsolescence issues, 57; precision strikes from, 22; propeller-driven, 36; reconnaissance from, 3, 66–67, 75; routing of, 5; surface weapons use versus manned or unmanned aircraft, 12, 251n11; swarm of, 12; target aircraft, 69; Tomahawk comparison, 63–65. See also fighter aircraft; pilots

aircraft carriers: ammunition carried by, 64, 251n11; automatic landing systems, 14; as base facilities, 3, 6, 29, 31–32, 252–53n3; battle group strategy, 5; cost to build and operate, 57–59; design of, 2–3, 4; flight deck operations and UCAVs, 13, 14; fueling requirements, 56–57; maintenance and spares, 56; maritime strategy and, 250n6; mass and dispersed precision attacks from, 25; naval warfare strategy and, 1–2; submarine warfare and, 56–57; supply line, length of, 1–2, 3–4; transfer of missiles at sea, 25, 64, 251n11; transformation of navy to carrier fleet, 35–36; unmanned vehicles flown from, 1–2

air-launched UAVs, 73

air-to-air refueling, 6, 12, 14, 65, 207–8

air-to-air weapons, 3, 249–50n5

Aist UAVs, 168

Aladin UAVs, 116, 119–20

Albatros UAVs, 184

Alenia UAVs, 146

Algeria, 19, 173, 174

ALO UAVs, 176, 177

Alouette helicopter, 142, 143

Aludra UAVs, 157

Amber UAVs, 90, 236
Angel UAVs, 100
Angola, 130
Anjian UAVs, 3, 101, 102
antiguerilla techniques, 22
antiradar missiles, 66, 119, 193
antisubmarine warfare, 43
APID UAVs, 178
AQM-34 drones, 92
AQM-91 drone, 38
Aquila UAVs, 79, 80, 86, 193, 243
Arcturus T-15, 10
Argentina, 96–98, 148
Ari UAVs, 183
armed reconnaissance, 30
Army, U.S.: Camcopter UAVs, 98; control of air vehicles, 71; interservice cooperation, 79; N-LOS missiles, 65–66; organization of units, 194; reconnaissance systems, 75–78, 79
ASIO UAVs, 147
ASN-15 UAVs, 102
ASN-104/105/106 UAVs, 102–3, 105
ASN-206/207/209 UAVs, 103, 104
asymmetric warfare, 18
ATLANTE UAVs, 176–77
Australia, 159, 222
Austria, 98, 174
automation: automatic takeoff and landing systems (ATLS), 73, 130; heroism, sacrifice, and, 50; human judgment and creativity and, 51–52, 53–54, 254–55n5, 255–56n9; military effectiveness and, 46–48; paths to, 48; target assignment and engagement and, 48–50
Autonomous Systems Technology Related Airborne Evaluation and Assessment (ASTRAEA), 75
AVE-C/AVE-D UAVs, 126–27

Backlight UAVs, 223
Banshee drone, 108, 110, 158
Barrakuda UAVs, 93, 117, 119, 120, 121
base facilities, 3, 6, 29, 31–32, 252n2
Bat UAVs: DP-7 UAVs, 224–25; KillerBee, 231
Bateleur UAVs, 100, 173–74
BATMAV, 247
battleships, 35–36, 253n4
Baykus UAVs, 182, 183
Bayonet UAVs, 224–25
Bayraktar UAVs, 182–83
Belgium, 78, 98, 139
Bird Eye UAVs, 132, 134, 145, 162, 163, 169
Black Lynx UAVs, 146
Black Shadow UAVs, 187

Black Widow UAV, 6, 246
Blue Horizon UAVs, 133, 134, 170
Boomerang UAVs, 224–25
Border Eagle Mk II UAVs, 159
Botswana, 134
BQM-34. *See* Firebee drones
BQM-74 UAVs, 79–80, 87
BQM-145 UAVs, 87, 240, 241
BQM-155 Hunter, 208, 243
BRAVE 200 UAVs, 193
Bravo UAVs, 158, 159
Brevel (Eurodrone), 118, 120–21
Broadsword UAVs, 222
Burraq UAVs, 159
Buster UAVs, 222–23
Butterfly UAVs, 133
Buzard UAVs, 113

Cabure UAVs, 96–97
Calere UAVs, 79
Camcopter UAVs, 96, 98, 99, 119
Canada: live-fire exercise, 30, 54; UAVs, 78, 98–100, 112, 137, 145, 238, 242
CARAPAS UAVs, 112, 115–16
Cardinal UAVs, 181
cargo aircraft, 73
Castor UAVs, 179–80
Cee Bee Project, 195
CEM-138 jammer, 193
Centurion UAVs, 197–98
CH-1 UAVs, 102
CH-3 UCAVs, 101, 102
China: DF-21 ballistic missiles, 253n1; guerrilla warfare, 19; ocean surveillance, 57; reconnaissance over, 82, 88, 89; UAV technology transfer, 132–33; UAVs, 3, 84, 100–106, 107, 163, 203; Vietnam War and, 17, 251–52nn3–4
Chukar drones, 79–80, 86, 94, 145, 148
Chung Shyang UAVs, 181
CK-1 UAVs, 102, 163
CL-89/289 drones, 71, 78, 95, 98–100, 115, 117, 145, 146, 181
close air support, 16, 17, 197, 199
Colibri UAVs, 168
combat air patrols (CAPs), 12, 50, 202
communication: bandwidth and reliability of, 46, 50–51, 52; cell phones and wireless networks, 22, 252n11; communication intelligence (COMINT), 85; data links, 65, 71, 93; radio communications, 38, 40
Compass Arrow UAVs, 89
Compass Cope UAVs, 87, 89–90, 91
Compass Dwell UAVs, 89

Compass Gull UAVs, 89–90

computer technology, 43–44, 48–49, 51–52, 53–54, 255–56n9

Condor UAVs, 90, 235

conventional warfare, 15–19

Cooperative Engagement Capability (CEC), 6, 13–14, 249n2

Copter 4 UAVs, 114

Corax UAVs, 190, 191, 192

Cormorant submarine UAVs, 195, 223–24

Corporal missile, 77

Coyote SL-UAVs, 244–45

CQ-10 Snow Goose, 214

Crécerelle UAVs, 95, 108, 110–13. *See also* Sperwer UAVs

Crex-B UAVs, 148

Croatia, 106, 134

cruise missiles, 8, 12, 13, 52, 57–58, 69–70

CT 20 jet target, 78, 107

Cyber Eye UAVs, 157–58

Cyber Shark UAVs, 157, 158

Czech Republic, 106–7

Czechoslovakia, 164

D-4RD UAVs, 103

D-21 Tagboard, 87–88

Dakota UAVs, 225

Dan-Baruk/Dan-M UAVs, 168–69

Dark Star UAVs, 9, 91, 193, 204–6

decentralized warfare, 16, 19–23

Denmark, 112

Dependable UAVs, 224

Desert Hawk UAVs, 159–60, 185, 190, 225–26

Dominator UAVs, 131–32

Doyosae UAVs, 155

Dozor UAVs, 167–68

DP series UAVs, 224–25

Dragon Drone UAVs, 227

Dragon Eye UAVs, 10, 95, 194, 214, 215–16

Dragonfly UAVs, 133, 134

Drone Anti-Submarine Helicopter (DASH), 34, 80, 94, 119, 122, 152

Drone de Reconnaissance au Contact (DRAC), 109, 114, 116, 118, 145

drones, 70

DUSTER program, 195

DVF 2000 UAVs, 114–15

Eagle 150 ARVs, 157

Eagle Eye PI/PII UAVs, 160

Eagle Eye tilt-rotor UAVs, 110, 195, 226–27

Eagle UAVs, 138

Eclipse UAVs, 186, 191

EFE UAVs, 183

Egypt, 86–87, 240, 243

Eitan UAVs, 137–38

electronic countermeasure (ECM) drones, 92

electronic intelligence (ELINT) and reconnaissance, 3, 12, 29–30, 84–85, 252n11

electronic support (ES), 12

electro-optical devices, 72

England. *See* United Kingdom

Épervier drones, 78, 98, 107

Euro Hawk UAVs, 119, 176, 208

Eurodrone (Brevel), 118, 120–21

Evolution UAVs, 10, 216

Excalibur UAVs, 227, 228

Exdrone UAVs, 227, 229

expeditionary warfare, 16, 24, 36–37

F-14 aircraft, 8, 35, 47, 253n2

F-15 aircraft, 36

F/A-18 Hornet, 252–53n3

Falco UAVs, 146–47, 149, 153, 158

Falcon UAVs, 153, 154, 181

Falconer UAVs, 75–77

Fancopter UAVs, 120, 122

Fantail ducted-fan VTOL UAVs, 172, 173

fast armed UAVs, 206

fighter aircraft: cost of, 34–35, 253nn2–3; jet fighters, 36; longevity of, 34–35; precision strikes, 35; propeller-driven aircraft, 36; swarm of, 12, 251n11; swarm of air vehicles and, 4, 249–50nn4–5; World War II use, 6, 34–35, 71, 249–50n5

FILUR UAVs, 179

Finder UAVs, 227–28, 229

Finland, 107, 108, 180

Fire Scout UAVs, 105, 119, 194, 195, 211, 212, 213, 232

Firebee drones, 70, 81–86, 89, 92–93, 94–95, 102, 129, 195, 240

Firebird UAVs, 187

Firefly UAVs, 81, 84, 102, 160

Flamingo UAVs, 161

FLAVIIR UAVs, 186, 191

Flying Forward Observation System (FFOS), 152–53

FM-07 UAVs, 157

forward edges of battle area (FEBA), 254n4

FoxCar UAVs, 246

France: Algeria, defeat in, 19; CL-89/289 drones, 99–100; combat experience with UAVs, 95; command and control capabilities, 39–40; international UAVs, 126–27; MidCAS, 75, 180; *mitrailleuse,* 37; offensive and defensive doctrines, 38, 39–40, 45, 253n5; tank development, 32, 39–41, 45; UAVs, 107–17, 137, 139; weapon sales to Israel, 86 free-fire zone, 254n4

French Indochina, 19

Gagam UAVs, 123–24

Gator UAVs, 224

Germany: blitzkrieg, 32, 38; bomber force, 39; bombing of German troops, 37; CL-89/289 drones, 99–100; combat experience with UAVs, 95; deceptive Soviet messages, 42, 254n7; fighter aircraft during World War II, 6, 71, 249–50n5; international UAVs, 126; MidCAS, 75, 180; offensive and defensive doctrines, 39, 41–42, 45, 253n5; rail communication, 15; resistance movements, 18–19; shock attack tactics, 38; tank warfare, 37–42; UAVs, 78, 93, 117–23, 137, 158, 208, 214

Global Hawk UAVs: automatic takeoff and landing systems (ATLS), 130; collision avoidance, 74; combat experience with, 95; development and specifications, 40, 71, 72, 74, 91, 193, 206–8; funding for, 204; Navy use of, 203; refueling of, 6, 7; system failures and, 250–51n10; UAVs similar to, 89, 100, 101, 204; use of by other countries, 119, 153, 171, 176

Global Observer UAVs, 198, 228–29, 230

Global Positioning System (GPS), 2, 7, 27, 28, 49, 64

GlobIHA UAVs, 183

Gnat UAVs, 90, 91, 92, 181–82, 194, 200, 202, 203

Golden Eagle UAVs, 173

GoldenEye UAVs, 229–30, 231

Gray Eagle UAVs, 202

Great Britain. *See* United Kingdom

Greece, 112, 123, 126–27, 130

ground fire as evidence of hostility, 15–16, 30, 54

ground forces: air coverage for, 5–6; economic issues, 34; equipment and resources for, 16; guerrilla forces, 17–19, 22; mass armies, 24, 251n2; mobility of forces, 44; nuclear weapons and, 75; organic firepower and, 24; size of, 16, 24, 30; stand-off support for, 30; UAV reconnaissance for, 66–67; UAV unit level designations, 72, 194; value of and confidence provided by, 23

Guardian UAVs, 96

guerrilla forces and warfare, 17–19, 22

Gufone UAVs, 148

Gulfstream aircraft, 130, 208

Harfang UAVs, 137

Harpy drones, 66, 69, 70, 95, 119, 128

Have Lemon Project, 93, 195

Helios UAVs, 197, 198

Heliquad UAVs, 158

Hellcat fighters, 35, 253n2

Hellfire missiles, 8, 9, 201

Hermes UAVs: development and specifications, 133–36, 137; JUSTAS, 98; UAVs similar to, 124, 185; use of by other countries, 129, 145, 162, 169, 170, 173, 185, 190

Heron UAVs, 98, 108, 119, 136–38, 139, 140, 182, 202

Heros helicopter UAVs, 106–7

HERTI UAVs, 187–88, 191

Hezbollah, 100, 129, 130

High Altitude Airship (HAA), 230, 231

high-altitude long-endurance aircraft (HALE), 72

high-altitude reconnaissance, 29–30, 87–92

HOB-bit UAVs, 162, 163

Honest John rocket, 75, 76, 78

Hornet UAVs, 117, 160, 161

Horus UAVs, 203

HoverEye UAVs, 108–9, 110, 173

HUAV/PERSIUS, 230

Huma-1 UAVs, 158, 160–61

Hummingbird UAVs, 147, 218–20

Hungary, 163

Hunter UAVs: Belgian Hunter (B-Hunter), 98, 139; BQM-155 Hunter, 208, 243; combat experience with, 95; French Hunter (F-Hunter), 139; Israeli UAVs, 138–39, 194, 208; MQ-5 Hunter, 139, 209–10; replacement for, 108; RQ-5 Hunter, 71, 139, 193, 202, 208–9

hunter-killer UAVs, 230–31

India, 8, 123–26, 137, 143

Indonesia, 126, 143

Insight UAVs, 238, 239

insurgency warfare, 15, 18, 19–23, 44, 252n10

Integrator UAVs, 232

international UAVs, 126–27

Iran, 53, 54, 127–29, 250n7, 255–56n9

Iraq: air defense coordination in, 249n4; air defenses of, 63, 64; air-to-air action over, 250n7; base facilities in, 6; combat experience with UAVs in, 95; guerrilla forces and warfare, 18, 19; insurgency warfare, 19–20, 21–23, 252n10; nuclear infrastructure, 16, 251n1; offensive and defensive doctrines, 41, 253–54n6; targets, attacks on, 16; UAV use in, 71; UAVs, 164

Irkut UAVs, 167, 168

ISIS airship, 232–33

Israel: antiguerilla techniques, 22; attack UAVs, 93; drone reconnaissance, 86; Harpy drones, 66, 69, 70, 95, 119, 128; UAVs, 66, 70, 79, 94–95, 101, 118, 119, 128, 129–45, 167, 169, 170, 173, 180, 194, 208; weapon sales to, 86

Italy: CL-89/289 drones, 99–100; international UAVs, 126–27; MidCAS, 75, 180; UAVs, 75, 76, 78, 86, 115, 145–52, 158, 203

I-View UAVs, 124, 139–40, 141, 145, 169

Japan, 19, 152–53
Jasoos Joined-Wing UAVs, 161, 162
Joint Strike Fighter (JSF), 51, 64–65
Jordan, 153, 154
Jupiter IRBM, 77

Ka-37/137 UAVs, 170
Kayarel UAVs, 183
KD2R drones, 76
Kelley, P. X., 193
Kestrel UAVs, 181, 190, 191
KillerBee UAVs, 198, 231–32
Kingfisher II UAVs, 232
Kiwit UAVs, 174
Korshun UAVs, 166, 168
K-UCAV, 153–54
KUS-7/KUS-9 UAVs, 156
KZO UAVs, 119, 120–21, 123, 194

L15 airship, 233
La-17 UAVs, 102, 163
Lakshya UAVs, 124, 125
LALE UAVs, 171
LAMPS (Light Airborne Multipurpose System), 34,
    80–81, 94
Lance rocket, 75, 78
Learjet, 74
Lehman, John F., 193
LEMV airship, 233
Libya, 159
Lipán UAVs, 96, 97
Little Bird UAVs, 110
loitering missiles, 27, 64, 65–66, 69–70, 119, 193
Long Haul Eagle UAVs, 101
low-altitude long-endurance (LALE) air vehicles, 72
LUNA UAVs, 121–22, 123, 158

Mabat UAVs, 86
Magpie UAVs, 181
Mako UAVs, 233–34
Malaya/Malaysia, 19, 157–58
Malazgirt UAVs, 183–84
Manta UAVs, 242
Mantis UAVs, 186, 188–89
Marine Corps, U.S.: aircraft use by, 195; Harrier use by,
    5; interservice cooperation, 79; Kandahar, base near,
    47, 48; organization of units, 194; support requests,
    response time for, 251n11; Vietnam War and, 23
MART UAVs, 107–8
Mastiff UAVs, 79, 94–95, 129, 130, 140–41, 142, 170, 193
MAV-1 UAVs, 171–73
Maveric UAVs, 234

medium-altitude long-endurance aircraft (MALE), 72
Mercury UAVs, 133, 197
Merlin UAVs, 109, 111, 116
Metcalf, James, III, 1
Mexico, 134, 145, 158, 159
Microglider UAVs, 240
micro-UAVs, 44, 69, 72
Midair Collision Avoidance System (MidCAS), 75, 180
Midge UAVs, 189
Milano UAVs, 176–77
Mini-Falcon UAVs, 135, 141
Minion UAVs, 234
Mirach UAVs, 75, 76, 78, 86, 87, 112, 148–49, 150
Mirador UAVs, 109–10
Mirsad UAVs, 129
missiles: control of, 13, 64; DF-21 ballistic missiles, 253n1;
    limitations of, 25; loitering missiles, 27, 64, 65–66,
    69–70, 119, 193; mass and dispersed precision attacks
    with, 24–25; naval forces use of, 25; strike missiles,
    control of, 11–12; surface weapons use versus
    manned or unmanned aircraft, 12, 251n11; transfer
    of at sea, 25, 64, 251n11. See also cruise missiles;
    Tomahawk strike missiles
model aircraft, 69
Mohajer UAVs, 128, 129
Mohawk UAVs, 77–78
Molynx UAVs, 146
Morphing UAVs, 223–24
Mosquito UAVs, 101, 109–10, 141, 173
MQ series UAVs, 193
MQ-1 UCAVs, 199, 200, 201–2. See also Predators
MQ-5 Hunter, 139, 209–10
MQ-9 UCAVs. See Reaper UAVs
MQM-33 Quail, 75, 76, 81, 145, 148
MQM-36 Shelduck, 76
MQM-57 Falconer, 75–77
MQM-170/171 UAVs, 222
MQ-Ma/Mb/Mc UAVs, 199
MQ-X UAVs, 198–99, 200, 220–21, 236
Multi-Purpose Loitering Missile, 27

nano-UAVs, 69, 70, 197, 198
Nart UAVs, 168
naval warfare strategy, 1–2
Navy, U.S.: Acoustic Rapid COTS Insertion, 57; bomb
    guidance systems, 28; Broad Area Maritime
    Surveillance (BAMS), 203, 208; Cooperative
    Engagement Capability (CEC), 6, 249n2; fighter
    aircraft, number of, 34; interservice cooperation,
    79; interservice rivalries, 1; Marine Corps aircraft,
    responsibility for, 195; maritime strategy, 250n6;
    N-LOS missiles, 65–66; offensive tactics and

strategies, 42–43; Outer Air Battle, 251n11; propeller-driven versus jet aircraft, 36; reconnaissance systems, 76; scout and bomber squadrons, 254n1; short-range UAVs, 80–81; strike missiles, control of, 11–12; target assignment and engagement, 64–65; transformation of, 42–43

NB-X2 UAVs, 161, 162

Neptune UAVs, 10, 216–17

Netherlands, 108, 110–13, 119–20, 130

network-centric warfare, 2–3, 24, 26–28, 31–32, 45, 67

Neuron UAVs, 75, 112, 126–27, 151, 186

Nibbio UAVs, 115, 146, 149–50, 151

Night Intruder UAVs, 154–55, 156

NightEagle UAVs, 240

Nightjar UAVs, 191

Nirbhay UAVs, 125–26

Nishan II/X-1000 UAVs, 161–62

Nishant UAVs, 123, 124

Nite Panther/Nite Gazelle program, 94

Non–Line of Sight (N-LOS) missiles, 66, 69

North Atlantic Treaty Organization (NATO), 33, 41, 75, 78

Northern Ireland, 19

Norway, 120

Novel Air Capability Vision program, 186–87

NRUAV (Naval Rotary UAV), 125, 142, 143

nuclear weapons, 75

NX110m quad-copter UAVs, 109, 111

observe-orient-decide-act (OODA) loop, 24, 26, 38, 40, 48, 254n3

Observer UAVs, 76

ocean surveillance, 43, 57

Odysseus UAVs, 234–35

Orbiter UAVs, 142, 143, 145, 162–63

Orel (Oryol) UAVs, 165

Orion HALL UAVs, 235–36

Orka UAVs, 110, 113, 119

Osprey UAVs, 77, 78

Otus-B UAVs, 148

Outer Air Battle, 251n11

Outlaw UAVs, 222

Outrider UAVs, 107, 193, 210, 211, 222

OV-1 Mohawk, 77–78

Overseer UAVs, 77

Owl UAVs, 248

P-3/P-3C Orion, 36, 43, 95, 132, 243, 244

P-47 Thunderbolt, 36

P-51 fighters, 36, 249–50n5

PAAMS (Principal Anti-Air Missile System), 10

Pakistan, 22, 158–62, 203, 252n9, 252-253n3

Pathfinder/Pathfinder Plus UAVs, 93, 197

Patria UAVs, 107, 108

Patroller UAVs, 113–14

Pave Eagle UAVs, 88–89

Pawan UAVs, 123, 124

PAWS UAVs, 236, 237

Pchela UAVs, 165–66

Pegasus UAVs: Greek UAVs, 123; X-47A Pegasus, 14, 195, 196, 220

Peregrine UAVs, 87, 196–97, 198

Pershing missile, 77

persistent strike capability, 28–30

persistent surveillance, 28, 29–30

pervasive surveillance, 9–10, 11, 28, 31–32, 66–67

Phantom Ray UAVs, 236–37

Philippines, 19, 133

Phoenix UAVs, 95, 184, 185, 187, 189–90

Picador UAVs, 132, 133

picture-centric warfare. *See* network-centric warfare

pilots: control of air vehicles, 11–12, 66, 71, 200, 250–51n10; expertise of, need for, 13; fatigue of, 11, 18, 29, 52; flexibility of mission and, 48, 50; judgement and decision making, 7, 30, 46–47, 50, 53–54, 250n7, 254n2; manpower, machinery, and automation, 46–48; navigationally guided weapons and role of, 28; proficiency flying, 55, 56, 58; role in weapon systems, 51–54; safety of flights and, 52–53; target recognition by, 15–16, 30, 52, 54, 255nn6–8; training of, 57, 58, 254n1

Pioneer UAVs: combat experience with, 71, 95; development and specifications, 10, 132, 141, 142, 148, 193, 203–4, 205; retirement and replacement of, 194–95; UAVs similar to, 118

Pluton missile, 78

Pointer UAVs, 95, 116, 237

Poland, 19, 131, 162–63, 211

Polecat UAVs, 205–6

PQM-149/150 UAVs, 243

Praeire UAVs, 79

precision strikes, 17, 22, 24–25, 30–31, 35

Predators: combat experience with, 63, 71, 95; control of, 66, 71, 200, 250–51n10; crashes, 201, 202; development and specifications, 72, 90, 91–92, 94, 199–203, 204; Hellfire missiles carried by, 8, 9, 201; JUSTAS, 98; modifications to, 9; MQ-X UAVs, 199; reconnaissance with, 66, 67; speed of, 66; target assignment and engagement, 8, 11; UAV wing, 201; UAVs similar to, 101, 106; use of by other countries, 119, 145, 158, 185, 200, 203

Principal Anti-Air Missile System (PAAMS), 10

Proryv UAVs, 169

Prospector UAVs, 194

Prowler UAVs, 90

Puma UAVs, 237–38
PUNA UAVs, 126
PW-1/2 UAVs, 104

Qaeda, Al, 15, 20, 22
QF-4/16 UCAVs, 193, 199
QM series UAVs, 193
QU-22 Pave Eagle, 88–89
quad-copter (XM110m) UAVs, 109, 111
Quartz UAVs, 91, 205

R4E-40/50/100 UAVs, 243, 244
R20 drone, 86, 107
R-90 UAVs, 169–70
radar, 51–52, 72, 77, 80
radio communications, 38, 40
Raider UAVs, 87
Ranger UAVs, 180, 181
Rapid Eye UAVs, 235
RAPTOR program, 197
Raven UAVs: BUSTER, 223; replacement for, 245; RQ-11 Raven, 10, 162, 176, 214–15, 226, 237, 247; UK delta-wing UAVs, 188, 190, 191
Reaper UAVs: combat experience with, 63; development and specifications, 72, 94, 200, 212–14, 230–31; replacement for, 199; UAV wing, 201; UAVs similar to, 189; use of by other countries, 185–86, 212, 214
reconnaissance: from aircraft, 3, 66–67, 75; armed reconnaissance, 30; communication intelligence (COMINT), 85; electronic intelligence (ELINT) and reconnaissance, 3, 12, 29–30, 84–85, 252n11; high-altitude reconnaissance, 29–30, 87–92; limitations of, 3; network-centric warfare and, 2–3; ocean surveillance, 43, 57; permanent surveillance and sudden attacks, 67; persistent surveillance, 28, 29–30; pervasive surveillance, 9–10, 11, 28, 31–32, 66–67; real-time tactical reconnaissance, 78–80; tactical reconnaissance, 81–87; with UAVs, 66–67, 71–72, 75–95; warning provided to enemies during, 2, 3; weapon targeting and, 24, 26–28
Redstone missile, 77
Reliant Mauser UAVs, 190
Remez UAVs, 184
RemoEye UAVs, 96, 156–57
remotely piloted vehicle (RPV), 70
resistance movements, 18–19
Reys UAVs, 163, 164, 168
RMAX UAVs, 152, 153
Romania, 164, 211
RQ series UAVs, 193
RQ-14 UAVs, 10, 214, 215–16
Russia, 102, 163–70, 250n9

Rustom UAVs, 123, 124–25, 137
Ryan 147 drones, 81–86, 89, 92–93. *See also* Firebee drones
Ryan 154 drone, 38

S-4 UAVs, 158, 159
Saudi Arabia, 22
ScanEagle UAVs, 145, 158, 194, 198, 218, 238–40
Scarab UAVs, 87, 240, 241
Scorpio UAVs, 114–15, 118
Scout UAVs: development and specifications, 94–95, 129, 144; replacement for and improvement of, 138, 142, 193; use of by other countries, 130, 170, 173, 180
Sea ALL UAVs, 216
Seamos UAVs, 119, 122, 123
Searcher UAVs, 130, 132, 143–44, 145, 158, 162, 169, 170, 176, 181
Seeker UAVs, 173, 174, 175
Sentinel UAVs, 206
Sentry UCAV, 240, 241
Seraph UAVs, 100, 174–75
Sergeant missile, 77, 78
SH-1 UAVs, 104
Shadow Fox UAVs, 66
Shadow UAVs: collision avoidance, 74; Pakistani Shadow, 161, 162; RQ-7 Shadow, 129, 162, 193, 194, 195, 202, 210–12; Shadow 200 UAVs, 95, 131, 158, 210–11, 212; Shadow 400 UAVs, 212; Shadow 600 UAVs, 211, 212
SHARC (Scouting and Hunting Autonomous RotorCraft) UAVs, 122, 124
SHARC (Swedish Highly Advanced Research Configuration) UAVs, 179, 180
Shekarchi UAVs, 128
ships: battleships, 35–36, 253n4; naval warfare strategy and, 1; supply line, length of, 1–2, 3–4; transfer of missiles at sea, 25, 64, 251n11; unmanned vehicles flown from, 1–2
Shmel' UAVs, 165
shock attack tactics, 38
signal intelligence (SIGINT), 43
Silent Eye UAVs, 153, 154, 240
Silver Arrow UAVs, 111, 124, 132
Silver Fox UAVs, 95, 240, 242
Singapore, 130, 134, 143, 170–73
SIVA UAVs, 177
Skat UAVs, 169
Skeldar UAVs, 178–79
Skua drones, 173
Sky Owl UAVs, 243
Sky Rider UAVs, 130, 144
Sky Spy UAVs, 77
Sky Warrior UAVs, 199–200, 202, 210
Skyblade UAVs, 170–71

SkyEye UAVs, 243, 244
Skyforce UAVs, 242
Skylark UAVs, 10, 130, 144–45, 163
Skylite UAVs, 130, 145
Skylynx UAVs, 243
Skyraider UAVs, 242
Skywatcher UAVs, 242–43
Sky-X/Sky-Y UAVs, 150–51, 152
SLAM-ER missiles, 65
SL-UAVs, 199, 243–45
Smart Ball UAVs, 109
Smart Eye HALE aircraft, 96
SmartUAV, 156
Snooper UAVs, 77
Snow Goose UAVs, 214
Soar Dragon UAVs, 101
Soar Eagle UAVs, 101
SoFar UAVs, 162, 163
Sojka UAVs, 106, 107
solar-powered UAVs, 72–73, 187, 191–92, 197, 198, 230, 232–33, 234–35
Soldier UAVs, 109
SoLong UAVs, 235
sonobuoy tube-launched UAVs, 199, 243–45
sound surveillance system (SOSUS), 43
South Africa, 100, 130, 173–76
South Korea, 143, 145, 153–57, 159
Soviet Union: bomber flights near U.S. fleet, 250n7; deceptive messages, 42, 254n7; decoys and mass attacks, 7, 250n8; equipment and resources of, 16; naval strategy against, 42–43; offensive doctrine, 40–41, 47, 253–54n6; reconnaissance-strike complexes, 26, 252n1; resistance movements, 19; submarine warfare, 43; tank warfare, 40; UAVs, 102, 163–65, 168; Vietnam War and, 17, 251–52n4
SP2S craft, 197, 247
Spain: international UAVs, 126–27; MidCAS, 75, 180; UAVs, 120, 137, 143, 159, 176–77, 208
Sparrowhawk UAVs, 187
Sparrow-N UAVs, 133, 134
Sperwer UAVs, 71, 108, 110–13, 114, 177–78. See also Crécerelle UAVs
Spirit UAVs, 90
Spy Arrow UAVs, 110, 111
Spy Hawk UAVs, 218
Spyball UAVs, 147
Squadron UAVs, 170
Sri Lanka, 143
Stabileye UAVs, 187
Stalker UAVs, 245
STAR (Shipboard Tactical RPV), 80
state-based control, 11–12

state-on-state conventional war, 17, 19
stealthy design, 3, 5, 7–8, 197, 247
Stingray UAVs, 161
strike missiles, 11–12. See also Tomahawk strike missiles
Strix UAVs, 151–52
Stroy UAVs, 165, 166
submarine warfare, 38, 43, 56–57
submarine-launched UAVs, 195, 223–24
suppleness, 45
surface weapons, 12, 251n11
surface-to-air weapons, 3, 249n4
Surveyor 600/Surveyor 2500 UAVs, 115–16, 117
SW-1 UAVs, 104
SW-6 UAVs, 104–5
Swallow UAVs, 77
swarm concept: air activity protection by, 5; communication between vehicles, 11, 12, 13; control of air vehicles, 1, 4, 6, 11–12, 249n2, 250–51n10; fighter aircraft use against, 4, 249–50nn4–5; as forward base for strikes, 3–4; mass strikes by, 12; network-centric warfare and, 2–3; persistent strike capability, 28–29; position of UCAVs within, 4–5, 11–12; routing of UCAVs, 5; tactical implications of, 6–8, 32; target assignment and engagement, 4, 6, 12; testing of concept, 249n1; weapons on UAVs, 4
Sweden, 75, 107, 112, 126–27, 177–80
Swift UAVs, 215
Switzerland, 120, 126–27, 130, 180
Syria, 164

T-20 UAVs, 218
TACMAV UAVs, 234
Tactical Tomahawk, 8, 13, 47, 63, 64, 65, 66, 69
Tagboard drone, 165
tailless configurations, 14
Taiwan, 130, 143, 180–81
Talarion UAVs, 126, 127
Talash UAVs, 128
Taliban, 20–21, 47, 48, 252n9, 254n3
Talon LASH, 245
Talon UAVs, 197
tanks, 32, 37–42, 45
Taranis UAVs, 186, 187, 190–91
Tarantula UAVs, 185
TARES UAVs, 121
target aircraft, 69
targets: accuracy of weapons against, 27; assignment and engagement of, 4, 8–11, 12, 13, 26–28, 35, 48–50, 52, 63–65, 66–67, 249n2, 255nn6–8; concealment of, 16; conventional warfare, 15–18; dispersible precision weapons and, 24; effective targeting, 24; ground fire and, 15–16, 30, 54; importance of, rapid changes

in, 50; mass strikes against, 7, 12, 24, 31, 250n8; observed enemy behavior and, 22–23; persistent strike capability, 28–30; pop-up, moving targets, 31; precision strikes against, 17, 22, 24–25, 30–31, 35; quick responsive attacks on, 22–23; recognition of by pilots, 15–16, 30, 52, 54, 255nn6–8; reconnaissance and assignment of, 24, 26–28; strike planning, 48–49, 63–64; surprise attacks on, 22, 26, 67

Teal Rain program, 90

technology: computer technology, 43–44, 48–49, 51–52, 53–54, 255–56n9; investment in by enemy, 24; pace of combat and, 38, 41; pervasive surveillance and, 28, 31–32; reasons for investment in, 33–37; tactic and strategy change for use of, 39–41, 44–45, 253n5; transformation of military through use of, 1, 13, 32, 33–37, 43–45; for UCAS, 12–14; World War II, use of during, 1, 71

Tern UAVs, 10, 245–46

terrorist war, 15, 20, 22

Thailand, 143, 243

T-Hawk UAVs, 102, 114, 217–18, 229

TigerShark UAVs, 246

TIHA UAVs, 182, 184, 185

Tipchuk (Tipchak) UAVs, 166

Tomahawk strike missiles: aircraft comparison, 63–65; control of, 13, 65; cost of, 64; launch of, 52–53, 251n11; mission planning, 63–64; speed of, 66; Tactical Tomahawk, 8, 13, 47, 63, 64, 65, 66, 69; target assignment and engagement, 1, 63–65

Tornado bombers, 119, 161, 186, 190

Tracker (DRAC) UAVs, 109, 114, 116, 118, 145

TRPV-1 Doyosne UAVs, 155

Tu-123 Yastreb drone, 102, 163–64

Tu-141 UAVs, 164–65

Tu-143 UAVs, 102, 164, 165

Tu-243 UAVs, 164, 169

Tu-300 UAVs, 166, 168, 169

Tube Launched Expendable UAVs, 199

Tucan UAVs, 93, 117, 118, 120–21

TUMAV UAVs, 178

Turais UAVs, 248

Turkey, 104, 137, 158, 181–84, 200, 203, 211

U-2 reconnaissance aircraft, 81, 82, 87, 89, 206, 207

U8E UAVs, 105

UA 10 UCAVs, 199

Ugglan UAVs, 112, 113, 179

Ukraine, 184, 252n8

United Arab Emirates, 96, 98, 174, 178

United Kingdom: Aberporth, 114; Autonomous Systems Technology Related Airborne Evaluation and Assessment (ASTRAEA), 75; bomber force, 39; combat experience with UAVs, 95; decentralized warfare, 19; defensive doctrine, 41, 253–54n6; fire-control system, 254–55n5; Hermes UAVs, 134; Royal Air Force, 37; tank development, 32, 37, 39; UAVs, 69, 78, 184–92, 201, 212, 214, 222–23, 226; Watchkeeper program, 184–87, 190

United States: defense spending, 36–37; development of UAVs, 193–200; fighter aircraft during World War II, 71; funding for UAV/RPV program, 193, 194, 196–97; interservice cooperation, 79; interservice rivalries, 1; offensive doctrine, 41, 253–54n6; transformation of military, 1, 13, 32, 33–37, 43–45; UAV program structure, 199–200; UAVs, 200–248

unmanned air vehicles (UAVs)/unmanned combat air vehicles (UCAVs): advantages of UCAS over, 45; affordability of manned aircraft and, 168; aircraft carrier design and, 4; air-launched UAVs, 73; attack UAVs, 92–94; carrier flight deck operations and, 13, 14; categories of, 72; characteristics of, 70–71; collision avoidance, 52, 73–75, 180; combat experience with, 63, 71, 85–86, 95; communication between vehicles, 11, 12, 13; control of, 1, 4, 11–12, 13–14, 66, 67, 69, 70–71, 249n2, 250–51n10; cost of, 69, 71; cost of war and, 19; crashes, 71, 250–51n10; decentralized warfare and, 16; design of, 14, 72; development of, 37, 71; emerging types of, 72–73; flight and control of, 1; as forward base for strikes, 3–4; landing air vehicles, 65, 73; military interest in and development of, 195–96; persistent strike capability with, 29–30; real-time tactical reconnaissance, 78–80; reconnaissance from, 66–67, 71–72, 75–95; refueling of, 6, 12, 14, 65, 207–8; routing of, 5; security of roads and, 95; short-range UAVs, 80–81; size of, 44, 72; sniper role of, 8–9; speed of, 66–67, 71–72; stealth characteristics of, 3, 7–8; unit level designations, 72, 194; vulnerability of, 56, 71–72; weapons on, 4; weather conditions and, 94

unmanned combat air system (UCAS): advantages of over manned aircraft, 1–2, 5–6, 11, 29, 45, 47–48, 55–59; air presence with, 6–8; attrition, 56, 57; control system for, 1, 4, 11–12, 13–14, 50–51, 249n2, 250–51n10; cost of, 55–56, 58; development of, 1; fighter aircraft and, 249–50n5; integrated system of, 11–12; landing air vehicles, 65; landings, takeoffs, stress, and fatigue, 55–56; maintenance and spares, 55–56; naval warfare strategy and, 1–2; pervasive surveillance, 9–10, 11, 28, 31–32; practicability of, 14; self-defense capabilities of, 249–50n5; system aspect of, 1; tactical implications of, 6–8, 37; target assignment and engagement, 4, 8–11, 12, 13, 25, 49, 52, 66–67, 249n2, 255nn6–8; technology and capabilities for, 12–14; testing for combat readiness, 55; transformation of military through use of, 1, 33, 37, 45; vulnerability of, 56. *See also* swarm concept; X-47B air vehicle

Uqab (Uqaab) UAVs, 158, 160

USD UAVs, 75–77, 78

Vantage UAVs, 179

Vector UAVs, 161, 162

vertical take-off UAV (VTUAV), 195

Vigilante 502 UAVs, 246

Viking 400 UAVs, 246, 247

Vincennes, 7, 53, 54, 250n7, 255–56n9

Vision Mk I/II UAVs, 159

Voyeur SL-UAVs, 244–45

VR-2 Strizh UAVs, 164–65

VR-3 Reys UAVs, 163, 164, 169

Vulture program, 235

Vulture UAVs, 175–76

war: asymmetric warfare, 18; automation and military effectiveness, 46–48; conventional warfare, 15–19; cost of and UCAV use, 19; decentralized warfare, 16, 19–23; economic issues, 33–35, 253nn2–3; enemy losses and surrender, 48; expeditionary warfare, 16, 24, 36–37; guerrilla forces and warfare, 17–19, 22; heroism and sacrifice, 50; high-intensity warfare, 15–19; insurgency warfare, 15, 18, 19–23, 44, 252n10; low-intensity warfare, 15; naval warfare strategy, 1–2; network-centric warfare, 2–3, 24, 26–28, 31–32, 45, 67; pace of combat and technology, 38, 41; point of, 48; resistance movements, 18–19; submarine warfare, 38, 43, 56–57; support for and cost of, 19; tactical environment, changes in, 33

Warrior Alpha UAVs, 202

Warrior Block UAVs, 202

Warrior Eagle UAVs, 101, 106

Warrior UAVs, 71, 194

Wasp UAVs, 109–10, 197, 224, 246–48

Watchkeeper program, 184–87, 190

weapons: accuracy of, 27, 30; defense train wreck, 36–37; dispersible precision weapons, 24; GPS-guided, 2, 7, 27, 28; manpower, machinery, and automation, 46–48; nuclear weapons, 75; strategic bombing, 37, 38, 253n3; transfer of at sea, 25, 64, 251n11; on UAVs,

4; unmanned cargo aircraft to deliver, 73; weapon systems, 46–47; weapon systems, role of people in, 51–54

Whisper UAVs, 224

Wing and Bomb Bay Launched UAVs, 248

Wing Loong UAVs, 101, 103

WK-450 UAVs, 185

WZ-5 UAVs, 84, 102, 103

WZ-9/WZ-2000 UAVs, 105

X-13 UAVs, 123, 124

X-45A air vehicle, 14, 195, 196, 236, 237

X-45B air vehicle, 196, 236

X-45C air vehicle, 196, 236, 237

X-46A vehicle, 236

X-47A Pegasus, 14, 195, 196, 220

X-47B air vehicle: carrier flight deck operations and, 13; cost of, 58; development and specifications, 220, 221, 236; development of, 196; DUSTER program, 195; photo of, 2; refueling of, 208; stealthy design, 5; swarm concept, 6; target assignment and engagement, 25; UAVs similar to, 126, 199; as UCAS vehicle, 1, 2; weapon bays, 5. *See also* Unmanned combat air system (UCAS)

Xianglong UAVs, 100–101

XM-156 UAVs, 218

XMQ-17 Spy Hawk, 218

XPV UAVs, 245–46

Yabhon UAVs, 96, 97

Yagua UAVs, 96, 97

Yak-131/Yak-133 UAVs, 169

Yarará UAVs, 96, 97–98

Yilong, 105–6

YMQ-12 UAVs, 215

YMQ-18 UAVs, 218–20

YQM-94/98 UAVs, 89–90

YQM-121A Pave Tiger, 193

YQM-121B Seek Spinner, 193

ZALA 421 UAVs, 170

Zephyr UAVs, 187, 191–92, 235

Zond UAVs, 166–67

About the Author

Norman Friedman is a strategist known for his ability to meld historical, technical, and strategic factors in analyses of current problems. Author of thirty-three books, he often appears on television, writes a monthly column on world and naval affairs for the *Proceedings* of the U.S. Naval Institute, and is a frequent contributor to many other periodicals. His Cold War history, *The Fifty Year War: Conflict and Strategy in the Cold War*, won the 2001 Westminster Prize for the best military history book of the previous year, from the British Royal United Services Institute. His *Seapower as Strategy* won the Samuel Eliot Morison prize awarded by the Naval Order of the United States in November 2002.

Dr. Friedman has testified before the U.S. House and Senate on U.S. Navy programs, has lectured widely in forums such as the U.S. Naval War College, the Naval Postgraduate School, the Industrial College of the Armed Forces, the Air War College, the Australian and Canadian junior and senior national staff colleges, the Royal United Services Institute, the British Ministry of Defence, and at a series of seminars for the Naval Air Systems Command managed by the University of Virginia. In the fall of 2002 Dr. Friedman served as the Royal Australian Navy's Synott Professor, lecturing on seapower in several Australian cities. For some years he was Visiting Professor of Operations Research (for the naval architecture course) at University College, London, concerned mainly with the formulation and consequences of ship operational requirements.

Among Dr. Friedman's many books are *Naval Firepower*, which describes gunnery in the battleship era; *Terrorism, Afghanistan, and America's New Way of War*; *The Cold War Experience*, a short history of the Cold War with accompanying reproduced documents; *Seapower as Strategy*; *The Fifty-Year War: Conflict and Strategy in the Cold War*; *Seapower and Space*, an account of the role that space and information assets now play in naval warfare; five editions of *The Naval Institute Guide to World Naval Weapon Systems*; and his renowned illustrated design histories of U.S. warships (volumes on cruisers, destroyers, battleships, carriers, small combatants, amphibious ships and craft, and submarines).

Dr. Friedman's articles have appeared in *Joint Forces Quarterly*, *Jane's International Defence Review*, *Asian Pacific Defence Reporter*, *Defense Electronics*, the *Journal of Electronic Defense*, *Armada*, *ORBIS*, *Military Technology*, *Naval Forces*, *Signal*, the *Wall Street Journal*, the *Journal of Cold War Studies*, *Proceedings* of the U.S. Naval Institute, and many others.

A longtime consultant to the media, he frequently appears on national television, including specials on various forms of weaponry, on warships, and on the Gulf War, for the Discovery and History networks, and the "Warplanes," "Warship," and "Seapower" series, as well as NOVA, on the U.S. Public Broadcasting System.